TOGETHER WITH THE SUBURBS AS THEY ARE NOW STANDING, ANNO. DOM., 1707

JOHN GAY'S LONDON

JOHN GAY

JOHN GAY'S
LONDON

ILLUSTRATED FROM THE POETRY OF THE TIME

By WILLIAM HENRY IRVING

ARCHON BOOKS
1968

SBN: 208 00618 4
LIBRARY OF CONGRESS CATALOG NUMBER: 68-26933
PRINTED IN THE UNITED STATES OF AMERICA

TO

GEORGE LYMAN KITTREDGE

Et ce Londres de fonte et de bronze, mon âme,
Où des plaques de fer claquent sous des hangars,
Où des voiles s'en vont, sans Notre-Dame
Pour étoile, s'en vont, là-bas, vers les hasards.

Gares de suie et de fumée, où du gaz pleure
Ses spleens d'argent lointain vers des chemins d'éclair,
Où des bêtes d'ennui bâillent à l'heure,
Dolente immensément, qui tinte à Westminster.

Et ces quais infinis de lanternes fatales,
Parques dont les fuseaux plongent aux profondeurs,
Et ces marins noyés, sous les pétales
Des fleurs de boue où la flamme met des lueurs.

Et ces châles et ces gestes de femmes soûles,
Et ces alcools de lettres d'or jusques aux toits,
Et tout à coup la mort, parmi ces foules;
O mon âme du soir, ce Londres noir qui traîne en toi!

— Verhaeren.

Contents

Illustrations

Introduction

THE poetry of the eighteenth century is worth understanding, and this book is meant as a contribution to that end. Critics of yesterday or the day before were too apt to tag the period an age of prose, and to call its verse mechanic, because they failed to appreciate metrical fashions and conventions of style so different from their own. All niggers looked alike to them, from Pope to Erasmus Darwin, and their dull ears heard but one tune. We seem at last to have got somewhere beyond such fopperies. We are glad now to find variety of measure, and can meet a ballad without undue surprise; we can even enjoy a poem in the Spenserian stanza without dubbing it "romantic." We can talk sincerely of power, subtle fancy, breadth of imaginative suggestion, direct drive to the intellect, sensitive humanity, as casual features of this poetry, and illustrate our propositions without expecting contradiction. In other words, appreciation has finally taken the place of polemics.

Now, this book takes a part of the poetry of the period and makes use of it for a special purpose — to throw light on the way ordinary people lived in London at that time. Prose essays, letters, memoirs, the current drama, all help toward the same end and have been used in innumerable books. One would expect these other forms of literature to be freer from pose, and on the whole more successful in reproducing the important features of town life, than is verse; but it is not so. D'Urfey and Tom Brown, Ned Ward, Edward Moore, and even Addison, are useful, but they are often lurid. The student of social history wants an ordinary, dull gray sky, not the reds and purples of sunset. It seems in this case that the stricter form fuses, somehow or other, the visual imagination. Narrow the shutter for sharp detail. At any rate, the following pages will test the truth of this position.

One warning I must give to the man of taste. The great poetry of the eighteenth century is known, though not always appreciated. Little enough of that will appear in these pages, but possibly the study of hedge-side chance blades will help toward an understanding of differences. Do not expect to be corn-fed.

One naturally starts with *Trivia*. All the quotations come from *Trivia* — that is, in the books on the London shelves of the big libraries. From *Trivia* we range abroad in three main directions, gathering those poems — a large group — which derive from the Roman satirists, many others from the ever-popular street ballads, and, last of all, vignettes of town life which developed from the growing interest in topographical poetry. Four classical types touch the streets — the "Arts," Juvenal's Third Satire, the "Journeys," and the "Rake." The street ballads, as a sort of underground Saturnian current of literature, approach legitimate poetry at two points, the "Journeys" and the "Rake," while the vignettes are close kin to parts of Juvenal's Third Satire.

With this material and its criss-cross of relations it seemed advisable not to adhere too rigidly to any arrangement based on literary *genres*. The mass of pertinent reference is hugely overgrown in spite of limitation. Trivial matters have accumulated, like the notes of Mr. Casaubon. Doubtless our patient suffers from ascites and needs a more skilled or conscientious surgeon to do the tapping.

The first chapter contains a brief impression of London in the reign of Queen Anne and an equally brief account of John Gay and the literary men he knew. With the decks thus cleared, Chapter II describes and illustrates three of the classical types involved. Chapter III is an analysis of *Trivia* itself, with detailed pictures of the town in its dullest and most animated attitudes, the shabbiness and filth, the pavements, noise and odors, signs, lighting, water-supply, vehicles, the mob in action at marriages and funerals, on the Lord Mayor's day, on November 5, at the pillory and at Tyburn, the beggars and pickpockets, coney-catchers and jugglers. Chapter IV, by a natural transition, discusses the last of the classical types, the "Rake." With him we visit the tavern and the brothel, the gaming-house, the broker's office, the prison, and prepare our minds for the general account of the amusements of the town which follows in Chapter V. These are sufficiently varied, and include outdoor sports, games, boxing, wrestling, cudgelling, bear-baiting, sight-seeing, especially the enthusiasm for monstrosities, the parks and gardens, the outlying watering-places, the coffee-houses, the clubs, the taverns, and the playhouses. The last chapter is a general survey of what we may, for convenience, call the *Trivia* tradition in the whole field of English literature, with some attempt to show just how the main interests and the prevailing ideas of the different periods influenced the *genre* and gave it sometimes subtle variations of stress. Two appendices follow, one dealing with costume as it lends color to street life, the other listing and describing the early editions of *Trivia*.

The dates of Gay's life mark our period closely enough. This half-century (1685-1732) saw for statesmen the establishment of those principles which were at stake in 1688, and for men of letters the virtual creation of a reading public. With a record of accomplishment like this, the time deserves separate treatment. John Gay, more than all the poets of the Augustan Age, was the lover and the laureate of the city. His *Trivia* is without question the greatest poem on London life in our literature. It is not, perhaps, of epic length, but is sufficiently long to mention or describe at least sixty ways of earning a living, and more than thirty-five separate localities. It is full of the most varied and interesting detail. And, in addition, it shows real architectonic ability in the persistent success with which the framework of classical burlesque is handled. The author of *The Beggar's Opera* is surely a better patron for our efforts than Pope, whose physical disabilities made it impossible for him to know the town in any complete sense, or Swift, who hated and feared the Yahoos of the streets, or even Addison, who gives us studies of certain features of town life in his admirable essays, but whose pose of superiority would effectually bar him out from sympathy with some of the humors we shall be interested in here. Gay, on the other hand, might get lost in the town, and be glad of it, find friends in any odd corner, and return to his lodgings in Whitehall a wiser man, at any rate, for the experience. Let him call the toasts, then, and introduce the speakers! They will not all be so genial and entertaining as the master, but, as a group, they have the ability to bring us very close indeed to the life of the people, and may save us from the fate of those who

> Turn Caxton, Winkin, each old Goth and Hun,
> To rectify the reading of a pun.
> Thus nicely trifling, accurately dull,
> How one may toil and toil — to be a fool! [1]

[1] David Mallet, *Poetical Works* (Edinburgh, 1780), p. 12, ll. 37-40.

We all become idealists, or romanticists, or what not, when we consider things unseen, satirists with things immediately before us. It should not, then, occasion surprise to find that London streets are left for the most part to the good graces of satire. The whole *genre* with which we are to deal draws its inspiration from the Roman satirists, and is almost, though not quite, unknown in English literature until their writings began to leaven the Elizabethan loaf in the last decade of the sixteenth century. At that time love-poetry and Arcadian romance were giving way to an interest in realism and satire. Donne, Hall, Marston, Guilpin, and the rest imitate the matter and tone of Juvenal, the style of Persius, and capture many a stock figure from the pages of Horace. Their work is often counterfeit coin. London is inextricably confused with Rome in their minds, and their models seem altogether too familiar. However, though the types they use are timeworn, there is a certain freshness of illustration and imagery about the way they develop them, and their work is still readable. Jonson's influence was supreme:

> my strict hand
> Was made to seize on vice, and with a gripe
> Squeeze out the humour of such spongy souls
> As lick up every idle vanity.[1]

And following his lead, many a scribbler went about the town rampant for humors, until years later, after Randolph's death in 1638, his brother-in-law, Richard West,[2] could say of them,

> Their brains lye all in Notes; Lord! how they 'd looke
> If they should chance to loose their Table-book!

[1] Induction, *Every Man out of His Humour* (1600).
[2] Thomas Randolph, *Poems* (5th ed., 1668). Verses by West and others prefixed.

Chekov's *Man in a Case* would have been an anomaly. Their resourcefulness was infinite and untiring.

> For Humours to lye leidger they are seene
> Oft in a Taverne, and a Bowling-greene.
> They doe observe each place, and company,
> As strictly as a Traveller or Spie.
> And *deifying dunghills*, seeme t' adore
> The scumme of people, Watchman, Changling, Whore.
> To know the vice, and ignorance of all,
> With any Ragges they'le drink a pot of Ale;
> Nay, what is more (a strange unusuall thing
> With Poets) they will pay the reckoning;
> And sit with patience an houre by th' Heeles
> To learne the Non-sence of the Constables.
> Such Jig-like flim-flams being got to make
> The Rabble laugh, and nut-cracking forsake,
> They goe Home (if th' have any) and there sit
> In Gowne and Night-cap looking for some wit.

This satiric spirit assumes such a variety of forms that one must distinguish carefully. Milton, for instance, in the "Apology for Smectymnuus"[1] (1642) takes a very serious view of its nature:

> For a satyr as it was borne out of a tragedy, so ought to resemble his parentage, to strike high, and adventure dangerously at the most eminent vices among the greatest persons, and not to creepe into every blinde taphouse that fears a constable more then a satyr.

But we want to go into the blind tap-houses. We have no tragic *flair*, neither have we Donne's aloofness, as expressed so admirably in the first lines of his Satire II:

> Sir, though (I thank God for it) I do hate
> Perfectly all this town.

Marvell's lines will set the tone which is most likely to help us:

[1] John Milton, *Works* (ed. Mitford, 1851), III, 293.

> So thou and I, dear Painter, represent
> In quick Effigy, others Faults; and feign,
> By making them ridiculous, to restrain.[1]

By way of satire, then, in one vein or another, the interest in the life of the streets made its way into our literature. Juvenal's Third Satire, for instance, was the progenitor of many poems we shall be considering. He pictures Rome as a city of great buildings and streets, noise and confusion, where the rich alone sleep, where houses may fall, fires break out, or carts get overturned. We hear about mud and high prices, bandits and bullies, and get a sufficiently vivid idea of conditions, with the Horatian contrast of small house and garden in the country thrown in as an extra. The "Rake" appears here for the first time in full vigor, though Persius has a pale shadow of his figure in his best satire, the fifth.

Oddly enough, next to Juvenal's Third Satire, Horace's description of his trip to Brundisium was the most fruitful source of inspiration for poems on London life. Published for the most part in the late seventeenth and early eighteenth centuries, these poems describe rambles through various parts of the city. Although decidedly satirical, they are far from formal, and no doubt in many cases have no connection with this classical parallel, but owe their form to the most natural of story-telling reasons. Indeed, this "Visit to London" type was a popular one even with ballad-singers and their audiences, and we must not imagine, for instance, that the author of *The Norfolk Farmer's Journey to London* thought he was imitating Horace.

These ballads and fugitive tracts of one kind or another naturally contain many references to the streets

---

[1] Andrew Marvell, *Satires* (ed. G. A. Aitken), p. 34, "The Last Instructions to a Painter," l. 390.

and the life of the town. Many of them are popular in the technical sense of the term; all of them are popular in the sense of appealing to the masses, and it would be strange indeed if the commonplaces of everyday life did not creep into them. A worthy London 'prentice may well find himself the hero of the story, though his adventures take him as far afield as Turkey.

In addition to the formal satire and the street ballads, we find through the seventeenth and eighteenth centuries a growing amount of poetry that is descriptive of special places. The emphasis shifts gradually from the characters to the *milieu*. Topographical poetry appears as a stage in the movement toward a romantic feeling for localities. And, besides this, there is the delight in the usually brief verse-sketch of street life, popularized mainly by *Trivia*.

JOHN GAY'S LONDON

Chapter I

THE TOWN, GAY, AND GRUB STREET

IN the London that Queen Anne was supposed to manage, the main interest was commercial. It always had been so, but in her time the opportunities before young men in business were increasingly attractive, and even spectacular. Great financial schemes, such as the founding of the Bank of England, the institution of the National Debt, the renewal of the coinage, had just been carried through by the Guilds and Corporation of London in conjunction with the government, and these promised to shift the centre of influence from the landed gentry to the moneyed classes of the metropolis. The city at this time could boast a population of about three quarters of a million, and her business connections were expanding rapidly. The process of give-and-take had begun, and the corners of the earth were beginning to feel vibrations from this growing trade centre. France and Spain were shattered by the greed of autocrats. Holland — once so great commercially — had been forced to scatter her wealth in the struggle to remain independent. The whole board was swept clear for England; and while her soldiers fought with Marlborough at Blenheim and Ramillies, her merchants busied themselves in establishing the beginnings of trade in India and America. Commercial supremacy and imperial policies were dimly visible. Paper credit was making its first appearance, — surely a proper symbol in such a period, — but people viewed it with suspicion, and various frivolous arguments were brought forward against

its use. Pope satirized these suggestions with his usual
incisive humor: [1]

> Blest paper-credit! last and best supply!
> That lends corruption lighter wings to fly!

And amateur economists argued for a return to barter,
which gave the poet a wonderful chance for his polished
irony:

> His Grace will game: to White's a bull be led,
> With spurning heels and with a butting head.
> To White's be carried, as to ancient games,
> Fair coursers, vases, and alluring dames.
> Shall then Uxorio, if the stakes he sweep,
> Bear home six whores, and make his lady weep?
> Or soft Adonis, so perfumed and fine,
> Drive to St. James's a whole herd of swine?
> Oh filthy check on all industrious skill,
> To spoil the nation's last great trade, Quadrille!

Pope realized that, as a driving force in civilization,
the red bunting had given place to these soiled scraps of
paper, and for them — not for King or religion — the
soldiers of the future must die. The shopkeepers were
getting more and more important and they knew it.
Their ranks were recruited largely from the younger
sons of the gentry,[2] who, through the gateway of ap-
prenticeship to some trade or other, could see the pros-
pect of generous independence ahead, the possibility of
really outshining their elder brothers left behind fox-
hunting. Energy and a fair idea of economy alone might
lead them through.

Another class of young men prominent in the town
life were those who thanked the gods for special favors
of birth and wealth, and had nothing much to do but

---

[1] *Moral Essays*, III, "On the Use of Riches."
[2] Henri Misson, *Mémoires et Observations* (1698), p. 8.

attend the ladies, drink, fight, and live the gay life gen-
erally. Of these beaux a French observer says, "Les
théâtres, les Chocolat-houses, et la promenade du parc
au printemps, en fourmillent."[1] Most of them were
harmless fools who lacked the sense to see that idleness
is no fun; but others, of a bolder sort, formed themselves
into secret societies of the most baneful kind and sought
excitement by breaking windows, slitting noses, rolling
women about in barrels, and so on. The high birth of
these young desperadoes served to intimidate the watch,
then hopelessly inefficient. Even the parsimonious
Swift was forced by fear of them to spend a shilling on a
chair when returning from late dinner-parties and con-
versations with Oxford and Bolingbroke. Gay pub-
lished a humorous play on the subject in 1712, and refers
to them later in *Trivia:*

> Now is the time that rakes their revels keep;
> Kindlers of riot, enemies of sleep.
> His scatter'd pence the flying Nicker flings,
> And with the copper shower the casement rings.
> Who has not heard the Scowrer's midnight fame?
> Who has not trembled at the Mohock's name?

Most of these lively youths were admitted to the out-
skirts, at least, of the Court, and were ever on the watch
for lucrative posts of the kind which require neither
brains nor exertion. In the days of the Stuarts their
chances would have been good, but the Revolution of
1688 — quietly as it had been carried through — had
wrought changes of great importance in the govern-
ment of the nation. England had at last a ruler respon-
sible to the people, or at any rate to Parliament, which
was supposed to represent the wishes of the people. It
was necessary now to conciliate public opinion. Party

[1] Misson, *Mémoires et Observations* (1698), p. 28.

government developed, and the little group of men who from time to time held the reins of executive power found it very much to their advantage to favor those who, in some way or other, could really influence the political thought of the country and control votes. Electoral laws were, as may be supposed, in a bad state, and that, together with the almost feudal state of society in the small boroughs, led at once under the new system to an increasing amount of bribery and corruption.

But the landowners were not the only people at that time who could influence opinion, as the men in power, notably Robert Harley, Earl of Oxford,[1] soon discovered. A large and growing mass of independent political thinking was making its presence felt and could be turned one way or another by the pen of genius. The old patronage of letters was slowly dying out. Charles Montagu,[2] himself at one time a struggling student and writer, later the greatest man of affairs and statesman of William's reign, was indeed a patron of the old school. He was, if we may believe Pope, "fed with soft dedication all day long," and his like subsisted until Dr. Johnson snuffed out their flickering pretensions by his famous letter to the Earl of Chesterfield half a century later. But few of the great men of letters in Anne's time depended on such patrons for their living. Newspapers were on the streets, and people were reading them, — more people than any writer had ever dreamed of before as a "reading public," — and thus a new source of income and a way of deliverance from petty indignities were finally opened to men of literary talent. Oxford saw and Bolingbroke saw what Halifax had never quite real-

[1] Lord Treasurer, 1710–14.
[2] Lord Halifax made his reputation as joint author with Prior of *The Hind and Panther Transversed to the story of the Country-Mouse and the City-Mouse* (1687).

ized, that men like Defoe and Swift, Steele and Addison, even Roger L'Estrange and James Ralph, must be considered, that their attitude toward political questions was important. In this way, literature acquired, though at a heavy price, a new status. Writers were bought by the administration, and in return for their places and pensions were expected to set aside their personal opinions, and all other interests, in their extravagant support of government measures.

> Why mad for pensions, Britons young and old
> Adore base ministers, those calves of gold,
> Why witling templars on religion joke,
> Fat, rosy justices, drink, doze, and smoak,
> Dull critics on best bards pour harmless spite. . . .
> Methinks some Daemon answers — "'Tis the mode!"[1]

In spite of this appearance of rabid partisanship in the political world, the spirit of the age was against extremes. The Augustans felt disillusionment in the air, as we feel it, who pride ourselves on being modern. The pendulum had been swinging wide in morals, religion, and politics. To pass from puritanic severity to the license of Charles II's reign, from the Clarendon code to assumed toleration, from royal prerogative to responsible government and party politics, from the Caroline lyrists and Milton to wit-comedy and Dryden's satire, might well give pause to the leaders of Queen Anne's England and make them see, like Savile, the necessity of trimming the boat. And so the old enthusiasms were frowned upon as not in good taste. Religion and love both grew frigid. Deism was the popular creed in polite society, while outward conformity screened indifference and, sometimes, downright atheism. At Houghton Hall, Norfolk, for example, Walpole got up that "funny"

---

[1] Anon., *Fashion, a Satire*, in Dodsley, *Old Plays*, III, 320.

game of taking "not" out of the Commandments and putting it into the Creed. As for love, the reader of that literature might well imagine that it had gone out of fashion altogether. The most cynical ideas flourished quite properly in such an atmosphere, and Mandeville is perhaps the typical blossom of the time. Carlyle must have hunted far for his hero. Who could possibly qualify? Atterbury, Bolingbroke, Walpole, Addison, Pope, Berkeley? Great names, but not of heroic mould! The times made the men. Stock-taking follows the Christmas rush; the gay bunting comes down; the clerks get to work.

There was, then, this new political affiliation for men of letters to reckon with, and the changed spirit of the time. What price did poetry pay? It made a strategic retreat before prose, for one thing, and took up new lines of defence. The age was one primarily of criticism and satire. William Watson, in a poem on "Wordsworth's Grave," finds words which aptly express the change:

> A hundred years ere he to manhood came,
> Song from celestial heights had wandered down,
> Put off her robe of sunlight, dew and flame,
> And donned a modish dress to charm the Town.

All productions now must be judged by rigid standards of correctness. As Young writes to Pope:

> Our age demands correctness; Addison
> And you this commendable hurt have done.[1]

The writers produced what there was market for. Society, like its fine ladies, was fond of the mirror. It was amused and flattered sometimes even by distortions. It was intellectually keen enough to be critical, but not sufficiently virile to be creative in the romantically ex-

---

[1] Edward Young, *Poems*, II, 321, "Two Epistles to Mr. Pope" (1730).

aggerated sense of that word. Let us know the men
about us. Let us find in your verses the town, the clubs,
the streets, the taverns, the amusement places. Mock-
heroics, pastorals, may be clever, charming, even realis-
tic; but for the most part get down to the pavement on
which our heels grind. To this sort of expectation the
poets could give but one answer. Their only refuge was
satire!

Of all the writers who catered to the spirit of the age,
and they all did, John Gay reflects perhaps more popu-
lar fashions than anyone else. He wrote mock-heroics,
vers de société, pastorals, prose essays of the *Spectator*
variety, two of the very few good lyrics of the time,
fables, tragedies, comedies, operas, all thoroughly im-
pregnated with his own usually amiable kind of satire.

Modern criticism has conspired to damn practically
all the wits of his circle. Of the members of the Scrib-
lerus Club (1713), Parnell emerges unscathed from the
hands of Goldsmith; Arbuthnot is saved by a curious
combination of humor and combativeness; for the rest,
Pope is drawn with a character as crooked as his unfor-
tunate body, Swift has a Freudian complex, Congreve
is a wit posing ridiculously as a gentleman; for Atter-
bury, St. John, Harley, failure spells obloquy; and as
for Addison, who with Budgell may have had a guest's
card for the Club, Pope's "faint praise" has been echoed
by all succeeding writers. In Lord Morley's criticism
Gay becomes a mere lap-dog, and that he apparently
remains in the judgment of the scholars who have since
written about him. Now, Goldsmith wrote a *Life of
Parnell*. His father and uncle had known their poet
compatriot. He therefore speaks with the authority of
one who has listened to fireside talk about these men,
and his words sound strange indeed in our ears:

The friends, to whom, during the latter part of his life, he was chiefly attached, were Pope, Swift, Arbuthnot, Jervas, and Gay. Among these he was particularly happy, his mind was entirely at ease, and gave a loose to every harmless folly that came uppermost. Indeed it was a society, in which of all others, a wise man might be most foolish without incurring any danger of contempt.

Here we see them as men, but it so happened that they took satire as their field, and there they appear often more like leering gargoyles. Besides, they lacked high seriousness, and that was a sin Matthew Arnold and his contemporaries never learned to pardon.

Gay was the inventor of ballad opera, which has, alas! suffered a sea-change, but which is still and will be the favored amusement of the world's millions; the writer of fables which have been reprinted an astonishing number of times; and the author of a ballad loved then and now by everybody. In other words, he was a man who made his way to the hearts of the people and for that reason has a claim to greatness. Shall we think of him, then, merely as the pet of great ladies?[1] He was, as we know, a fat man[2] with no bump for practical finance. His fatness predisposed him to laziness, and his inability to look after his purse laid him open to the well-meant and no doubt necessary officiousness of his friends. Hence

---

[1] Gay writes to Swift, March 31, 1730: ". . . and I hate to be in debt; for I cannot bear to pawn five pounds worth of my liberty to a tailor or a butcher. I grant you this is not having the true spirit of modern nobility; but it is hard to cure the prejudices of education." Again, Dec. 1, 1731: "The motive to my parsimony is independence."

[2] Breval, *The Confederates* (1717), p. 17:
"For by the clumsie tread it should be Gay."
Of Gay's size, by the way, Nichols thinks we have an interesting sidelight in Hogarth's "South-Sea Bubble" print (*Biog. Anec. of Hogarth* [3d ed., 1785], pp. 177–178). He says that Pope "is represented with one of his hands in the pocket of a fat personage, who wears a horn-book at his girdle. For whom this figure was designed, is doubtful. Perhaps it was meant for Gay, who was a

the lap-dog! Like many of his circle, he persisted in his refusal to take life seriously, which is intensely irritating to certain temperaments. With him, "Life is a jest." But even Gladstone, when the news of Parnell's death was brought to him as he was about to address a great meeting in the north, exclaimed, "Shadows we are and shadows we pursue!" And Pope implicates himself and two other great names in the same heresy:

> If, after all, we must with Wilmot own,
> The cordial drop of life is love alone,
> And Swift cry wisely, "Vive la Bagatelle!"
> The man that loves and laughs, must sure do well.[1]

Addison was clear-headed enough in his dealings with men, at any rate, not too apt to overlook the weaknesses even of friends, and yet Joseph Warton tells us that he

was informed by Mr. Spence, that Addison, in his last illness, sent to desire to speak with Mr. Gay, and told him he had much injured him; probably with respect to his gaining some appointment from the court: but, said he, if I recover, I will endeavor to recompense you.[2]

Gay had ridiculed *Cato* in the *What d'ye Call It*, and yet Addison in the most serious circumstances had this tribute of respect for him. A little before the passage just quoted Warton had been telling how "the sweet-

---

fat man, and a loser in the same scheme." And Pope, too, gives a sample of what the fat man always has to endure from his friends:

> "At Leicester Fields a house full high,
>   With door all painted green,
> Where ribbons wave upon the tie,
>   (A milliner, I mean;)
> There may you meet us three to three,
>   For Gay can well make two of me."
>   *The Challenge*, 1717.

[1] Pope, *Imitations of Horace: Epistles*, Bk. I, Ep. 6 (1737).
[2] Joseph Warton, *An Essay on the Genius and Writings of Pope* (5th ed., 1806), II, 246.

ness and simplicity of Gay's temper and manners, much endeared him to all his acquaintance, and made them always speak of him with particular fondness and attachment." This indeed is the universal testimony.

Even so critical a visitor as Voltaire was captivated by his charm. The famous Frenchman spent three years in England, 1726–29, and his impression of this group of friends is interesting. A certain Major Broome, who died so lately as 1826, at the age of eighty-nine, dined once with Voltaire at Ferney in 1765, and has left a brief account of their talk that day at table.[1]

March 16th, 1765 (Geneva). — Dined with Mons. Voltaire, who behaved very politely. He is very old, was dressed in a robe-de-chambre of blue sattan and gold spots in it, with a sort of sattan cap and blue tassle of gold. He spoke all the time English. . . . His house is not very fine, but genteel, and stands upon a mount close to the mountains. He is tall and very thin, has a very piercing eye, and a look singularly vivacious. He told me of his acquaintance with Pope, Swift (with whom he lived for three months at Lord Peterborough's), and Gay, who first showed him the *Beggars Oppora* before it was acted. He says he admired Swift, and loved Gay vastly. He said that Swift had a great deal of the "ridiculum acre."

Gay's friends are of course unanimous. Pope forgets his artificiality, Swift his cynicism, when speaking of him. Swift leaves the letter announcing Gay's death unopened for five days, from a premonition of serious disaster, and anyone who imagines his letter to the Duchess of Queensberry, later, to show coldness, knows little of Swift's mentality. One does not win affection from men like these, or from women like Queensberry, for that matter, by mere compliance. That more often wins contempt.

[1] This passage is an extract from the MS. Journal of Major Broome, the most intimate friend of Sir Henry Grattan, Speaker of the Irish House of Commons. Printed in *Notes and Queries* (Nov. 18, 1854), X, 403.

This group of friends with whom it was Gay's good fortune to fraternize ranks among the most distinguished in literary history, and one gathers from reference after reference that it was Gay's good-nature which to a very large extent cemented the curious brotherhood together. Pope photographs some of the friends in an early poem, "A Farewell to London in the Year 1714."[1] Here the place which Gay had made for himself is clearly suggested:

> Farewell Arbuthnot's raillery
>   On every learned sot;
> And Garth, the best good Christian he,
>   Although he knows it not. . . .
>
> Still idle, with a busy air,
>   Deep whimsies to contrive;
> The gayest valetudinaire,
>   Most thinking rake alive. . . .
>
> Luxurious lobster-nights, farewell,
>   For sober, studious days!
> And Burlington's delicious meal,
>   For sallads, tarts, and pease!
>
> Adieu to all but Gay alone,
>   Whose soul, sincere and free,
> Loves all mankind, but flatters none,
>   And so may starve with me.

This was written just before Pope retired to devote himself to the composition of his Homer (1715–20). About the same time Swift had begun an adaptation of the Sixth Satire of Horace's Second Book, the latter part of which was added by Pope years afterwards and first printed in 1738. Swift's relations with the group are pleasantly recorded in the earlier part. From day to day they met, and exchanged the gossip of the hour:

[1] *Works* (ed. Warton), II, 360.

Or, "Have you nothing new to-day
From Pope, from Parnell, or from Gay?"

Goldsmith tells us in his *Life of Parnell* [1] that Gay was
obliged to Parnell upon another account, "for being
always poor, he was not above receiving from Parnell
the copy-money which the latter got for his writings."
Goldsmith learns this from an undated letter from Pope
to Parnell (quoted on page xii of the *Life*): "My hearty
service to the Dean, Dr. Arbuthnot, Mr. Ford, and the
true genuine shepherd, J. Gay of Devon, I expect him
down with you." Pope then speaks of publishing Par-
nell's *Zoilus:* "Inform me also upon what terms I am to
deal with the book-seller, and whether you design the
copy-money for Gay, as you formerly talk'd." [2]

Gay always seems like the good angel, if that is not
too extravagant language, of these rather difficult people
among whom he moved. He gave quite as much as he
received. The charming familiarity which existed be-
tween him and Pope is perhaps suggested most deli-
cately in Pope's "Epistle to the Same [Mrs. Blount] on
her leaving the Town after the Coronation": [3]

So when your Slave, at some dear idle time,
(Not plagu'd with head-achs, or the want of rhyme)
Stands in the streets, abstracted from the crew,
And while he seems to study, thinks of you;
Just when his fancy points your sprightly eyes,
Or sees the blush of soft Parthenia rise,
Gay pats my shoulder, and you vanish quite,
Streets, Chairs, and Coxcombs rush upon my sight;
Vex'd to be still in town, I knit my brow,
Look sour, and hum a Tune, as you may now.

---

[1] Prefixed to the 1770 edition of Parnell's *Poems*, p. ix.

[2] This *Life of Parnell* is full of interesting anecdotes. One of the best is
that about the walking party to Lord Burlington's country house, and the
chase to defraud Swift of the best bed.

[3] *Works* (ed. Warton), II, 323. This poem was first published in 1727.

Gay, indeed, seems to have had a marvellous faculty for friendship.[1] He was the bond between Pope and Swift, and as long as he lived there was no hint of coldness in their relations. Lord Orrery is not inclined to be complimentary to Swift or to any of his friends, yet we learn from his *Remarks on the Life and Writings of Dr. Jonathan Swift* [2] how great was the confidence between these two men:

Gay's letters have nothing in them striking or recommendatory. His sentiments are those of an honest, indolent, goodnatured man. He loved Swift to a degree of veneration: and the friendship was returned with great sincerity. Swift writes to him in the same strain as he would have written to a son: and seems to distinguish him as the correspondent to whom he had not the least grain of reserve.

But it was not only by the immediate circle of the Scriblerus Club that Gay was beloved. He was welcome in many circles to which not one of his more distinguished friends would have been *persona grata*. The passing hint often tells a bigger and truer story than a long poem. Dr. John Armstrong, for example, in the last lines of "An Epistle to John Wilkes,"[3] mentions Gay casually as one of his familiar friends:

> There lively, genial, friendly Gay, and I,
> Touch glasses oft to one, whose company
> Would — but what's this? . . .

Those violently hostile to Pope frequently had some kind reservations to make when the name of Gay crept into their verses. Leonard Welsted, who, with James Moore-Smythe, wrote the "Epistle to Mr. A. Pope,

---

[1] The best list of Gay's friends is his own poem, "Mr. Pope's Welcome from Greece" (1720).
[2] Fourth ed. (1752), p. 253.
[3] *Poetical Works* (1807), p. 120.

occasion'd by Two Epistles lately published" (1730),
pities Gay as the victim of his associations:

> 'Midst this vain tribe, that aid thy setting ray,
> The Muse shall view, but spare ill-fated Gay:
> Poor Gay, who loses most when most he wins,
> And gives his foes his fame, and bears their sins;
> Who, more by fortune than by nature curs'd,
> Yields his best pieces, and must own thy worst.

In case his allusions should be misunderstood, he adds
this note: "Mr. Gay, not thought to be the entire au-
thor of *The Beggar's Opera*, and ordered to own *Three
Hours after Marriage*."[1] Welsted had earlier written a
satire on *Three Hours after Marriage*, which he called
Palaemon to Caelia at Bath; or, the Triumvirate (1717).
In this he has a reference to Gay's failure with *The Wife
of Bath:*

> To see their first essay, the House was full;
> None fear'd a secret to make Chaucer dull.

And here he also pays an ill-tempered tribute to Gay's
popularity:

> Thy friend, unrival'd, undisturb'd by me,
> Gleans an insipid fame, from envy free;
> His verse, like countries nor polite nor rude,
> Keeps the dull medium between bad and good;
> As other works for energy and strength,
> His are, like May-poles, famous for their length:
> Canorous trifles let him still pursue;
> Second to none but Arbuthnot or you.

This is the poet, by the way, whose *Apple Pye* insi-
pidity led Pope to parody Denham's lines:

---

[1] Leonard Welsted, *Works* (ed. by John Nichols, 1787), p. 193, ll. 24–30.
This note may have been inserted by Nichols.

Flow, Welsted, flow! like thine inspirer, Beer,
Tho' stale, not ripe; tho' thin, yet never clear;
So sweetly mawkish, and so smoothly dull;
Heady, not strong; o'erflowing, tho' not full.[1]

Welsted is also the hero of Thomas Cooke's "The Battle
of the Poets" (1725). He does not properly appreciate
his own position in the scale of dulness, though his poem
"On the Death of John Phillips"[2] assigns the lowest de-
gree without any misgivings:

Ye Criticks, that like locusts vex the press,
With little reason damn, and write with less;
Ye honourable Bards, that sung of old
The mighty stories Greece or Athens told;
And thou, the worthiest of th' inspired host,
The pride of Isis and thy St. John's boast;
Be witness to the sacred vow I make;
And when, by verse debauch'd, that vow I break,
Pure unenlightened Dullness on my head
The soul and quintessence of Blackmore shed!

The famous *Twickenham Hotch-Potch for the use of the
Rev. Dr. Swift, Alexander Pope, Esq. and Company, being
a Sequel to The Beggar's Opera* (1728), written by Caleb
D'Anvers (pseudonymous for Nicholas Amhurst), is vir-
ulent enough in its treatment of Gay, but the criti-
cisms show that straining for the clever phrase which so
easily and so often vitiates fair judgment. The writer
quotes first from Dennis, whose similes in this case are
crudely extravagant. Especially is this true when, after
speaking of various writers, Dennis finally comments on
Congreve's retirement in the following manner: "And
those nice great Persons, whose squeamish Palates re-
fused Quails and Partridges, have pined ever since in
such a Dearth, that they greedily feed upon Bull-Beef,

[1] Pope, *Works* (ed. Warton), V, 197.
[2] 1710. Welsted, *Works* (ed. Nichols), p. 25.

alias, the *Beggars* Opera." The distinguished group of friends is characterized as "An impertinent Scotch-Quack, a Profligate Irish-Dean, the Lacquey of a super-annuated Dutchess, and a little virulent Papist." This curious sheet contains also some ribald verses by D'Anvers, called "A New Ballad," and beginning,

> Of all the Belles that tread the Stage,
> There's none like pretty Polly,

and has a reference to the controversy over the morality of *The Beggar's Opera* and Parson Herring, "A mighty weak sucking Priest, who to show his Theological Capacity, preached a Sermon at Lincoln's-Inn-Chapel against the Deism of the Age and the *Beggar's Opera*." It may be worth while recalling Dr. Johnson's dictum on this last topic:

> At the same time I do not deny that it may have some influence by making the character of a rogue familiar and in some degree pleasing! Then collecting himself as it were, to give a heavy stroke: There is in it such a *labefactation* of all principles as may be injurious to morality.

But whatever effect *The Beggar's Opera* may have had on the public morality, it certainly hit the public fancy. Satire on Walpole henceforth was pretty sure to be reminiscent of this play,[1] especially as Walpole called unnecessary attention to his wounds by prohibiting *Polly* in the following year. The Duchess of Queensberry took the field as Gay's champion, and her pretty bit of petulance at Court was celebrated in many a pamphlet. It was harmless news anyway, and good advertising for the poet. In *The Female Faction: or, the Gay Subscribers* (1729), D'Anvers is called upon to retire in favor of Gay

---

[1] See *An Epistle from Matt of the Mint, lately deceased, to Captain Macheath* (1729).

as critic of the Court; the episode with the Lord Chan-
cellor is related, Queensberry praised, and other ladies
scorned.

> Then G[ay]! all *future* Trophies wisely scorn,
> And Glory, Thou'rt to *present* Statues born;
> By Nations deify'd be Homer's Shade;
> He smiles unconscious of the Honours paid:
> Thy Works, whilst *Here*, sublimest Columns raise,
> From Woman's Bounty, and from Woman's Praise;
> The *brightest Sex* Thy Worth in Rev'rence hold,
> And load Thee *living* with *Renown* and *Gold*.

The Banished Beauty; or, a Fair Face in Disgrace re-
peats the same story, but it is surely interesting to note
that the absurd little poem went through three editions
in 1729.

It is not easy to find adverse criticisms of Gay either
as a man or as a writer. Welsted's remark [1] about the
What d'ye Call It, that it was an attempt "to raise
preposterous mirth from human woes," is unfair. The
same writer, however, finds *Three Hours after Marriage*
easy prey for his sarcasm:

> "That Play," retorted Fopling, "was so lewd,
> Ev'n Bullies blush'd, and Beaux astonish'd stood;
> But gentle Widows with soft Maids prevail,
> And kindly save the Alligator's tail."

In 1733, following the production of Gay's posthumous
ballad opera, Burnet published *Achilles Dissected, being
a Compleat Key of the Political Characters in that new
Ballad Opera, written by the late Mr. Gay* . . . Burnet
has some harsh things to say of this very commonplace
opera, but he prefers to think it the joint production of
the Pope circle, "as I am very well satisfied Mr. Gay
could not deviate into so much dullness." He perpetu-

---

[1] See Welsted, *Palaemon to Caelia at Bath* (1717).

ates the old rumor that Gay had been imposed upon by his friends:

> It is no Secret how often he was obliged to own what he never wrote, when the Success did not answer; and that others took the Reputation of what was approved of, and he willingly resigned Fame to Interest or Friendship.

This kind of talk is no compliment either to Gay or to his friends, and deserves no attention except to show what a wasps' nest Pope had managed to stir up. Burnet's real spite finds vent in the addendum to this "Key," *The First Satire of the Second Book of Horace, Imitated in a Dialogue between Mr. Pope and the Ordinary of Newgate*. This is dull enough, and need detain us only long enough to notice an amusing reference to Ward, the distinguished author of *The London Spy*. Pope is speaking to the Ordinary:

> Oft has my Verse been lame, I can't but say,
> Like Ward, I've spun *a Thousand* in *a Day!*

"The Battle of the Poets, an heroic poem in two cantos . . . " (1725), by Thomas Cooke, contains naturally several references to Gay and his work. They are not especially complimentary. Ancients and moderns prepare for the grand combat:

> There's not a Bard but panted for the Day,
> From Pope and Philips, down to Trapp and Gay.

The combinations are surely very strange, compared with our modern rearrangements:

> Three Captains next appear, Trapp, Cibber, Gay,
> Heading a Thousand Witlings of a Day.

The heroes of modernity have a very hard time of it:

> Cibber, and Gay, upon the Ground are thrown,
> And all their Labours perish, — all their own.
> One cries aloud upon a noble Peer;
> The other wishes that his Chief were near.

A little later there is a reference to *The Captives:* [1]

> Gay swears to Beckingham, but all in vain,
> He'll ne'er attempt the Tragick Scene again.

Gay wrote no other tragedy, but certainly not because of the failure of this one, for *The Captives* was acted seven times and received the approbation of Royalty.

From some quarters praise is condemnation. Such is the patronage of a man like J. Mitchell, who prints the following consolatory lines in a poem "To the Right Hon. Charles, Earl of Lauderdale." [2]

> Tho' Homer shone the mighty Soul of Verse,
> The *minor Poets* sweetly could rehearse.
> Without Hill's Strength, and Pope's harmonious Flow,
> The Muse's Fire in Gay and *Me* may glow.

In 1730, the office of poet-laureate was given to Colley Cibber, whose literary gifts were not so remarkable as to let the honor pass unquestioned. Evidently, some thought Gay would have lent more lustre to the position: [3]

> Nor could Gay, the coy minstrel of nature and art,
> Tho' by Queensbro' led in, move the chamberlain's heart;
> Whoe'er meanly hopes in the household to settle,
> No, not e'en on a dunghill must raise a *court nettle.**
>
> * *The Beggar's Opera.*

Nor had the jests at Cibber's expense altogether died out three years later, when an anonymous poem, called "On Poetry, a rapsody," appeared,[4] for this writer talks about "harmonious Cibber" entertaining the Court

---

[1] Produced at Drury Lane, Jan. 15, 1724.

[2] *Poems* (2 vols., 1729), I, 276.

[3] "The Gardener's Congress on Colley Cibber's being appointed Poet Laureat," later republished in *The Fugitive Miscellany* (1774–75), II, 60.

[4] Printed Dublin, reprinted London, 1733. Evidently written before Gay's death (Dec. 4, 1732), by Swift.

with annual birthday strains. He also suggests the continued propriety of panegyric:

> Attend ye Popes, and Youngs, and Gays,
> And tune your Harps and strow your Bays.
> Your Panegyricks here provide,
> You cannot err on Flatt'ry's Side.
> Above the Stars exalt your Stile,
> You still are low ten thousand Mile.

In 1734, some verses were written "Occasion'd by a Report that Mr. Butler's Monument in Westminster-Abby, is to be remov'd, to make Room for One to be set up to the Memory of Mr. Gay": [1]

> To this immortal Poet's awful Dust,
> Did Barber raise a monumental Bust. . . .
> Great Hudibras I'll undertake to say,
> Would never to Mackheath have given Way,
> Why should his Author then make Room for Gay?

As a matter of fact, Dean Stanley, in his *Historical Memorials of Westminster*,[2] tells us that Butler's bust was removed to its present position to make room for Gay's monument "by permission of Alderman Barber." But the Town was far more interested in Gay than in Butler, and the erection of the Queensberry monument in his honor was, no doubt, generally applauded.

Allusions to Gay after his death continue to be both affectionate and respectful. In 1734, Dodsley wrote "An Epistle to Pope, Occasion'd by his Essay on Man," in which he pays a pleasant compliment to Gay:

> This Simile drawn out, I now began
> To think of forming some Design or Plan,
> To aid my Muse, and guide her wand'ring Lay,
> When sudden to my Mind came honest Gay.
> For Form or Method I no more contend,
> But strive to copy that ingenious Friend.

---

[1] *The Honey-Suckle* (1734), p. 105.   [2] Third ed. (1869), p. 315.

Dodsley's lines on pedantry in the same poem are very good:

> And come ye solemn *Fools*, a numerous Band,
> Who read, and read, but never understand!

In 1735, a gentleman of the University of Cambridge wrote "An Epistle to Sir J--r--y S--b---k," whoever that may be, and in it showed as plainly as possible that *Trivia* still had readers:

> Haply just rhyming an Epistle,
> (As for Amusement some Folks whistle)
> By some rude Porter I am tost,
> With broken Elbow, 'gainst a Post,
> And then what pretty Thoughts are lost!
> The flourish'd Whip, from rattling Hack,
> Now makes me start with sudden Smack;
> I mend my Pace, as much dismay'd
> As on myself the Whip were laid.
> Full in my Face some spiteful Girl
> Her drizzly Mop contrives to twirl.
> Another, while I musing trail,
> Discharges an unlucky Pail.
> And now I dodge a spouting Dray,
> That totters with uncertain Sway;
> And now a Cart, with nodding Load
> Of Clinking Ir'n, or Clatt'ring Wood:
> One single Plank on 't, let me tell ye,
> Good Knight, wou'd jamm me to a Jelly;
> And after all Expense and Pains,
> Strew *London* with Poetic Brains.
>   Such sad Annoyances, and mo',
> Attend upon the Foot-Pad Beau.
> In pity *Gay*, Himself a Wit,
> Compell'd to trudge, his *Trivia* writ.
> Thus for Convenience-sake I dwell
> An Anchorite in College-Cell.

In 1734, Gerard wrote a disgusting "Epistle to the egregious Mr. Pope in which the Beauties of his Mind

and Body are amply displayed." In this he recalls the
old scandal about the *Three Hours after Marriage* and,
like the rest, exempts Gay from all blame:

> Thou once club'st Nonsense for dramatic Stuff,
> And there thy Folly met a just Rebuff;
> Th' indignant Town cou'd easily divine
> The Grain of Wit was Gay's, the Mass of Scandal thine.

The neglect under which Gay always thought himself
languishing [1] is echoed in "The Church Yard, a Satirical
Poem," published anonymously in 1739:

> See Gay, with Innocence and Genius blest,
> Forgets ungrateful Courts, and sinks to rest.

In 1744, the year of Pope's death, there appeared a
collection of poems called *The Norfolk Poetical Miscel-
lany, to which are added Some Select Essays and Letters
in Prose . . . by the Author of the Progress of Physick.*
This contains "Fidelio to Machaon, an Epistle; occa-
sion'd by his desiring the Author to write a Poem on
Health," which has the following curious contemporary
estimate of poetic values:[2]

> Restless to Shades — to Books I run —
> Myself — the worst of Foes — to shun:
> Wit, Sense, and Pope, — no longer please;
> Nor Homer's Strength — nor Waller's Ease —
> Tasteless alike, the wide Extremes
> Of Addison's — and Bunyan's Dreams —
> The Bell-Man's, or the Laureat's Lay,
> "And Sonnets trim of gentle Gay." [3]
> Vain e'en Philosophy I find,
> That boasted Med'cine of the Mind!

---

[1] Swift, *Poems* (Bohn, 1910), I, 320, "A Libel" (1729):
> "Thus Gay, the hare with many friends,
> Twice seven long years the court attends."

[2] Vol. II, p. 42.   [3] Gay's Prologue to *The Shepherd's Week* (1714).

Evidently Gay's reputation as a poet was thoroughly established in his own time. The minor versifiers had no doubts on the matter. William Whitehead praises "Gay's ingenuous Stile."[1] Nicholas James begins his curious poem on "Wrestling"[2] with the following lines:

> The modest bard attempts no lofty theme,
> But to his little mind confines his aim;
> No army he directs, and steers no fleets,
> Nor treads with skilful Gay Augusta's streets;
> His Foot pervades Cornubia's heathy ways:
> That Heath, alas! is destitute of Bays.

Later in the century the same tone continues. In 1778, William Heard published *A Sentimental Journey to Bath, Bristol, and their environs; a descriptive Poem. To which are added miscellaneous pieces.* In this he pays a perhaps undeserved compliment to one phase of Gay's descriptive power, and proposes

> To paint the manners of the rural scene,
> The fruitful valley, and the velvet green.[3]

[1] *An Essay on Ridicule* (1743).

[2] *Poems on Several Occasions* (Truro, 1742).

[3] This poem contains some amusing examples of the characteristic bathos of the eighteenth century. Here are some lines describing the climbing of the "Sugarloaf" — hill-climbing *à la mode* eighteenth century:

> "But, ah! the hill's steep height! She toils and sighs,
> And views the summit with desponding eyes;
> When gentle fortune favouring our intent,
> A horse to meet us on the hill, was sent.
> I blessed the omen, seized the willing steed,
> (What gratitude for help in utmost need!)
> On the kind beast I place my bosom fair,
> Who, with a smile rewards my tender care.
> While, by his humble halter, up the height,
> I lead the bearer of my heart's delight."

They meet some children, who splutter Welsh, and, like the bounding roe, "trip up the steep, and *Tiperary* cry."

As late as 1790, a writer in *The Bystander; or, Universal weekly expositor by a literary association* (page 196), makes the following estimate of Gay and his work:

Gay's pastorals, his fables, his *Trivia*, and many other of his admirable works, prove him a most beautiful versifier, and an intuitive poet; and though *Oliver* [Samuel Johnson] in complaisance to a lady, will not allow him to have been more than of the *lower order* — which expression one would think the World has imitated — yet I will venture to say if he himself could have boasted half his lyric merits, he would have maintained a much higher rank in poetic fame.

Joseph Warton and Hazlitt have high praise for Gay. In *An Essay on the Genius and Writings of Pope*,[1] Warton writes:

Our nation can boast also, of having produced one or two more poems of the burlesque kind, that are excellent; particularly *The Splendid Shilling* . . . the *Muscipula* . . . the *Scribleriad* of Mr. Cambridge, the *Machinae Gesticulantes* of Addison, the *Hobbinol* of Somerville, and the *Trivia* of Gay.

In this passage, one must confess that *Trivia* is not in very good company; therefore let us hear his special commendation of that poem (II, 49):

The point of the likeness consists in describing the objects as they really exist in life, like Hogarth's paintings, without heightening or enlarging them, and without adding any imaginary circumstances. . . . In this also consists the chief beauty of Gay's *Trivia*, a subject Swift desired him to write upon, and for which he furnished him with many hints.

Hazlitt is still more unreserved in his praise:[2]

If good sense has been made the characteristic of Pope, good-nature might be made (with at least equal truth) the characteristic of Gay. He was a satirist without gall. He had

---

[1] 1756. Fifth ed. (2 vols., 1806), I, 242.
[2] *Collected Works* (ed. Waller and Glover, 13 vols., 1902–06), V, 107–109, and 373.

a delightful placid vein of invention, fancy, wit, humour, description, ease and elegance, a happy style, and a versification which seemed to cost him nothing. His *Beggar's Opera* indeed has stings in it, but it appears to have left the writer's mind without any.

The poets of the late eighteenth century, minor and major, speak of Gay with respect. J. Caulfeild, in *The Manners of Paphos; or The Triumph of Love* (1774), mentions him and his *Trivia:*

> The modest Gay appears on foot,
> Wrapt in his virtue and surtout;
> While *Trivia*, with a golden lyre,
> Supports him at his own desire.[1]

Further on in the same poem, Gay's name is introduced naturally, in company with the highest:

> Say, wander'd ye in Windsor's shade,
> With Contemplation, lonely maid,
> In Kensington, or Hampton Court,
> Where Lansdown, Gay, and Pope resort; —
> Or on Parnassus' top reclin'd,
> Say, were ye feasting then the mind?[2]

Chatterton, too, mentions him in "February, an Elegy," published eight years after the young poet's shocking death:[3]

> Begin, my Muse, the imitative lay,
> Aonian doxies sound the thrumming string;
> Attempt no numbers of the plaintive Gay,
> Let me like midnight cats, or Collins sing.

With the exception of *The Beggar's Opera*, Gay's most popular work has undoubtedly been the *Fables*, two of which were translated by Cowper into Latin verse,[4] the

---

[1] Canto III, ll. 55–58.   [2] Ibid., ll. 154–159.
[3] *Miscellanies in Prose and Verse* (1778), p. 72.
[4] *Poems* (ed. J. C. Bailey, 1905), p. 657.

"Lepus multis Amicus" and "Avarus et Plutus." A mul-
titude of fables appeared from time to time in direct imi-
tation of Gay's style. Some of the most interesting of
these may be found in a book called *Parodies on Gay, to
which is added The Battle of the Busts* (*ca.* 1810). The sort
of thing this unknown writer was capable of doing may
be observed by comparing his fable of "The Officer and
his Poor Parent" with its original in Gay, "The Barley
Mow and the Dunghill."[1] The parody begins:

> As cross the Park, at early dawn,
> The happy Monarch sought the lawn;
> A shining multitude appears,
> Of brave and faithful Volunteers;
> A loyal zeal each bosom warms;
> They greet their King presenting arms.

The subject is adapted from the original, but the imi-
tator deserves credit for his clever reproduction of the
spirit and style.

"The Battle of the Busts," presumably by the same
author, is a decidedly spirited poem. Its references to
most of the distinguished names in English literature,
and to some foreign men of letters, are often very amus-
ing. In this poem Gay and Wyatt take a leading part in
a dispute over precedence, which is described with con-
siderable verve and even an attempt at characterization.

> Addison now prepar'd to say
> Something to end the mighty fray,
> "For Falconer," said he, "will join
> His efforts, I am sure, with mine."
> When lo! an accident occurr'd,
> Which settled all without a word.

A mob outside the house, too impatient to wait for
candles, throw a volley of sticks and stones and cinders

---

[1] (Ed. Underhill), II, 109, No. 35.

through the windows, and reduce the contending literary figures to their common dust.

Gay's fatness and supposed laziness did not prevent him from writing the best poem in our literature on London streets. Warton speaks very highly of it, calls it "the best of his poems, in which are many strokes of genuine humour and pictures of London life, which are now become curious, because our manners, as well as our dresses, have been so much altered and changed." [1] Perhaps the highest compliment paid to it was one which Gay and his friends failed to appreciate. Their retort courteous is to be found in the *Three Hours after Marriage*, in which, according to the *Biographia Dramatica*,[2]

Phoebe Clinkit was said to be intended for the Countess of Winchelsea, who was so much affected with the itch of versifying, that she had implements of writing in every room in her house that she frequented. She was reported also to have given offense to one of the triumvirate, by saying, that Gay's *Trivia* showed he was more proper to walk before a chair, than to ride in one.

James Heywood, unlike the Countess, paid his compliments direct. He wrote some very flattering lines, "To Mr. Gay, on his Poem entitled *Trivia, or, the Art of Walking the Streets of London*":[3]

O Gay! my grateful Thoughts do crowd my Mind,
To tell you what harmonious Lines I find
In this thy *Trivia;* such Beauties shine,
I'm pleased to see a Wonder in each Line:
So much thy tow'ring Thoughts my Fancy fire,
The more I read, the more I still admire.

---

[1] Joseph Warton, *An Essay on the Genius and Writings of Pope*, II, 244.
[2] (Three vols., 1812), III, 333, paragraph 108. But see Prof. George Sherburn's article in *Mod. Philol.* (Aug., 1926), p. 91, "The Fortunes and Misfortunes of *Three Hours after Marriage*."
[3] *Poems and Letters on several subjects* (1724), p. 17.

What Critick with his stabbing Pen, can stain
Thy tuneful Verses, or eclipse thy Fame?
The very Momus which insults thy Name,
Envies thy Genius, tho' thy Verses blame.
Thy useful Hints direct the rural 'Squire,
His Steps from wand'ring Females to retire.
To hoary Heads thou'rt an indulgent Friend,
And those which under heavy Burthens bend.
When jostling busy Crowds walk in the Street,
And helpless Objects, Blind and Lame, we meet,
Thou dost instruct us what Respect to pay,
To give the Wall, and when to take the Way.
These Men with thankful Voice will give thee Praise,
Pray for thy Health, and wish thee prosp'rous Days.
   Whether by Phoebus's Meridian Light,
Or in the gloomy Horror of the Night,
I walk, in winding Alleys, Streets unknown,
And lose my Way in this great Hive, the Town,
By thy Directions, I shall fear no Ill,
No panick Terror shall my Bosom fill:
Whilst I walk Streets, thy Precepts I'll imbibe,
Trivia shall be my Convoy, and my Guide.

The memoir prefixed to the 1803 edition of the *Works* of Richard Owen Cambridge, by his son, contains a letter to the poet from Henry Berkeley, who praises *Trivia* along with the *Dunciad* and the *Dispensary:* "I have always thought that expressing the common accidents, and business, and actions of life in elegant verse, was the most difficult matter in poetry, and required the greatest industry."

The tribute to our guide and patron having been thus generously paid, it will be useful now to trace the curve in the history of professional men of letters through the century following the Revolution, with the idea always of getting them properly established in our minds as observers of and actors in this *revue* of town life.

The period may be divided, perhaps too neatly, into three sections.[1] I state the facts in general and then reinforce them by contemporary testimony. The years from 1660 to the coronation of William and Mary in 1689 were probably, for authors, the most difficult time in what is ordinarily called modern English history. Men of letters were then dependent almost entirely on titled patronage, and the subserviency which this involved left its mark on their product and on their lives. Since they wrote to please the profligate, their writings were frequently obscene; and because their income was so shockingly uncertain, their lives were irregular. No possible condition of affairs could have been more detrimental to any sense of personal dignity or *esprit du corps*. With the passing of the old order at the Revolution, the profession, if one may call it so, experienced a refreshing change. Instead of hanging about for scraps in the lobbies of nobility, writers found themselves courted and caressed by the powerful. The emoluments of office were theirs, and in many cases the dignity and social conscience which should accompany wealth. Addison, for example, wrote *The Campaign* (1705) and became Under-Secretary of State. The political conditions which brought about this change are not specially our concern here.[2] The fact is plain enough. There was a

[1] Alexandre Beljame, *Le Public et les Hommes de Lettres en Angleterre au dix-huitième Siècle* (1881).

[2] See "A new satyrical Ballad of the Licentiousness of the Times," *Bagford Ballads*, II, 715. All talk politics, the republican, the bully, the cit, the knight, the cobbler, the women.

King William, however, paid scant attention to writers. See Sir Richard Blackmore, *Poems* (1718), "The Kit-cats" (printed 1708):

"He shun'd the Acclamations of the Throng,
And always coldly heard the Poet's Song.
Hence the great King the Muses did neglect,
And the meer Poet met with small Respect."

much-needed calm after stormy seas in the literary
world, and an opportunity for writers to establish their
profession. The recess from old tribulations lasted until
the accession of Walpole to power in 1721. This great
minister economized on poets. Men of letters noticed at
once a marked decline in the number of posts available,
and must perforce look about for other means to pre-
serve their independence. From that time to the middle
of the century, success in letters from the worldly point
of view, making it pay, was partly a matter of cultivat-
ing a large circle of friends as prospective subscribers,
but, more than that, the possession of keen sense for the
value of advertisement and ability to drive a good bar-
gain with one's bookseller.

The hopeless condition of the hacks in the first of our
periods (1660–89) is reflected in Oldham's poem "Upon
a Printer that exposed him by Printing a Piece of his
grosly mangled and faulty." [1] In this he describes him-
self as

> Born to chastise the Vices of the Age,
> Which Pulpits dare not, nor the very Stage.

Satire is for him his only province and delight; he wears
a pen as others do their swords. Even the humblest
have some means of defence against the assaults of the
world:

> Strumpets of *Billingsgate* redress their Wrongs
> By the sole noise, and foulness of their Tongues.

He then proceeds to utter the most stupendous curse he
can think of against the printer who has so misused him:

> Thou, who with spurious Nonsence durst prophane
> The genuine issue of a Poets Brain,
> May'st thou hereafter never deal in Verse,

[1] *Works* (6th ed., 1703). Written about 1681.

But what hoarse Bell-men in their Walks rehearse,[1]
Or *Smithfield* Audience sung on Crickets hears:
May'st thou print H—, or some duller Ass,
Jorden, or him that wrote *Dutch Hudibras:*
Or next vile Scribler of the House, whose Play
Will scarce for Candles, and their snuffing pay:
May you each other Curse; thy self undone,
And be the Laughing-Stock of all the Town.
May'st thou ne'er rise to History, but what
Poor *Grubstreet* Penny Chronicles relate,
Memoirs of *Tyburn* and the mournful State
Of Cut-purses in *Holborn* Cavalcade,
Till thou thy self be the same subject made.
Compell'd by Want, may'st thou print Popery,
For which, be the Carts Arse and Pillory,
Turnips, and rotten Eggs thy Destiny.
Maul'd worse than *Reading*, *Christian*, or *Cellier*,
Till thou, daub'd o'er with loathsome filth, appear
Like Brat of some vile Drab in Privy found,
Which there has lain three Months in Ordure drown'd.
The Plague of Poets, Rags, and Poverty,
Debts, Writs, Arrests, and Serjeants, light on thee;
For others bound, may'st thou to Durance go,
Condemn'd to Scraps, and begging with a Shoe.

[1] Ballads such as Swift tells of in "The Metamorphosis of Baucis and Philemon burlesqued, from the 8th Book of Ovid" (*Poems*, I, 70). Two saints visit a poor man's cottage, and in return for kindness make it over into a church, with the good man as rector:

> "The ballads pasted on the wall,
> Of Joan of France, and English Mall;
> Fair Rosamond, and Robin Hood,
> The little Children in the Wood,
> Now seem'd to look abundance better,
> Improved in picture, size, and letter."

Itinerant poets also furnished verses for prints, specimens of which may be seen under some of Hogarth's engravings. "Your print," says he, "is a taking one, and why won't you go to the price of a half-crown Epigram" (Nichols, *Biog. Anec.* [3d ed., 1785], p. 123).

Cf. Richard Ames, *A Dialogue between Claret and Darby-Ale* (1692.) Two gentlemen meet on Ludgate Hill and discuss in prose town *vs.* country life. Then one reads a poem:

> "*Claret:* But I yet never heard you could Inspire,
> Except some Smithfield poets when they Write,
> And sad and Lamentable Songs Indite."

Between the lines of this passage one can easily read the progress of many a poet in Charles II's reign.

Oldham likes to depreciate his trade. There is a certain crude energy about his railings, which is partly temperamental, and partly the result of his intimate knowledge of the town. One of his Satyrs introduces Spenser, "dissuading the Author from the Study of Poetry; and shewing him how little it is esteem'd and encourag'd in this present age."[1]

> I'd be a Porter, or a Scavenger,
> A Groom, or anything, but Poet here:
> Hast thou observ'd some Hawker of the Town,
> Who thro' the streets with dismal Scream and Tone,
> Cries Matches, Small-coal, Brooms, Old Shoes and Boots,
> Socks, Sermons, Ballads, Lies, Gazetts, and Votes?
> So unrecorded to the Grave I'd go,
> And nothing but the Register tell, who:
> Rather that poor unheard of Wretch I'd be,
> Than the most glorious Name in Poetry,
> With all its boasted Immortality:
> Rather than He, who sung on *Phrygia's* shore,
> The *Grecian* Bullies fighting for a Whore:
> Or he of *Thebes*, whom Fame so much extols
> For praising Jockies, and *New-market* Fools.
>   So many now, and bad the Scriblers be,
> 'T is scandal to be of the Company:
> The foul Disease is so prevailing grown,
> So much the Fashion of the Court and Town,
> That scarce a man well-bred in either's deem'd:
> But who has kill'd, been often clapt, and oft has rhim'd . . .
> So Oats and Bedloe have been pointed at,
> And every busie Coxcomb of the State:
> The meanest Felons who thro' Holborn go,
> More eyes and looks than twenty Poets draw:
> If this be all, go have thy posted Name
> Fix'd up with Bills of Quack, and publick Sham;
> To be the stop of gaping Prentices,
> And read by reeling Drunkards when they piss.

[1] Cf. Juvenal, VII.

Poems once popular are now thrown into Duck-lane
shops:

> A Poet would be dear, and out o' th' way,
> Should he expect above a Coach-man's pay.

He is compelled to flatter, and even this does not always
save him from starvation. Cowley and Waller both suf-
fered; Butler more than all:

> Reduc'd to want, he in due time fell sick,
> Was fain to die, and be interr'd on tick.

The playwrights are no better off. Sedley was rich, but
Settle and the rest who write for pence have a hard time
of it, and get but scant reward for their labors. "The
vile Emp'rick, who by Licence kills," the trading sot,
the punk, the pandar, and the bawd, are all more com-
fortable than he. Become a lawyer, parson, anything
at all,

> Be all but Poet, and there's way to live.

Then, if this advice is disregarded,

> May'st thou go on unpitied, till thou be
> Brought to the Parish-Badg, and Beggary:
> Till urg'd by Want, like broken Scriblers, thou
> Turn Poet to a Booth, a *Smithfield* Show,
> And write Heroick Verse for *Barthol'mew.*
> Then slighted by the very Nursery,
> May'st thou at last be forced to starve, like me.

The taste of the public was not to be depended upon—
by no means an extraordinary state of affairs. Neither
Court nor Commons could tell good work from bad, and
if by chance they approved the good, it was always for
the wrong reason.

> At ev'ry Shop, while *Shakespeare's* lofty Stile
> Neglected lies, to Mice and Worms a Spoil;
> Gilt on the Back, just smoking from the Press,
> Th' Apprentice shews you *Durfey's Hudibras,*

Crown's Mask, bound up with *Settle's* choicest Labours,
And promises some new Essay of *Babor's*.
If you go off, as who the Devil would stay,
He cries, Sir, Mr. *Otway's* last new Play,
With th' Epilogue, which for the Duke he writ,
So lik'd at Court by all the Men of Wit:
I heard an Ensign of the Guards declare,
That with him *Shadwell* was not to compare;
He lik'd that scene of *Nicky Nacky* more,
Than all that *Shadwell* ever writ before.[1]

Again and again in later poems occur references to the sad stories of really great writers. Butler and Otway are the stock examples of this neglect of genius, but they are by no means isolated in their despairs. There were no great patrons of letters. Rochester posed as one, but, though his taste was good, he allowed the freakishness of his character to lead him into strange literary company. The noble dabbler in poetry must be pleased, either by fulsome flattery or by catering to the fashions of the moment. Those lines that Dryden wrote about plays have a much wider application:

You now have Habits, Dances, Scenes, and Rhymes;
High Language often; Ay, and Sense, sometimes . . .
But blame yourselves, not him who writ the Play;
Though his Plot's Dull, as can be well desir'd,
Wit stiff as any you have e'er admir'd:
He's bound to please, not to write well; and knows
There is a Mode in Plays as well as Cloaths.[2]

The poet at all times is bound to please, though he has on occasion been put to strange shifts to do it. Prior to the Revolution the circle of readers was so small that it would scarcely be proper to speak of a "reading public." An author never expected to get any money from the

---

[1] "A Satire," *Poems on State Affairs*, III, 110.
[2] Prologue to *The Rival Ladies*, acted 1664.

sale of his books on the stalls. His gains were limited to
the subscription list and what the good-nature of his
patron might afford him. It was just the same in Ben
Jonson's time. He cared little whether his books sold
or not. An immense sale would add to his fame, no
doubt, and thus indirectly better his position, but for
the moment the worries of distribution were largely the
concern of his bookseller. The following "Epigram to
my Booke-seller" makes this clear:[1]

> Thou that mak'st gain thy end, and wisely well,
>   Call'st a book good, or bad, as it doth sell,
> Use mine so too; I give thee leave: but crave,
>   For the luck's sake, it thus much favour have,
> To lie upon thy stall, till it be sought;
>   Not offer'd, as it made suit to be bought;
> Nor have my title-leaf on posts or walls,
>   Or in cleft-sticks, advanced to make calls
> For termers, or some clerk like serving-man,
>   Who scarce can spell th' hard names; whose knight les can.
> If, without these vile arts, it will not sell,
>   Send it to Bucklers-bury,* there 't will well.[2]

* To the butter-man.

Swift's life is typical of the new day in the fortunes
of literary men, as Otway's is of the old, and Pope's or

---

[1] Jonson, *Works*(ed. by W. Gifford, 9 vols., 1816), VIII, 154.
[2] Cf. Henry Fitzgeffrey, "To his Book-binder," *Certain Elegies* (1620):
>   "If thou behold a Courtcast *Satten*-show,
>   Fallen from the Fashion a Degree or two:
>   *One* as goes purueing vp and downe for *Tales*,
>   To Jest his hungry stomacke into *meales:*
>   That with a merry pocket-*Pamphlet* will,
>   For a weeke after Laugh his *Belly-full.*
>   Send him to Soiourne with Duke *Humfrey.*
>   Let him starue ere hee get a bitt of mee.
>   Least lying (*Read*) neglected in his *Slop*,
>   I bee conueyed vnto the *Brokers*-shop.
>   Or by his theeuish *Page* discouered
>   Quickly conuerted into *Ginger-bread.*"

Johnson's of that still to come. Starting as tutor and
private secretary in a wealthy family, Swift became
within a few years one of the most powerful men in the
country, the confidant of prime ministers, and distribu-
tor of political patronage, better able to serve others
than himself. Such a beginning with such a conclusion
was extraordinary:

> Harley, the Nation's great support,
> Returning home one day from Court,
> (His mind with public cares possest,
> All Europe's business in his Breast)
> Observed a Parson near Whitehall,
> Cheapning old authors on a stall.[1]

That was all there was to begin with. To-day there
would be nothing remarkable about a career like his.
Many a clever young man starts out in life as a tutor
and finds his way at last into some conspicuous position.
No need for a black cat, either! But in Charles II's time
an ascent like that was unthinkable. It may be as well
to notice just what the fate of such a person might then
be. And again we follow Oldham, this time in "A Satyr
Address'd to a Friend that is about to leave the Uni-
versity, and come abroad in the World."[2] The poet ad-
vises his friend not to become a parson, a schoolmaster,
or a tutor:

> you'll hardly meet
> More Porters now than Parsons in the street.

But the blindest of all alleys is the tutor's position in a
noble family. The favorite footman is better paid.

> Some think themselves exalted to the Sky,
> If they light in some noble Family:

[1] Swift, "To Lord Oxford, A.D. 1713; In Imitation of Horace, Epistles
I, 7," *Poems*, II, 159.
[2] *Works* (6th ed., 1703), p. 388.

Diet, an Horse, and thirty pounds a year,
Besides th' advantage of his Lordship's ear,
The credit of the business, and the State,
Are things that in a Youngster's Sense sound great.
Little the unexperienc'd wretch does know,
What slavery he oft must undergo:
Who, tho in Silken Scarf, and Cassock drest,
Wears but a gayer Livery at best:
When Dinner calls, the Implement must wait,
With holy words to consecrate the Meat:
But hold it for a Favour seldom known,
If he be deign'd the Honour to sit down.
Soon as the Tarts appear, Sir *Crape*, withdraw!
Those Dainties are not for a spiritual Maw:
Observe your distance, and be sure to stand
Hard by the Cistern with your Cap in hand:
There for diversion you may pick your Teeth,
Till the kind Voider comes for your Relief.
For meer Board-wages such their Freedom sell,
Slaves to an Hour, and Vassals to a Bell:
And if th' enjoyment of one day be stole,
They are but Pris'ners out upon Parole:
Always the marks of Slavery remain,
And they, though loose, still drag about their Chain.
    And where 's the mighty Prospect after all,
A Chaplainship serv'd up, and seven years Thrall?
The menial thing perhaps for a Reward,
Is to some slender Benefice preferr'd,
With this Proviso bound, that he must wed
My Lady's antiquated Waiting-Maid,
In Dressing only skill'd, and Marmalade.
Let others who such meannesses can brook,
Strike Countenance to every Great Man's Look:
Let those that have a mind, turn slaves to eat,
And live contented by another's Plate:
I rate my Freedom higher, nor will I
For Food and Raiment truck my Liberty.
But, if I must to my last shifts be put,
To fill a Bladder, and twelve yards of Gut;

Rather with counterfeited wooden Leg,
And my right Arm ty'd up, I'll chuse to beg.[1]

The main facts are here. Truewit's philosophy, "What's six kicks to a man that reads Seneca?"[2] would certainly be needed in a situation like this. For Swift, however,

[1] Cf. John Hall, "A Satire," *Poems*, 1646, in Saintsbury, *Minor Poets of the Caroline Period* (1906), II, 188:

> "Who if some lowly carriage do befriend,
> May grace the table at the lower end,
> Upon condition that ye fairly rise
> At the first entrance of th' potato pies,
> And while his lordship for discourse doth call
> You do not let one dram of Latin fall;
> But tell how bravely your young master swears,
> Which dogs best like his fancy, and what ears;
> How much he undervalues learning, and
> Takes pleasure in a sparrow-hawk well mann'd,
> How oft he beats his foot-boy, and will dare
> To gallop when no serving man is near."

Also cf. Macaulay, *Works* (1875), I, 256; *Tatler*, Nos. 255 and 258; Scott, *Rob Roy:* "But here comes cheese, radishes, and a bumper to Church and King — the signal for ladies and chaplains to retire"; Swift, "Mrs. Frances Harris's Petition," 1699, in *Poems* (2 vols., Bohn, 1910), I, 36. Also cf. Juvenal, VII:

> "Haec, inquit, cures, et cum se verterit annus
> Accipe victori populus quod postulat aurum!"

and Hall, *Satires* (Oxford, 1753), II, 6, p. 33:

> "A Gentle squire would gladly entertaine
> Into his house some trencher-chaplaine;
> Some willing man that might instruct his sons,
> And that would stand to good conditions.
> First, that he lie upon the truckle-bed,
> Whiles his young maister lieth o'er his head.
> Second, that he do, on no default,
> Ever presume to sit above the salt.
> Third, that he never change his trencher twise.
> Fourth, that he use all common courtesies;
> Sit bare at meales, and one halfe rise and wait.
> Last, that he never his yong maister beat,
> But he must aske his mother to define,
> How manie jerkes she would his breech should line.
> All these observ'd, he could contented bee,
> To give five markes and winter liverie."

[2] Jonson, *The Silent Woman*, IV, 2.

such reflections were quite alien, and he doubtless chafed under the indignities of his position in Sir William Temple's family. Fortunately for him, conditions in London were now vastly different for the man who could write, and even Grub Street hacks were comparatively prosperous. The tutor must come up to the city. There with ability and character he was assured of success. Without much of either he could live. Take the case, for instance, of Tom Brown, the voluminous author of essays on London life, whose character Addison gives in the *Tatler* (No. 101):

The merry Rogue said, when he wanted a Dinner, he writ a Paragraph of Table-Talk, and his Book-seller upon Sight paid the Reckoning. . . . Poor Tom! He is gone — But I observed, he always looked well after a Battle, and was apparently fatter in a fighting Year.

The news-sheets, at all events, were open to the ambitious. The writers in these, like George Ridpath of *The Flying Post*, Abel Roper of the *Post Boy*, and John Tutchin of the *Observator*, were pedestrian enough in their styles, but at last they had found a public interested in their ideas, and they made the most of the discovery. The indispensable element in their equipment was rabid party spirit.

No matter whether false or true,
Take Pattern by D[e]F[oe]'s *Review;*
Let it be Scandal and 't will do . . .
Fling Dirt enough, and some will stick.[1]

The same qualification is implied in some amusing verses from the Lewis *Miscellany*,[2] "On the death of Abel Roper and George Ridpath, Authors of the Post-Boy and Flying-Post: who dyed both on the same Day."

[1] Ward, *Hudibras Redivivus* (4th ed., n. d., first publ. 1708,) Part II, p. 11.
[2] 1726. P. 209.

Roper and Ridpath both at once, we read
In the same self-same Paragraph, are dead!
No longer each, his Party to amuse,
For Infant Whispers hunts, and early News:
No more, as Whig or Tory most prevails,
Repines, or triumphs; or commends, or rails;
With Politicks profound no longer vexes,
No longer curious Innocents perplexes.
But weary'd both and spent, with fruitless Jar,
To others leave th' Hereditary War.
Lye they, where-e'er they lye, at last in Peace;
Where-e'er they lye, their Epitaph be this;
Roper and Ridpath, long to fame well known,
Were Twain when living, but in Death are One.

It was, indeed, the golden age of the pamphleteer, especially if he could wield the keen sword — or broad-axe, perhaps better — of satire. Pope's claim in his *Imitations of Horace: Satires*, II, 1, was true neither of himself nor of most of his friends, including Swift:

Satire's my weapon, but I'm too discreet
To run amuck, and tilt at all I meet;
I only wear it in a land of Hectors,
Thieves, Supercargoes, Sharpers, and Directors.[1]

They did run amuck, Pope more noticeably than any, and were often much inclined to misuse their new-found power. Pope and most of the others claimed a magnanimity and public spirit which they did not possess.

Down, down, proud Satire! though a realm be spoil'd,
Arraign no mightier thief than wretched Wild;
Or, if a court or country's made a job,
Go drench a pickpocket, and join the mob.[2]

---

[1] "Dialogue between Alexander Pope and a Learned Council" (1733), *Works*, (ed. Warton), IV, 71.

[2] Pope, *Seventeen Hundred and Thirty-Eight*, Dialogue II (ed. Elwin and Courthope), III, 474.

Thomas Cooke knew them better than they knew themselves, and in Canto I of "The Battle of the Poets" (1725) he has a description of Pope and Swift, with an imaginary conversation.

Swift: Call them, without Reserve, Dog, Monkey, Owl,
And splutter out at once Fish, Flesh, and Fowl.
Pope: To him thus Pope: waste not thy Breath again
To give Advice to whom Advice is vain.
Who better knows than I his Dirt to throw?
To wound in Secret either Friend or Foe?
Go preach to Gay, and such as are inclin'd
Less to exert an enterprising Mind,
Who, slothful to pursue our glorious Ends,
Lag as if willing to make all their Friends.

All these writers would have been better off, had they digested Young's wise warning:[1]

Satire recoils whenever charg'd too high;
Round your own fame the fatal splinters fly.

And some of them at least deserved Blackmore's reproof:[2]

Those, who by Satyre would reform the Town,
Should have some little Merit of their own,
And not be Rakes themselves below Lampoon.

Pope was not a rake; he was a cripple, and he doubtless feared the dunces quite as much as they feared him. Lady Mary Wortley-Montagu addressed a poetical epistle "To the Imitator of the First Satire of the Second Book of Horace" (1733), in which she charged that even benefits failed to check Pope's hand. Rancorous enough is Lady Mary.

It was the Equity of right'ous Heaven,
That such a Soul to such a Form was giv'n.

[1] "Love of Fame" (1728), *Poems*, II, 322.
[2] "A Satire upon Wit" (printed 1700), *Poems* (1718).

Nearly as savage is "An Epistle from a Nobleman to a
D.D. in Answer to a Latin Letter in Verse, written from
H[ampton] C[our]t" in the same year, by Lord Hervey:

> But had he not, to his eternal Shame,
> By trying to deserve a Sat'rist's Name,
> Prov'd he can ne'er invent but to defame:
> Had not his *Taste* and *Riches* lately shown,
> When he would talk of Genius to the Town,
> How ill he chuses, if he trusts his own.
> Had he, in modern Language, only wrote
> Those Rules which *Horace*, and which *Vida* taught;
> On *Garth* or *Boileau's* Model built his Fame,
> Or sold *Broome's* Labours printed with P[o]pe's Name:
> Had he ne'er aim'd at any Work beside,
> In Glory then he might have liv'd and dy'd;
> And ever been, tho' not with Genius fir'd,
> By *School-boys* quoted, and by *Girls* admir'd.

This was the sort of arena into which the writer —
no matter how great — must descend in Pope's time.
Some attained with rapidity a success merely of scandal,
and enjoyed it.[1] Grub Street lodgings were at a pre-
mium, and the methods that their tenants used to pro-
mulgate their wares were more than questionable.

> Who'd be the man leud Libels to indite,
> Yet fears to own what he ne'er fears to write?
> And meanly sneak his Lampoons into th' world,
> Which are i' th' streets by porters dropt and hurled,
> Or else by Julian 'mong the Bullies spread,
> Which with his pimping brings him in his bread?[2]

Baker speaks in *Tunbridge Walks* (1703) of lawyers
turning poets:

---

[1] See "An Epistle from a Gentleman at Twickenham, to a Nobleman at
St. James's. Occasion'd by an Epistle from a Nobleman, to a Doctor of
Divinity" (1733?).

[2] *Poems on Affairs of State, continued to 1697* (1709), I, 60.

For since the Lawyers are all turn'd Poets, and have taken
the Garrets in Drury-Lane, none but Beaux live at the Tem-
ple now, who have sold all their Books, burnt all their Writ-
ings, and furnish'd the Rooms with Lookinglass and China.

But the beaux and ladies also took their turn at the
game of letters. No preparation was necessary to write,
therefore, have at you for a play, or a poem! Char-
acters such as the one portrayed in the Prologue to *Ig-
noramus* [1] were by no means unknown. The writer of
this complains that Ignoramus has been throughout
life changeable like Proteus.

> First in one Dress, and then another seen.
> Howe'er this Play confines him to the Bar,
> He ranges, and by Turns is ev'rywhere.
> Sometimes upon a Stage exalted high,
> He either couches, or puts out an Eye.
> Now glares in gilded Chariot, and anon
> Ascends a Tub, and proves a stiff *Non-Con.*
> Then he will dress, and drink, and swear, and fight,
> And lose a thousand Guineas in a Night.
> Next runs against a Post, and breaks a Shin,
> Yet gravely tells you of the Light within.
> Soon after the Poetic Maggot bites,
> He calls for Paper, Pen, and Ink, and writes,
> No matter what, Dramatics, Epics, Lyrics,
> Ballads or Odes, Lampoons or Panegyrics.
>   Thus have I oft the various Frenzy view'd,
> Thro' every Scene the shifting Fool pursu'd,
> 'Till tir'd with all the Changes he had shown,
> His genuine Figure he resolv'd to own,
> Of *Dev'reux* Court, his proper Sphere, possest,
> *Free-Thinker* turn'd — and there he stands confest.

No one was more acutely conscious of the heat of this
literary fever than Edward Young, himself among the
afflicted:

[1] 1711. Publ. in Lewis, *Misc.*, p. 166.

> Some future strain, in which the Muse shall tell
> How science dwindles, and how volumes swell.
> How commentators each dark passage shun,
> And hold their farthing candle to the sun.[1]

The disease was epidemic. His crisp phrases come home
forcibly to us in these days:

> Pursuit of fame with pedants fills our schools,
> And into coxcombs burnishes our fools.[2]

Shortly after this, Young wrote "Two Epistles to Mr.
Pope concerning the Authors of the Age" (1730), in
which he gives salutary advice to aspirants:

> Write, and re-write, blot out, and write again,
> And for its swiftness ne'er applaud your pen.[3]

And even more forcefully:

> Think frequently, think close, read nature, turn
> Men's manners o'er, and half your volumes burn.[4]

Moreover, unlike some critics, Young is willing to ac-
knowledge his own sins:

> Who's this with nonsense, nonsense would restrain?
> Who's this (they cry) so vainly schools the vain?
> Who damns our trash, with so much trash replete?
> As, three ells round, huge Cheyne rails at meat?

The most glaring example of this plethora of wit is Sir
Richard Blackmore, of whom Tom Moore once wrote:

> 'Twas in his carriage the sublime
> Sir Richard Blackmore used to rhyme,
> And if the wits don't do him wrong,
> 'Twixt death and epics passed his time,
> Scribbling and killing all day long.

---

[1] "Love of Fame" (1728), *Poems* (2 vols., 1852), II, 136.
[2] *Ibid.*, p. 137.
[3] *Ibid.*, p. 320.
[4] *Ibid.*, p. 322.

But the Authors of the Town are so numerous that
the satire which bears that name (1725) can suggest only
a few types, and gossip a bit about their methods. They
are satisfied with any subject. Dr. John Byrom — by
no means a dunce — actually wrote a poem "On In-
oculation" when it first began to be practised in Eng-
land, and that theme will do as well as another if only
public attention can be caught:

> If next Inoculation's Art spreads wide,
> (An Art, that mitigates Infection's Tide)
> Loud *Pamphleteers* 'gainst *Innovation* cry,
> *Let Nature work* — 'T is natural to die.

To politics or to Tyburn they indifferently turn their
thoughts:

> If Ruin rushes o'er a Statesman's Sway,
> Scribblers, like Worms, on tainted Grandeur prey;
> While a poor Felon waits th' impending Stroke,
> Voracious Scribes, like hov'ring Ravens, croak.
> In their dark Quills a dreary Insult lies,
> Th' Offence lives recent, tho' th' Offender dies;
> In his last Words they suck his parting Breath,
> And gorge on his loath'd Memory after Death.

To the critics this satirist is equally rude:

> None unprefer'd in Parliament more loud!
> No worn-out Fair more peevish, or more proud!
> No City-Dame, when to the Birth-Night drawn,
> More vain of Gems! — (Some female Courtier's Pawn!)
> Proud as a Judge, when Equity's a Trade,
> Or Lord, whose Guilt was with a Title paid.

The profession draws recruits from all quarters.

A Blade whose Life a Turn of Humour takes,
Cocks smart, trims fine, treats Harlots, scours with Rakes!
When his drained Purse no new Expence supplies,
Fond Madam frowns, each dear Companion flies!
Duns clamour, Bailiffs lurk, and Clothes decay,

Coin ebbs, he must recruit. — He writes a Play.
"Bold task! a Play? — Mark our young Bard proceed!
"A Play? — Your Wits in Want are Wits indeed."
Here the Punk's Jokes are for Politeness wrote,
Some inconsistent Novel forms a Plot.
In the Gallant, his own wise Conduct glares!
Smut is sheer Wit! — Each Prank a Merit wears!
Bright Youth! He steals, to make the Piece entire,
A Cuckold, Beau, pert Footman, and a Squire.

This satire on the Authors of the Town is of special interest to us here because, among the many praised or reviled, John Gay has the most prominent place. Two pages at least are devoted to him.

> *Johnny's* fine Works at Court obtain Renown!
> *Aaron* writes Trash — He ne'er collogues the Town.

Johnny gets hints from La Fontaine, and something more than hints from "that bright Genius that has charm'd the Age." He writes a play:

> New Thoughts they hatch! — but *Johnny* holds the *Name*.

This probably refers to Gay's tragedy, *The Captives*, which was acted for *seven* nights following January 15, 1724, at Drury Lane.

> Thus thro' nine Nights loud Party-Praises roar,
> Then die away at once, to noise no more.

The author tells us, too, how

> Cabals are form'd, our *Johnny's* Debts to clear.

The piece is inscribed to the author of *The Universal Passion*, who had, as we have just seen, prepared some bitter drafts for young versifiers. Sir Richard Blackmore, who wrote *A Satyr against Wit* (3d edition, 1700), shared his ideas.

> Our Learning daily sinks, and Wit is grown
> The senseless Conversation of the Town.

Precautions should have been taken earlier:

> Had but the People scar'd with Danger run
> To shut up *Will's*, where first this Plague begun:
> Had they the first infected Men convey'd
> Strait to *Moorfields*, the Pest-house for the Head;
> The wild Contagion might have been supprest,
> Some few had fal'n, but we had sav'd the rest.

He recommends an Academy to restrain extravagance:

> Set forth your Edict, let it be enjoyn'd
> That all defective Species be recoyn'd.
> *St. E[vre]m[on]t* and *R[yme]r*, both are fit
> To oversee the Coining of our Wit.
> Let these be made the Masters of Assay,
> They'll every Piece of Metal touch and weigh,
> And tell which is too light, which has too much Allay.
> 'Tis true, that when the coarse and worthless Dross
> Is purg'd away, there will be mighty Loss.
> Ev'n *C[ongrev]e*, *S[outhern]e*, manly *W[ycher]ly*,
> When thus refin'd will grievous Suff'rers be.
> Into the melting Pot when *D[ryde]n* comes,
> What horrid Stench will rise, what noisome Fumes?
> How will he shrink, when all his lewd Allay,
> And wicked Mixture shall be purg'd away?

Literary men always think the shelves overstocked. A hundred years before this time they were complaining. Even the fop then professed learning, and for the diurnal-maker writing was a disease. In *The Return from Parnassus* (1606), the beau gives his final instructions to his page: "Sirrah, boy, remember me when I come in Paul's Church yard, to buy a Ronsard, and Dubartas in French; and Aretine in Italian, and our hardest writers in Spanish." The news-sheet was appearing on the streets, a frivolous débutante of letters. Cleveland, in his *Character of a Diurnal-Maker* (1644), defines the diurnal as a "puny Chronicle, scarce Pin-feather'd with the Wings of Time"; and as for its maker,

Writing is a Disease in him, and holds like a Quotidian; so
'tis his Infirmity that makes him an Author, as *Mahomet* was
beholding to the Falling-sickness to vouch him a Prophet . . .
they tug at the Pen, like slaves at the Oar, a whole Bank to-
gether; they write in the Posture that the *Swedes* gave fire in,
over one another's heads.

In the volume called *Certain Elegies* (1620), Henry Fitz-
geffrey has a few things to say about this excess literary
baggage:

> Who'd not at venture *Write?* So many waies
> A man may prove a *Poet* now a daies!
> Does *Nature* witt afford to breake a Jest?
> This is a *Poet;* and his friends protest
> He is to blame he *Writes* not: when (indeed)
> Th' Illiterate Gull can neither *write* nor *read.*
> Let *Nature* faile! Takes he but so much *Paine,*
> To *write obscurely;* adding so much *Braine,*
> As end his crabbed sencelesse verse in *Rime;*
> This might a *Poet* beene in *Perseus* time.

There seems to have been a general feeling of this sort
among writers in the early seventeenth century; so that
in this respect also we must not think our own age
peculiar. Cowley [1] writes in *Davideis* as any thoughtful
man might to-day:

> I' th' *Library* a few choice *Authors* stood;
> Yet 'twas well stor'd, for that small Store was *good;*
> *Writing,* Man's *Spir'tual Physick,* was not then
> *Itself,* as now, grown a *Disease* of Men.
> *Learning* (young Virgin) but few *Suitors* knew;
> The common *Prostitute* she lately grew,
> And with the *spurious Brood* loads now the Press;
> *Laborious Effects* of *Idleness!*

We have the poet of love rhymes, whom Rowlands
notices in his *Terrible Battell betweene Time and Death.*[2]
Death speaks:

[1] 1656. Bk. I, paragraph 52, p. 315 (ed. 1707).
[2] No date; according to Gosse, 1606.

This Poet thus a sonneting we found,
Riming himselfe even almost out of breath,
Cupid (quoth he) thy cruell Dart doth wound,
Oh graunt me loue, or else come gentle *Death:*
I heard him say, come gentle death in Jest;
And in good earnest graunted his request.

This specialist in love lines is not perhaps so terrible
as another figure, whom the same satirist calls "Signieur
word-monger, the Ape of Eloquence," and whom he
ridicules in the familiar lines beginning, "As on my way
I itinerated." The journalist had his innings in the civil-
war period, and it was for him that Sir Francis Wortley
wrote the following epitaph in his *Mercurius Britannicus,
his Welcome to Hell* (1647). This particular Mercury
was Marchmont Needham.

Here lies *Britannicus*, Hell's barking cur,
That son of *Beliall*, who kept damned stir;
And every Munday spent his stocke of spleen,
In venomous railing on the King and Queen.
Who, though they both in goodnesse may forgive him,
Yet (for his safety) wee'l in hell riceive him.

The writers about 1600 begin to claim a property in
the products of their wit, and we find frequent com-
plaints about plagiarism. Marston in his first Satire
(1598) growls over the man who is "but broker of
another's wit," neglecting to mention that the phrase
is dangerously like Sidney's "pick-purse," an obvious
borrowing from Petrarch. Donne waxes pornographi-
cal in his condemnation of literary thievery in Satire II
(1593). Jonson also has some lines in *The Staple of
News* (1625), I, 1, which show that men were disapprov-
ing of the popular practice:

I pray thee tell me, Fashioner, what authors
Thou read'st to help thy invention! Italian prints?
Or arras hangings? they are tailors' libraries.

Books were sold not only in the regular shops, but by venders through the streets as to-day; evidently the door of the playhouse was a profitable stand for such persons, for in a play called *The Ordinary*, by William Cartwright,[1] Vicar Catchmey says:

> I shall live to see thee
> Stand in a play house door with thy long box,
> Thy half-crown library, and cry small books:
> "Buy a good godly sermon, gentlemen,"
> "A judgment shown upon a knot of drunkards":
> "A pill to purge out popery": "The life
> "And death of Katherine Stubbs."

The overcrowding of the profession in the early eighteenth century partly accounts for the numerous tirades against dulness which are so characteristic a feature of the period. Dryden's superb creation of the form in *MacFlecknoe* had evidently made a real impression, and the times offered unusually wide scope for its application. Pope's *Dunciad* is merely the most famous representative of a large number of similar satires. Smedley uses the idea long before Pope:[2]

> How long shall *Dulness*, dreaming God, sustain,
> In this fair Island, his inglorious Reign?
> Behold! what Pranks he plays; behold him range,
> The darling Deity, around the '*Change*;
> Where Pun-full Misers jest, and cheat, and cant,
> And wallow in the Riches, which they want.
> See! how his awful Godhead does dispence
> At *Child's* and *Will's*, his solid Influence!
> How willy-whisps P[op]e's senses quite astray;
> And sheds his whole collected Force on G[a]y!
> How puzzles pert Ar[buthno]t's Learned Head;

[1] 1634. Dodsley's *Old Plays* (ed. 1875), II, 272.

[2] "Cloe to Mr. Tickell, occasioned by his Avignon Letter," on p. 81 of *Poems on Several Occasions* (1721). Cf. Sir Richard Blackmore, *The Kit-Cats* (ed. 1709), p. 8.

Who, tho' to *Recipe's* and Pulses bred,
His former Studies, dozing, now reverses,
Writes Madrigals, Cracks Puns, and Clubs for Farces.

It was certainly an age of unlimited verbosity. Every-
body had something to say and hastened to say it, many
to write it. This gave the satirists a good chance:

Lo! in the *Church* my mighty Pow'r I shew,
In Pulpit preach, and slumber in the Pew:
The *Bench* and *Bar* alike my influence owns;
Here prate my *Magpies*, and there doze my *Drones*.
In the grave Dons, how formal is my mien,
Who rule the Gallipots of *Warwick-Lane!*
At Court behold me strut in *purple pride.*
At *Hockley* roar, and in *Crane-Court* preside.[1]

If with encouragement dulness was so rampant, if
political patronage had packed Grub Street, what
might one expect to happen when posts and pensions
dissolved in thin air, as many of them did with the com-
ing to power of Walpole in 1721?[2] A certain amount
of suffering and discouragement, doubtless, but not so
serious a situation as one might fear. The twenty fat
years had yielded store for the future of a very satis-
factory kind in the possibility of profit from sales to an
ever-increasing and sufficiently critical public. Pope had
made a fortune from the sale of his Homer,[3] an unheard-

---

[1] Paul Whitehead, *The State Dunces* (1733). Cf. Griffith Morgan D'Anvers
(M.A., formerly of Jesus College, Oxford), *Persius Scaramouch, or, a critical
and moral satire on the orators, scribblers, and vices of the present times in imi-
tation of the 1st Satire of Persius by way of dialogue betwixt the said Mr.
D'Anvers and Mr. Orator Henley of Lincoln's Inn Fields* (1734; dedicated to
Pulteney; rather clever satire).

[2] Oliver Goldsmith, *An Enquiry into the Present State of Polite Learning
in Europe* (1759), p. 130.

[3] Breval's satire in *The Confederates* (1717) about the sales of this book is
unfounded. On p. 32 Lintot is represented as saying:

"Look on your Homer, there, behind the Door.
Thou little dream'st what Crowds I daily see,
That call for Tickell, and that spurn at Thee!

of thing, and now disdained any entanglement with government.[1] The dunces must go, certainly. Moreover, until reputation was made, the booksellers were apt to be unfair, though some were reputed generous. In Breval's *The Confederates*, Lintot asks for a copy of Cibber's *Cid:*

> For who in *Fleetstreet*, or in *Warwick Lane*,
> Rewards like me the Labours of the Brain?

Writers of established fame might, as to-day, lend a helping hand to the less fortunate. Edmund Curll evidently, and reasonably, needed some encouragement to bring out Thomas Newcomb's *Ode Sacred to the Memory of that truly Pious and Honorable Lady*, *The Countess of Berkeley* (1717), for he prints an advertisement from Young in the preface:

MR. CURLL,

 I have perus'd the Poem which you receive with this, with much Pleasure, and I believe you will find your Advantage considerable in Printing it.

Yours, etc.

E. YOUNG

Haslemere, *May* 26, 1717.

But with reputation once established, financial returns were by no means despicable. Nichols [2] reprints

---

> Neglected there, your Prince of Poets lyes,
> By Dennis justly damn'd, and kept for Pyes."

Lintot is said to have paid fifty guineas for *Three Hours after Marriage*, the very play Breval is here condemning.

[1] Swift, *On Poetry, a rapsody* (1733), p. 18, l. 309:
> "Harmonious Cibber entertains
> The Court with annual Birth-day Strains;
> Whence Gay was banish'd in Disgrace,
> Where Pope will never show his Face;
> Where Y[oung] must torture his Invention,
> To flatter Knaves, or lose his Pension."

[2] *Literary Anecdotes of the 18th Century* (1814), VIII, 296.

from a small memorandum book, which formerly be-
longed to Lintot, the amounts paid to Gay for the copy-
right of his works. The list contains — it is to be noticed
— £16 2s. 6d. for *The Battle of the Frogs,* Parnell's con-
tribution to the flat purse of his friend:

1713, May 12, *Wife of Bath*	25	0	0
1714, Nov. 11, *Letter to a Lady*	5	7	6
1715, Feb. 14, *The What d'ye Call It*	16	2	6
1715, Dec. 22, *Trivia*	43	0	0
1715, Dec. 22, *Epistle to the Earl of Burlington*	10	15	0
1717, May 4, *Battle of the Frogs*	16	2	6
1717, Jan. 8, *Three Hours after Marriage*	43	2	6
Revival of the *Wife of Bath*	75	0	0
[*The Mohocks,* a farce, 2–10–0: Sold the *Mo-hocks* to him again]			
	234	10	0

This is not by any means an indifferent sum, consid-
ering the change in the value of money.[1]

The copyright laws were still very loose. Gay com-
plains of the rascality of Henry Hills:

> While neat old Elzevir is reckon'd better,
> Than Pirate Hills' brown sheets and scurvy letter.[2]

And Nichols [3] tells us of efforts made by government to
check this piracy:

Henry Hills, a notorious Printer in Black Fryars; who reg-
ularly pirated every good Poem or Sermon that was published;
a circumstance which led to the direction in the Act of 8
Anne, that *fine paper copies* should be presented to the Public
Libraries.

---

[1] Lintot's stand was at the Cross-Keys and Cushion, next Nando's Coffee
House, Temple Bar.

[2] See "On a Miscellany of Poems to Bernard Lintott," printed in Lin-
tot's *Miscellaneous Poems* (1712), p. 173.

[3] *Literary Anecdotes,* VIII, 168.

Men of letters had serious distress as well as petty annoyances to endure. Some of the booksellers played the slave-driver in too realistic a fashion. William Whitehead's *Charge to the Poets* in 1762 would not be very encouraging to young writers:

> Lords of their workhouse see the tyrants sit,
> Brokers in books, and stock-jobbers in wit,
> Beneath whose lash, oblig'd to write or fast,
> Our confessors and martyrs breathe their last!
> And can you bear such insolence? — away,
> For shame; plough, dig, turn pedlars, drive the dray;
> With minds indignant each employment suits,
> Our fleets want sailors, and our troops recruits;
> And many a dirty street, on Thames's side,
> Is yet by stool and brush unoccupied.[1]

But even this tyranny of the booksellers must have been preferable to the tyranny of the noble numskull which characterized Charles II's reign. The bookseller

---

[1] Cf. "A Satyr upon the Poets" (a translation of Juvenal, Satire VII), printed in *Poems on Affairs of State to the year 1703*, II, 138:

> "By Verse you'l starve: *John Saul** cou'd never live,
> Unless the Bellman made the Poet thrive;
> Go rather in some little Shed by *Pauls*,
> Sell *Chevy Chase*, or *Baxter's* Salve for Souls,
> Cry Raree-Shows, sell Ballads, transcribe Votes,
> Be *Care*, or *Ketch*, or anything but *Oates*. . . .
> Were I, like these, unhappily decreed
> By Penny Elegies to get my Bread,
> Or want a Meal, unless *George Croom* and I
> Could strike a Bargain for my Poetry,
> I'd damn my Works to wrap up Soap and Cheese,
> Or furnish Squibs for City Prentices
> To burn the Pope, and celebrate Queen *Bess*."

> * Bellman at Cambridge.

But, once touched with the fever of art, a man forever burns to write:

> "So practis'd Thief oft taken ne'er afraid,
> Forgets the Sentence, and pursues the Trade.
> Tho yet he almost feels the Smoaking Brand,
> And sad *T. R.* stands fresh upon his Hand. . . .
> More I could say, but care not much to meet
> A Crabtree Cudgel in a narrow Street."

had to please his public, but that public was, on the whole, more just in its discriminations than most patrons of former days. There was small decrease in scurrility, and some of the sensational productions of the mid-century are unrivalled for crude obscenity and sloppy sentiment. But many readers did appreciate good poetry and virile prose, and would have no other kind. The great authors were well known, and not so quickly forgotten as Swift's verses would suggest: [1]

> Some country Squire to Lintot goes,
> Inquires for "Swift in Verse and Prose."
> Says Lintot, "I have heard the name;
> He died a year ago." — "The same."
> He searches all the shop in vain.
> "Sir, you may find them in Duck-Lane;
> I sent them with a load of books,
> Last Monday to the pastry-cook's."

Depraved tastes did, of course, find caterers. The name of so great a writer as Charles Churchill is be-smirched by some stuff of this kind; and the circle of hacks who passed as his friends were guilty of the most nauseous varieties of filth imaginable. Arthur Murphy in the opposing camp was not guiltless, though his description of his enemies, in *The Expostulation*, published with *An Ode to the Naiads of Fleet-Ditch*, is vigorous enough to make us forgive some at least of his multitude of sins:

> See Grub-street opens her ten thousand doors,
> See Billingsgate unsluices all her stores;
> See essays, fables, puns, assist the fray,
> Abuse descending from confed'rate Say; [2]
> See authors on all sides desert their dens,
> New edge their blunted wits, and nib their pens:

---

[1] *Verses on the Death of Dr. Swift* (Nov., 1731).
[2] Printer of the *Gazetteer*.

All who in distant Hockley-hole reside,
The men who drink, Fleet-ditch, thy sable tide!
Who in Moorfields have scrawl'd a darken'd cell,
In the King's Bench, or in the Compter dwell;
On Ludgate-Hill, who bloody murders write,
Or pass in Fleet-street supperless the night;
The bards who doze around an alehouse fire,
Who tipple drams, or fatten with entire;
Thick as when locusts o'er the land appear,
And ruin all the promise of the year;
Thick as when pismires crawl along the plain,
Or half-starv'd crows around some ripen'd grain,
They form their ranks; they rail, they doom me dead,
And the press aims its thunders on my head.

Murphy had been attacked by Shirley in the *Murphiad*, and by Churchill and Lloyd elsewhere. His reply to these attacks was called *The Examiner* [1] (1761), which, while it may be very sound as a diatribe against his enemies, is interesting to us only because it contains an occasional hint about London life:

Cast but your eye around you, and survey
Books once admir'd, now with'ring in decay;
Whole poems, for their time delightful found,
All now transferr'd to grocers by the pound.
Verse, that could once a lady's toilet grace,
'Gainst a dead wall attracts the livried race.
Else to *High Holborn*, or *Moorfields* consign'd,
'Midst other still-born embryos of the mind,
It lies for ages doom'd, in silence deep,
With *Shirley's Pepin*, or *Black Prince*, to sleep.

His remarks about Churchill have enough truth in them to cut:

At fairs he cudgell'd, and with porters drank;
In ev'ry low dexterity he dealt,
Broughtonian fame, and judgment *at a belt*. [2]

---

[1] *The Expostulation* was first called *The Examiner*, to mislead enemies. See advertisement to the 1761 edition, printed for J. Coote.
[2] A game, "Pricking at the belt."

> At wheelbarrows for apples cogg'd the dice,
> In ev'ry ale house gather'd ev'ry vice.

Hogarth evidently shared Murphy's opinion of Churchill. He had once drawn a picture of his own head in a cap, a pug-dog, and a palette with a line of beauty. Afterwards he erased his own head and inserted that of Mr. Churchill, under the character of a bear, in its room.[1] Lines about this picture before the alteration occur in *The Scandalizade* (1750):

> There elbowing in 'mong the Crowd with a Jog,
> "Lo! good Father *Tobit*, said I, with his Dog!—
> But the Artist is wrong; for the Dog should be drawn
> At the Heels of his Master in Trot o'er the Lawn."—
> "To your idle Remarks I take leave to demur,
> 'Tis n't *Tobit*, nor yet his canonical Cur,
> (Quoth a Sage in the Crowd) for I'd have you to know, Sir,
> 'Tis *Hogarth* himself and his Friend honest *Towser*.

The enemies of Churchill did their best for him in a horrible poem called "Churchill Dissected" (1764), which describes a post-mortem on the satirist. The writer gives a fairly sane account of the functions of satire and is willing to admit the power of his adversary.

> Such Ease, such Vigour flowing in his Verse,
> As *Pope* or *Dryden* might with Pride rehearse;
> Witty as *Butler*, and like *Mulgrave* clear,
> As *Denham* strong, than *Oldham* more severe:
> Envy must own his Works almost divine,
> Would he but blot out each offensive Line.

But the usual tone of the pamphlet is more like the following extract, or worse:

> His Person — all will know him by the Print
> *Hogarth* has giv'n, with such arch Meaning in 't.

---

[1] Nichols, *Biog. Anec.* (1785), pp. 295, 296.

His drunken Attitude, his *leering Eyes*,
His Bear-Skin, and his Staff stuck round with Lies:
He travels with a Trull he calls his Wife,
By him seduc'd to Infamy for Life:
His Muse bred up in *Billinsgate*, his Muse
A vixen Jade, instructed to abuse;
A vixen Jade (but not to do her wrong)
With Wit, Skill, Spirit, all the Powers of Song;
With Strumpet Air, drest in a Negligée,
A Prostitute each Hour, for a Fee.

The poet then calls on the flowers — Milton fashion —
to mourn for Churchill's death, but they lift high their
heads in scorn.

Battles among the wits were as common in the eight-
eenth century as flytings in the Middle Ages, or quarrels
among Renaissance scholars. Mathias's long poem, *The
Pursuits of Literature*, had been revised for a third edi-
tion in 1797, and received the honor of reply from Thomas
Dutton in the following year. Dutton's poem, *The Liter-
ary Census*, includes free and candid strictures on *The
Pursuits of Literature* and on its anonymous author.

If flattery [says a note on the first page of this publication],
if flattery, as Mr. Gay informs us in the dedicatory address to
his fable of *The Lion, the Tiger, and the Traveller*, be in verity
"the nurse of crimes" — and who can for a moment doubt
the truth of this position? — the present rage for satirical
publications, in preference to the "dulcet strains of pane-
gyric lore" should seem to augur most propitiously to the
morals of the rising generation.

Dutton had read his Milton and his Pope, and in the
year of the *Lyrical Ballads* could produce this:

A wider range presents, a bolder sight,
The realm of Chaos and primeval Night.
Realms, where the sun of Genius never shines,
Nor breath of Heaven the sluggish air refines.

Where jarring elements refuse to blend,
And in eternal strife for rule contend.
Where Dulness rears her throne; and from the schools
Enlists grave pedants and pragmatic fools.
Where each against his fellow whets his claws,
But makes in self-defence one common cause.
If but the vilest scribbler you attack,
You straight have all the legion on your back.
Then helter-skelter, blockheads herd together,
And dunce hugs dunce, like vermin in cold weather.
Critics and authors (then no longer foes)
With quacks and learned M.D.'s suspend their blows.
Playwrights and managers their squabbles hush:
And leagued with Attic bards bum-bailiffs rush.
With Charles, proud R.A. — dawbers make a sally,
And join their brother-artists in Harp Alley!
Ev'n politicians on each other fawn,
And prim conventiclers and priests in lawn.

Enough has been said to accomplish the purpose of
this chapter. The changed spirit of the times in com-
merce and politics and the influence of this gradual rev-
olution on the world of letters have been suggested.
Gay and his friends along with the throng of Grub
Street writers have been introduced and set free to take
their places in the crowded streets. The rise and fall in
their fortunes has been sketched. In this, fulsome eu-
logy, lying partisanship, and personal jealousies have
been inferred if not mentioned. The final observation
which may be permitted in a discussion of this sort is
the complete independence of circumstance which the
spirit of poetry insists on showing. Pegasus pretends
submission to patron, politician, editor, bookseller, in
turn, but shows small regard for times or persons when
the moment comes to strike fire from flint.

Chapter II

LONDON IN CLASSICAL TYPES

I. The "Arts"

GAY calls his poem *Trivia: or The Art of Walking the Streets of London*. The fancy for naming poems in this way comes down to us from Horace's *Art of Poetry* and Ovid's *Art of Love*, and was decidedly popular at the time. Dr. William King (1663–1712), for instance, has an *Art of Cookery*, an *Art of Love*, and even an *Art of Making Hasty-Pudding*.[1]

This Dr. King (not the archbishop) proves himself a close observer of London life, and his *Journey to London* (1698) is an unusually interesting contribution to the prose literature of the subject. His *Art of Cookery* has, strange to say, little to do with cookery and much to do with streets and the humors of the town. He has the expected things, however, to say about onions, shell-fish, and other eatables of more or less unsavory reputation. He ridicules French recipes, their mushrooms —

> O how could *Homer* praise their Dancing Dogs,
> Their stinking Cheese, and Fricasy of Frogs!

But most of the time he manages somehow or other to relate food to people and to places. In one passage, for instance, he suggests characteristic menus for youth and age, and in a few lines takes us with him into some of the favorite resorts of the gay young men of fashion and the tired business man:

[1] Not published separately. See William King, *Miscellanies in Prose and Verse*.

A General View of the City of London, next the River Thames

The smooth fac'd Youth that has new Guardians chose
From Play-House steps to Supper at the *Rose*,
Where he a Main or two at Random throws:
Squand'ring of Wealth, impatient of Advice,
His eating must be Little, Costly, Nice.
  Maturer Age to this Delight grown strange,
Each Night frequents his Club behind the *Change*,
Expecting there Frugality and Health,
And Honour rising from a Sheriff's Wealth:
Unless he some Insurance Dinner lacks,
'Tis very rarely he frequents *Pontacks*.

This writer finds it easy to look with amusement on
magisterial dignity and aldermanic bumptiousness, espe-
cially when these are exhibited on great occasions like
the Lord Mayor's banquet. There's food at Islington,
too, and why should not the poet take us there to laugh
with and at the young players out for a good time and
all the rest of the holiday crowd:

When the young Players get to *Islington*,
  They fondly think that all the World's their own:
Prentices, Parish-Clerks, and Hectors meet,
He that is drunk, or bullied, pays the Treat.
Their Talk is loose, and o'er their bouncing Ale,
At Constables and Justices they rail.
Not thinking Custard such a serious thing,
That Common Council Men 'twill thither bring,
Where many a Man at variance with his Wife,
With soft'ning Mead and Cheese-Cake ends the Strife.
Ev'n Squires come there, and with their mean Discourse,
Render the Kitchin, which they sit in, worse.
Midwives demure, and Chamber-Maids most gay,
Foremen that pick the Box and come to play,
Here find their Entertainment at the Height,
In Cream and Codlings rev'ling with Delight.

He tells of the origin of street cries and of their partial
suppression by law; after all, turnips, pippins, pease,
oranges, currants, gooseberries, flounders, sprats, cucum-

bers, gingerbread, milk, and mackerel either are cooked
or may be cooked. He even lists the favorite athletic
sports of the town by advising the ill-nourished individ-
ual to abstain from them, or change his cook:

> He that of feeble Nerves and Joints complains
> From Nine-pins, Coits, and from Trap-ball abstains;
> Cudgel avoids, and shuns the wrestling place,
> Lest *Vinegar* resounds his loud Disgrace.

And, by way of simile, introduces an Irish funeral:

> So at an *Irish* Funeral appears
> A Train of Drabs with mercenary Tears;
> Who wringing of their Hands with hideous Moan,
> Know not his Name for whom they seem to groan.

In spite of us, he will sometimes wander into descrip-
tions of food — very good ones, too, though he is much
better with his eye off the cook book and his imagina-
tion free. In his *Orpheus and Eurydice* (first printed in
1704), he gives us a delightful description of the food of
the fairies. This deserves comparison with Tickell's
efforts of the same sort in *Kensington Gardens* (1722). It
is that kind of charming filigree work which Pope
brought to such high perfection in *The Rape of the Lock*
(1712), and it looks back for inspiration to some pas-
sages from *A Midsummer Night's Dream*.

> Sir, a roasted Ant that's nicely done,
> By one small Atom of the Sun.
> These are Flies Eggs in Moon-shine poach'd,
> This a Flea's Thigh in Collops scotch'd,
> 'Twas hunted Yesterday i' th' Park,
> And like t' have scap'd us in the dark.
> This is a Dish entirely new,
> Butterflies Brains dissolv'd in Dew;
> These Lovers Vows, these Courtiers Hopes,
> These to be Eat by Microscopes:
> These sucking Mites, a Glow-worm's Heart,
> This a delicious Rainbow-Tart.

One thinks of Mercutio, or Drayton, or Herrick:

> A little mushroome-table spred,
> After short prayers, they set on bread;
> A Moon-parcht grain of purest wheat,
>   . . . which done,
> His kitling eyes begin to runne
> Quite through the table, where he spies
> The hornes of paperie Butterflies:
>   . . . what wo'd he more,
> But Beards of Mice, a Newt's stew'd thigh,
> A bloated Earewig, and a Flie;
>   . . . to these, the slain-Stag's teares;
> The unctuous dewlaps of a Snaile;
> The broke-heart of a Nightingale
> Ore-come in musicke. [1]

But enough of the fairies! Dr. King also wrote an *Art of Love* (1709), in imitation presumably of Ovid, though the actual resemblance is confined to the title. In this also he shows his major interest. His description of the midnight adventures of a drunken bar-tender is inimitable, while the picture of the boy with the kite is almost as good. He gives his women ideas about wealth and the odor of bank-notes, and tells us how they like to get a little start on the fashions:

> Your goldsmiths now are mighty neat;
> I love the air of Lombard Street.
> Whate'er a ship from India brings,
> Pearls, diamonds, silks, are pretty things:
> The cabinet, the screen, the fan,
> Please me extremely if Japan:
> And what affects me still the more,
> They had none of them heretofore.

Besides, whether in reality or as a factitious reflection from material in the Roman satires, women seem to have

---

[1] Robert Herrick, *Poetical Works* (ed. F. W. Moorman, Oxford, 1915), p. 119.

been shaking themselves loose from the trammels of at least some of the old conventions. King, for example, describes their appearance in the Park:

> Some prance like Frenchwomen, who ride,
> As our lifeguard men, all astride.[1]

Richard Tickell wrote *The Wreath of Fashion, or The Art of Sentimental Poetry*; Robert Dodsley brought forth *The Art of Preaching*, a poem which betrays at least a casual acquaintance with homiletic discourses:

> Should some strange Poet, in his Piece, affect
> *Pope's* nervous Stile, with *Ward's* low Puns bedeck'd;
> Prink *Milton's* true Sublime, with *Swift's* true Wit;
> And *Blackmore's* Gravity, with *Gay's* Conceit;
> Would you not laugh? Trust me that Priest's as bad,
> Who in a Stile now grave, now raving mad,
> Gives the wild whims of dreaming Schoolmen vent,
> While drowsy Congregations nod assent.[2]

Poor Ward, who suffers here, had previously complained about the same sort of preaching:

> For Gesture is the Life and Glory
> Of Nonsense preach'd for Oratory.[3]

Dodsley tells us that

> If Pastors more than twice five Minutes preach,
> Their sleepy Flocks begin to yawn, and stretch.

[1] Cf. *Female Taste: A Satire*, by a Barrister of the Middle-Temple (1755), p. 57:

> "On horseback, flaunting it astride,
> In manly buskins when you ride,
> Trust me, 't will do your fame no hurt
> To change your smock into a shirt."

[2] *London Evening Post*, August 24, 1738:

> "This Day is Published
> *The Art of Preaching*. In Imitation
> of Horace's *Art of Poetry*.
> By R. Dodsley."

[3] *Hudibras Redivivus* (1707), Part II, p. 22.

He praises Sherlock, the Bishop of London, and advises young preachers to copy Young's pointed sense and Atterbury's style, just as

> Young Lawyers copy *Murray* where they can;
> Physicians *Mead*, and Surgeons *Cheselden*.

He enumerates some of the qualifications for chaplain in a noble family:

> When Dukes or noble Lords a Chaplain hire,
> They first of his Capacities enquire.
> If stoutly qualify'd to drink and smoke,
> If not too nice to bear an impious Joke,
> If tame enough to be the common Jest,
> This is a Chaplain to his Lordship's Taste.

And Dodsley knew; the Muse in Livery speaks. Swift knew also, and gives us other characteristics of the country parson in his "Baucis and Philemon" fable. The yeoman here for his good deeds is turned into a parson:

> His talk was now of Tithes, and Dues,
> Could smoak his pipe, and read the news;
> Knew how to preach old sermons next,
> Vampt in the preface and the text.
> At Christ'nings well could get his part,
> And had the service all by heart;
> Wish'd women might have children fast,
> And thought whose sow had farrow'd last.
> Against Dissenters would repine,
> And stood up firm for right divine.
> Found his head fill'd with many a sistem,
> But classick authors he ne'er miss'd them.

Probably the town preacher was more apt to be guilty of that unforgivable sin which John Byrom denounced in his poem "On Clergymen preaching Politics." Of course, the outstanding popular "divine" of the day was "Orator" Henley, to whom Pope refers good naturedly in the *Dunciad:*

> O great restorer of the good old stage,
> Preacher at once, and Zany of thy age.

He it was who engaged in a public controversy with Foote, the comedian, in the Haymarket, and beat him at his own trade. Preaching without notes was uncommon when John Byrom wrote his "Lancashire Dialogue."[1]

John Durant Breval, who published under the pseudonym of Joseph Gay, wrote a poem called *The Art of Dress* (1717), in which, after an elaborate and fanciful account of the historical evolution of costume, he ends his discourse by recommending simplicity in the matter of paint and jewels, warns the ladies against lacing too closely, lest they swoon at the ball, and wins modern prophylactic approval by suggesting,

> In polishing your Teeth be wond'rous nice.

More detailed suggestions about cosmetics are given in *The Art of Beauty,* a poem of twenty-two pages humbly addressed to the Oxford toasts and sent forth to an expectant public in 1719. The poet believes that what nature gave may be improved by art, especially her art, and is unselfish enough to tell people in an advertisement where the best lotions can be obtained — from "a gentlewoman up one pair of stairs at the sign of The Celebrated Anodyne Necklace for Children's Teeth, without Temple-Bar. Cream 2/6 a pot." We no longer write poems to celebrate our wares.

Beauty, or the Art of Charming (1735) is disinterested; at any rate, the author is not trying to sell cold cream. He praises the beauty of various great ladies, especially of Gay's Queensberry.

[1] John Byrom, *Miscellaneous Poems* (Manchester, 1773), p. 147.

James Bramston's poem on *The Art of Politicks* (1729)
contains at least one well-known couplet:

> What's not destroy'd by Time's devouring hand?
> Where's Troy, and where's the Maypole in the Strand?

Bramston sticks much more closely to his subject than
Dr. King.   Indeed, he gives us a very clever sketch of
conditions in the political world of the time, and that
rottenness for which it has long been the custom to
blame Walpole. He has the trick of mordant satire and
is quite merciless as he swings the club. Personalities
are scattered abundantly through his lines. He ridicules
Heidegger, the famous patron of masquerades, even
poking fun at his extraordinarily ugly features:

> Nay, I would sooner have thy phyz, I swear,
> *Surintendant des Plaisirs d'Angleterre.*[1]

His denunciation of the scurrilous pamphleteer is ad-
mirable:

> Wrap up your poison well, nor fear to say
> What was a lye last night is truth today;
> Tell this, sink that, arrive at Ridpath's praise,
> Let Abel Roper your ambition raise.

He gets off his political track sometimes and indulges in
literary comparisons, which are amusing:

> Though no great connoisseur, I make a shift
> Just to find out a Durfey from a Swift;
> I can discern with half an eye, I hope,
> Mist from Joe Addison, from Eusden Pope:
> I know a farce from one of Congreve's plays,
> And Cibber's Opera from Johnny Gay's.

[1] Cf. W. E., *Horace, Satires*, I, 6 (1738):
> "I ramble unobserv'd where'er I please,
> To Change, to Court, to Heidegger's repair,
> Or to the Mall, and view the Market there."

No man can be a wit unless he is fit for Newgate or
Bedlam, and the only way to show a genius, some think,
is to show a spite. Everybody talks politics these days,
and taverns as well as newspapers take sides. The poli-
tician must forget all ideas of moderation or judgment
and vote plumb:

> Stick to your friends in whatsoe'er you say;
> With strong aversion shun the middle-way;
> The middle-way the best we sometimes call,
> But 'tis in politics no way at all.
> A Trimmer's what both parties turn to sport,
> By country hated, and despis'd at Court . . .
> Who would in earnest to a party come,
> Must give his vote, not whimsical, but plumb.
> There is no medium; for the term in vogue
> On either side is, Honest Man, or Rogue.
> Can it be difficult our minds to shew,
> Where all the difference is, Yes, or No?

When the author starts to describe his serious Member
of Parliament,[1] he shows his knowledge of both town
and human nature. While the session is on, this scrupu-
lous man of business neglects his ordinary diversions:

> A Man of Bus'ness won't till evening dine,
> Abstains from women, company, and wine:
> From Figg's new Theatre he'll miss a night,
> Though cocks, and bulls, and Irish women fight.

[1] The country gentleman gets his measure taken pretty closely in Mar-
vell's *The Last Instructions to a Painter about the Dutch Wars* (1667):

> "Nor could all these the Field have long maintain'd
> But for th' unknown Reserve that still remain'd;
> A Gross of English Gentry, nobly born,
> Of clear Estates, and to no Faction sworn,
> Dear Lovers of their King, and Death to meet
> For Country's Cause, that glorious thing and sweet;
> To speak not forward, but in Action brave,
> In giving generous, but in Council grave;
> Candidly credulous for once, nay twice;
> But sure the Devil cannot cheat them thrice."

See also Mark Akenside, *To the Country Gentlemen of England* (1758).

Nor sultry sun, nor storms of soaking rain,
The man of bus'ness from the House detain:
Nor speaks he for no reason but to say,
I am a Member, and I spoke today.

One melancholy story repeats itself again and again in the poetry of this time, and we find it here in Bramston, the ruin which dabbling in politics so often brings:

Tag, rag, and bobtail to Sir Harry's run,
Men that have votes, and women that have none;
Sons, daughters, grandsons, with his Honour dine;
He keeps a Publick-House without a sign.
Coblers and smiths extol th' ensuing choice,
And drunken taylors boast their right of voice.
Dearly the free-born neighbourhood is bought,
They never leave him while he's worth a groat:
So leeches stick, nor quit the bleeding wound,
Till off they drop with skinfuls to the ground.[1]

Thus, as Bramston says, the interest that everybody was beginning to take in politics was largely mercenary. Patriotism might be the day's conversation, but the sweet dreams were of preferment. And besides, what better subject for conversation than politics? Judgment in politics,

like criticism, requires no knowledge of the subject, no study or pains to be master of it, but enters imperceptibly, like in-

---

[1] Cf. *Folly*, By the Author of *The Female Rake* and *The Rake of Taste* (1737):

"Drinks with a cobler, to a tinker bows,
Asks how his children do, how fares his spouse?
Prays that his service may not be forgot,
And calls, for honest *Tom*, another pot."

Compare also Thomas Nevile's imitation (1769) of Persius, Satire IV:

"Cease then, while yet a youth, by name to hail
Each dirty Voter, fawn, and wag the tail;
Or, as you pass, with hands uprais'd to pour
On the maz'd multitude a silv'ry show'r.
Let Cleon's heir, agog for public praise,
Fell all his woods to purchase rank huzzas."

spiration, into the mind of the man who gives his mind to it. Else how could such persons, who in every Coffee-house, Ale-house, and Cellar, we may hear settling the affairs of the nation, have their knowledge?

This sort of sentiment is very much *A New Tale of an Old Tub*, and was as true in 1752 as it is to-day. The party idea in government had caught on well with the ale-house politician and with the poet.

> Besides, on Parties *now* our Fame depends,
> And frowns or smiles, as these are Foes or Friends.
> Wit, Judgment, Nature join; you strive in vain;
> 'Tis keen Invective stamps the current Strain.
> Fix'd to one Side, like *Homer's* Gods, we Fight,
> These always Wrong, and these forever Right.[1]

Since this was the general attitude, the "trimmer" would get, as usual, small consideration. In spite of Savile, he was looked upon as a monster:

> Hang out your cloth, and let the trumpet sound,
> Here's such a beast as Africk never own'd.
> A twisted brute, the Satyr in the story,
> That blows up the Whig-heat and cools the Tory.
> A Stale Hermaphrodite, whose doubtful lust
> Salutes all parties with an equal gust.[2]

Neuter Neither-side of No-land, Esq.[3] found himself much misunderstood in the early eighteenth century. Fortunately, besides the party-heeler and the trimmer there was always the steady pragmatist, with his eye on realities, willing to do his share of the work of the world and rather doubtful about the importance of all these political bogeys. The year 1745 was an eventful one, but *Tom the Porter* carried on as usual — a very good fable his!

---

[1] William Whitehead, *The Danger of Writing Verse* (1741).

[2] *Character of a Trimmer* (1683).

[3] *Raven and Owl: a politico-polemico-sarcastico-historical dialogue*, by Neuter Neither-side of No-Land, Esq. (1739).

> As Tom the Porter went up Ludgate Hill,
> A swinging shower obliged him to stand still;
> So, in the right-hand passage through the gate,
> He pitched his burden down, just by the grate,
> From whence the doleful accent sounds away,
> "Pity—the Poor—and Hungry—Debtors—pray."

A half-drowned soldier joins him, tells how the High-landers have got as far as Derbyshire from Preston-pans. A prisoner behind the grate breaks excitedly into the conversation: England is doomed. Tom is unmoved; he will go on with his daily work, and leave "country" and "religion" to take care of themselves.

The matter of the succession was the usual subject for division in Queen Anne's reign. Whigs and High-Flyers threw out pamphlet after pamphlet, some pleasantly fabulous or epistolary, some acrid and almost treasonable. In 1710 the Tories had their way with the electorate, and from that time till the Queen's death, four years later, the Jacobites, in spite of acts of succession, dared to hope, while the Whigs played what looked to be a losing game, with the courage of desperation. Some of the verses were popular enough to run into several editions — address from one side and answer from the other, first part and second part, as occasion or, rather, demand suggested. *The Apparition* (1710) is a fair example of the type. Here the Devil comes, in the shape of an old college bed-maker, to the doctor's room. Some of his sentiments are just; he might well repeat them to-day under similar circumstances:

> Democracy (a Noisy Patriot Fool,
> The Rabble's *Idol*, and the Statesman's *Tool*),
> After her sawcy and familiar way,
> Doctor, I'm Yours; Yours heartily, She'll say;
> How fares on Earth the *Jus Divinum?* Dead?
> Do the *Patricii* the *Plebes* dread?

Almost — then fling this *Mitre* at that *Monarch's* Head
Sedition loud, to *Tumult* mad, shall bawl;
And Welcome Thee to Satan's gloomy Hall.
Slander with all her Snakes shall hiss thy Praise;
Treason leave all her Plots on Thee to gaze:
Lewdness with *Deism* shall Record thy Name,
And *Envy* shall not envy Thee thy Fame.

This poem has some caustic lines on writers alive and dead. Satan brings kind messages from hell (I fill out the initialed blanks):

John Dryden, with his Brethren of the Bays,
His love to *Garth*, Blaspheming *Garth*, conveys;
And Thanks him for his *Pagan* Funeral Praise.
Hopes *Wycherley*, whose Christian Name is *Will*,
Continues very Witty, Wicked still:
The like of *Congreve*, *Vanbrugh*, and the Rest,
Who Swear, that *all Religion is a Jest*.

The first *Apparition* gave birth to a second within the same year, stuffed as compactly with satire on the Jacobites, the Devil this time disguised as Sacheverell.[1]

The Ballad of the King shall enjoy his own again: with learned Comment thereupon, at the request of Capt. Silk, dedicated to Jenny Man (1711) is announced as by the author of *Tom Thumb*, and contains, in addition to sixteen pages of verse, a prefixed letter to Jenny Man, the proprietress of the famous tavern in Whitehall.

The Junto (1712) celebrates the Sacheverell trial with sufficient particularity to cover forty-six pages. The preface contains some references to the best Whig poet, Addison. Then we pass, in the poem itself, to an account of Sacheverell's speech in St. Paul's, to his trial before the Peers, its unfavorable outcome and the sentence to

---

[1] See *A Collection of Hymns and Poems for the Use of the October Club*, By Dr. S——l, Dr. A——y, Dr. S——e, Dr. M——ss, and little T——p of Oxford, Ch——ns to the said Club (1711; Bodleian Library, G. P. 1278).

three years' silence, the big popular demonstrations, the fall of government, praise of the Tory ministers and the Queen, consternation over the attempt on Harley's life.

The year 1714 was the crucial time, and one of its political shows was celebrated by Edward Ward in *The Republican Procession, or the Tumultuous Cavalcade*. This also went through a second impression, with additional characters. It is in Hudibrastic verse, and gives detailed descriptions of all the absurd figures in the throng — cobblers, tailors, baptists, distillers, canting Scots, independents, factious priests, small-coal men, quacks, a Presbyterian mercer of Ludgate, a Quaker, the Kent Street mob, the doctor, a leather-selling Roundhead, a brewer, an independent wizard who deals in coffee, tea, and Whiggish news, a wild rabble, and finally, the coach and six with the Idol, — Marlborough, of course, — and his Mate in it, supported in following coaches by city elders, managers, and Bank directors, king-killers, monarchy electors, and votaries for Lord Protectors. They pass through Kent Street, smashing the windows of St. George's Church, and by way of Southwark to the bridge, where a loyal chemist attacks the brewer with a shovel; the shop front is broken, but the chemist remains victor undaunted; through Gracechurch Street to St. Dunstan's in the West, the author, like his procession, trudging along an unmapped course.

Both sides found their poets, and the list of pamphlets on this political question is interminable, lasting down through 1745, when the last hopes of the Stuarts must have faded. Very few of the pamphleteers show anything like the balance or judgment of Tickell, whose *Epistle from a Lady in England to a Gentleman in Avignon* passed to its third edition in 1717, and must

have seemed exceedingly sensible to most men of good
will. The lady has done her best for the absent prince:

> Thy Female Bands, O Prince, by Fortune crost,
> At least more Courage than thy Men may boast:
> Our Sex has dar'd the Mugg-House Chiefs to meet,
> And purchas'd Fame in many a well-fought Street.
> From *Drury-Lane*, the Region of Renown,
> The Land of Love, the *Paphos* of the Town,
> Fair Patriots sallying oft have put to flight
> With all their Poles the Guardians of the Night,
> And bore, with Screams of Triumph, to their Side
> The Leader's Staff in all its painted Pride.
> Nor fears the Hawker in her warbling Note
> To vend the discontented Statesman's Thought.
> Tho' red with Stripes, and recent from the Thong,
> Sore smitten for the Love of sacred Song,
> The tuneful Sisters still pursue their Trade,
> Like *Philomela* darkling in the Shade.
> Poor *Trott* attends, forgetful of a Fare,
> And Hums in Concert o'er his Empty Chair.

But the agitation has gone on so long now with nothing
accomplished that the lady is discouraged and thinks
the signs have failed her:

> Was it for this the Sun's whole Lustre fail'd,
> And sudden Midnight o'er the Noon prevail'd!
> For this did Heav'n display to Mortal Eyes
> Aërial Knights and Combates in the Skies!
> Was it for this *Northumbrian* Streams look'd Red!
> And *Thames* driv'n backward show'd his Secret Bed!
> False Auguries! th' insulting Victor's Scorn!
> Ev'n our own Prodigies against us turn!
> O Portents constru'd on our Side in vain!
> Let never Tory trust Eclipse again!

And the sum of all her argument leads her to the conclu-
sion which a majority of the nation had already found
satisfactory:

To James my Passions and my Weakness guide,
But Reason sways me to the Victor's Side.

Allowing gradually the Pretender and his claims to slip from mind, men sought other cause for argument. If we may not have tyrants as our Kings, God save us from them in subordinate posts. Marlborough was feared as the Modern Whig Dictator as early as 1702, and Walpole must have fairly well answered that description in later years. In general, Walpole allowed the versemongers to vent their spleen with impunity:

Yet upon some you may securely joke,
Who are insensible to Satire's Stroke.
Walpole is easy, when, to please the Mob,
You call him *Knave*, his *Honour*, or plain *Bob*.
But drunk with *Helicon*, be more discreet,
Than, Bully-like, to fall on *All* you meet.
Consider wisely o'er and o'er again,
Who draws a *Sword*, or who can wield a Cane:
Lest by one dreadful Blow across the Pate,
Apollo and the *Muses* quit their Seat.[1]

The topics for satire on Walpole were threefold: the first and most delectable, his "tother fair charmer;" the second, his corrupt political practices; and the third, his too sane foreign policy. Two of these, at least, are handled with disgusting rudeness and vulgarity — especially when one remembers that the second lady had just died — in a pamphlet called *The Rival Wives, or, the Greeting of Clarissa to Skirra in the Elysian Shades* (1738). Skirra, it appears, is notorious even in hell:

So when to Tothill, or to Clerkenwell,
Some nymph is sent, for crimes too vile to tell;
If with lac'd cap, or silken gown she's blest,
Due reverence she claims from all the rest;

[1] *The Art of Poetry* (1741).

> A more than usual noise the dungeon rends,
> Which louder still from cell to cell descends:
> The Keeper cries, "Make room for Madam there,"
> While all the hungry, starving wretches stare.

The two favorites meet and fall upon one another with vituperation. It is almost impossible to suppose anyone capable of such bad taste as the author of this curious stuff seems to possess. It is like pushing an old man over with a dung-fork. He gets to work at the foreign policy presently:

> "Skirra! thy love occasion'd this," I'll cry.
> "See where the once fam'd Empress of the Main,
> By Pirates robbed, from vengeance does refrain;
> See Europe's scum defy her falling Pow'r,
> Her ruling flag insulted, mock'd, and tore;
> Lethargic slumbers all her spirits seize,
> And see, she sinks to nothing by degrees;
> Her sons with ardour burn, each bosom glows,
> And would revenge the insults of her foes."

The conclusion is a very pleasant little *memento mori* for the Prime Minister.[1] The ladies have heard their doom:

> Yet both confess their sentence is not hard,
> Knowing what torment's for their lord prepar'd.

The man strong enough to overlook scurrility of this sort must be admired.

The Voice of Liberty, or a British Philippic, appeared in the same year. It was written in Miltonic verse, and was "occasioned by the insults of the Spaniards and the preparations for war." This poem was prefixed by a copper-plate etching representing the sufferings of our captive sailors in a Spanish prison.

Walpole — needless to say — had his supporters, but he seems to have taken little interest in the war of wits.

---

[1] Cf. *The Rival Wives Answer'd: or, Skirra to Clarissa* (1738).

He fought for the most part with other weapons. At
this distance one sympathizes readily with his friend,
the author of *A Panegyric on a Court* (1739):

> To guard our liberty is Sylla's aim,
> From madmen that usurp a Patriot's name;
> Who rail in loud harangues against the Court,
> In country towns to make the rabble sport,
> Insinuate that virtue's in disgrace,
> And none without corruption get a place,
> That Liberty now breathes her latest hour,
> And falls a sacrifice to Sylla's power.

The gloves were off about this time, and there is a kind
of grim humor in Walpole's strategy at the end. Read
An Ode to Mr. Pulteney (1739), which contains an in-
sulting translation of a Latin epitaph published in *Old
Common Sense*, February 3, 1738, and now adapted to
Walpole; and remember, at the same time, the amusing
hoist with his own petard which the sturdy old states-
man gave Pulteney [1] a year or two later.

Electioneering methods were, it is to be hoped, some-
what different from our own. Nichols, in his *Biographi-
cal Anecdotes of William Hogarth*,[2] prints a rather long
poem, in four cantos, called "The Humours of an Elec-
tion Entertainment" and illustrating, shall we say, some
prints by Hogarth on the same subject. The first canto
describes the banquet given by the candidates, the
music, the presents for the ladies, the toasts, the bribes.
The second tells of the canvassing for votes:

> But here's a Porter; what's the news? —
> Ha, ha, a load of billet-doux!
> Humbly to sue th' Electors' favour,
> With vows of *Cato*-like behaviour.

[1] See also Mark Akenside, *Epistle to Curio.*
1785. P. 338.

There is an interesting debate between a cobbler and a barber, and from that we pass, in the third canto, to the actual polling at the hustings. Strange voters appear — the pensioner with one arm and one leg, the wretch without a nose, the blind man led by a boy. Finally, in the fourth canto, we have the chairing of the successful candidates with due ceremony:

> When *London* city's bold train-band
> March, to preserve their tract of land,
> Each val'rous heart the *French* defying,
> While drums are beating, colours flying,
> How many accidents resound
> From *Tower-hill* to th' *Artillery-ground!*
> Perhaps some hog, in frisky pranks,
> Unluckily breaks through their ranks,
> And makes the captain storm and swear,
> To *form* their soldiers, *as they were.*

Some of these raw recruits[1] pop the ramming into a by-stander's ear, others forget to draw the rammer:

> See from the Town-hall press the crowd,
> While rustic Butchers ring aloud!
> There, lo, their cap of liberty!
> Here t'other side in effigy!
> A notable device, to call
> The Courtier party blockheads all:
> Aloft True-Blue, their ensign, flies,
> And acclamations rend the skies.

Hogarth is not the cause of much wit in this writer, but perhaps the lines help, since the prints are not before us.

---

[1] Baker, *Tunbridge Walks* (1703), Act V:
"*Penelope* to *Squib:* 'We must go a Visiting together, and to *Hyde-Park* together, and be extremely Fond for a Month: Then, Captain, My Aunt, and I must go to the *Artillery-Ground* o' Training Days, that the Soldiers may let off their Muskets, and cry, Heav'n Bless the Noble Captain's Lady.'"
Before this, in Act IV, Squib has been wooing Hillaria, who has too much worldly wisdom to be enthusiastic. "Then, shou'd you be kill'd in a Battle one must Sneak to the Government, for a Pension of twenty Shillings a Week to Subsist half a Score Children, and hammer out the rest with Washing, and Starching."

An anonymous poem, called "The Fatigues of a Great Man" (1734), suggests much of the discomfort and chagrin of the political chase. Though successful, the great man repents the trouble he has taken:

> How has he been compell'd to cringe and bow,
> To court the surly Peasant at the Plough?
> To creep into the *Cobler's* filthy Stall;
> To dandle after the Innkeeper's Call;
> To be affronted, contradicted, nos'd;
> To be bamboozled, ridicul'd, expos'd;
> All this, and more, with Patience forc'd to bear,
> To gain his Point: — Is this *no Toil* and *Care?* [1]

One should compare with these verses Pope's description of the politician in action: [2]

> But if to power and place your passion lye,
> If in the pomp of life consist the joy;
> Then hire a slave (or if you will, a Lord)
> To do the honours, and to give the word;
> Tell at your Levee, as the Crowds approach,
> To whom to nod, whom take into your coach,
> Whom honour with your hand: to make remarks,
> Who rules in Cornwall, or who rules in Berks:
> "This may be troublesome, is near the chair:
> That makes three members, this can chuse a Mayor."
> Instructed thus, you bow, embrace, protest,
> Adopt him son, or cozen at the least,
> Then turn about, and laugh at your own jest.

Strange comment on political conditions is furnished also by a once-popular satire called *The Causidicade . . . on the strange Resignation and Stranger Promotion* (1743). In this poem we have the story of the Inquisitor General's resignation, followed by a long account of the claims of various people to succession. The worthy and unworthy enlarge upon their merits:

---

[1] Bound with Edward Ward's *Vulgus Britannicus* (1710), p. 13.
[2] *Imitations of Horace: Epistles*, I, 6 (1737).

When strait a weak voice was heard, crying out
Like some poor old Woman's pent up in a Butt.

After a long and wearisome session no agreement has
been reached:

When lo! a loud Noise! — stand clear there — make Room
For my L[or]d first C[o]mm[i]ss[ione]r — Hoa, there! is come.
The President, staring, look'd devlishly sick,
As tho' the new M[ini]st[r]y play'd him a Trick,
And had put in C[o]mm[i]ss[io]n Great Britain's Gr[ea]t S[ea]l,
(Which, if they had done, they had done very well)
But seeing 'twas one, tho' not easily wrought on,
In Bulk and in Strength, more a Rival for Broughton,
(Yet with good useful Talents sufficiently stor'd,
Tho' not proper, perhaps, for an Adm[ira]lty Board;
But Talents in Courts are ne'er misapply'd)
His spirits recover, and terrors subside.
With dignify'd Port he advanc'd thro' the Hurry,
Before wav'd his Ensigns, behind him tripp'd M[urra]y:
So march'd thro' old Sherwood in Nottinghamshire,
Robin Hood in the front, Little John in the rear.
The President met him and crouch'd like a Spaniel,
"Pray what is your Pleasure," quo' he, "my Lord D[anie]l?
Be pleas'd to command." — "*I come to encourage
Yon brave bonny Sco*i, *my Kinsman by marriage;
For th' Inquisitor's post he's set up by the Court,
And is ready to shew he is qualify'd for 't.*"
"Then you'd have it be so" — "*Yes, truly, I'd fain.*"
"'T'oppose what you're bent on, I'm sure is in vain."
Then M[urra]y prepar'd with a fine Panegyrick
In Praise of himself, would have spoke it like Garrick;
But the President stopping him, said, "As in Truth,
Your Worth and your Praise is in ev'ry one's mouth;
'T is needless to urge what's notoriously known,
The Office, by Merit, is your's all must own.
The Voice of the Publick approves of the Thing,
Concurring with that of the Court and the K[in]g." [1]

---

[1] Fielding, much to his annoyance, was credited with the authorship of this scurrilous pamphlet. The Murray mentioned is William Murray, first Earl of Mansfield (1705–93), solicitor-general, 1742.

The poem in this group of *Arts* which, apart from *Trivia*, is most successful in its would-be classicism is *The Art of Dancing*, written by that curious eccentric, Soame Jenyns, and published in 1730.[1] Like Gay's poem, it contains an announcement of the subject in the style of the *Aeneid*, an appeal to the appropriate Muse, an expressed desire "to tread in paths to ancient bards unknown" and thus win immortality. Its author "mythologizes" on the invention of the fan, as Gay does about the invention of the patten.[2] Gay's clever lines at the close of *Trivia* are parodied in *The Art of Dancing* with considerable success. The material, too, is interesting, the satire delicately amiable. We should expect some of his directions to be unnecessary, while others have a very modern, up-to-the-last-minute flavor.

> For why should I the gallant spark command,
> With clean white gloves to fit his ready hand?
> Or in his fob enlivening spirits wear,
> And pungent salts to raise the fainting fair?
> Or hint, the sword that dangles at his side,
> Should from its silken bondage be unty'd?
> Why should my lays the youthful tribe advise,
> Lest snowy clouds from out their wigs arise:
> So shall their partners mourn their laces spoil'd,
> And shining silks with greasy powder soil'd.

He recommends care about the buckles on the shoes, and then comes to a crucial matter, on which his complaints must have won him the popularity of all the young men about town:

> Dare I in such momentous points advise,
> I should condemn the hoop's enormous size;
> Of ills I speak by long experience found,

[1] Dodsley, III, 168.
[2] Cf. *The Thimble, an Heroi-comical Poem*, in four cantos, By a Gentleman of Oxford (1743). The author acknowledges his debt to Pope and Gay.

> Oft' have I trod th' immeasurable round,
> And mourn'd my shins bruis'd black with many a wound.
> Nor should the tighten'd stays, too straitly lac'd,
> In whale-bone bondage gall the slender waist.

Toward the close there is a delightful description of a ballroom, and some wise advice about drinks:

> But ever let my lovely pupils fear
> To chill their mantling blood with cold small-bear . . .
> Destruction lurks within the pois'nous dose,
> A fatal fever, or a pimpled nose.[1]

Many other poems of less distinction than those we have discussed use this same popular trick of title. We are interested, of course, only in those which to some extent reflect London life.

In 1731, James Miller published a poem which he called *Harlequin-Horace: or, The Art of Modern Poetry*. In this he recommends propriety and correctness in poetry, notes how society staggers under the craze for speculation, and ridicules the foreign fashions in the theatre.

> Since *South-Sea Schemes* have so enrich'd the Land,
> That *Footmen* 'gainst their *Lords* for *Boroughs* stand;
> Since *Masquerades* and Op'ras made their Entry,
> And *Heydegger* and *Handell* rul'd our Gentry;[2]
> A hundred different Instruments combine,
> And foreign *Songsters* in the Concert join.

The clown has displaced the tragic muse:

> Long labor'd *Rich*, by Tragick Verse to gain
> The Town's Applause — but labour'd long in vain;
> At length he wisely to his Aid call'd in,
> The *active Mime* and *checker'd Harlequin*.

---

[1] Cf. "The Downfall of Dancing" in *The Foundling Hospital for Wit* (1749), No. II, p. 46 (by Chas. Hanbury Williams?). Also Budgell, in the *Spectator*, No. 67, and Addison, in the *Tatler*, No. 88.

[2] In the 1741 edition this line stands,
     "And *Heydegger* reign'd *Guardian* of our Gentry."

The mob wants spectacle. A *quantum sufficit* of smut
and profanity will bring crowds of applauders to the
dullest plays, while plenty of tragic rant, grim ghosts,
and a generous use of Dennis's thunder will ensure com-
plete success. Miller's references to our early drama are
a little disconcerting. He seems to mix his periods sadly:

Our antient Tragedy was void of Art,
Shewn by some merry *Briton* in a Cart;
Whose naked Tribe of *Saxons*, *Scots*, and *Picts*,
Sung Songs like *L[everid]ge* and like *R[ic]h* play'd Tricks.[1]

There is a reference to *The Beggar's Opera* (1728) and to
Cibber's misfortune:

Poor *Bay's*[2] Opera scarce would bear *one* View,
But *Gay's*, repeated *Sixty-times*, was new.

And at the end we find a cynical bit of advice to play-
wrights and producers, which incidentally brings theatre
conditions pretty sharply before us:

'T is likewise requisite you some should hire,
On the first Night, your Labours to admire;
Some that will stamp, and rave at every Line,
And swear 't is charming! exquisite! divine!
Applaud when *Chair*, or *Couch*, is well brought in,
And clap the very *Drawing* of the *Scene*;
And next old *Dennis* with a Supper treat,
He'll like your *Poem* as he likes your *Meat*;
For, give that growling *Cerberus* but a *Sop*,
He'll close his Jaws, and sleep like any Top.[3]

The same writer, James Miller, published an *Art of Life*
in 1739, in which he declaims on the vicissitudes of life,

---

[1] This line read, in 1741,

   "Sung Songs like *Cary*, and like *Lun* play'd Tricks."

[2] Cibber's name appears in the 1741 edition.

[3] Compare the experience of the poet whom Roderick Random finds in
the Fleet. John Byrom tells in his Diary how he and his friends arranged to
applaud Charles Johnson's *Hurlothrumbo*.

and, by way of illustration, notes some of the changes
that have recently taken place in the town:

> There's nought so fix'd but what a Change must prove,
> Lo, to *Fleet Ditch Stocks-Market* must remove!
> And in its room some future Age will see,
> If haply *rival Masons* may agree,
> A tow'ring Mansion for the good Lord-Mayor,
> Tho' not *the Alderman that's next the Chair.*
> Whilst that drain'd barren Sluice, whose sable Streams
> "Late roll'd her Tribute of dead Dogs to *Thames*,"
> Prolifick now, the neighb'ring Ward supplies
> With the rich Offspring of th' indulgent Skies.[1]

He also makes sympathetic allusion to Stephen Duck,
the illiterate farm-hand turned poet, who had a short
time before attracted the attention of the critics:

> Not but sometimes, should *Phoebus* deign his Fire,
> A *Duck* or *Dodsley* may to Rhyme aspire.

Even physicians entrusted their valuable counsels to
verse, among them John Armstrong, who published his
Art of Preserving Health in 1744. This professional gen-
tleman disapproves of the city most heartily:

> Fly the rank city, shun its turbid air,
> Breathe not the chaos of eternal smoke
> And volatile corruption, from the dead,
> The dying, sick'ning, and the living, world
> Exhal'd, to sully Heaven's transparent dome
> With dim mortality.

At Richmond he sees a hundred villas rise, rural or gay.
Hampstead, Greenwich, Dulwich, and the Kentish hills
are recommended, but not marshy Essex. His advice is,
on the whole, very sensible. Be frugal in your cups, take
plenty of exercise, live in the sunlight as much as possi-
ble. He is no faddist on diet:

> Each creature knows its proper aliment.

---

[1] A market was built over the upper end of Fleet Ditch in 1733.

For exercise, both toil and sports are wise. The garden brings health to many a man. The foils, tennis, the dance, fowling, are all good in moderation, though he has nothing but scorn for the "athletic fool":

> The men of better clay and finer mould
> Know nature, feel the human dignity,
> And scorn to vie with oxen or with apes.

His doctrine about study would hardly do for a graduate school. "Toy with your books," he says;

> While reading pleases, but no longer, read.

Solitude is apt to breed melancholy.

No theories about fit subjects for poetry seem to have occurred to these eighteenth-century enthusiasts. To have a bright idea was the only necessary prelude for an appeal to the appropriate Muse. Bevill Higgins wrote *A Poem on Nature* in 1736, in imitation of Lucretius, to which he added a description of the foetus in the womb. Some nameless Gideonite wrote a forty-seven-page poem in 1746 on *The Art of Stock-Jobbing*, dedicating it comfortably to all the Gentleman Stock-Jobbers at Jonathan's. But more interesting than these, and a really entertaining poem, is one on the art of ringing, by William Woty, whose pen-name was "Jemmy Copywell." He called it *Campanalogia, a poem in praise of Ringing*, by the author of *The Shrubs of Parnassus* (1761). It is a burlesque of the heroic style, done this time in blank verse with generous echoing phrases from Milton. The author tells first how to learn the art of ringing, suggesting a technique similar to what an amateur typist finds necessary. Then he grows rhapsodical over the virtues of well-known practitioners of the art, sentimentalizes over various great holidays associated in his mind with ringing, such as the day of Queen Charlotte's arrival, and concludes by assigning to bells an important rôle in the tremendous business of preserving the nation's stability.

Probably sufficient examples of the popularity of this sort of poem have already been given. They keep on appearing in pamphlet literature down through the century, sometimes indescribably bad. There is one called *The Art of Eloquence*, a didactic poem published in 1785. From the opening section on "general precepts," it goes bravely through bar, senate, and pulpit, argumentative, ornamental, to a decidedly pathetic fourthly. It is written in blank verse bad enough to make more than Sam Johnson sweat; and most of its pages in the Bodleian copy are still, I suspect, uncut.

In direct imitation of *Trivia* is James Smith's poem, *The Art of Living in London* (1768). In Charles Lamb's copy of this *Art of Living in London*, by the way, there is a note in his writing stating that the author of the poem was Oliver Goldsmith. It is rather long, — forty pages, — and has many curious things to tell us. Poets are beginning to realize that it is well to hide good intentions:

> How hard his task, who does not fear to tell
> He means instruction, more than writing well?

The writer advises strangers to lodge near Temple Bar midway between Court and City, and thus save coach-hire and shoes. Take an upper room, not a first floor. Learn from the morning cries when to get up.

> Leave to the loiterer his simp'ring tea.

Eat gruel made with milk or water. Don't bother with the hairdresser. Get shoes shined by the boys at the street corner. Then spend the morning reading Virgil, Newton, Swift, Steele, Addison, and Pope. Dine at the

Cock, Threadneedle Street, behind the Exchange. This
is a steak-house with an excellent host. Many other
choices are given, in the manner of Ames or Ned Ward
— the Bull up north in Bishopsgate, or, along the east-
ern road, Kenton's at Whitechapel. Westward are all the
extravagant eating-houses, Cambell's, Wood's, Stacey's.

> Facing that street where Venus holds her reign,
> And *Pleasure's* daughters, drag a life of *pain;*
> There the *Spread-eagle* . . .

This he recommends, although so near the notorious
Catherine Street, Strand, or the Dog in Holy-well. What
did these "poets" get from the innkeepers? Probably
a good dinner gratis, occasionally, would do the busi-
ness. Smith's visitor is a country cully with not much
money. He is advised to avoid early vegetables for the
health of his purse, and for the same reason he must not

> indiscreetly stray
> Where *Giles's* ruins mark the broaden'd way;
> Where, for what end, most obviously appears,
> The knives are chain'd, and ladder forms the stairs;
> Or to *Moorfields*, where wretched paupers ply
> Round clothless tables in an open sky.

In the evening he will visit the coffee-houses to read the
prints and study mankind, or, if it is summer-time, the
gardens of Knightsbridge, Chelsea, Kensington (founded
by William III), Bagnigge, or Cromwell's Gardens near
what was once the great man's house, where nowadays
one may get a dish of tea. But at night the town shows
lurid. Drunken coachmen neglect their fare; the hap-
less housewife and antique maid seek the fortune-teller;
Drury nymphs are abroad.

> Their lofty garrets Drury's nymphs forsake;
> Down the dark alley pants the batter'd rake:
> The drowsy watchman hobbles to his stand,
> Prepar'd to free the thief who gilds his hand.

Gamesters meet, robbers of mankind; common cheats abound; even among the wealthy the sharper plays his tricks; he knows the mysteries of Breslaw the juggler, and plunders under the guise of friendship. Whores gather

> In shameless groupes, along the lengthen'd Strand.

Their terms of address are given: "My life, my love, my charmer, or, my dear." To get rid of this nuisance the author recommends that whores be "dismissed instant" to some single street, as in parts of Italy and Holland. And let them wear a badge. Episode comes next, of course: the story of Palaemon, drunkenness, harlotry, disease. Then we pass to the theatre. Not too much on this! The lord and cit are both there. Shakespeare, Otway, Rowe are praised for tragedy; for comedy, Congreve, Cibber, Steele, and Gay. Smith has been reading his Milton:

> Oh! how shall words, immortal bard! display
> The warbling sweetness of thy woodland lay?

Presently we are back among the eating-houses. Two of the same ones are praised again, as if the author wished to say before closing his work, "Now don't forget, these are the places to go." The amateur politician of the tavern is described very well:

> Now on the *colonies* profoundly treats,
> And from the daily-prints at large repeats.

The son of Mars is here with rather shrunk shanks, *pace* Goldsmith:

> Now he expatiates o'er battles won,
> Of plunder'd provinces, and towns undone,
> In his spill'd porter, martial lines advance
> 'Gainst the united pow'rs, of Spain, and France . . .

With bread and cheese, a parapet he rears,
While broken pipe-stems cannonade by tiers.

With prospects of such society, why worry about Almack's and Soho, about the Rose and Shakespear. Here you can pay your debts and be happy.

II. JUVENAL'S THIRD SATIRE

Dependent as the Augustans were on classical inspiration, they would in all probability never have produced half of the material used in this study had Juvenal not written his Third Satire. It will be wise, therefore, to make a careful examination of this great poem and of the most important translations and adaptations of it in our literature.

The purpose of the satirist was to portray conditions in Rome as he saw them: not only the external realities of her streets, but the influences which were working insidiously enough, he thought, upon the character of her people. He planned a discussion of such questions as immigration, race mixture, graft, the crime wave. Now, this all sounds like the material for a newspaper paragraph, not for a poem. How did he manage, with such a subject, to produce a work of art? It seems almost as difficult a task as that which Verhaeren or some modern Americans have undertaken, to create poetry from the whirr and grind of machinery.

In the first place, Juvenal sets his poem in a charming framework of narrative. Umbricius is leaving the city, disgusted with the excesses he has witnessed there, and confident that it is no place for a poor and honest man. He stops his cart at the Conduit Gate and tells his friend the poet why he intends to settle in the country for good. In Rome he sees people from the very lowest classes making fortunes out of disgraceful occupations, rising by their servile flatteries to affluence, and crowding out their more scrupulous neighbors by unblushing hypocrisy.

> Knaves who in full Assemblies have the knack
> Of turning Truth to Lies, and White to Black;
> Can hire large Houses, and oppress the Poor
> By farm'd Excise; can cleanse the Common-shoare;
> And rent the Fishery; can bear the dead;
> And teach their Eyes dissembled Tears to shed,
> All this for Gain; for Gain they sell their very Head.[1]

This was true certainly for the Rome of Juvenal's day; it has also a far broader application, as every observer of modern cities knows. The scions of old and cultured families give way these days to the sons of the street, who start life selling newspapers and cleaning lamps, and let no outworn conventions stand between them and the power or wealth they want. Or, as Oldham back in 1682 puts it, once grooms, or footboys, they become rich with the spoils of spendthrift heirs, they make their way as plot-mongers, and in the hope of preferment many a man is willing to set

> His wife, his conscience, or his oath to let.

And a little later Defoe writes, in "The True-Born Englishman," [2]

> Innumerable City-Knights we know,
> From *Bluecoat Hospitals* and *Bridewell* flow:
> Draymen and Porters fill the City Chair,
> And Footboys Magisterial Purple wear.
> Fate has but very small Distinction set
> Betwixt the Counter and the Coronet.
> Tarpaulin L[or]ds, Pages of high Renown,
> Rise up by Poor Mens Valour, not their own.
> Great Families of Yesterday we show,
> And Lords, whose Parents were the Lord knows who.

[1] Dryden, 1693.
[2] Part I, p. 17 (1708).

Juvenal's poem is truly dramatic; his Umbricius is a real man, who burns with righteous indignation as he tells his friend about his wrongs. Many of the things he talks about refer to special conditions of the time and place, or at any rate are abuses which no longer worry us; yet that does not in the least prevent our imaginative sympathy, or keep the active mind from continually ranging for modern variations on the old themes. Human nature is before us, and the idea of progress retreats to its proper corner. That is the essential greatness of the poem.[1] That is the reason, too, why Oldham and Dryden and Johnson find it so easy to drift from old saws to modern instances, as soon as they star^ to translate it. The term "translation," indeed, can be applied only to Dryden's version. Oldham's poem is an adaptation of Juvenal revised to date with the utmost particularity, while Johnson's (1738) is rather conspicuous for omissions than for the illustrative material he uses, though this is frequently interesting.

Oldham's malcontent is willing to go anywhere rather than stay in London:

> The *Peake*, the *Fens*, the *Hundreds*, or *Lands-end*,
> I would prefer to *Fleetstreet*, or the *Strand*.

His friend, the poet, meets him,

> Hard by *Mile-end*, the place so fam'd of late,
> In Prose and Verse for the great *Factions Treat*.

The time when Oldham was writing must have been difficult enough for the flatterer. One recalls the per-

---

[1] An interesting discussion of this Satire and its relation to the adaptations by Boileau (I and VI) and Mathurin Regnier (III) may be found in chap. 2 of Auguste Widal's *Juvenal et ses Satires* (1870). He mentions the famous appearances of the flatterer in classical literature: Theophrastus, *Characters*, II; Terence, *Eunuchus*, II, 4, III, 1; and Plutarch, *De discriminatione amici et adulatoris*, chap. 13.

vading excitement and distrust[1] which followed the revelations and fabrications of Titus Oates in 1679 — how politicians and others swung from side to side in the political whirlpool; how some, slipping too near centre, disappeared in the wildest part of the maelstrom. Oldham complains that he is no astrologer,

> To tell the minute, when the King shall die,
> And you know what — come in: nor can I steer,
> And tack about my Conscience, whensoe'er,
> To a new Point I see Religion veer.

Oldham's *saeva indignatio* against the sins of the town certainly reaches its highest point in his imitation of the Eighth Satire of Boileau (1682). Here he puts man down as the greatest fool in nature. None of the brutes can compete. Man busies himself with trades either vain or villainous. Money is the only mark of success, and all that a young man needs to make his way in the world is a case-hardened conscience, *Irish proof*. The pedant is the acme of futility, and does not know it. Better

> Go, practise with some Banker how to cheat,
> There's choice in Town, enquire in *Lombard-street*.

Let's suppose an ass were given speech:

> What would he say, were he condemn'd to stand
> For one long howr in *Fleetstreet*, or the *Strand*,
> To cast his eyes upon the motly throng,
> The two-leg'd Herd, that daily pass along;

[1] Cf. Oldham, "The Careless Good Fellow" (1680), *Works*, p. 408:

> "A Pox of this fooling, and plotting of late,
> What a pother and stir has it kept in the State?
> Let the Rabble run mad with Suspicions, and Fears,
> Let them scuffle and jar, till they go by the ears:
> Their Grievances never shall trouble my pate,
> So I can enjoy my dear Bottle in quiet."

To see their old Disguises, Furs, and Gowns,
Their Cassocks, Cloaks, Lawn-sleeves, and Pantaloons?
What would he say to see a Velvet Quack
Walk with the price of forty kill'd on's Back;
Or mounted on a Stage, and gaping loud,
Commend his Drugs, and Ratsbane to the Crowd?
What would he think on a Lord Mayor's day,
Should he the Pomp and Pageantry survey?
Or view the Judges, and their solemn Train,
March with grave decency to kill a Man?
What would he think of us, should he appear
In Term amongst the crowds at *Westminster*,
And there the hellish din, and Jargon hear,
Where J[effreys] and his pack with deep mouth'd Notes
Drown *Billinsgate*, and all its Oyster-Boats?

"The Town-Life"[1] is an imitation of Juvenal's Third
Satire, and in the opening lines expresses a similar cyni-
cism. The writer first tells of his discontent with condi-
tions in the city and his intention to get away from it all:

I cannot veer with ev'ry Change of State,
Nor flatter Villains tho' at Court they're great:
Nor will I prostitute my Pen for hire,
Praise *Cromwell*, damn him, write the *Spanish Fryar*:
A *Papist* now, if next the *Turk* should reign,
Then piously transverse the *Alcoran*.

The approximate date of the poem and the writer's poli-
tics are evident. He then goes on to outline the usual
round of duties and pleasures for the Spark — the
Mall, high mass, Locket's gossip, the play, the Park,
cards, the Drawing-Room:

The *English* must not seek Preferment there,
For *Mack's* and *O's* all Places destin'd are. . . .
Thus Sparks may dress, dance, play, write, fight, get drunk,
But all the mighty pother ends in Punk.

[1] *Poems on Affairs of State, 1660–1688* (6th ed., 1716), I, 190.

Dryden had passed through the same troublous times, but in his old age, bitter as some of his memories must have been, he preferred to leave these scars untouched, and to confine himself to translation. Johnson, on the other hand, was writing in better days. Walpole had given the nation peace and efficient government for many a long year when *London* appeared, though there was still corruption enough in politics and society, superfluity of naughtiness certainly, to provide a great satirist with abundance of illustrative material. Johnson really missed his chance. His poem is full of clever phrases, with some apt allusions — better, on the whole, than contemporary essays of the same sort, but a failure compared with its original. Even the couplet, which most people think so effective, about the Frenchman in London, —

> All sciences a fasting Monsieur knows,
> And bid him go to hell, to hell he goes, —

is an irresistible adaptation of the corresponding line in Dryden. Johnson did not have, or failed to use, the imaginative grasp which would do for London what Juvenal had done for Rome. Possibly he was handicapped in such a task by his enthusiastic love of the city. His work is an exercise in translation with a change of names. He speaks of falling houses, though this must have been an unusual occurrence in London, whereas the houses in Juvenal's Rome were very high and flimsy and did collapse occasionally.[1] Instead of poets on street corners, a female atheist talks him dead. The exile leaves in a wherry from Greenwich. Masquerades, excise, lotteries, and eunuchs provide material for the grumbler. "What hope remains for me?" he cries, "for I

[1] See M. L. Friedlaender, *Darstellungen aus der Sittengeschichte Roms*, pp. 3, 4, 5.

> Despise a fool in half his pension dress'd,
> And strive in vain to laugh at H[erve]y's jest."

Bribes cannot tempt him, however large,
    All Marlb'rough hoarded, or all Villiers spent.

He sees London invested with French parasites [1] as Rome was with Greek. One fancies that Johnson might have been more genuinely indignant here, had he introduced the Scotch [2] instead of the French. His prejudice against the northerners is almost instinctive, and we even find among his opening lines a satire on the poverty of Scotland slyly disguised as a hint of preference:

> For who wou'd leave, unbrib'd, Hibernia's land,
> Or change the rocks of Scotland for the Strand?
> There none are swept by sudden fate away,
> But all whom hunger spares, with age decay.

From the time of James I down, London had been the happy hunting ground for needy Scotchmen. We know from Smollett's stories how prominent they had made themselves in the life of the town. They did not excite, however, the virulence[3] of popular feeling that would make them possible as modern protagonists for Juvenal's Greeks. The French were, no doubt, better.

Riots against the foreigner had been for a long time the sport of successive generations of Londoners. Jews

[1] For lampoons against Dutchmen see Defoe, *The True-Born Englishman*, and Tutchin, *The Foreigners*. Both are printed in *Poems on Affairs of State*, II, 7 and I respectively. See also *Humorous and Diverting Dialogues between Monsieur Baboon, a French Dancing-master (but lately come over) and Jack Tar, an English Sailor* (1755).

[2] Lord Holland did use the Scotch in place of Juvenal's Greeks in his *Imitations* (1798–99).

[3] Cf. *Baboon-à-la-mode, A Satyr against the French*. Also the ballad, "The French Dancing Master and the English Soldier" (1666; Luttrell Collection), quoted in Ashton, *Humour, Wit and Satire of the Seventeenth Century*, p. 377.

and Flemings in turn had felt the weight of clubs. In the mad May Day [1] of Queen Katherine's time, the 'prentices were "out" for the Spaniards.

The story of this ill May Day is told in a ballad of the time,[2] along with the account of how Queen Katherine begged the lives of two thousand London 'prentices. The trouble arises over the discontent caused by the unusual influx of Spaniards. Slaughter of the foreigners is uncontrolled on the streets until finally troops from the Tower arrive:

> Hundreds were hangd by martial law
>   on sign posts at their masters doores,
> By which the rest were kept in awe,
>   and frighted from such lewd vproars.
> Some others who their fact repented,
>   two thousand prentices at least,
> Were all before the king presented,
>   as Maior and magistrates thought best.
> And two and two together tyde,
>   through Temple Bar and Strand they goe
> To Westminster there to be tryde,
>   with ropes about their neckes also:
> But such a crye in euery streete
>   till then was neuer heard nor knowne,
> By mothers for their children sweete
>   vnhappily thus ouerthrowne.

The Queen intercedes, and the King graciously grants her request:

> Thou has thy boone, and they may liue
>   to serue me in my Bullein warre.

---

[1] Cf. Jonson, *The Silent Woman*, IV, 1: "*Morose:* You sons of noise and tumult, begot on an ill May-day, or when the galley-foist is afloat to Westminster." This was May Day of 1517. "Galley-foist" is the Lord Mayor's barge.

[2] J. P. Collier, *Broadside Black-letter Ballads* (1868), p. 96.

Oldham complains of the French:

> But leaving these *Messieurs*, for fear that I
> Be thought of the *Silk-Weavers Mutiny*.

And to-day, with the same intolerance that Juvenal expressed, the cry is "America for the Americans," for one knows perfectly well that no good can come from these foreigners.[1] It is true that Juvenal's bitter indictment is supported step by step in history. The Greeks and Orientals who swarmed into Rome during the first century were evidently a bad lot. Horace and Cicero both complain of them.[2] Men of all trades, they wormed their way into the houses and secrets of the great. Theophrastus never guessed that his description of the flatterer [3] would three hundred years later be so justly applied to his own countrymen. Juvenal's Greek is Tartufe off stage.[4]

Juvenal shows his *humanitas* far more clearly in the splendid passage which follows, on the inequalities and injustices of the social order. A man is not judged by what he is but by what he has:

> The Question is not put how far extends
> His Piety, but what he yearly spends:

[1] Cf. Gay's "Epistle to Pulteney," *Works* (ed. Underhill), I, 192.

[2] Horace, *Epistles*, II, 1, 156; Cicero, *Pro Flacco*.

[3] Cf. Lodge, *A Fig for Momus* (1595), Satyre I:

> "He is a gallant fit to serue my Lord,
> Which clawes and soothes him up at euerie word,
> That cries, when his lame poesie he heares,
> 'T is rare (my Lord) 't will pass the nicest eares,"

and Marston, *Satires*, I (1598):

> "Holding him on as he through Paul's doth walke,
> With nodds and leggs and odde superfluous talke;
> Making men thinke thee gracious in his sight,
> When he esteemes thee parasite."

[4] Cf. Molière, *Tartufe* (1667), V, 6.

> Quick, to the Bus'ness; how he Lives and Eats;
> How largely Gives; how splendidly he Treats:
> How many thousand Acres feed his Sheep,
> What are his Rents, what Servants does he keep?[1]

Juvenal proves himself here what he has been aptly called, the advocate of the disinherited classes. In our English literature Goldsmith takes the torch from his hand:

> If to the city sped — What waits him there?
> To see profusion that he must not share;
> To see ten thousand baneful arts combin'd
> To pamper luxury, and thin mankind;
> To see each joy the sons of pleasure know
> Extorted from his fellow creature's woe.
> Here, while the courtier glitters in brocade,
> There the pale artist plies the sickly trade;
> Here, while the proud their long-drawn pomps display,
> There the black gibbet glooms beside the way.
> The dome where Pleasure holds her midnight reign,
> Here, richly deck'd, admits the gorgeous train;
> Tumultuous grandeur crowds the blazing square,
> The rattling chariots clash, the torches glare.
> Sure scenes like these no troubles e'er annoy!
> Sure these denote one universal joy!
> Are these thy serious thoughts? — Ah, turn thine eyes
> Where the poor houseless shivering female lies.
> She once, perhaps, in village plenty bless'd
> Has wept at tales of innocence distress'd.

Both writers understand well enough the bitterest portion of the poor, that *paupertas ... ridiculos homines facit.* One may justly claim, I think, some improve-

---

[1] Oldham puts the case well in his "Satyr touching Nobility out of M. Boileau" (*Works*, p. 387):

> "But he that's rich is prais'd at his full rate,
> And tho he once cry'd *Small-coal* in the street,
> Tho he, nor none of his e'er mention'd were,
> But in the Parish-Book or Register."

ment in the attitude of most men toward poverty and misfortune to-day. Such conditions no longer appeal to us as funny. Few indeed would be caught joking about torn clothes, hunger, homelessness, or idiocy. The minute, however, the matter is moved one step higher in the social order, away from the tragic stage, that sort of poverty is just as vain as ever, and toward it the flood-gates of humor may open. Competition with one's neighbors, for instance, in the buying of cheap cars is a modern form of a very old disease.

In Dryden's day humanitarianism had not begun its work. He translates Juvenal's phrases with literalness and sees nothing incongruous in them. Men still laughed at the poor. Oldham makes his illustrations extremely up to date. No one, he says, respects the poor:

> One takes occasion his ript Shooe to flout,
> And swears 't has been at Prison-grates hung out:
> Another shrewdly jeers his coarse Crevat,
> Because himself wears *Point:* a third his Hat,
> And most unmercifully shews his Wit,
> If it be old, and does not cock aright.

The poor are insulted, even in church. Everyone is ashamed to wear woolen:

> Only, the Statutes Penalty to save,
> Some few perhaps wear Wollen in the Grave.

The hint for this comes also from Juvenal, for he speaks of certain parts of the country where none but dead men wear gowns. Pope puts the idea to better use than any of them in the passage about Mrs. Oldfield in *Moral Essays*, I, "Of the Knowledge and Characters of Men":[1]

> "Odious! in woollen! 't would a Saint provoke,"
> (Were the last words that poor Narcissa spoke),

[1] (Ed. Warton), III, 207, l. 246.

"No, let a charming Chintz and Brussels lace
Wrap my cold limbs, and shade my lifeless face;
One would not, sure, be frightful when one's dead —
And — Betty — give this Cheek a little Red." [1]

Johnson, as one would expect, enters with full sympathy into Juvenal's advocacy of the poor. The insults they suffered touched his heart. He had endured much himself, and had observed even more:

By numbers here from shame or censure free,
All crimes are safe, but hated poverty.
This, only this, the rigid law pursues,
This, only this, provokes the snarling muse.
The sober trader at a tatter'd cloak,
Wakes from his dream, and labours for a joke;
With brisker air the silken courtiers gaze,
And turn the varied taunt a thousand ways.
Of all the griefs that harass the distress'd,
Sure the most bitter is a scornful jest;
Fate never wounds more deep the gen'rous heart,
Than when a blockhead's insult points the dart.

The poor have no money to forward their schemes. If they want to see some man of influence, they must first bribe all his understrappers, as Oldham reminds us:

His Porter, Groom, and Steward must have Fees,
And you may see the *Tombs*, and *Tow'r* for less.

Then follows in the Juvenal the famous description of the fire:[2] the poor man in his garret near the tiles and

---

[1] See *Gentleman's Magazine*, March, 1731. Betty is supposed to be Mrs. Saunders.

[2] Cf. *Trivia*, III, 353; Dryden's *Annus Mirabilis* (stanzas 209 ff.). J. O. Halliwell catalogues a ballad (CLXX) called "The Londoners Lamentation, wherein is contained a sorrowfull Description of the dreadfull Fire, which happened in Pudding-lane, next beyond Fish-street Hill, on the second of September, 1666, betwixt twelve and one of the clock in the morning, being Sunday, and continued till the Thursday night following. With an account of the King and the Duke of York's indeavours with several Peers of the Land for the quenching of the same; Also the manner of doing it, and the

the pigeons, the contrast between his fate and that of
his rich neighbor, whose losses are so abundantly re-
paired by his friends and parasites that one suspects
him of setting the fire. Johnson leaves out altogether
the description of the poet's garret; his friend, Gold-
smith, evidently saw the opportunity and used it in his
"Description of an Author's Bedchamber": [1]

> He views with keen desire
> The rusty grate unconscious of a fire;
> With beer and milk arrears the frieze was scor'd,
> And five crack'd teacups dress'd the chimney board;
> A nightcap deck'd his brows instead of bay,
> A cap by night — a stocking all the day!

Dryden's translation of this section of the poem is ex-
cellent. It has keen pathos without sentimentality, and
shows virtuous indignation without loss of dignity.
With this highly important reservation, it is almost
tractarian in its championship of the proletariat. We
may congratulate ourselves that, in spite of ultra-
modern reactions from humanitarianism and a tendency
to regard pity as a weakness, we no longer leave the poor
unaided after fire and famine, and the rich man who
took Martial's [2] old-time suggestion would soon regret
it, unless, indeed, he regard the insurance companies as
his public, as in one sense they are.

name of every particular place where the fire did stop." See also Jeremiah
Wells, *Poems* (1667), p. 112, "On the Rebuilding of London"; John Allison(?),
Upon the late Lamentable Fire in London (1667).

[1] This sketch was sent by Goldsmith from Switzerland in a letter to his
brother Henry, in 1755. Cf. Mark Akenside, *The Poet*, Bk. I, p. 293, in
the Aldine edition.

[2] Cf. Martial, *Epigrammata*, III, 52, "Ad Tongilianum, de Utili
Incendio":

> "Empta domus fuerat tibi, Tongiliane, ducentis:
>   Abstulit hanc nimium casus in urbe frequens.
> Conlatum est deciens. Rogo, non potes ipse videri
>   Incendisse tuam, Tongiliane, domum?"

Juvenal advises a retreat to the country:

> Est aliquid quocumque loco, quocumque recessu,
> Unius sese dominum fecisse lacertae.

Or, as Molière's *Alceste* has it:

> Chercher sur la terre un endroit écarté,
> Où d'être homme d'honneur on ait la liberté.

Then follows that part of the poem which is of most interest to us. The inconveniences and dangers of the city are discussed with so much detail and vivid picturesqueness that the Rome of those long-past years lives before us. Things are told about here which the dignity of history passes by. One feels as if digging in the graves of buried civilizations, so close does one get to the very bodies of the people. The poet's words are the "Open, Sesame!" and touch the secret springs of imagination. They can do that only because the things they connote remain much the same throughout the generations. The noise of the great city still grinds mercilessly into the ears of the poor. From their bedroom windows they can almost touch the shrieking trains as they pass. Juvenal's catalogue of noises sounds almost idyllic to us moderns, while Oldham's seventeenth-century variations are no more exciting:

> The noise of Shops, with Hawkers early Screams,
> Besides the Brawls of Coach-men, when they meet,
> And stop in turnings of a narrow Street,
> Such a loud medley of confusion make,
> As drowsie A[rche]r [1] on the Bench would wake.

But all this never disturbs the rich. Their homes are far from these congested centres, and they pass through the crush and confusion in litters or limousines. Crowds

---

[1] "Arche" in 1720 and 1722 editions of Oldham's *Poems*. Oldham refers to John Archer, justice of the Common Bench in Charles II's time.

were probably no more ill mannered and clownish in the
Roman market-place than they are to-day in the New
York subway. The poor have to endure both their
familiarities and their insults. They have to slide around
on the greasy paving-stones, or eat "beef stew" in dingy
restaurants. If any accident occurs, they are usually the
ones to suffer. Their houses fall; it is on them that the
overturned cart flings its load of great timbers; for them
the household waits and the chair stands empty.

When Oldham comes to this passage, he thinks of the
huge cut stones now passing through the streets toward
the new St. Paul's, and draws his illustration thence:

> Next a huge *Portland* Stone, for building *Pauls*,[1]
> Itself almost a Rock, on Carriage rowls.

What the poor have not suffered through the history
of modern industrialism would be a far shorter story
than their injuries. Nor need we be too complaisant
about present conditions. When machinery breaks
down, the wealthy shareholder is not by. Our theatres
collapse; not the Opera House or His Majesty's, but
some down-town music hall or "movie palace." This
part of the Satire, about the dangers of the streets for
the pedestrian, should be compared with Horace, *Epis-
tles*, II, 2, which Pope imitates (1737):

> But grant I may relapse, for want of grace,
> Again to rhyme; can London be the place?
> Who there his Muse, or self, or soul attends?
> In crowds, and courts, law, business, feasts, and friends?
> My counsel sends to execute a deed:
> A Poet begs me, I will hear him read:

---

[1] Edward Ward, *Hudibras Redivivus*, Part I, Canto II:
"I strol'd among the *Bibliopolae*,
Where Pamphlets lay in Shops and Stalls,
Pil'd up as thick as Stones in *Paul's*."

In Palace-Yard at nine you'll find me there —
At ten for certain, Sir, in Bloomsb'ry-Square —
Before the Lords at twelve my Cause comes on —
There's a Rehearsal, Sir, exact at one. —
"Oh but a Wit can study in the streets,
And raise his mind above the mob he meets."
Not quite so well however as one ought;
A hackney-coach may chance to spoil a thought;
And then a nodding beam, or pig of lead,
God knows, may hurt the very ablest head.
Have you not seen, at Guildhall's narrow pass,
Two Aldermen dispute it with an Ass?
And Peers give way, exalted as they are,
Ev'n to their own S-r-v-nce in a Car?
Go, lofty Poet! and in such a crowd,
Sing thy sonorous verse — but not aloud.

Also with Horace, *Epistles*, I, 14, in the excellent imitation done by Thomas Nevile (1758):

I grant you, here no coffee-house affords
The sight of saunt'ring fops, or prating lords;
No bagnio, brothel, for nocturnal hour,
No watch to bully, and no streets to scour.
"Who, that the Belles of Ranelagh has seen,
With rose-cheek'd flirts could circle Clarehall green,
Or who, once happy in a masquerade,
Could bear to ramble in a rook'ry's shade?"

Juvenal next pictures the dangers of the streets at night, and here his imitators in Stuart England can follow him with conviction. The possibility of petty annoyances and serious mishap was doubled with the going down of the sun. An occasional flickering lamp served only to make darkness visible. Neither the people nor the corporation had any traces of social conscience, so that ordinary prohibitions and precautions, which we take for granted to-day as absolutely necessary if people are to live in such close proximity, were altogether ne-

glected. Besides, — to let Milton still flavor our para-
graph, — the sons of Belial were then abroad, flown
with insolence and wine.

We may give Juvenal's "Rake" scant courtesy in this
chapter, since he was responsible for at least a *petit genre*
in the literature of Gay's time, and we shall get better
acquainted with him later, when these poems are before
us. Here we must notice the exquisite genius which our
Roman poet shows in placing this full-fed scion of the
wealthy beside the poor wretch he is bullying on the
street, and making him talk about food. The pitiful in-
justice of the whole thing comes out with amazing clear-
ness. The wolf addresses the lamb. There is no redress.
Justice tips the scale with gold and a jest on your rags.[1]
The extraordinary force of this indictment on society is
but heightened by the complete absence of bitterness.

It is interesting to note in this connection how com-
pletely Oldham misses the whole point of his original
here, and thus shows a marked crassness and lack of
poetic sense:

> *Who's there?* he cries, and takes you by the Throat,
> *Dog! are you dumb? Speak quickly, else my Foot*
> *Shall march about your Buttocks: whence d'ye come,*
> *From what bulk-ridden Strumpet reeking home?*
> *Saving your reverend Pimpship, where d'ye ply?*
> *How may one have a Job of Lechery?*

Oldham really does much better for the rake in his
imitation of the Thirteenth Satire of Juvenal. Here
Juvenal tells the story of a man who has been deceived
by a friend, to whom he has lent money. His indig-
nation runs high, and makes him forget how common

---

[1] *A Poem on the Civil-Wars of the Old-Baily; Occasion'd by a Late Dispute,
between the Sheriffs and Students of the Law* (1713):
  "Not far from *Newgate*, stands a lofty Pile,
  Where Justice Frowns, but brib'd she kindly Smiles."

his experience is. But the poet, to comfort him, dilates most vividly on the pangs of conscience, and deprecates revenge:

> But, Oh, Revenge more sweet than Life! 'T is true,
> So the unthinking say, and the mad Crew
> Of hect'ring Blades, who for slight cause, or none,
> At every turn are into Passion blown:
> Whom the least Trifles with Revenge inspire,
> And at each spark, like Gunpowder, take fire:
> These unprovok'd kill the next Man they meet,
> For being so sawcy, as to walk the street;
> And at the summons of each tiny Drab,
> Cry, Damme! Satisfaction! draw, and stab.[1]

However, these young bullies, "who cannot sleep without a Braul," [2] never interfere with the rich.

Satire III goes on to discuss the increase of crime since the good old days when one prison sufficed for the whole city. Now there is hardly iron left for the goads and ploughshares.

> The Ruffian Robbers by no Justice aw'd,
> And unpaid cut-Throat Soldiers, are abroad;
> Those Venal Souls, who, harden'd in each ill,
> To save Complaints and Prosecution, kill.

Oldham echoes his complaint, while Johnson sees such crowds at Tyburn that it is hard to get hemp enough to supply the fleet.

Things are, no doubt, better to-day in our great cities. One may, at any rate, go about them at night without danger of being bullied by the drunken sons of the wealthier classes. There are not many streets in either

---

[1] Cf. John Duer, The Third Satire of Juvenal, translated, to which are added Miscellaneous Poems, original and translated (1806).

[2] Cf. Shadwell, Bury Fair (1689), IV, 2: "Gertrude: Well, I am of opinion, that a lady is no more to be accounted a beauty, till she has killed her man, than the bullies think one a fine gentleman, till he has killed his."

London or New York where a man need fear to wander, even though he has a full purse. Yet there are disquieting things going on; desperate games are played for the same old stakes. One hesitates to think what the research student of the future may produce, should he base his judgment of our social conditions too exclusively on newspaper files. Crime pulsates, and generally the reasons for the variations in the "curve" are *post facto* evident. Rome in the time of Augustus was an unusually well-governed city. In Juvenal's day all that splendid system of watch and ward had collapsed. At present we seem to be passing through a similar period.

And now, to complete the picture, Umbricius takes leave of the poet and turns his face away from the hated town:

> More I cou'd say, more Causes I cou'd show
> For my departure; but the Sun is low:
> The Waggoner grows weary of my stay;
> And whips his Horses forwards on their way.
> Farewell; and when, like me, o'rewhelm'd with care,
> You to your own *Aquinum* shall repair,
> To take a mouthful of sweet Country air,
> Be mindful of your Friend; and send me word,
> What Joys your Fountains and cool Shades afford:
> Then, to assist your Satyrs, I will come;
> And add new Venom, when you write of *Rome*.

III. "Journeys" about Town

The "Wanderer" is a familiar type in every literature. With the lyrical outpourings of his loneliness we can have nothing to do here; but we must notice him when he descends from his airy nothings to tell us about commonplace journeys from place to place, the things seen and the accidents worth recording. This was done in Roman poetry at least as early as Lucilius, who describes his journey to Capua and thence to the Straits of Messina in Book III of his *Satura*, fragments only of which survive. The possibility of using everyday themes and conversational looseness of structure in poetry having been once accepted, — Lucilius called his poems *Sermones*, — nothing could be more natural than the introduction of verse travelogues; for, after all, no one who has had a good time on a holiday goes home and says nothing about it. Horace followed the example of the older poet, and his *Journey to Brundisium* [1] serves too readily as a label for this type of poetry wherever we find it.

In English literature there is a vast amount of verse which may be grouped under this heading: stories of pilgrims, whether bound for Canterbury or making *The Golden Journey to Samarkand*, long and patriotic descriptions of places like the *Polyolbion*, or rambling accounts of rambles like Braithwaite's *Drunken Barnaby's Four Journeys* (1638). Sometimes the journey is eulogistic. Dr. Robert Wild, for instance, celebrates the Restoration in a poem which he calls *Iter Boreale*, *attempting something upon the Successful and Matchless March of the Lord General George Monck from Scotland to London* (1660). This contains far more eulogy than topography, and the verses describing the landing of Charles show fallacies that are pathetic enough:

> Methinks I see how throngs of people stand
> Scarce patient till the Vessel come to land,
> Ready to leap in, and if need require
> With Tears of Joy to make the water higher:
> But what will *London* do? I doubt Old *Paul*
> With bowing to his Soveraign will fall.

[1] See Cowper, *Poems* (ed. by J. C. Bailey, 1905), p. 617; Horace, *Satires*, I, 5, in iambic tetrameter couplets; or Thomas Creech, *Odes, Satyrs, and Epistles of Horace* (5th ed., 1730).

A Curious Pump, near Bishopsgate Street

The mermaid figure at the top was constructed to be used on festal days as a
fountain, to discharge wine or other liquors at the breasts.

> The Royal Lyons from the Tower shall roar,
> And though they see him not, yet shall adore:
> The Conduits will be ravish'd, and combine
> To turn their very water into wine.

Sometimes the poet brings his wanderer into the town and allows him to exhaust his restlessness among the streets themselves. The old poem, "London Lickpenny," is the lineal progenitor of most of these verses, though the classical tradition no doubt exerts its influence even before we reach the time of Gay and the imitators of his "Journey to Exeter." [1]

A late and very close imitation of "London Lickpenny" may be found in "There's Nothing to be had without Money," possibly by Martin Parker.[2] In this poem, the wanderer finds himself well treated at the Royal Exchange and in Cheapside:

> For my contentment, once a day,
>   I walkt for recreation
> Through Paul's, Ludgate, and Fleet-street gay,
>   To raise an elevation:
> Sometimes my humour is to range
> To Temple, Strand, and New Exchange,
> To see their fashions rare and strange;
>   *But God a' mercy, penny.*

He may go to Westminster Hall, or to the Abbey:

> And having seene the sights most rare,
> The water-men full ready were
> Me ore the river of Thames to beare;
>   *But God a' mercy, penny.*

He likes, also, to visit the Globe on the Bankside, and the gardens on that side of the river:

---

[1] 1715. *Poems* (ed. by Underhill), I, 186.
[2] *Roxburghe Ballads*, II, 565.

> Both tapsters, cookes, and vintners fine,
> With other jovial friends of mine,
> Will pledge my health in beere or wine;
>   *But God a' mercy, penny.*

"The Norfolk Farmer's Journey to London,"[1] by
Edward Ford, tells about a country couple and their
visit to London to see some relatives. They wander
through the streets delighted with the strangeness of
their surroundings, though Sisly has her doubts about
all this brawling and brabbling and thinks most of the
folk must find their way sooner or later to Hogsden.
They get along as far as Fleet Street, where Thomas is
pushed about by the crowd till he is quite in a sweat and
almost angry. The throngs of people surprise him, too,
for it is just after the plague.

> At length, quoth she, good husband, stay,
> And tell me what this place is, pray,
> Where things are carried as they may?
>   I never saw the like.
> For yonder's one doth ride in state,
> And here's a begger at a gate,
> And there's a woman that will prate
>   for nothing.
> See, here is one that soundly beats
> And thumps his hemp until he sweats;
> And there's another greedy eats —
>   I fear hee'l choak himselfe.
> And yonder goes a gallant bilk,
> And there's a woman winding silk,
> And here's another fetches milk
>   at Hackney.

The tall woman with the little husband excites her won-
der, and later, the beggar who has apparently lost both

---

[1] *Roxburghe Ballads* (ed. by Wm. Chappell, 1871), II, 169. Collier thinks
ca. 1603, but possibly later, *ca.* 1625.

hands in the wars disturbs her sense of justice. At the Exchange they see a world of people fine; Sisly good-naturedly envies their luck, but soon turns her attention to the pretty pictures on the stalls. The rat-catcher comes by, then a gentlewoman masked. The churches seem to them empty. They pass an old man bent under a load of wood, while young men are loafing on the street-corners. Presently they decide that they must hurry on to find their friends, who all prove too busy to be bothered with them, so that they have to leave, disgusted with the town and its people.

Among the *Roxburghe Ballads* is one called "The Great Boobee."[1] The title tells the tale here, as it does in "London Lickpenny." The hero visits all the places of interest which Baedeker would have recommended had he been living then, climbs the tower of Paul's, sees the tombs at Westminster, wanders back to Pye Corner, where he helps himself to the roast meat exposed for sale there, and is appropriated by a whore in Smithfield, who picks his pockets at the nearest tavern. Then he pays his respects to the portraits of the Kings in the Royal Exchange, "negotiates" the bridge on his way to Paris Gardens, where he is maltreated by an unruly bull, and finally on his return falls into the river, to be rescued, fortunately, by a public-spirited waterman. He thinks he might make a name for himself if he could only get a license to play before the bears.

D'Urfey's *Wit and Mirth, or Pills to Purge Melancholy*[2] contains three ballads of the same sort. One, which from its first line we may call "At London che've bin," makes use of the conventional dialect marks of the

[1] *Roxburghe Ballads*, VII, 273. Written before 1641, for bear-baiting was suppressed between 1641 and 1647.
[2] (Fourth ed., 1714), I, 286.

Southwest. This probably added to the humorous appeal it might hope to exert with the very miscellaneous audience which on ordinary occasions formed the only patrons of these literary ventures. This particular coney is much impressed with his view of the King and Queen, the lords and earls:

> Che've seen the Lord-Mayor,
>   And Bartoldom-Fair;
> And there che met with the *Dragon*,
>   That St. *George* that bold Knight,
>   Fought and killed out-right,
> Whilst a Man could toss off a Flaggon.

He goes to see the Monument also, but finds the girls in Cheapside far more interesting.

There is another, called "The North-Country Man's Song on the View of London Sights," which is credited to a Mr. Akeroyde:[1]

> When Ize came first to *London-Town*,
> Ize wor a Noviz, as many mo Men are.

He manages to lose his hat when up in Paul's tower, and his purse in Westminster Hall among the lawyers. He stares in wonder, but not too long, at Jacob's Stone:

> Ize staid not there, but down with the Tide
>   Ize made great haste, and Ize went my way,
> For Ize was to zee the Lyons beside,
>   And the *Paris-Garden* all in a day.

Still another,[2] called "Oh, London is a fine Town," describes the progress and other doings on Lord Mayor's Day. The grand display as the mayor journeys to Westminster to take the oath, the return and landing at Paul's Wharf, the banquet, all form part of the great celebration. Nor do we leave the worthy gentleman

---

[1] Cf. *Pills to Purge Melancholy*, II, 96.   [2] *Ibid.*, II, 40.

there. His subsequent duties and amusements are detailed; his holiday at Greenwich, his inspection of weights and measures, his attendance at sessions, at bear-baitings, at church once a year, how he entertains a courtier, and even how he hunts foxes in Essex.

"The Countriman's Bill of Charges"[1] puts the old idea into a new framework. It contains a reference to the silencing of the bells during the Puritan régime which gives some idea of the date.

> Imprimis, coming into towne,
> and at my Inne alighting,
> I almost spent a noble crowne
> in potting and in piping.

He has his pockets picked, gets into trouble with a wench, with coney-catchers, with a lawyer. The wine is bad — all foam — and expensive. His horse is half starved.

There is one poem about a journey to London in time of plague. This is the "Iter Orientale, A Journey from Oxford to London, Begun Apr. 23, 1666, being St. George's Day" (printed 1667). Its author, the Reverend Jeremiah Wells, describes in detail the itinerary of two students, through Shotover and Wheatley, where they meet the parson on his lean horse, and the usual debauch that night at Beaconsfield; in the morning, they move on to Uxbridge and Acton, where they see the smoke of London, and begin to feel dismayed by the number of pest-houses. They take lodgings in a house upon the Bridge:

> Where Buildings on this contradiction stand,
> On endless strifes like the whole World, sustain'd:
> And like high Heav'n, with a becalmed brow,
> Securely smile on petty Jarrs Below.

[1] *Roxburghe Ballads*, I, 458.

Strangely enough, the presence of the plague does not seem to disturb their good time:

> Next Morn we wandred wildly up and down,
> Surveighing all the Rarities o' th' Town.

The Exchange is apparently open for business, and after seeing that,

> We take a boat, lest surly Thames should grow
> Incens'd to see himself neglected so.

By this time it is mid-day and they must start for home.

The same writer, who was a Fellow of St. John's College in Oxford, and Curate of All Hallows, Barking, London, produced Latin verses on the plague in 1665, and on the fire in 1666.

Of London streets in time of plague, John Taylor, the "Water-poet," gives about as graphic an account as any, in "The Fearefull Summer":[1]

> In some whole streete (perhaps) a Shop or twayne
> Stands open, for small takings, and lesse gaine.
> And euery closed window, dore and stall,
> Makes each day seeme a solemne Festiuall.
> Dead Coarses carried, and recarried still,
> While fiftie Corpses scarce one graue doth fill.
> While *Lord have mercie upon us*, on the dore,
> Which (though the words be good) doth grieue men sore.
> And o're the doore-posts fix'd a *crosse* of *red*,
> Betokening that there *Death* some blood hath shed.

Six years later the plague appeared again. It is in connection with this visitation that Henry Crouch gives us his account of one kind of treatment that seemed to work a cure. In *London Vacation and the Countries*

---

[1] *Works* (collected ed., 1630), p. 59. Cf. Thomas Sprat, *The Plague of Athens, which happened in the second year of the Peloponnesian War. First described by Thucydides, then Lucretius*, 24 pp. (1709).

Tearme,[1] he tells of a traveller who discovered "God's tokens," the blue spots, on his arm:

> He spurs his horse, and speedily he rides
> To the next town, and there all night abides.
> But yet before he went to bed, 't is said,
> In's chamber he a good fire causde be made:
> So, when the Chamberlain had made a fire,
> A payle of water he did then desire:
> Then cal'd he for the best sheet in the Inne,
> The which he wet, and wrapt himself therein.
> The sheet being wet, and he stark naked in it,
> About his body he did straitway pinne it;
> Which being done, away to bed he went.
> The morning being come, and the night spent,
> He found himself well, and his body cleare
> From all those spots which before did appeare.

A curious poem of the ramble type was published in 1682 by Alexander Radcliffe, the author of *Ovid Travestie* (1680). It is called *The Ramble: an anti-heroick Poem, together with some Terrestrial Hymns and Carnal Ejaculations.* This time it is the ramble of a rake. The hero awakens late in the day when duns are knocking at his door, gets away, and, after a "bracer" at the tavern, goes to the Duke's House to see the play. When the play is over, he calls a link, and, hoping to improve his financial condition, he throws a main or two at a gaming-house. Unfortunately he is drawn in by a bully, and loses twenty shillings before a friend rescues him by carrying him off to the Green Dragon in Fleet Street. Here, with the aid of wine and bacon, he becomes exceedingly profane and quarrelsome:

> Then I cry'd up *Sir Henry Vane*,
> And swore by God I would maintain
> Episcopacy was too plain
> A juggle.

[1] H. C[rouch?], 1637.

The friends find their way into another room, where a
Bacchanalian club is in session. The company talk of
Maestricht. A barrister offers his opinion, to which the
captain objects on the general ground that a barrister
has no right to form any judgment on military ques-
tions. A spruce young squire supports the barrister,
and the bully finds a quack doctor to strengthen his side
of the dispute. Personal histories of an unsavory kind
are aired. Everybody gets exasperated, and a general
mêlée follows:

> The Youngster first desir'd a Truce,
> Because Cravat from Neck hung loose.

Our hero now leaves the tavern, falls into the hands of
the watch, gets them drunk, too, and finally staggers
home.

The last decade of the seventeenth century brought
forth some curious accounts of London haunts in verse.
Thomas D'Urfey's *Collin's Walk through London and
Westminster*, published in 1690, preserves the old tra-
dition of the country cully on a visit to the city. This
time he has "the Major" as guide, philosopher, and
friend. They visit the Royal Exchange, view the grand
procession, — for it is Lord Mayor's Day, — see the
fireworks, get into trouble with the watch, are thrust
into the Roundhouse, from which the major soon ex-
tricates them by the timely use of a shilling or two.
They then wander over to Westminster, where they
are involved in a riot. They dine with a physician
who turns out to have Jesuitical affiliations, and whose
brother, a member of that order, appears at dinner dis-
guised as a girl. Heated arguments arise. Finally, the
major takes Collin away to the playhouse, where he
quite properly gets entangled with skirts and has his
pockets picked.

Long jaunts and liquor appealed with about equal force to Richard Ames, a once-popular writer but now so well forgotten that even his name does not appear in the *Cambridge History of English Literature*, or in the *D.N.B.* He shows almost an antiquarian delight in finding out unusual places and introducing them into his none too sprightly verse. We can feel the enthusiasm of the chase as he follows the stranger to "The Jacobite Conventicle" (1692), and share his curiosity:

> Thus I in *Temple-Cloysters* walking,
> O're-heard a Man t' himself a talking . . .
> But I myself being somewhat curious,
> Did follow this *Old Huncks Penurious*,
> Through *Streets, Lanes, Alleys*, and *By-ways*,
> More than are found in *Stow's Surveys*,
> Traversing almost as much Ground,
> As on *New-Market Heath* is found,
> Leading me such a dainty jaunt,
> As if one on an Errand sent,
> Missing his way, which did not hap well,
> Should go by *Lambeth* to *White-Chappel*;
> How're at last, in *Lane of Fetter*,
> Than which, there is not many better,
> In *Magpye-Court*, or *Yard*, or *Alley*,
> For which 't was, *Faith*, I cannot tell ye,
> He stopt at Door.

The seditious gossip he hears, the distorted service and political sermon, the invasion by King's officers, and the following arrests need not detain us here. This writer's most famous effusion is *The Search after Claret; or, a Visitation of the Vintners*. Two editions were published in 1691, and in the same year, *A Farther Search after Claret* and *The Last Search after Claret in Southwark*. With the reader's patience, we shall follow the rambler in his search. Along with a friend he makes the round of the ale-houses in the East Side, from Tom Jolly's

through White Chapel to the Castle, where he finds
that the butchers have drunk too much wine:

> But seeing they all were ingag'd *Snicker-Snee*,
> We thought fit to march off, and keep our skins free.

He passes through Aldgate to the King's Arms, which

> Did so like an *Alsatian* Tavern appear,
> That to taste of their *Wines* we were almost afraid,
> And so crossing the Kennel went to the *Naggs-Head.*

All the barmaids suggest port and forget that they ever
knew anything about French wines. Even "*Lewis* of
Cornhill scorns *Lewis* of *France*." Along Cheapside to
the Swan he goes:

> He must surely have more than the Brains of a Man,
> Who at *Change-time* can suffer the noise of the *Swan*.[1]

Some of the taverns are blacklisted by this laureate of
the long neck; for example, the Bull-head over on the
other side of Cheap. Here he observes

> how Cullies and Cracks flockt by Pairs
> To the House, as the Unclean Beasts did into the Ark.

His remarks on the Nagshead, too, are hardly calculated
to encourage business:

> At the *Nagshead* of good we were sure to despair,
> When we spy'd a young Female asleep at the *Bar*,
> When the Inches of Candles were twinkling in Sockets,
> And the Drawers stood yawning with hands in their
> Pockets.

[1] The Exchange itself was a noisy place, according to a little poem by
Horace and James Smith, "The Unanswerable Query," in *Horace in London*
(1813), No. 18, in Bk. II:

> "Oh! say what means this deafening din,
> A thousand Babel voices shout;
> Bears leagued with Bulls rush roaring in,
> And limping lame Ducks waddle out."

Past the Tory Taver, a gathering-place of the 'prentices, they hurry on to Paul's Church-Yard, where they find drapers, chair-makers, some Christian, some Quakers, but no claret among them all. Then they go through Ludgate to the Widows, and, crossing the street, enter the Vulture and George.

> When we askt him for *Claret*, he had not a Drop,
> For the *New River-Water Men* drank it all up.

Their way now leads over the Fleet Bridge, and on to the Globe, where they find the drawers engaged in a free fight. At the Horn they are taken for government informers and have to beat an inglorious retreat. Always unsuccessful, the friends begin to get discouraged:

> At the *Queens-head* the Porters were letting down *Wines*,
> And at the Ropes, stumbling, my Friend hurt his Shins . . .
> By the noise of *Port, Port*, which the Drawers all made,
> One would guess the *Three-Tuns* had a thund'ring great Trade,
> But *Claret* was *Hebrew* and *Greek* to their Ears,
> Tho' they know it as well as they do their Neck Verse.

By this time the day is over and they have to be satisfied with Nottingham ale. In the second canto, they start unfatigued on another search:

> Wisht morning arriv'd, where Men Ply for their Fares,
> We took *Oars*, and were Landed at *Parliament-Stairs;*
> Having finisht our Business in *Westminster-Hall*,
> Where the Lawyers do *Billinsgate* loudly out-baul . . .

They make the round of the taverns in that quarter, and then wander up through Whitehall, past Charing Cross, to Covent Garden and the famous Rose:[1]

[1] Cf. *Rake Reformed* (1718), p. 12:
> "Not far from thence appears a pendant Sign,
> Whose Bush declares the Product of the Vine,
> Where to the Travellers Sight the full-blown *Rose*
> Its dazling Beauties doth in Gold disclose,
> And painted Faces flock in Tally'd Cloaths."

The last Tavern we came to, was that of the *Rose;*
At the Door of which stood such a parcel of *Beau's,*
Who in Eating and Drinking great Criticks commence,
And are Judges of everything else but of Sense,
When we saw 'em make Faces, and heard one or two Swear,
That the Wine was the Devil they lately drank there;
We rely'd on their word, and ne're stept o're the Groundsil,
But thought they spoke truth like General Council.

A Farther Search after Claret has no fresh inspiration,
but plenty of fresh detail. It is dedicated satirically to
all master vintners who know how to revive old wines,
to barkeepers, to cellar-men, and so forth. This time a
friend carries the author with him down to Billingsgate
— not a very promising district, one would suppose, but
the friend is positive.

When we entred the *Gun*, and arriv'd at the Bar,
More confusion of Tongues did old *Babel* ne're hear;
Some *Singing*, some *Dancing*, some *Swearing*, some *Roaring*,
Some *Ranting*, some *Drinking*, some *Gaming*, some *Whoring*,
Such a Medley of Noises, like strings out of Tune,
Made both of us quickly afraid of the *Gun*.

At the Mermaid — not the one, let us hope, of lyric
fame [1] — they find six fat oyster-wives sitting,

Who over cool *Quarterns* were smoaking and spitting.

They range about all over this section. Even at Pon-
tack's they cannot get what they want:

At *Puntacks* the famous French Ord'nary, where
Luxurious Eating is never thought dear,
We expected to meet with a Glass of that same
Wine, which properly carries the Masters own Name.

Past the Stocks Market, through King's Street, into
Wood Street, — where the friend has personal reasons

---

[1] Shakespeare's Mermaid was on Cheapside, between Friday Street and
Bread Street. It is mentioned as early as 1462. See Pendrill, *London Life
in the 14th Century* (1925), p. 29.

for hurry, though he insists that he fears no arrest, —
until finally they reach the Dog full of Spots, where
night-walkers are. The host here is an Irishman.

> *By* St. *Patrick* (says *Symon*) *how has it been wi' thee?*
> *Dee'l tauke me now Joy, if I joy not to see thee.*
> *By my Shoul — of good Wine thou shalt have a brauve Glash,*
> *For by my Shoulvation thou hast a sweet Faush.*
> We declin'd his *Teague-cant*, and to keep free from harms,
> Left his House, and directly went to the *Queens-Arms*.

They have worked their way over toward Newgate
now, and out into Smithfield: [1]

> At the Taverns in *Smithfield* we were sure to despair,
> For both good and bad's drank in time of the *Fair*,
> When each House is a *Brothel*, and delicate work,
> Is produc'd by bad *Wine, Cully, Punk, Pig,* and *Pork* ...
>   On *Snow Hill* at the *Castle*, two Fellows in *Halters*,
> Just going to *Tyburn*, and reading their *Psalters*,
> Made the Cart stop, and Drank off a Pint of *Canary*,
> To attend their sad Fate with a Countenance Merry.

They then make the circuit through Holborn, to Lin-
coln's Inn Fields and Covent Garden, back to Fleet
Street by coach, with no better results for themselves
and little interest for us.

The last poem in this series takes us over to South-
wark:

> Took Coach and were hurried down to the *Old Swan*,
> Where a *Waterman* who will a thousand Lyes tell ye,
> Soon wafted us over to *Old Pepper-Ally*.
>   Through stinks of all sorts, both the Simple and Compound,
> Which through narrow Allies our Senses do confound;
> We came to the *Bear*.

[1] Tom Brown, quoted in Stephenson's *Shakespeare's London*, p. 229:
"Smithfield is another sort of place now to what it was in the time of honest
Ben, who, were he to rise out of his grave, would hardly believe it to be the
same numerical spot of ground where Justice Overdo made so busy a figure;
where the crop-eared Parson demolished a gingerbread stall; where Nightin-
gale of harmonious memory sung ballads; and fat Ursula sold Pig and Bot-
tled Ale."

They visit the King's Bench, to see a poor friend who
was suspected of debt, and the Mint also, where there
are debtors of all descriptions, mostly old vintners. A
violent argument arises, and soon a general scuffle, in
the midst of which the poem, if such it may be called,
abruptly ends.[1]

The law against French importations was finally dis-
carded in 1712. In that year *Brooke and Hellier*, a satire
of thirty-two pages, was published. The poet recalls the
blind laws made for prohibition, when no more claret
could be drunk, and complains that with the passing of
good wine fancy had faded. Dryden would have hanged
himself like Creech without the powerful charm of wine:

> Had not our liquor been so foul,
> How could bright Garth have e'er been dull.
> Great Philips never had been willing,
> To stoop his head to *Splendid Shilling*.
> But once a famine of good wine,
> No wonder Wit should starve and pine.

Garth, Congreve, Addison, and Montagu are all dumb.
But now, better times are coming:

> The work's begun, the long eclipse of wine
> Wears off, the native bright begins to shine;
> And men begin again to taste the vine.
> The Nation damned to dulness and decay,
> Drinks Brooke and Hellier now to lead the way,
> And bright champaign will come to close the day.

But we are not quite through with Richard Ames and
his pathetic ramblings. His best poem, *Islington Wells,
or the Threepenny Academy* (1691), was reprinted in
1861, by J. O. Halliwell. It is also of the "journey"

---

[1] See *To the October Club on the Bill for Importing French Wines* (n.d.),
Bodleian Library, Godwin Pamphlets, 1278.

type, and relates how the author left his bed by six in the morning, and, with nothing but a clipped half-crown in his pocket, wonders how he had best spend the day.

> At last could pitch on nothing else,
> But Islington's renowned Wells,
> Where twice or thrice a week most duly,
> In months of May, June, August, July,
> The doctor and his sly Jacall,
> Whom some the pothecary call,
> Lawyers, divines, civilians, quakers,
> Some cuckolds, but more cuckold-makers,
> Sharpers, decoys, trapans and bullies,
> Designing cracks, and sneaking cullies,
> Fine modish sparks, and dressing beaus,
> Who charm the women with their cloaths;
> Ladies, some chast, and others common,
> Young, old, and many other women;
> The tradesman and his lovely spouse,
> Th' enamour'd youth and 's dear Queen Blouze,
> Taylors and other trades which rack
> Invention to adorn the back,
> Go there to make their observation,
> Upon the dresses of the Nation,
> Of either sex whole droves together,
> To see and to be seen flock thither,
> To drink, and not to drink the water, —
> And here promiscuously they chatter.

The rambler has an excellent opportunity to observe the humors of the place:

> By this time company repair,
> As thick as to a wake or fair:
> No broacher of a new religion,
> Nor flat-noz'd quack, nor stage physitian,
> Nor Indian King, unto his Palace,
> Nor knots of Highway-men to th' gallows,
> More followers have ever known,
> Than come to Wells of Islington.

The old governess, with the two young things who call her aunt, the beau bedaubed with lace, the tawdry punk, the semptress from the Exchange in negligée,

> In an undress so loose and strange,
> That she was thought by every man,
> To come from China or Japan;

the old-maid sisters, the soldiers;

> A Doctor then with twirling cane,
> Well skill'd in each disease and pain,
> Which do the corps of man assail,
> From Crown of head to Great-Toe-nail,
> And can of all the plants tell stories,
> From Saffron down to stinking Orrice;

the fop from the city;

> Then half a dozen of the fry,
> Who can so neatly cogg a dye —

all these types get ample justice. He notes also the freaks of fashion in talk, the popularity of French words and phrases:

> To say they've melancholly been,
> Is barb'rous; no, they are chagrin;
> To say a ladies looks are well,
> Is common; no, her air is Belle.[1]

The ladies gossip about one another's clothes:

> "Sure that commode was made, I' faith,
> In days of Queen Elizabeth;
> Or else it was esteem'd the fashion
> At Charles the Second's coronation;
> The Lady by her Manteaus Forebody,
> Sure takes a pride to dress like nobody;"

---

[1] Cf. Charles Jenner, *Town Eclogues* (1772), II, 11:
"Whilst Miss despises all domestic rules,
But lisps the French of *Hackney* boarding-schools;
And ev'ry lane around *Whitechapel* bars
Resounds with screaming notes, and harsh guittars."

When at the very selfsame time
She's taxt by others for the crime,
Of dressing of her hair so high,
As if she would with steeples vye,
Or rival with her modish skill,
The Monument on Fish-Street Hill.

Some go to the Wells to drink the waters, some to the raffling shop for dice, some to the Royal Oak;

Others who would cheap pleasures choose,
To coffee-house to read the news,
Retire, and there devoutly prate,
Of Luxemburgh and Catinat,
And talk as briskly as Commanders,
Who now are at their posts in Flanders,
As if in heats and colds and rains,
They'd past together some Campaigns,
When they had never crost the seas,
But in a Map with Compasses.

There is dancing and music, perfumes and plum-cakes. The quietest place at hand is actually the spring itself, which is hemmed in by iron railings and where two old women dispense the water gratis.

"The Long Vacation" (1691) seems to have been a fruitful subject for the minor poets of the time. They treat the topic in various ways, but Ames, as usual, takes a walk about town. The judges are on circuit, and the young law-clerk left in the city has nothing to do.

But come, let's leave this wrangling crew,
And step to Fair of *Bartlemew*,
Where 't is not thought the greatest curse,
To eat lean Pigs were starv'd at Nurse.

He finds there punks, merry-andrews, pickpockets, drummers, fruit-women. The road is filled with cits going to Tunbridge, Epsom, or Sturbridge Fair, to sell goods that are not vendible in the city. Duns are there, making the best of their opportunities; attorneys also, with their tattered clients; the love-sick girl, and the young squire doing general treats. A little satire on the fox-hunters creeps in:

> What shew on yonder Hill appears?
> They seem a *Troop* of *Mountaineers*,
> And by the swiftness of their Pace
> To be of the true *Irish* Race. . . .
> A Leg or Arm is often Cur'd,
> But no Man's Neck was e're Ensur'd.

He makes his way back into London. Coaches and horsemen are all leaving the town, yet "Peccadilly" still swarms with people. Westminster Hall,[1] though, is deserted:

> But where the *Sages* of the *Law*
> Did use to sit, were *Boys at Taw*.

He starts for his rooms in Lincoln's Inn:

> But when I came to *Charing-Cross*,
> Sitting on Steps by *Horse* of *Brass*,
> Saw *Splitcause* the *Solliciter*,
> Expecting, like some humble Cur,
> What scraps or bones would fall for Dinner.

He takes him to dinner, but gets rid of him only to meet another crony out at elbows, with whom he drinks altogether too many bumpers, so that the friend gets vociferous and has to be sent home in a hackney coach. After kicking out of the way an impudent young beggar, our puisne finally gets in at the Temple Gate, past a beau, who

---

[1] Cf. Robert Lloyd, "The Law Student," *Poems* (1762), p. 135:
> "'T is not enough each morn, on Term's approach,
> To club your legal threepence for a coach;
> Then at the Hall to take your silent stand,
> With ink-horn and long note-book in your hand."

> would with *Tooth-Pick* fixt in Mouth,
> Stand three full hours by th' Clock in troth
> At *Temple-Gate*, with Roguish Leering,
> Ogling all women who came near him.

The vacation soon passes, however, and Cowley, Waller, Oldham, Cleveland, and his beloved *Hudibras* have to be laid aside for the study of actions.[1]

Davenant's early poem on the same subject, "The Long Vacation in London,"[2] is crude, but highly entertaining, and may be noticed here by way of comparison. Everything about the town is very quiet. The town wit has gone on a journey to the country; the old husband returns to the shop to find his young wife off to Islington; the whore and the hack are idle, and the bright dresses must go to the pawn broker's:

> Now wight that acts on stage of Bull,
> In skullers' bark does lie at Hull,
> Which he for pennies two does rig,
> All day on Thames to bob for grig:
> Whilst fencer poor does by him stand,
> In old dung-lighter, hook in hand;
> Between knees rod, with canvas crib,
> To girdle tide, close under rib;
> Where worms are put, which must small fish
> Betray at night to earthen dish.

The mayor rides off to the fair, while the aldermen play at quoits. The lean attorney and the aged proctor shoot arrows all day at Finsbury.

> Now Spynie, Ralph, and Gregorie small,
> And short hayr'd Stephen, whay-fac'd Paul
> (Whose times are out, indentures torn,
> Who seven long years did never skorne,

---

[1] Cf. Edward Ward's *Walk to Islington* (1701).
[2] Chalmers's *English Poets* (1810), VI, 433. Published also in *Wit and Drollery* (1661), p. 87.

> To fetch up coales for maid to use,
> Wipe mistresses', or children's shooes)
> Do jump for joy they are made free;
> Hire meagre steeds, to ride and see,
> Their parents old who dwell as near,
> As place call'd Peake in Derby-shire.
> There they alight, old croanes are milde;
> Each weeps on cragg of pretty childe:
> They portions give, trades up to set,
> That babes may live, serve God and cheat.

The performers at Bartholomew are off now to cheat the country louts of their hard-earned pence:

> Now man of war with visage red,
> Grows chollerick and sweares for bread.

He has to borrow money from a friend, but is straining his credit to the breaking-point, as the poet already has done:

> But stay my frighted pen is fled;
> Myself through fear creep under bed;
> For just as Muse would scribble more,
> Fierce city dunne did rap at door.

In 1693, John Lewkenor published a poem which he called *Metellus his Dialogues, The First Part, Containing a Relation of a Journey to Tunbridge-Wells* . . . This gentleman was the son of Sir John Lewkenor of West Deane in Sussex, and had been entered as a gentleman commoner at Christ Church in 1673.

In this poem five friends start out for Tunbridge Wells, four of them riding two and two by different routes, and the odd one travelling by coach. They finally get together at the journey's end in front of the fire in a pleasant cottage, and Acer tells the story of his experiences in the coach on the way down. It has taken him twelve hours to travel the thirty-six miles, and he has found the journey tedious:

When I to this Etherial Life return,
From that Death of bad Company; that Urn
Of foetid Coach; ere I from Crew so curst
Transmigrate well, I must drink *Lethe* first.

He had overslept, and having thus missed the society of his friends, was forced to be satisfied with the coach:

Not to too hard, but too soft Fate was left
Of Stage-Coach-Company, and Gossips prate.

He is one lone man among three women. After some delay, caused by the heavy weight of classical allusion under which the poet is laboring, the coach rolls along out of town:

As soon as we were off the jolting Stones,
First things they utter'd were some sighs and groans.

Then, out of courtesy, the ladies unmask their faces, and begin to talk about the sins of man, of the married state, of liberty of conscience. Though marriage may turn out to be all and more than was expected, yet

to a blessing to be chain'd and ty'd,
Is for the Blessed to be Devilify'd.

They are sadly interrupted by the jolting of the coach:

For *Rhadamanth* had harassed our brains,
With dismal Jolts, and not unlike Hell's pains.

At last they come to a fairer way, and then to an astonishingly steep hill.

The Coach-man like a *Rhadamanthus* sate,
Hurried us downward at such Devilish rate,
And uncontroulable, the Plea, Hold, Hold,
Signify'd nothing, he was hot and bold.
Th' inexorable fury was come on,
His Breast by Ale, he whipt like *Tisyphon*.

Next comes a long digression in praise of ale.

> On Market-days, the heavy Country Clown
> This rouzes up to moule his Landlord down.
> Hence first Rebellion hisses in the street;
> This makes the Uproar, makes the Rabble meet.
> This makes the blunt and brawny Carmen croke,
> And the exalted Coachman to provoke.

It is getting on toward the middle of the afternoon when they draw into Seven Oaks and pull up at the inn.

> Hostess and Host advance, pursue us in,
> With all the Household-Devils of an Inn.

They get the northern lady fixed in an armchair, between her two companions. The ladies appear delicate; they forbear

> Their hunger then; cry'd 't is too late to eat,
> What shou'd they do with all this greasie Meat?

However, the gentleman orders dinner and pays half the scot. It is here that they notice the first approach of the "Tunbridge fairies," who haunt every coach; these fair "dippers" are anxious to engage the favor of passengers in advance. The coach drives on through delightful country, to the beauties of which the poet seems really sensitive. The pastures, the flowers, the corn, the vast woods, which "in looking wild look pleasantly," the cheerful sun, and the birds, — everything disposes the traveller to forget his disagreeable companions and to revel in nature's charms. They pass through ugly Tunbridge and up the hill beyond, from which they gain a splendid prospect. He notices the flimys houses as of cards built for a three-months occupation, and then finds himself, after a grand furious sweep down the hill, at last at the Wells.[1]

---

[1] Cf. John Byrom, *Miscellaneous Poems* (Manchester, 1773), p. 10: "A Full and True Account of an Horrid and Barbarous Robbery, committed on Epping Forest, Upon the Body of the Cambridge Coach." The thief here is exorcised by the magic of Byrom's shorthand script.

The second dialogue describes the town and its spring, the Upper Walk bordered with trees and fine shops:

> The Buyer sees
> City in Countrey, *Cheapside* among trees.

Music and sober conversation here provide delights enough for the morning. There is also an Under Walk with a fine market:

> The Lady, without wetting of her Shooe,
> May chuse her Dinner, while her Gallants wooe.

Fruits, veal, and fish, "so fresh they offend no Nose," mix here in the poem with discourse on painted faces, and talk about the pretty new ale-house. Thence we saunter — no hurry whatever — back to the end of the Upper Walk and descend to the Wells themselves. These are in sandy ground and surrounded by heath and rocks, and hills of just the correct height:

> Yet not too high, too horrid, nor too near.

The poet thinks of the Well as the ancient mother of the place, and the scene around it reminds him irresistibly of various Biblical pools. It is walled in, but always keeps an open gate. Crowds of patients walk about:

> Twice twenty Nymphs still round about her stand,
> Fair Country Maids, each with a Glass in hand,
> Reaching her Bounty forth, give with good Grace
> Full Cups, bestow'd by th' Goddess of the Place.

At this point, the poet strains the Bible and classic myth to adorn his descant on the virtues of the waters; and, having exhausted, literally, that theme, he attacks the characters — poet, lover, philosopher, student, hero, statesman, merchant.

> The Ladies round the pleasant Country fly,
> As if they had kind of Ubiquity.

He tells of the dance, the picnic, the lute solo, the song.

> Pity that every Winter shou'd deface
> That which at Summer is so sweet a place.

He thinks that the whole thing is quite beyond the power of words to describe. Indeed, he is hard put to it at times in his attempt, and he finally gives up, with the recommendation that the name of the charming place be changed, for he dislikes the connection with dirty Tunbridge. The next dialogue is to be on concubinage. Rochester's "Satire on Tunbridge Wells" is, needless to say, a good corrective for the overdose of enthusiasm that one gets in this poem. Both are about equally exaggerated. Rochester's poem is dated June 30, 1675, and gives a lively account of the various groups of people that he sees in this celebrated resort.

> Bless me! thought I, what Thing is Man, that thus,
> In all his Shapes, he is ridiculous.[1]

James II's precipitate departure from England was made the subject for a poem called "The Royal Ramble" (1697). The introductory lines of this piece might wellserve as a general summary of the possibilities of the journey type:

> Of Ramblings and Follies you oft have been told,
> Since (their wits and their language confounded of old)
> Our fathers Knights Errant from Babylon stol'd.
> The Macedon ranged for Drink, Women, and Glory,
> And Caesar for matter to pen a fine story.
> Ambition and love sent old Tony a madding;
> And people will fancy why Sheba went gadding.
> Next Chivalry flourish'd, till Fate proving kind,
> The Heroes and Lovers to Bedlam confin'd:

[1] *Poems on State Affairs* (6th ed., 1716), I, 218. Compare also "Tunbridgialia: or the Pleasures of Tunbridge," by Mr. Peter Causton, Merchant, *Ibid.*, p. 202. Also John Byrom, *Miscellaneous, Poems* (Manchester, 1773), p. 5, "A Description of Tunbridge in a letter to P. M. Esq."

Then Mankind with wandering Devotion possest,
To relicks and shrines weary journeys addrest,
On Pilgrimage holy. The Loretto Church
Bilkt her lodgings, and left the poor Turk in the lurch.
Of Byrnham Wood travels, Scotch Chronicles talk,
And Kynaston Hill (as Stow tells us) did walk.
Sticks and stones may prove blockheads, and keep a
    damned stir,
But things that have reason and sense should not err.
Will our Nephews believe, that a Prince should outrun
(And no Friend to withhold him) his country and throne?
'Tis nonsense so obvious, they never will bear it;
Though Glanvile should write it, or Titus Oates swear it.

The itch to throw their wandering lucubrations into
this singularly appropriate form affected most of the
scribblers of the day. It was epidemic. Ned Ward suf-
fered acutely, and — to vary the metaphor — spills his
multitudinous lines over our heads till we despair of
rescue. And people liked his verses, called for second
and third editions, I suppose because they saw them-
selves and their neighbors in them and enjoyed the
spectacle. We may look at *A Journey to Hell* as an ex-
ample. A second edition of this poem appeared in 1700.
It is not like Dante; that is sure. No subtlety of thought,
no universal significance, certainly! A few lines from it
will show just how it found readers. The poet wants to
pay a visit to the Devil and comes down to the riverside
to cross. But Charon will not row one passenger alone,
and no fine talk will move him:

> But all my soft Persuasions would not make,
> The grim Tarpaulin his old Custom break,
> Who gently row'd his Ferry to and fro,
> Bauling aloud, *Hey, downward, downward ho.*

A bevy of lawyers arrives presently, the boat is trimmed,
and off they go.

Charon now tir'd, his labouring Oar forsook,
A Dram of some infernal Spirits took,
And 'twixt his Jaws a Pipe of flaming Sulphur stuck;
Then to his Oars himself again apply'd,
And to his Fare the merry Slave thus cry'd,
"Chear up, ye sullen Shades, and be not dull."

A Thames waterman must have had something pecu-
liarly devilish about him.   On with his story Ward
goes, always using figures familiar to every dirty-faced
child in the street.   The hell-bound lawyers refuse to be
cheered,

But hung their thoughtful Heads, look'd *al-a-mort*,
Like sullen Convicts in a *Tyburn*-Cart.

The poet himself still diffuses some rays of innocence,
and passes unquestioned by the guards,

As he that visits *Bridewell*, with intent
To Goodness learn from others Punishment,
Does fearless thro' the Prison confines rove,
Whilst guilty Slaves are to Correction drove.

Here kings are punished, who on earth waged unneces-
sary war.   From one circle to another he goes.   Vicious
priests get three pages of satire.   Then venal lawyers;
counter-rats, with great beards and dirty hands; quacks,
profusely blessed with two talents, who

seem'd to study least, what they profest,
In earnest Poetry, and Physick but in jest;

scribblers from Poet Ninny to the worthy Bays; print-
ing pirates; booksellers, who first get a writer in debt to
them, then awe him by their frowns,

And buy him as their Slave by lent Half-Crowns;

vintners and coopers who adulterate wine—all these and
more are pictured in their appropriate torments.   One

sees the writert hrough his lines, as Tory, high-church-
man, vender of pills and poetry, host of the King's Arms.

*A Trip to Nottingham, with a Character of Mareschal
Tallard and the French Generals* is a fourteen-page
pamphlet published anonymously in 1705. It reads as
if it might have happened, but that scarcely makes it
more exciting. The start through the High Gate, dinner,
supper, bed, amorous adventures, travelling compan-
ions, political talk, lead us finally to Tallard and the
captured generals just starting on a hunt.

*A Trip lately to Scotland, with a true Character of the
Country and People* appeared in 1705. Some of its plati-
tudes are still on our lips:

> Biggots with fiery zealots disagree,
> And the devil dances to the harmony.

Or better:

> Every mechanick schismatick can wrest
> The Holy Writ, to prove his cause the best.

In politics, a similar argumentativeness is evident:

> The very barber while he shaves shall prate,
> And charm your ears with some intrigues of state.
> Censure a parliament for want of care;
> And trim the Court proceedings to a hair.

This writer's modesty is amusing and, we'll hope, genu-
ine, for it should be

> Equipt for journey, mounted on a steed,
> That sprung (I guess) from Hudibras's breed;
> A foundered Pegasus, as e're was rid;
> As old and blind as ever man bestrid;
> Some baker's drudge he'd been for many years;
> And like his master too, had lost his ears.

The poet does get to Edinburgh, however, and there
his main impressions concern beggars, lice, sedition, and

long sermons. A prose "Character of a Scot" is inserted.

Another crazy horse, this time called Rosinante, finds place in Ned Ward's poem, "The Poet's Ramble after Riches." On him the poet starts his journey. Grandmother has died and he hopes for the best. The description of a low-class inn is very good, but beyond this there is little of interest in the poem, and the reader is not so disconsolate as the rambler at its close.

Ned Ward is the author, also, of *The Field-Spy: or, the Walking Observator*, a thirty-eight-page pamphlet published in 1714. He imagines a need for contemplation, starts out northward to the fields, moralizes on clouds and sunshine with little conviction, finds a house of entertainment with music and dancing, nine-pins and card games. St. Martin's Garretteers spend their money at All-fours, while their wives are looking for them, eager "to destroy the Devil's books and scold them home." New Tunbridge Wells is neglected; men are fishing near the basin which supplies the droughty town. The Spaw, Old St. John's and its archery practice, Black Mary's little Sodom, and finally the prison, are described with his usual zest. Bowling-greens and betting, grenadiers and Bedlam, whores, bedraggled beaux stolen from the confines of the Fleet, gangs of butchers, a poet who reads his fable of the Frogs, the Log, and the Stork, — a rather curious comment on the political situation in 1714, — these are the topics of his verse, and in the midst of such riotous allusion the poet, like ourselves, gets tired and stops.

It must have been about this time that Ned Ward wrote his *Vade Mecum for Malt-Worms* — possibly two years earlier, as this is apparently the poem referred to twice in an anonymous satire of 1712 called *Brooke and Hellier* from the names of two well-known wines.

> How has the virtue of their wine appeared
> In vintner's verse, from famous dogrell W—d.
> The poet honest in the very letter,
> If theirs had been good wine, had mocked them better.

The other reference is not surprising:

> If he write Satyrs none regard,
> Just as the vintners hire Ned Ward.

For Ward's *Vade Mecum* is a catalogue, in the *Search after Claret* style, of the ale-houses of the town, with comments often of an interesting character. It also is cast in the form of a journey. One wonders sometimes how even a hardened sinner could get a third of the way on such a pilgrimage, and again how much the Grub Street writer was paid for some of his very valuable advertisements. We pass through Rosemary Lane,— where, as in Monmouth Street, women stand selling coats, suits, and breeches, second-hand, — down in the direction of the river.

> Hence to *Cloak-lane*, near *Dowgate-hill*, we steer,
> And at *Three Tuns* cast Anchor for good Beer;
> Since, in Sea-Terms, 't is proper to accost,
> The Tenement of this Seafaring Host.

Now up to Smithfield, and away through a particularly noisy quarter called Turnmill Street:

> Now to the Street where Rabble Rout reside,
> Let me from *Smithfield* my Companion guide,
> Thro' the Throngs of Scolds that every Nook frequent,
> And give their restless Tongues eternal Vent.
> Here sits you many a Matron at her Door
> Calling her *Virtuous* Neighbour *Bitch* and *Whore*.

Passing by Shoe-lane, evidently a camping-ground for naughty wenches, we come to Newman's Tipple House, a favorite rendezvous for the young law-students:

> Here in the Evening, after Six, are seen,
> Loit'rers, 'till then, from Five, in *Lincoln's-Inn*.

Moorfields, to the northeast, was the great athletic field, rifle range, and general recreation ground of the city, and to this interesting place our malt-worm takes us in his second book.

> In Moor's most pleasant Field, where Northern Lads
> With Western Youths, contend for broken Heads,
> And where our Wealthy Citizens repair
> To lengthen out their Lives with wholesome Air:
> Joining to Trotter's famous Castle, stands
> A noted Mansion built by artful Hands;
> Where Young and Old, at small Expense, may find
> Delightful Pastimes to refresh the Mind.
> Hither the sprightly Genius has recourse,
> To practise riding on the Flying-Horse;
> Where, Danger-free, he thro' the Air may scow'r,
> And, void of Wings, fly fifty Miles an Hour;
> Nor that has this Courser, tho' he runs so fast,
> One living Leg to expedite his hast,
> Yet carries double, treble, if requir'd,
> But never stumbles, or is ever tir'd.

A bit farther on in this book there is a melancholy description of a new arrival in the King's Bench prison, and after that, an account of a rousing scene in an ale-house. About this time, no doubt, the author has imbibed all that he can comfortably carry away with him from the taverns; he stops, and for our part we may sympathize with his satiety.

In 1715, John Gay enjoyed a trip to his boyhood home in Devonshire, at the expense of Lord Burlington, his friend and patron. His "thank you" note took the form of a poem called "A Journey to Exeter."[1] This is a very

---

[1] Cf. "Scarborough, a Poem in Imitation of Mr. Gay's Journey to Exeter," in *The Scarborough Miscellany* (1734).

interesting production, especially because it shows how little the humors of the countryside change in two hundred years. True, the Macheaths have largely disappeared, and the elections in the small village amount to little since the days when a vote might bring as much as sixty pounds; but the country inns are much the same to-day as they were when Gay took mental note of their curiosities. The landlords look the same and have the same line of talk. Each village had, and has, its own pet gossip. Gay is much more interested in the people than in the scenery. He likes the shepherd better than the unbounded plain, even though he no longer, like Amaryllis, "chaunts alternate lays." Salisbury Cathedral with its lofty spire is mentioned, but along with it such plebian matters as scissors and riding-hoods, boarding-schools and kisses. Dorchester, its fair meadows and silver brooks, appears all right, but how vaguely compared with the companion pictures of the poet in the "pub," tracing names on glasses, Kit-Cat fashion,[1] while his friends snore; and later the laundry operations at Axminster, and the shave, with the lady of the golden chain and soft touch officiating. To put the distinction briefly, Gay has very little in common with Thomson: he is the Hogarth of verse.

There is a rare and curious imitation of Gay in the Harvard Library called *A Walk from St. James's to Convent Garden, the Back-Way, Through the Meuse: in Imitation of Mr. Gay's Journey to Exeter, in a Letter to a Friend.* It was published anonymously by James Roberts in 1717, and seems more like an imitation of *Trivia* than of the "Journey." Starting through Pall-Mall,

> whose friendly Surface scorns
> To hurt the gouty Feet or horny Corns,

[1] On toasts, see *Tatler*, Nos. 24 and 31.

the author passes through the Haymarket,[1]

> Where Grooms smell over *Pots* of *Ale*, and *Hay*;
> Waggons and Carts, ill-crowded in the Throng
> Reminded me of *Suckling's* glorious *Song*.

The beggar meets his eye:

> A blinded *Woman* with some Lines at Breast,
> That both her Parish, and her Age confess'd;
> On Stool she sat and mournful mov'd her Head,
> And seem'd to say give Money — that gives Bread.

Soon the walker gets over among the merchants, whose efforts to gain his attention and trade annoy him as they must have many others at the time:

> But lo! the Passage widens, and behold
> The *Norwich* Stuff-dealers in Night-gowns bold.
> Vain Men, who think that each that meets their Eye,
> Is certain Prey and destin'd there to buy;
> I pass'd their Cringes and their Bows in pain,[2]
> And hasten'd thro' the Turning with disdain.

Now to Covent Garden, which we know so well in Hogarth's print — a place of contrasts, St. Paul's Church beside Tom King's ramshackle beer-garden.

> For as to *Convent-garden* I drew near
> Two fighting Females in a Mob appear;
> A Hand of Carots was the Prise, which both
> Claim'd as their own Propriety, by Oath.

---

[1] Haymarket Theatre was opened on April 9, 1705, with "a translated Opera, to Italian musick, called the *Triumph of Love*." The Prologue was by Dr. Garth, spoken by Mrs. Bracegirdle:

> "Your own magnificence you here survey,
> Majestick columns stand where dunghills lay,
> And carrs triumphal rise from carts of hay."

[2] See Samuel Rowlands, *Greenes Ghost Haunting Conie-Catchers* (1602; no pagination), section called "A notable exploit performed by a Lift," on 18th leaf of this pamphlet: "There are another sort of Prentices, that when they see a Gentlewoman or a countriman minded to buy aniething, they will fawne upon them, with their cap in hand, with 'what lacke you Gentlewoman? what lacke you Countriman? See what you lacke.'"

Like the fashionable ladies, the author wanders care-
lessly through the shops, and enjoys the process of
cheapening various wares though he purchases none.
The passage on the bookshops and the wits is particu-
larly suggestive:

> But I digress, — the *British* Bards Divine
> Tow'r high above, and rise from Line to Line;
> The Plays and Poetry of *Dennis* here,
> Had long contended for the highest Sphere,
> But vain their Labour, for still *Chevy-chase*
> And *Guy of Warwick* held the topmost Place.
> From the dead Wits my willing Course I steer
> To see Collections of the *Living* near,
> At *Button's* or at *Tom's* pretend to read
> The Northern News and beat the coming *Swede;*
> Meantime with listning Ear aside recline,
> And every pensive Statesman's Thought Purloin;
> Catch Fragments scatter'd by the Critics Tongue,
> And grace with others Wit my next *New* Song.

Covent Garden, the goal of this interesting journey,
was the background for many a strange scene in the
verse and caricature of the time. No one makes more
entertaining use of it than Hogarth, to whom we have
occasion so often to refer. One of his prints is called
"Rich's Glory, or his Triumphant Entry into Covent
Garden," and represents the removal of Rich's company
and chattels from Lincoln's Inn Fields to the New House
in 1733. The area of this famous centre of London life is
all there, and passing over it the grand procession: the
cart loaded with thunder and lightning, the performers,
Rich himself riding with his mistress in a chariot and in-
vested with the skin of the famous dog in *Perseus and
Andromeda.*[1] The chariot is driven by Harlequin and
drawn by Satyrs.

[1] Cf. Nichols, *Biographical Anecdotes of Hogarth* (1785), p. 161, "Perseus
and Andromeda. With the rape of Columbine; or, the Flying Lovers." In

> Not with more glory through the streets of *Rome*,
> Return'd great conquerors in triumph home,
> Than, proudly drawn with Beauty by his side,
> We see gay R[ich] in gilded chariot ride.

There are allusions, more or less subtle, to Quin, Ryan, Walker, Hall, Johnny Gay, and the "Man of Taste," possibly Pope.

Along with "The Delights of the Bottle," by Ned Ward (1720), were published "A South Sea Song upon the Late Bubbles," and "The Merry Travellers, or a Trip upon Ten-Toes from Moorfields to Bromley." The last describes a walk through the town from open country to open country, north to south, and back by coach. Starting early, the jolly friends meet the coaches of wealthy vintners, who during the long vacation send their wives and daughters out to their Hampstead houses. Then they pass through Islington, which now

> by dint of Grace, 't is grown,
> A Pious Quarter of the Town,[1]

into Gracechurch Street,

> Where wealthy Quakers live in Fame;

onward through the middle of the town, still with the energy of morning upon them,

> Downwards we almost run a Race
> To *Fishstreet-Hill*, that noted Place,
> Where shoals of Lobsters lay in view.

---

five interludes; three Serious, and two Comic. The Serious compos'd by Mons. Roger, and the Comic by Mr. John Weaver, Dancing-Masters " (1728).

[1] Of Finsbury and Moorfields, Pennant writes: "Here too, I lament to say, that religion set up its stage itinerant, beneath the shade of the trees; and here the pious, well-meaning *Whitefield* long preached so successfully, as to steal from a neighboring *charlatan* the greater part of his numerous admirers, in defiance of the eloquence of the doctor, and the witty sallies of his pied attendant" (Thomas Pennant, *Some Account of London* [2d ed., 1791], p. 252).

RICH'S GLORY, OR HIS TRIUMPHANT ENTRY INTO COVENT GARDEN

Thence past Thames Street,

> Till we proceeded to that ridge
> Of arched Stones, call'd *London-Bridge*,
> Where wooden Houses tott'ring stood
> On Props, above the raging Flood.

They find the pavement of Southwark very trying, and, like Gay, are forced to keep an eye on traffic:

> And to the wracking of our Bones,
> Slid on from greasy Stones to Stones,
> Giving, like civil Men, the way
> To Hackney Coach and Brewer's Dray,
> Or lab'ring Horses that came nigh us,
> Loaded from Tan-yard and from Dye-house.

Now through Southwark Market, with its multiplicity of dogs, they go, by the Debtors' Prison, into Kent Street, famous for its broom men, and out among the gardens on the way to Tunbridge Wells. Presently they meet a jolly parson and a nonconformist preacher, and with them a little satire has a chance to creep into the story. Then they breakfast at a small country inn, where hogs and hens and broken-backed chairs are more numerous than guests. The friend is fat and drowsy, and much doubtful humor is indulged in at his expense. The jolting of the coach on the return journey bothers him. His misadventures, however, are not half so interesting as the description of the Irish servant at the tavern who objects to being laughed at:

> Which *Teague*, observing, shook his Skull,
> And cry'd, *You take me for a Fool,*
> *But by St. Patrick, look me thorow,*
> *You'll find I was not born to Morrow.*

A poem by Elizabeth Thomas should also be mentioned here among the "journeys." It is called *The Metamorphosis of the Town, or a View of the Present*

Fashions, and was published in 1730. An old knight of the "reformed rake" type comes to town to view progress and grieve over changes. The impudence of the boys annoys him. He is surprised at the decay in business, which the shopkeepers at the Exchange tell him is due to the popularity of the peddlers. He dines with his friend at Pontack's, the guinea ordinary, and marvels at the menu, which certainly is sufficiently curious and contains, among other items, bird's-nest soup, ragouts of fatted snails, bantam pig one day old, frogs, ambergris, shrimp, chickens — "they've not been two hours from the shell." They go to one playhouse and see *The Beggar's Opera*, which the old man criticizes as a "Clitter-Clatter of Ballad Fragments, without Matter," leave to try their luck at the other, and there see old *Doctor Faustus*. Everything displeases the old man. The Abbey is the same, of course, as in the days of his youth, but the Park, and the ladies! He thinks their manners like those of country wenches, and the fashionable dishabille which some of them wear is only less shocking than the men's attire that others affect. If they will wear such clothes,

> Then let them bravely mount astride,
> And like true *Amazonians* ride.

Occasionally, the rambles recorded are more real than imaginary, like the one which Nichols writes about in his *Biographical Anecdotes of William Hogarth* (page 502): "An Account of what seemed most remarkable in the Five Days' Peregrination of the Five Following Persons, viz. Messieurs Tothall, Scott, Hogarth, Thornhill, and Forrest. . ."[1]

> Our march we with a song begin;
> Our hearts were light, our breeches thin.

Saturday, May 27, to May 31, 1732.

HOGARTH'S FIVE DAYS' PEREGRINATION

A. The Fisherman shaving.
B. Mr. Thornhill.
C. Mr. Tothall shaving himself.

D. Mr. Hogarth drawing this drawing.
E. Mr. Forrest at breakfast.
F. Mr. Scott finishing a drawing.

We meet with nothing of adventure
Till *Billingsgate's Dark-house* we enter;
Where we diverted were, while baiting,
With ribaldry, not worth relating,
(Quite suited to the dirty place):
But what most pleas'd us was his Grace
Of *Puddle Dock*, a porter grim,
Whose portrait *Hogarth*, in a whim,
Presented him in caricature,
He pasted on the cellar-door.
   But hark! the Watchman cries "Past one!"
'Tis time that we on board were gone.
Clean straw we find laid for our bed,
A tilt for shelter over head.
The boat is soon got under sail,
Wind near S. E. a mackrel gale,
Attended by a heavy rain;
We try to sleep, but try in vain,
So sing a song, and then begin
To feast on biscuit, beef, and gin.

These are the most graphic lines in the poem, which contains nine hundred and sixty-five, and ends with our travellers back in the Bedford Arms, Covent Garden, having a farewell glass, and auditing their accounts, with many thanks to the treasurer.

A note may be here in place on the various imitations of Horace's Satire on "The Impertinent" (Book I, Satire IX). This was used by Jonson in *The Poetaster*, and later imitated by Sprat. In 1666, Alexander Brome produced an interesting adaptation of the idea to London life. He represents the journey as starting in the West End and directed toward the Tower, a sufficiently remote quarter. Finally, the ill-sorted companions come over against the Guildhall, where a bailiff seizes the bore.

But in the *Hall* we so great tumult find,
Such heaps of *Women* follow'd us, and *Boyes*,
That I with ease escapt amidst the noise.

The next year John Oldham attempted an imitation.[1]
In this the poet is walking in the Mall, where he meets
an impertinent fop, who talks to him about the drought,
the price of hay, the comet at The Hague,

> Names every Wench that passes through the Park,
> How much she is allow'd, and who the Spark
> That keeps her: points, who lately got a Clap,
> And who at the *Groom-porters* had ill hap
> Three nights ago, in play with such a Lord.

The bore invites the poet to a bottle; but no, his journey
lies to Lambeth. On this, he proceeds to discuss his own
qualifications as a writer and dancer. By this time tor-
tured and torturer have arrived at Westminster, where
the fop says he has a case, which, however, he will ne-
glect for such good company. He talks of Titus Oates,
of religion, inquires after His Grace, and seeks an intro-
duction. The poet's friend, a doctor, arrives on the
scene but fails to help, and the unhappy man remains
defenceless, until finally "a brace of Bailiffs clap the
Rascal on the back."

Thomas Creech, a classicist of Dryden's time, gives a
very good transcription of the Satire in his *Odes, Satyrs,
and Epistles of Horace*,[2] and his work on the text is fol-
lowed in 1754 by a more individual and virile version by
Richard Owen Cambridge. This writer takes the two
strollers over into the Billingsgate neighborhood:

> But now his voice, tho' late so loud,
> Was lost in the contentious croud
> Of Fishwives newly corporate,
> A Colony from *Billingsgate*.

The prejudices of the market people appear:

> Our talk, which had been somewhat loud,
> Insensibly the market croud

---

[1] *Works* (6th ed., 1703), p. 175.   [2] Fifth ed. (1730).

> Around my persecutor drew;
> And made 'em take him for a *Jew*.

Cowper did the "Rome to Brundisium" Satire in iambic tetrameter couplets, and then continued his work on Horace with "The Impertinent." [1] He makes his idlers cross the Thames, and refers to Gray and Mason, and Beard the singer. The picture of the arrest, with the mob around huzzaing, is effective.

[1] (Ed. Bailey, 1905), pp. 617 and 622.

Chapter III

TRIVIA AND THE LIFE OF THE STREETS

TRIVIA was first published in an octavo volume of ninety-six pages, on January 26, 1716. Bernard Lintot was responsible for the issue, and the price was one-and-sixpence, though some special large-paper copies were sold by subscription at one guinea. This edition did not contain the Cloacina incident, which appeared first in the 1720 volumes of Gay's *Poems*. The poem is divided into three parts: the first describes the implements for walking the streets and the signs of the weather; the second tells of walking the streets by day; and the third, of walking the streets by night. The whole thing is cast in a framework of burlesque classicism, some of which is amusingly done, none of it by any means stupid, though Warton disliked the Cloacina episode and blamed Swift's muddy mind for that suggestion. Not arms and the man, but streets and crowds, are to be sung. Not the Muse, but Trivia, the Goddess of the Three Roads, will aid; and the poet shows the proper enthusiasm for his task, even though vulgar minds may consider it very much of a middle flight on which he intends to soar. Each book begins with the expected compliments, while the peroration at the end is humorously magnificent. There are, besides, about fifteen parodies of the classical simile, some of which have the true Virgilian ring. Moreover, the main business of the poem is interrupted by two episodes, one describing the invention of the patten, the other, the introduction of the bootblack to London streets. The latter should not really be styled an interruption at all, for after an extremely short visit to "Jove's eternal throne" we continue our wanderings about the streets; and, though we may not like the company of the dirty goddess with her fantastic decorations, we may be sure that she is by no means so conspicuous among her earth-born sisters as we might fear.

When this poem was published, London was well on its way to the million mark in population. It had gone through the great fire and was doubtless a much finer city in consequence. Its mediaevalism was less evident, at any rate. Its rapid growth was astonishing the citizens, and ineffectual efforts were being made to limit expansion by refusing building permits except under special circumstances. As early as Elizabeth's time there were proclamations designed to stop the erection of new buildings within three miles of the city gates, and forbidding more than one family to live in the same house.[1] This seems an odd expedient now, and brought just those results which common sense would prophesy, but which were apparently unforeseen at the time. Fortunately, laws are brittle, and break down before the force of human necessity. For a time, the poor were thrust into the most miserable hovels and unbelievably crowded, but soon the houses spread out through the open fields and London went out of town. As James Bramston says in his *Art of Politicks* (1729):

> Pease, Cabbages, and Turnips once grew, where
> Now stands new *Bond-street*, and a newer Square;
> Such Piles of Buildings now rise up and down;
> *London* itself seems going out of *Town*.
> Our Fathers cross'd from *Fulham* in a Wherry,
> Their Sons enjoy a Bridge at *Putney-Ferry*.

[1] See H. T. Stephenson, *Shakespeare's London* (New York, 1905), p. 70.

What modern writers delight to call the illusion of
progress deepens into very hard outlines when one con-
siders the growth of a great modern city. Writers in the
midst of affairs are apt to see improvements through a
purple mist of delighted appreciation, and to exclaim,
as Dr. William King does in his *Art of Cookery* (1708):

> What Cavalier wou'd know St. *James's* Park?
> For *Locket's* stands where Garden's once did spring,
> And Wild-Ducks quack where Grass-hoppers did sing.
> A Princely Palace on that Space does rise,
> Where *Sidley's* [1] noble Muse found Mulberries.

Such writers are very often blind to the disagreeable
features in their environment which to us, looking back-
ward from our eminence of superior accomplishment,
appear all too evident. One might imagine, for instance,
that the nearness of the open fields would be a blessing
to the town dwellers of Gay's time; that there the chil-
dren of the poor might play in the midst of green grass,
with the clean odors of the soil about them. The reality
was a far different thing, even down so late as 1772,
when Charles Jenner wrote his *Town Eclogues*. In the
fourth of these he describes the poet sitting on a stile at
the crossroads on the way to Highgate and Hampstead
Heath:

> He labour'd not for that vain meed renown,
> But fill'd the stated sheet for half a crown;
> And, all regardless what the critics said,
> The churlish bookseller was all his dread.

His struggles for poetic conception are fruitless, and he
begins to think he had better turn to novel-writing, like
Noble and Bell:

> In vain, alas, shall city bards resort,
> For past'ral images, to *Tottenham-court*;

---

[1] Sir Charles Sedley (1634?–1701), author of *The Mulberry Garden* (1668).

For droves of sheep, consign'd from *Lincoln* fens,
That swearing drovers beat to *Smithfield* penns,
Give faint ideas of *Arcadian* plains,
With bleating lambkins, and with piping swains.
I've heard of *Pope*, of *Phillips*, and of *Gay*,
They wrote not past'rals in the king's highway:
On *Thames'* smooth banks, they fram'd the rural song,
And wander'd free, the tufted groves among;
Cull'd ev'ry flow'r the fragrant mead affords,
And wrote in solitude, and din'd with lords.
Alas for me! what prospects can I find
To raise poetic ardour in my mind?
Where'er around I cast my wand'ring eyes,
Long burning rows of fetid bricks arise,
And nauseous dunghills swell in mould'ring heaps,
Whilst the fat sow beneath their covert sleeps.
I spy no verdant glade, no gushing rill,
No fountain bubbling from the rocky hill,
But stagnant pools adorn our dusty plains,
Where half-starv'd cows wash down their meal of grains.
No traces here of sweet simplicity,
No lowing herd winds gently o'er the lea,
No tuneful nymph, with chearful roundelay,
Attends, to milk her kine, at close of day,
But droves of oxen through yon clouds appear,
With noisy dogs and butchers in their rear.

In Jenner's day people were beginning to realize the unnecessary squalor of the fields about their city. He merely voices what no doubt everybody was thinking. When this happens, improvement quickly follows. Gay, however, writing half a century earlier, has little to say about the outskirts save for a reference to their dangers, but he does come back again and again to the condition of the streets themselves. With a realism that is unparalleled in his time except by Swift, he describes the wretched condition of the pavements, rough cobblestones with the gutter in the middle of the street, and frequently, as in the Strand by St. Clement's, with no posts to protect pedestrians from the encroachments of traffic.[1] Pall-Mall running along the north of St. James's Park is praised because of the smoothness of its pavement, for there one need not fear a sprained ankle turned on slippery stones. In Dodsley (III, 197) there is an anonymous poem called "The Modern Fine Lady" (*ca.* 1735), in which, after many disheartening adventures, the heroine is compelled to retire to her country estate. The hired coach passes through what we now call Oxford Street:

> For lonely seat she's forced to quit the town,
> And *Tubbs* conveys the wretched exile down.
> Now rumbling o'er the stones of Tyburn-road,
> Ne'er pressed with a more grieved or guilty load,
> She bids adieu to all the well-known streets,
> And envies every cinder-wench she meets.

This "rumbling" accounts in large measure for Gay's repeated complaints against the noise of the city. The "dying thunder" of wheels is recalled at least six times throughout his poem. These recurring references show that in parts of the city, at any rate, the din of traffic was excessive. It was, no doubt, the constant accompaniment of all the lesser sounds, never silent except when snow had padded the rough pavements. Tiles rattling in a rainstorm, clicking pattens, the bawling bootblacks, the sound of coins in their pockets, the oaths of the car-men, apprentices shouting at shop doors, the doleful appeals of beggars, the impudent footman pounding away at the brass knocker, all added variety to the town chorus.[2] Here and there, on a quieter corner, one

[1] There were a few raised pavements for crossings. See *Trivia*, III, 188.
[2] Cf. Jonson, *The Silent Woman* (1609), IV, 2. Haughty suggests a visit to the noisiest places in town: "to Bedlam, to the China-houses and to the Exchange." And Morose will go to any extremes to get rid of his wife: "So it would rid me of her! — and, that I did supererogatory penance in a belfry,

would find the ballad-singer still popular. Off some-
where else, the drummers might perhaps be torturing
the timidity of the new-made bride,[1] while down an-
other alley, an unwary pedestrian might find himself
rudely pushed about by a crowd of apprentices madly
chasing a football, making the sashes of the penthouse
rattle as they smashed into it, and wildly shouting to
keep up their enthusiasm.[2] Even the nights were dis-
turbed, for then the rakes were abroad, "enemies of
sleep." [3]

An interesting account of the multitudinous variety
of street noises in an earlier period may be found in a
description of the man of one phrase in Edward Guil-
pin's poem, *Skialetheia* (1598):

> As *Caius* walks the streets, if he but heare
> A blackman grunt his note, he cries *oh rare!*
> He cries *oh rare!* to heare the *Irishmen*
> Cry pippe, fine pippe, with a shrill accent, when
> He comes at Mercers chappell; and *oh rare!*
> At *Ludgate* at the prisoners plaine-song there:
> *Oh rare!* sings he to heare a Cobler sing,
> Or a wassaile on twelfe night; or the ring
> At cold *S. Pancras* church, or anything:
> He'le cry *oh rare!* and scratch the elbow too
> To see two Butchers curres fight; the cuckoo

at Westminster-hall, in the Cockpit, at the fall of a stag, the Tower-wharf —
what place is there else? — London-bridge, Paris-garden, Billingsgate, when
the noises are at their height, and loudest. Nay, I would sit out a play, that
were nothing but fights at sea, drum, trumpet, and target."

[1] D'Urfey's *Pills to Purge Melancholy* (ed. of 1714), V, 189, contains a
ballad about "A Jolly Young Grocer of London Town" (Anon., n.d.), who
falls in love with his maid and marries:

> "The morning after they marry'd were,
>   The Drums and the Fiddles came,
> Then Oh what a thumping and Scraping was there,
>   To please the new marry'd Dame."

Cf. Steele, in *Spectator*, No. 364.
[2] Gay, *Trivia*, II, 347.   [3] *Ibid.*, III, 321.

Will cry *oh rare!* to see the champion bull,
Or the uictorious mastife with crown'd skull:
And girlanded with flowers, passing along
From *Paris* garden; he renewes his song,
To see my L. Maiors Henchman; or to see,
(*At an old Aldermans blest obsequie*)
The Hospitall boyes in their blew œquipage;
Or at a carted bawde, or whore in cage.
He'le cry, *oh rare!* at a Gongfarmers cart,
Oh rare! to hear a ballad or a fart:
Briefly so long he hath usde to cry, *oh rare!*
That now that phrase is growne thin and thred-bare,
But sure his wit will be more rare and thin,
If he continue as he doth begin.

One feature of street noise deserves special notice —
indeed, books have been devoted to it; that is, the cries
of London. They have not disappeared altogether from
the modern city, but the weird sounds which now occa-
sionally astonish the stranger are but insignificant echoes
of the medley which continually assailed the ears of Gay
and his friends. Dr. William King gives a good descrip-
tion of their development in his *Art of Cookery* (1708,
p. 99):

Tom Bold did first begin the Strolling Mart,
And drove about his Turnips in a Cart:
Sometimes his Wife the Citizens wou'd please,
And from the same Machine sell Pecks of Pease.
Then Pippins did in Wheel-barrows abound,
And Oranges in Whimsey-boards went round.
Bess Hoy first found it troublesome to bawl,
And therefore plac'd her Cherries in a Stall;
Her Currants there and Gooseberries were spread,
With the enticing Gold of Ginger-bread:
But Flounders, Sprats, and Cucumbers were cry'd,
And ev'ry Sound, and ev'ry Voice was try'd.
At last the Law this hideous Din supprest,
And order'd that the Sunday should have rest,

And that no Nymph her noisy Food should sell,
Except it were new Milk or Maccerel.[1]

The extraordinary variety of the street vender's stock-in-trade[2] may best be realized by an examination of the prints and their accompanying legends in J. T. Smith's *The Cries of London* (1837).[3] Gay undertakes to note the seasons by the cries:

Successive cries the seasons' change declare,
And mark the monthly progress of the year.
Hark, how the streets with treble voices ring,
To sell the bounteous product of the spring!
Sweet-smelling flowers, and elders early bud,
With nettle's tender shoots, to cleanse the blood:
And when June's thunder cools the sultry skies,
Ev'n Sundays are profaned by mackerel cries.

Walnuts, blue plums, and pears appear in autumn, and oranges later; rosemary and bays, holly, laurel green, and sacred mistletoe brighten the Christmas-time. The barrow people, men and women, begin early; with the opening of the shops,

All the streets with passing cries resound.

[1] Thomas Britton, the musical sma'l-coal man (died, 1714), kept shop in Aylesbury Street, Clerkenwell. He was in one sense a patron of the arts, and even received quality in his garret: Cf. John Hughes, *Poems* (1735), p. 143:
"Tho' mean thy Rank, yet in thy humble Cell,
Did gentle Peace, and Arts Unpurchas'd dwell.
Well-pleas'd *Apollo* thither led his Train,
And *Musick* warbled in her sweetest Strain:
Cyllenius so, as Fables tell, and *Jove*,
Came willing Guests to poor *Philemon's* Grove.
Let useless Pomp behold, and blush to find
So low a Station, such a liberal Mind."

[2] Cf. *The London Spy* (Part VI, pp. 130–131): "We mov'd on till we came to *Fleet-Bridge*, where *Nuts, Ginger-Bread, Oranges* and *Oysters*, lay Pil'd up in Moveable Shops that run upon Wheeles, attended by ill-looking Fellows, some with but one Eye, and others without Noses." Oysters might be had from barrow men at 12*d.* a peck.

[3] Cf. *Spectator*, No. 251.

News, one remembers, was hawked, as well as oysters.[1] Moreover, when Gay wants an anecdote to give color to his picture of the frost-fair on the Thames, he uses the story of the apple-woman's disaster, and describes her as crying "pip-pip-pip" when she breaks through the ice, like Orpheus calling Eurydice on Heber's banks.

The literature of the streets has naturally much to tell us about these cries. An early ballad by W. Turner (1662), called "The Common Cries of London"[2] describes many of them.

> The fish-wife first begins:
>   Anye muscles lilly white!
> Herrings, sprats or place,
>   or cockles for delight.
> Anye welflet oysters!
>   Then she doth change her note:
> She had no need to have her tongue be greas'd
>   for she rattles in the throat.

The taylor, the broom man, the costermonger (hot pippin pies!), the milkmaid, the bootblack, all receive attention. Nor should the waterman be forgotten, the noisiest of all London bawlers:

> Mark but the waterman attending for his fare,
> Of hot and cold, of wet and dry, he alwaies takes his share:
> He carrieth bonny lasses over to the playes,
> And here and there he gets a bit,
> And that his stomach stays.[3]

An eighteenth-century ballad gives a very detailed account of "The Cries of London."[4] The most remarkable

---

[1] Cf. Jonson, *The Silent Woman* (1609), I, 1: "I entreated a bear ward, one day, to come down with the dogs of some four parishes that way, and I thank him he did; and cried his games under Master Morose's window: till he was sent crying away, with his head made a most bleeding spectacle to the multitude."

[2] Collier, *Book of Roxburghe Ballads*, p. 207.

[3] John Taylor, *Works* (coll. ed., 1630), p. 266.

[4] *Roxburghe Ballads*, VII, 57 (*ca.* 1759).

among the long lists of street cries given here refer to "singing-birds," "I'll change you pins for coney-skins," "Here's an express from Admiral *Hawke*,"[1] "Maids, have you any hair to sell?" "new prunes, two pence a pound," "lights for your cats," "butter, sixpence a pound." Perhaps it is worth while to introduce here a proposal for the employment of players, which may be found in *A New Tale of an Old Tub, or the Way to Fame* (1752):

I have laid out several Trades they are to exercise and I think with great judgment suited them to their capacities. For instance, Mr Q[ui]n I think by the deepness of his voice, and the solemnity of his Expression, Progression, — other Qualifications, seems by nature intended to cry, Buy my Flounders, buy my Flound-o-o-o-o's, or Old Chairs to mend, Knives or Scissors to grind. Mr G[entlema]n if he pleased might employ himself in crying Green Hastings, and Colly-Flowers. Mr. B[arr]y I would have rival the famous Tiddy-Doll, of Musical Melody, and sell Ginger-Bread, which the sweetness of his voice would enable him to sing melodiously. Mr. M[ac]k[li]n's Voice is very adapted to the cry of Potatoes, or Newcastle Salmon. Mr. R[ya]n Old Cloaths. Mr. W[oodwar]d might serve his country in the capacity of a tinker, and continue to make more noise than Work. Mr Be[rr]y might cry Rabbits, or Corns to Cure, or Work for a Cooper. As to the Ladies, Mrs. W[offingto]n, I think, is very well qualified to cry hot Green-Peas hot, or Dumplings ho. Miss B[ellam]y would cry Milk' or Macrell extremely well. Mrs. P[ritchar]d, I think, would shine in the occupation of a Merchant in Kitchen Stuff. And Mrs C[ibbe]r would be particularly excellent in crying Murders and Dying Speeches. As for Mrs. C[liv]e, if she's fit for anything, it must be to cry Brick-dust, or Cabbage-nets, and Save-alls.

Frequently odors give a more characteristic tone to a place than sounds, and Gay was well aware of this. London smells in Queen Anne's time are by no means an

---

[1] Admiral Hawke defeated Conflans in Quiberon Bay on Nov. 20, 1759.

attractive subject for either poetry or prose. People seemed to imagine them unavoidable and accepted them with equanimity, just as we do the presence of abattoirs, meat-packing establishments, soap factories, and so forth, in our cities. Dicky, in Farquhar's *Sir Harry Wildair* (1701), I, 1, sniffs with delight "the sweet smoke of Cheapside, and the dear perfume of Fleet Ditch." The constant feature in the town's olfactory bouquet was no doubt caused by the primitive street-cleaning arrangements. Young's city dame, for instance, finds the country irksome,

> Black kennels' absent odours she regrets,
> And stops her nose at beds of violets.[1]

These kennels, or gutters, as we would call them, ran through the middle of the streets, and were evidently sufficiently deep and wide to be a cause for uneasiness to all but the young and active. Stow's story of the young man who was drowned in the kennel near Dowgate refers to a much earlier time, but it shows that Gay's warning against too much confidence in crossing the streets among carts and coaches was not unnecessary:

> Yet do not in thy hardy skill confide,
> Nor rashly risk the kennel's spacious stride.

Stow had been describing the old wall, and comes finally around to Dowgate:[2]

The next is Downe gate, so called of the sudden descending or down-going of that way from St. John's church upon Walbrooke unto the river of Thames, whereby the water in the channel there hath such a swift course, that in the year 1574, on the fourth of September, after a strong shower of rain, a

---

[1] *Love of Fame* (1728), II, 103.
[2] John Stow, *Survey of London* (ed. by H. B. Wheatley, Dent, n.d.), p. 39.

lad, of the age of eighteen years, minding to have leapt over
the channel, was taken by the feet, and borne down with
the violence of that narrow stream, and carried toward the
Thames with such a violent swiftness, as no man could rescue
or stay him, till he came against a cart-wheel that stood in the
water-gate, before which time he was drowned and stark
dead.

In spite of the scavenger's cart these kennels were con-
tinually clogged with filth, overflowing their banks in a
rainstorm and at such times generating a fresh variety
of odors; in winter they were frozen and banked up with
the accumulated offscourings of the crowded houses that
surrounded them.

William Whitehead,[1] whom Churchill called "Dul-
ness and method's darling son," grows romantic on the
subject of the sweepers, though it might have been more
to the point for him to curse them for their carelessness
and inefficiency. Goldsmith's work had preceded this
poem, or we might think it but a cumbrous joke on pov-
erty to tickle the ears of the prosperous. It is largely
that, but an occasional phrase shows a more generous
spirit:

> Hail, unown'd youths, and virgins unendow'd!
> Whether on bulk begot, while rattled loud
> The passing coaches, or th' officious hand
> Of sportive link-boy wide around him dash'd
> The pitchy flame, obstructive of the joy ...
> Let others meanly chaunt in tuneful song
> The blackshoe race, whose mercenary tribes
> Allur'd by halfpence take their morning stand
> Where streets divide, and to their proffer'd stools
> Solicit wand'ring feet; vain pensioners,
> And placemen of the croud! Not so you pour
> Your blessings on mankind; nor traffic vile
> Be your employment deem'd, ye last remains

[1] *Plays and Poems* (1774), II, 239.

> Of public spirit, whose laborious hands,
> Uncertain of reward, bid kennels know
> Their wonted bounds, remove the bord'ring filth,
> And give th' obstructed ordure where to glide.

All ages and all tempers find occupation here:

> . . . I too have oft
> Seen in our streets the wither'd hands of age
> Toil in th' industrious task.

Evidently their conduct was not always virtuous. He
warns them against losing the precious hours assigned
to toil in fruitless brawls, and from the serene heights of
two hundred a year and a keg of Madeira cautions them
against vice:

> . . . For should ye, youths,
> When blood boils high, and some more lucky chance
> Has swell'd your stores, pursue the tawdry band,
> That romp from lamp to lamp — for health expect
> Disease, for fleeting pleasure foul remorse,
> And daily, nightly, agonizing pains.
> In vain you call for Aesculapius' aid
> From White-cross alley, or the azure posts
> Which beam thro' Haydon-yard: the god demands
> More ample offerings, and rejects your prayer.

And then, to emphasize his lesson, and incidentally to
lengthen his poem considerably in the fashionable man-
ner, he tells the story of Lardella and her misfortunes,
which need not harrow our feelings here, though the
description of the Whitehall gate is worth quoting:

> Lardella once was fair, the early boast
> Of proud St. Giles's, from its ample pound
> To where the column points the seven-fold day.
> Happy, thrice happy, had she never known
> A street more spacious! but ambition led
> Her youthful footsteps, artless, unassur'd,
> To Whitehall's fatal pavement. There she ply'd
> Like you the active broom. At sight of her

The coachman drop'd his lash, the porter oft
Forgot his burthen, and with wild amaze
The tall well-booted sentry, arm'd in vain,
Lean'd from his horse to gaze upon her charms.

Poor Collin[1] in the excitement of the Lord Mayor's
Show gets thrown into the kennel, where he is "sowc'd
o're Head and Ears." Receiving the refuse from these
kennels were open sewers, which in turn discharged
their unsavory burdens into the Thames, or into the
rapidly filling, and at last notorious, Fleet Ditch, which
ran through Holborn to the river between Bridge and
Tower. This vile-smelling and germ-disseminating sink
was left entirely open until the year following Gay's
death, 1733, when the Corporation granted permission
for the erection of a market over the upper end of it. It
was not entirely covered until between 1760 and 1768,
at the time of the building of Blackfriars Bridge. The
most vigorous description of it is in the *Dunciad* (1728): [2]

> *Fleet-Ditch* with disemboguing streams
> Rolls the large tribute of dead dogs to *Thames*,
> The King of dykes! than whom no sluice of mud
> With deeper sable blots the silver flood.

Swift refers to it in the "City Shower" (1710).[3] As the
greatest of "common shores," it figures largely in the
Cloacina incident of *Trivia*. It even became a stock
figure for Grub Street verse. Robert Lloyd uses it in
that way in his "Epistle to C. Churchill": [4]

> Lest we should flounder in some Fleet-Ditch Ode,
> And sunk forever in the lazy flood
> Weep with the Naiads heavy drops of Mud.

And his enemy, Arthur Murphy, writes an "Ode to the
Naiads of Fleet-Ditch" (1761).

---

[1] D'Urfey, *Collin's Walk through London and Westminster* (1690).
[2] Bk. II, l. 269.
[3] *Poems*, I, 78.   [4] *Poems* (1762), p. 190.

In addition to these obscene odors from the city
sewers there were the no less disagreeable smells of de-
caying animal and vegetable matter in the low streets
around Billingsgate along the riverside, or up north by
Smithfield Market. Gay describes with sufficient par-
ticularity all the steams

> That, in mixed fumes, the wrinkled nose offend.

He is thinking of Thames Street, which ran from Black-
friars to the Tower, and mentions the odors from the
chandlers' cauldrons, from the stale fish and meats, from
the hogsheads of oil and the piles of Cornavian cheeses.
In *Hudibras Redivivus*[1] the hero visits the fair at Smith-
field:

> No sooner had I pass'd the Gate,
> Where fetter'd Villains dread their Fate,
> And enter'd into *Gilt-Spur Street*,
> But such a Nosegay did I meet,
> Arising from the Pig and Pork,
> Of greasy Cooks at sweating Work,
> Enough to 've made a faithless *Jew*,
> Or freckly *Scotch*-man Keck or Spew.

But perhaps the above quotations are enough to sug-
gest the possibilities. Exhaustive research in this cor-
ner is not attractive. Writers like Thomas Brown and
Edward Ward seem to us frequently pornographic; in
many cases they are merely realistic. Gay celebrates
"fair Pell-Mell" not only because its pavements are
safe, but because "grateful is thy smell." No wonder
the plague visited every generation!

Other disturbing features of the London streets at
that time should be noted. Mud or dust, in quantities
varying with the weather and the amount of traffic,

---

[1] Edward Ward, Part III, vol. II, Canto III (1708).

must be endured at all times. No gentleman could possibly get through a day without having his shoes cleaned at least four or five times, so that the prominence given to the bootblack in Gay's picture is by no means out of proportion. Moreover, the lack of proper building regulations made possible the existence of alleys, which, though in general cleaner than the more crowded thoroughfares, had their own peculiar dangers, especially at night. The following permission recorded in official reports of the Royal Hospital tells its own story (1647): [1] "No man shall cast urine or ordure in the streets afore the hour of nine in the night. Also he shall not cast it out but bring it down and lay it in the channel." Besides, loose tiles might fall; cellars were frequently left open with no warning lights; even turnstiles still existed, to ram the soft spots of one's anatomy. Balconies overhung the streets, from which the careless passenger might conveniently be sprayed with dirty water, especially when "Saturday's conclusive morn appears." Penthouses, in which various kinds of goods were exposed for sale, were permitted to jut out in front of the main line of buildings, and were frequently built so low that the walker must bow his head to get under them. This was, of course, one of many reasons why the "wall" was at such a premium in a rainstorm.

About this Martin Parker recommends moderation in asserting one's rights: [2]

If thou see a Gentleman strive for the wall,
And hazard his life for a phantasie vaine,
This is the occasion for many a brawll;
But he that's a wise man from that will refraine:

---

[1] Quoted by H. T. Stephenson, *Shakespeare's London* (1905), p. 71.
[2] "Fayre Warning," *Roxburghe Ballads*, I, 370.

'␣t is better give place
        to one that's more base,
Then hazard thy life in so desperate a case.
O happy is he whom other men's harmes
Can make to beware, and to shun Satan's charmes. . . .

If thou seest a drunkard come reeling i' th' street,
And cutting crosse capers oft times through the durt,
Still ready to quarrell with all he doth meet,
Whereby he goes seldome to bed without hurt . . .

In *Trivia*, Gay gives full directions when to keep the wall and when to give way.[1] What might happen to the inexperienced is well described by Sir John Davies in an appendix to his *Epigrams* (1590):[2]

I tooke the wall, one thrust me rudely by,
And tould me the King's way did open lye.
I thankt him that he did me so much grace,
        to take the worse, leave me the better place;
For if by th' owners wee esteeme of things,
        the wall's the subjects, but the way's the King's.

The higher rank was always favored, and Nash could say with astonishment, in his attack on Gabriel Harvey, that he made "no bones of taking the wall of Sir Philip Sidney, in his black Venetian velvet." We need not imagine any very careful calculation of respective ranks whenever two men met on the streets. The general grades into which society was divided were clear enough, and for the rest, no doubt the man with assertive instincts found the wall promptly in most cases, as he does the street-car seats to-day.

Gay recommends the worst wig for rainy weather! Gutters to carry off the water from the roofs were by no means universal, and where they did exist, the spouts

---

[1] *Trivia*, II, 45, 59; III, 205.
[2] Cf. *Two Centuries of Epigrammes*, written by John Heath, Fellow of New College (1610), Epigram 17; and *Witts Recreations* (1640), Epigram 247.

Old Bulk Shop, Temple Bar

were apparently carefully trained to deluge those pass-
ing below. Swift describes such a scene in his "City
Shower." [1] Some suggestive lines on the same subject
occur in Fielding's "Tom Thumb": [2]

So have I seen, in some dark winter's day,
A sudden storm rush down the sky's highway,
Sweep through the streets with terrible ding-dong,
Gush through the spouts, and wash whole crouds along,
The crouded shops the thronging vermin skreen,
Together cram the dirty and the clean,
And not one shoe-boy in the street is seen. [3]

Winter had other pleasures in store for the hapless
Londoner. The smooth surface of the kennels provided
constant temptation to the boys to stage their still-
unforgotten tricks.

Why do ye, boys, the kennel's surface spread,
To tempt with faithless pass the matron's tread?

To the poet winter often means frost-fairs on the
Thames. Gay devotes over forty lines to this subject,
and references to it might be multiplied from the works
of his contemporaries. Edward Ward mentions it: [4]

And Rivers chang'd to Rocks of Ice,
That working Tradesmen and their Spouses,
Forsook their *Terra firma* Houses,
And with old Blankets, Poles and Sheets,
On Frozen *Thames* built Lanes and Streets.

He has humanity enough to remember that the severe
weather meant something far different from gaiety to
many poor people:

[1] Written Oct., 1710; fiirst printed in the *Tatler*, No. 238; published in
Miscellanies (1711). See *Poems* (Bohn), I, 78.
[2] 1730. *Works* (ed. G. H. Maynadier, New York, 1905), XII, 95.
[3] Cf. Addison's *Cato* (1713), end of Act I.
[4] "British Wonders," in *A Collection of Historical and State Poems, Satyrs,
Songs, and Epigrams*, vol. V of *Miscellanies*, p. 23 (1717).

> Beggars crept up and down, poor Souls,
> Cursing the Price of Bread and Coals.

Jonathan Smedley, to whom Swift was pet aversion, stops to point out the celebrities in the scene for us:[1]

> Lo! there a sleek *Venetian* Envoy walks,
> And there an Alderman, more proudly, stalks;
> There goes the *French* Ambassador; that's He:
> And there is Honest Squire and Captain *Lee.*
> Here's *Rue St. Jaque*, and yonder is the *Strand;*
> In this Place *Noyer* plies; that's *Lintott's* Stand.[2]

But to return to the streets and their complications. The overhanging signs grew so numerous and so elaborate that finally, in 1762, the law had to interfere and they were removed. Gay speaks of their swinging with a creaking noise as a portent of rain. They served as landmarks to strangers in the absence of numbers and printed names on the street corners. Edward Ward tells us, in his "Delights of the Bottle" (1720):

> Thus Signs, when first they came in fashion,
> Denoted each Man's Occupation.

And Addison recommends a reasonable consistency:

> I would enjoin every Shop to make use of a Sign which bears some Affinity to the Wares in which it deals. . . . A Cook should not live at the Boot, nor a Shoemaker at the Roasted Pig; and yet, for want of this Regulation, I have seen a *Goat* set up before the Door of a Perfumer, and the *French* King's Head at a Sword-Cutler's.[3]

---

[1] *Poems on Several Occasions* (1721), p. 34.

[2] The most astonishing frost that one hears about occurred on Dec. 23, 1684. J. O. Halliwell catalogues a ballad (CLIX) about this, called "Sad News from Salisbury, and other Parts of the West of England, being an Account of a most sad and dreadful Frost and Snow, which hapned on the 23d. of December, 1684, in and about most Parts of the West of England, which Froze to Death many poor passengers who Travelled the Rode, besides many Beasts, incredible to believe, but that some who were in the same storm are alive to justifie the truth thereof, the like scarce ever being known in this Kingdom." [3] *Spectator*, No. 28.

Later, the connection between sign and occupation be-
came very hazy, although the device sometimes re-
mained significant. The author of the *Vade Mecum for
Malt-Worms* gives a curious list of public-houses with
their signs and, like Addison, mentions a few anomalies.
In Rosemary Lane, for instance,

> Near to the Place where *Frippery-Women* stand
> With *Stays, Coats, Suits,* and *Breeches,* second hand ...
> There stands a House, wherein if Fame not lies,
> The Stars at Noon-day to Men's Sight arise,
> And *Charles* his Wain in Sun-shine greets their eyes.[1]

Sometimes the sign suggested political affiliations. Thus
Bramston in *The Art of Politicks* (1729):

> The love of Politicks so vulgar's grown,
> My Landlord's Party from his Sign is known:
> Mark of *French* wine, see *Ormond's* Head appear,
> While *Marlborough's* Face directs to Beer and beer:
> Some *Buchanan's,* the *Pope's* Head some like best,
> The *Devil Tavern* is a standing jest.

St. George was ever popular:

> St George that swinged the Dragon, and e'er since
> Sits on his horseback at mine hostess' door.[2]

J. O. Halliwell catalogues a ballad (CLXIX), called
"London's Ordinarie, or Every Man in His Humour,"
which, he says, contains curious information about
London inn signs. This is printed by Ebsworth.[3] It
enumerates the London signs as they were in James I's
and Charles I's reigns. It was, however, reprinted in
Charles II's reign, so that the signs must have remained
approximately the same.

---

[1] Cf. Bramston, *Art of Politicks* (1729):
> "Who in the *House* affects declaiming Airs,
> *Whales* in *Change-Alley* paints: in *Fish-Street,* Bears."

[2] *King John,* I, i.

[3] *Roxburghe Ballads,* II, 24.

Through the Royall Exchainge as I walked,
Where gallants in sattin doe shine;
At midst of the day they parted away
To severall places to dine.

The Gentry went to the King's-Head,
The Nobles unto the Crowne;
The Knights went to the Golden Fleece,
And the Plough-men to the Clowne. . . .

The Cheater will dine at the Checker,
The Picke-pockets in a blind Ale-house,
Till taken and tride, then up Holborne they ride,
And make their end at the Gallowes.[1]

There is also a very curious list of inn signs in an
early poem by William Elderton called "A New merry
Newes" (1606): [2]

But chiefly in London at the Salutation.
And at the Bores head, hard by London stone,
And the swan at Dowgat a tauerne well knowne,
The Myter in Cheape, and then the Bull head,
And many like places to make Noses red,
The Castel in Fishstréet, thrée Cranes in the Vintry,
And now of late at S. Martins in the Sentry,
And so in generall in many a good towne,
Where gallants be gaging the cups vp & downe.[3]

Merchandise itself was exposed as the most effective
kind of advertisement — frequently things which in
this germ-invested age we prefer to see under glass, or
at least protected from the dust of the street in some
fashion. Gay speaks of combs dangling in one's face in
the narrow pass of St. Clement's on the Strand.[4]   In
another place,

    [1] John Taylor, *Travels and Circvlar Perambvlation* . . . (1636); reprinted
by the Spenserian Society. This contains a description of tavern signs.
    [2] Hazlitt, *Fugitive Tracts.*
    [3] See on this subject Philip Norman, *London Signs and Inscriptions* (1893).
    [4] *Trivia*, III, 22.

> On hosiers poles depending stockings tied,
> Flag with the slacken'd gale, from side to side.

The "nailed hoop" was apparently the warning sign for fresh paint, while lanterns were used as to-day around danger spots in the streets.

The street-lighting system in the London of the early eighteenth century was frequently praised by strangers, and evidently the English capital was considered a city of "white ways." From our point of view in this later age, conditions must have been intolerable. All too few oil-lamps, burning not half the night and concealing their insufficient rays behind smoked glass, provided this blaze of light which astonished the Parisians. They had, of course, to be replenished and lit by hand, — to add "cleaned" would be merely facetious, — and the lamp-lighters were familiar figures on the streets. Their efficiency in general may be surmised from the sketch of one of them which Hogarth gives us in his series on "The Rake's Progress."

Wooden pumps at intervals supplied the town with water, and provided also a means of summary punishment when the good-nature of the citizens had been too rudely irritated by the vagaries of pickpockets, whores, and bailiffs. Gay describes such a scene, the sleights of the petty thief, the hue and cry, the capture:

> Seized by rough hands, he's dragg'd amid the rout,
> And stretch'd beneath the pump's incessant spout:
> Or plunged in miry ponds, he gasping lies,
> Mud chokes his mouth, and plasters o'er his eyes.

D'Urfey, in *Collin's Walk through London and Westminster*,[1] tells of Collin's disapproval of the nude statues on a clock near St. Dunstan's; how the mob ill digested

[1] (1690), p. 59.

his criticisms and, but for the major's interference, would have "pumped" him.[1]

> Pump'd in my sense, is cooling Courage;
> When th' People for diversion, or rage;
> Do punish Pick-pockets, or Whores,
> For filching, or too fond Amours:
> A decent Guerdon too for Bayliffs,
> That lurk in close By-Lanes and Alleys,
> Or lye perdue in some blind Alehouse,
> To nab some needy honest Fellows:
> But being seiz'd and hamper'd first;
> Are carri'd straight to quench their Thirst,
> To a strange Wooden kind of Fountain,
> That doth great store of Water contain;
> And there without a cup to fill,
> Are forc'd to drink against their Will.

Evidently the Londoners of that time were not the tame asses that most city dwellers are to-day; lawless, perhaps, yet in whimsical fashion strenuous upholders of law. They needed to be, for the watchmen in the scattered sentry-boxes counted for little in emergencies.

D'Urfey's reference to the bailiffs serves to remind us of the ubiquity of these unpopular officials. References to them are frequent in the poetry of the time and are always uncomplimentary.

Thus Joseph Mitchell in his "Congratulatory Verses" marks them as one of the nuisances of the streets:

> No cursed *Bribery* corrupts the Chair,
> No *Duns*, no *Catch-poles*, ever enter there.
> No *Cart*, no *Coach*, no *Chimney-sweeper*, seen,
> To break your Rest, or edge you off the Green.[2]

---

[1] Cf. *The Bow-Street Opera, in Three Acts* (written on the plan of *The Beggar's Opera*), p. 28: "The thief that steals trifles is duck'd in the streets."

[2] *Poems* (1729), II, 4.

St. Dunstan in the West, Fleet Street

And the author of the *Parodies on Gay* has evidently had his experiences:

> One morn, o'er head and ears in debt,
> As forth he slowly walk'd, he met
> Two bailiffs at Spring Garden gate,
> And skulks to shun impending fate;
> He stops, he starts, he racks his wits,
> He pants, he smiles, and frowns by fits;
> And to mislead pursuing duns,
> Thro' many a lane and alley runs.[1]

One of the *Roxburghe Ballads* (VII, 10) is called "The Poet's Dream, Or The Great Out-cry and Lamentable Complaint of the Land against Bayliffs and their Dogs." This actually names some of them. We learn that the tallyman at the tavern usually kept one handy, and also that many rogues who had been branded at the Old Bailey for pilfering turned bailiff.

> Ten groats the fees, and a crown the [arrest,
> and three round ooo's for a writ beside . . .
> The Jayl-fees many are bound to rue,
> The garnish, bed, and Turn-key too.

This was written before 1680.

Taylor, in *The Water Cormorant his Complaint* (ed. 1630), gives us a good picture of this unpopular gentleman's operations (page 10):

> The *Serieant* I before the *Jaylor* name,
> Because he is the dog that hunts the game:
> He worries it, and brings it to the toyle,
> And then the *Jaylor* liues vpon the spoyle.
> I'ue knowne a *Serieant*, that foure houres hath sate,
> Peeping and leering through a tauerne grate,
> His Yeoman on the other side the way,
> Keeping the like *watch* both for one poore prey.

[1] *Parodies on Gay* (*ca.* 1810), p. 22.

But to return from bailiffs to pumps, for, after all, their connection is but transitory. The larger conduits must have been centres for the town gossips in much the same way as the fountain in the French village is to-day, or as the town pump was in old New England times. The verse-makers of the streets no doubt submitted their compositions to the judgment of such audiences, and hated with professional jealousy those happier rivals who basked in the sunlight of noble patronage:

> All these hate Verses, and Verse-makers fly,
> That Beast the *Poet* comes, *'ware horns*, they cry:
> To make the People laugh, these Fellows use
> Not to regard what *friends* they do abuse,
> And whatso'ere they write, they forthwith to
> The *Politicians* of the *Conduit* shew,
> Or at the *Bake-house*, that Old Women and
> The roguing Boys their jests may understand.[1]

The water-supply was then large enough for the ordinary purposes of the Londoner. When fires occurred, however, the supply was often hopelessly inadequate. One thinks at once of Dryden's description of the nights and days of terror during the great fire of 1666. A reasonably good account of this catastrophe may be found in a poem by John Allison, called *Upon the late Lamentable Fire in London* (1667). This describes the diminutive start of the blaze, its progress along the riverside, the downfall of Gresham's famous building [2] and Paul's, the burning of Newgate, with the release of the prisoners. The great fire, too, has its place among the "British Wonders" which Ward tells about in his *Collection of Historical and State Poems, Satyrs, Songs, and Epigrams.*[3]

---

[1] Alex. Brome, *The Poems of Horace, rendred in English and paraphrased by Several Persons* (3d ed., 1680), *Satires*, I, 4.
[2] The Royal Exchange was opened in 1570, and faced Cornhill.
[3] Vol. V of *Miscellanies* (1717).

Various signs and monuments commemorated the event. The naked boy, made of wood and standing on a column at Pie Corner, corner of Wood and Giltspur Streets, was one of them. The inscription he bore has been long since obliterated: "This boy is in Memory Put up for the late Fire of London, occasioned by the Sin of Gluttony, 1666." [1] There could be no doubt about the cause. "No, my beloved; it was occasioned by the sin of gluttony, for it began at Pudding Lane and ended at Pie Corner." [2] The column that Pope speaks of was a fire monument, and bore an inscription importing that the city was burnt by Papists.

> Where London's column, pointing at the skies
> Like a tall bully, lifts the head, and lies.[3]

This severe experience must have taught the lesson of preparedness, for Gay's description of the fire in *Trivia* shows a rather elaborate system of engines, ladders, explosives, and so forth, in use. In this connection, the imitations of Juvenal's Third Satire noted above should be reconsidered, for the work of the great Roman poet colored the imagination of many an English writer when he came to picture the town in flames.[4]

Having seen how small was the space left in London streets for traffic, one must leave the imagination free to crowd these narrow, crooked thoroughfares with a multitude of coaches, sedan-chairs, and carts of all descriptions. Coaches became common about 1601, though their advent was violently opposed, especially by the watermen, whose business was at stake:

---

[1] Cf. Thomas Pennant, *The Antiquities of London* (2d ed., 1818), p. 23: "As it begun in *Pudding-lane*, it ended in *Pye-corner*, which might occasion the inscription with the figure of a boy on a house in the last place, *which attributes the fire of London to the sin of gluttony*."

[2] Philip Norman, *London Signs and Inscriptions* (1893), p. 8.

[3] *Moral Essays*, III, 339–340.

[4] Cf. Simon Ford, *The Conflagration of London* (1667).

> Carroaches, Coaches, Iades and Flanders Mares,
> Doe rob vs of our shares, our wares, our Fares:
> Against the ground we stand and knocke our heeles,
> Whilst all our profit runs away on wheeles.[1]

In 1613, a maximum of 430 was suggested, and in 1626 Sir Sanders Duncombe was given a monopoly of sedan-chairs for fourteen years, ostensibly because the streets were "so encumbered with the unnecessary multitude of coaches that many of our subjects are thereby exposed to great dangers and the necessary use of carts and carriages for provisions thereby much hindered." And moreover, the coach had quite the same uncanny ability to pauperize as the motor-car has now. Among the *Roxburghe Ballads* there is one called "Mock-begger Hall," [2] in which the following lines occur:

> There's some are rattled thorow the streets,
> *Probatum est,* I tell it,
> Whose names are wrapt in parchment sheets,
> It grieves their hearts to spell it;
> They are not able two men to keepe,
> With a coachman they must content be,
> Which at play house doores on his box lies asleep
> *While mock-begger hall stands empty.*

In this same collection there is another ballad, "The

---

[1] John Taylor, "A Thiefe," *Collected Works* (1630), p. 111. See Major Norman G. Brett-James, "London Traffic in the Seventeenth Century," in *Nineteenth Century and After*, November, 1925. See also John Taylor, *World runs on Wheels* (1622), p. 232 of the first collected edition (1630); and Stow, *Survey of London*, p. 77 (first published in 1574): "But in the next year [after Wat Tyler's rebellion, 1381], the said King Richard took to wife Anne, daughter to the King of Bohemia, that first brought hither the riding upon side-saddles; and so was the riding in wherlicoates and chariots forsaken, except at coronations and such like spectacles; but now of late years the use of coaches, brought out of Germany, is taken up, and made so common, as there is neither distinction of time nor difference of persons observed; for the world runs on wheels with many whose parents were glad to go on foot."

[2] *Roxburghe Ballads*, VI, 762, and II, 132 (Anon., *ca.* 1636–42).

Coach's Overthrow," [1] which mentions the arrival of the
sedan-chair.

> The Sedan does (like Atlas) hope
> To carry heaven pick-pack.

The coachman was better appreciated in the country.
There he had a real place to fill. No one needs to be re-
minded of old Hobson, or of Milton's charming elegy
on him (1631). There is in Sorbière's *A Voyage to Eng-
land* a description of an English coachman, which de-
serves notice. Sorbière made his trip in 1664.

> J'allay de Douvre à Londres dans un coche, ou pour mieux
> dire, dans un chariot. Il estoit traîné par six chevaux attelez
> l'un à la queuë de l'autre, et conduit par un charretier, qui
> marchoit à costé de son chariot. Cét honneste homme estoit
> monté comme un S. George, habillé de noir. Il avoit la grosse
> botte remonté, faisoit l'homme d'importance, et paroissoit
> fort satisfait de sa personne. [2]

Gay thinks Venice fortunate, for there

> No carts, no coaches shake the floating town!

His numerous references to coaches show, I think, some-
thing of the poor man's rather silly chagrin in the midst
of what seems to him unmerited prosperity. He is tre-
mendously impressed by their color and gilding, and
allows his imagination too readily to play about the sins
of their owners. [3] About chairs, too, our poet is a bit

---

[1] *Roxburghe Ballads*, III, 333 (1636).

[2] Samuel Sorbière, *Relation d'un Voyage en Angleterre* (1667), p. 12. First
published in 1664, and first translated in 1709, though Dr. William King had
used it in his burlesque *Journey to London in the Year 1698*.

[3] He was influenced, no doubt, by Juvenal III. Cf. Pope, *Imitations of
Horace: Satires*, II, 1, 107:

> "Dash the proud Gamester in his gilded Car."

Cf. also J. Mitchell, *Poems* (1729), I, 262, "To the Rt. Hon. Charles, Earl of
Lauderdale":

> "How *mimick Patriots* in gilt Chariots, ride,
> Forget the *Dunghils*, and *themselves*, thro' Pride."

spleeny. They cost but a shilling a mile, and though they had been used in London for half a century, had evidently only at this time grown common. To the carts and heavy wagons of various kinds Gay gives less attention, though the coaches were forced always to give them right of way or regret it. Gay was, like Hogarth, awake to the cruelty daily practised on the horses. He refers to it twice, and is in this also, no doubt, the spokesman of a growing public feeling. Thomson expressed himself forcibly on the question in *The Seasons* (1726-30), and not many years were to pass before Horace Walpole would resent bitterly the slaughter of stray dogs on the streets. He wrote to Lord Strafford on September 4, 1760:

> In London there is a more cruel campaign than that waged by the Russians: the streets are a very picture of the murder of the innocents — one drives over nothing but poor dead dogs! The dear, good-natured, honest, sensible creatures! Christ! how can anybody hurt them? Nobody could but those Cherokees the English, who desire no better than to be halloo'd to blood: — one day Admiral Byng, the next Lord George Sackville, and to-day the poor dogs!

Soame Jenyns even claimed to believe in the transmigration of souls and disapproved of hunting.

Herds of cattle might still be driven through the streets of London to market. Asses were led about in Gay's time and milked before the doors of consumptives:

> Before proud gates attending asses bray,
> Or arrogate with solemn pace the way;
> These grave physicians with their milky cheer,
> The love-sick maid and dwindling beau repair.

So that under these circumstances, the cow that ate Tom Thumb would not be such an extraordinary portent after all:[1]

---

[1] Henry Fielding, *Works* (ed. Maynadier, New York, 1905), XII, 113.

Whilst from my garret, twice two stories high,
I look'd abroad into the streets below,
I saw Tom Thumb attended by the mob;
Twice twenty shoe-boys, twice two dozen links,
Chairmen and porters, hackney-coachmen, whores;
Aloft he bore the grizzly head of Grizzle;
When of a sudden through the streets there came
A cow, of larger than the usual size,
And in a moment — guess, oh! guess the rest! —
And in a moment swallow'd up Tom Thumb.

The asses themselves take part in Bacco's celebrations: [1]

Bacco was drawer at The Sun,
And had his belly like his tun.
For blubber-lips, and cheeks all bloated,
And frizzled pate, the youth was noted.
He, as his custom was, got drunk,
And then went strolling for a punk.
Six links and lanterns, 'cause it was dark yet,
He press'd from Covent-Garden-Market;
Then his next captives were the Waits,
Who play'd lest he should break their pates.
But as along in state he passes
He met a fellow driving asses;
For there are sev'ral folks whose trade is
To milk them for consumptive ladies.
Nothing would serve but get astride,
And the old bellman too must ride.
What with their houting shouting yell
The place had something in it of hell.

The London mob was fond of exhibitions of this sort,
and delighted to take part in them. Shakespeare gives
a vivid conception of the townsmen *en masse* in his de-
scription of the coronation scene in *Henry VIII* (1612).
Less familiar is "Jack of Lent's Ballad, On the Welcom-
ing of Queen Henrietta Maria" (1625): [2]

[1] "The Art of Love" (1709), in *The Poetical Works of William King*
(Edinborough, 1781), p. 131.
[2] By John Eliot. See *Bagford Ballads*, II, 1010. Reprinted by J. W.
Ebsworth, in *Choyce Drollery* (1656), p. 25.

From thence in order two by two
As we to *Pauls* are us'd to goe,
　To th' Bridge we will convey her,
And there upon the top o' th' gate,
Where now stands many a Rascal's pate,
　I mean to place a player.
And to the Princess he shall cry,
May't please your Grace, cast up your eye
　And see these heads of Traytors;
Thus will the City serve all those
That to your Highnesse shall prove foes,
　For they to Knaves are haters.
Down Fishstreet hill a Whale shall shoot,
And meet her at the Bridges foot,
　And forth of his mouth so wide a
Shall *Jonas* peep, and say, for fish,
As good as your sweet-heart can wish,
　You shall have hence each Friday.

Troops of Graces, the Fates, Spain's Infanta, follow; a pair of gloves is given; the lord mayor and his lady meet the royal party and accompany them beyond Temple Bar; many of the merry-makers stay behind at the Devil Tavern.

Admiral Deans's funeral is described elaborately in the same volume, oddly enough in ballad verse, with the refrain, "which no body can deny." All the landmarks are noted — Greenwich, London Bridge, the Old Swan, the Globe, Tom Godfrey's bears, Queenhithe, Paul's Wharf, Blackfriars ("where now the players have little to do"), Temple Chambers, Essex House, Strand Gate, Somerset House, the Savoy, the Exchange, Durham House, Whitehall, Westminster, with its Chapel of Henry VII.

A funeral might thus give occasion for real sport. We know this also from *A Tale of Two Cities* and from strange and painful echoes that come down to us about Garth's performances at Dryden's funeral.

An anonymous *Description of Mr. D[ryde]n's Funeral*
appeared in 1700. The service, such as it was, was held
from the College of Physicians.

> The Day is come, and all the Wits must meet
> From *Covent-Garden* down to *Watling-street;*
> They all repair to the Physicians Dome,
> There lies the Corps, and there the Eagles come.

Tonson was there, and the playhouse sparks, with gen-
erous numbers from the musical mob of the streets.

> It much affected every tuneful Ringer,
> But most of all the jolly Ballad-singer,
> Who now at a Street's Corner must no more
> A Play-house Song in equal Numbers roar.

The boys from Paul's were dumb.

> With Tag-Rag, Bob-Tail was the Room full fill'd,
> You'd think another *Babel* to be built;
> Not more Confusion at St. *Batt's* fam'd Fair,
> Or at *Guild-Hall* at choice of a Lord Mayor.
> But stay my Muse, the learned *G[ar]th* appears,
> He sighing comes, and is half drown'd in Tears.

At this point in the ceremonies Garth delivers his ora-
tion, which is followed by the singing of an Ode from
Horace instead of a hymn:

> Next him the Sons of Musick pass along,
> And murder *Horace* in confounded Song.

Then the mixed, disorderly mob starts on the way to
the Abbey, with hautboys before the hearse and more
dismal plaints than at an Irish funeral:

> Now, now the time is come, the Parson says,
> And for their *Exeunt* to the Grave he prays:
> The Way is long, and Folk the Streets are clogging,
> Therefore my Friends away, come let's be jogging.[1]

---

[1] This should be compared with contemporary accounts of the riot at the
funeral of Francis Chartres, 1731. See the satirical Epitaph by Arbuthnot;

Funerals took place regularly at night in those earlier times, and for this reason we find Gay's description of their solemn vanities[1] in his third book, "On Walking the Streets by Night."

As for weddings, they were not properly solemnized without some sort of charivari or masque.[2] Most of them were suspect, it is true, like the one Gay tells of in the twelfth fable (1727), for Cupid had little to do with them:

> When, says the Boy, had I to do
> With either your affairs or you?
> I never idly spent my darts;
> You trade in mercenary hearts.
> For settlements the lawyer's fee'd;
> Is my hand witness to the deed?
> If they like cat and dog agree,
> Go rail at Plutus, not at me.

This made no difference to the crowd seeking excitement. Neither did it matter whether the "parties" were rich or poor. The beggar might have as good a time as Suckling's lord,[3] and the list of guests might be even larger, as one may see from the old ballad called "The Beggars' Wedding, or The Jovial Crew," printed with allowance, October 19, 1676.[4]

see also Part XVIII of *The London Spy* (1704–06) and Hogarth's Plate I of "The Harlot's Progress."

[1] Cf. Alexander Brome, *The Poems of Horace*, etc. (1680), *Satires*, II, 5:

> "And if th' *interrment* should be left to thee,
> Be sure thou do't with *pomp* and *decency;*
> The *Neighbours* all about will celebrate
> A *Funeral* that's manag'd in great state."

[2] Cf. Jonson, *The Silent Woman* (1609), III, 2. "*Haughty:* Pardon me, sir, I must insinuate your errors to you; no gloves? no garters? no scarves? no epithalamium? no masque?" See also *Trivia*, II, 17.

[3] Suckling, "A Ballade upon a Wedding" (1646), *Poems* (ed. by A. H. Thompson, 1910), p. 29.

[4] *Bagford Ballads*, II, 872. Ebsworth quotes a large part of this piece.

Then *Tom a Bedlam* winds his *Horn* at best,
Their Trumpet 't was to bring away their Feast;
Pickt Marybones they had, found in the Street,
Carrots kickt out of Kennels with their Feet;
Crusts gather'd up for bisket, twice so dry'd,
Alms, Tubs and *Olla Podrida's*, beside
Many such Dishes more; but it would cumber
Any to name them, more than I can number.
Then comes the Banquet which must never fail
That the Town gave, of whitebread and strong Ale.
All were so Tipsie, that they could not go,
And yet would Dance, and cry'd for *Musick Hoe:*
With Tonges and Gridirons they were play'd unto,
And blind Men sung, as they are us'd to do.
Some whistled, and some hollow sticks did sound,
And so melodiously they play around:
Lame men, lame women, manfully cry Advance,
And so all limping, Jovially did Dance.

Any occasion might serve for mirth, or mischief, for the assembling of the London mob together was not always innocent. The ballad-singer's auditory, for instance, formed a good stalking-ground for the pickpocket:

As dothe the Ballad-singer's auditory,[1]
Which hath at Temple-barre his standing chose,
And to the vulgar sings an Ale-house story:
First stands a Porter: then an Oyster-wife
Doth stint her cry, and stay her steps to heare him;
Then comes a Cut-purse ready with a knife,
And then a Countrey-clyent passeth neare him;
There stands the Constable, there stands the whore,
And, listening to the song, heed not each other;
There by the Serjeant stands the debitor,
And doth no more mistrust him than his brother:
Thus Orpheus to such hearers giueth musick,
And Philo to such patients giueth physick.[2]

---

[1] Cf. *Trivia*, III, 77.
[2] Cf. Sir John Davies, *Works* (ed. Grosart, 1869), I, 340.

It might be the frequent fires that brought the crowds together; it might be merely the quack doctor selling pills:

> No sooner had the gaping *Zany*
> Turn'd Fool, but there appear'd a many;
> Boys left their Hustle and Trap-ball,
> And scowr'd, at *Merry Andrew's* Call.
> Fat Ale-wives, and their Campaign Wenches,
> Forsook their Brothel Doors and Benches.
> Porters, whose Shoulders were opprest
> With Burthens, stood to hear a Jest.
> Each bulky Dray-man stopp'd his Dray,
> To take a Hau, Hau, by the way.
> Young Vagabonds, and stroling Women,
> Lame Mumpers, and disabled Seamen,
> Some scratching in their lousy Rags,
> Some hobling on their wooden Legs;
> All scamper'd with what speed they cou'd,
> T' increase the growing Multitude.[1]

The doctor then commands his black to open the bag of medicines, and proceeds to lecture on his pill.[2]

Fights were welcomed, whether real, as in *Trivia* (III, 36), or shammed (III, 252) to encourage trade in watches and cambric pocket handkerchiefs. Lord Mayor's Day was the great day of the year. Then were the streets strewn with fresh gravel and everybody looked for a good time. The pageants which delighted the mob are described with technical precision by Settle, in his *Triumphs of London*,[3] and by others, but I think that for graphic quality old Ned Ward is better. His description comes in Part VI, volume II, Canto VI, of the *Hudibras Redivivus* (1708):

---

[1] Edward Ward, *Hudibras Redivivus* (1708), Part I, vol. II, Canto I.
[2] Pope, *Imitations of Horace: Epistles*, II, 1 (1737):
　　"Ward try'd on Puppies, and the Poor, his Drop."
[3] See Bentley's *Miscellany* (1848), XXIV, 603.

Thro' dirty Kennels did I wade,
To view the pompous Cavalcade,
Beheld with Pleasure and Amazement,
From Sash, Balcony,[1] and from Casement;
I came at length into *Cheapside*,
Where beauteous Dames in all their Pride,
Appear'd aloft, to grace the Show,
That march'd along in State below.

In the gorgeous procession passes the great sword, carried by a man in a huge, brimless hat:

But since it is too big by far
For Human Arm in bloody War,
We'll leave the huge pacifick Sword
To awe the Mob, and guard my Lord
To Church, or, if he thinks it fitting,
To the Jews Synagogue, or Meeting.
For since the Ruff of Moderation
Is brought of late so much in Fashion,
I shall be careful how I steer
My Betters, either here or there,
But let 'em free from Poet's Quill
Be d——d or sav'd, which way they will.

The lord mayor himself follows, then the aldermen in gowns, with heavy chains, wigs, and "broad, umbrella, pot-lid hats." The remarks of the spectators are suggested:

Some cry'd, *Look how Sir* Humphry Waddle
Sits like a Hog upon a Saddle!
Whilst others, more intent upon
The Horses, than the Men thereon,
Cry'd, *There's a pretty Nag, how well
He carr's his Head, and waves his Tail!*
'T is true, the Women in the Crowd
Would now and then cry out aloud,

---

[1] Cf. Austin Dobson, *De Libris* (1908), p. 38: "Cóntemplate," said Rogers, "is bad enough; but bálcony makes me sick."

There goes a handsome Man, I'll swear,
Pointing with Finger to the M[ayo]r,
Passing that Compliment of Old,
Which ev'ry weeping Oyster Scold
Does on each whining Wretch they see
Drawn backwards to Eternity.

From *Wit and Drollery* (1661, page 45), "Upon my Lord Mayors day, being put off by reason of the Plague," we get some disappointed holiday-maker's complaint. There will be no fife on the Thames, or any wild fire tost; the pageants will be useless; even the mighty whale, on which the players were to be mounted, will not swim through Cheapside. The banquet is cancelled and the mayor will not take barge for Westminster.

It is pleasant, however, to know that even in those early days there were sometimes a few cynics in the crowd.

On a Day of great Triumph, when Lord of the City
Does swear to be honest and just, as he's witty;
And rides thro the Town, that the Rabble may shout him,
For the wonderful Merits he carries about him;
Being an honester Man, I'll be bold for to say,
Than has sat in the Chair this many a day:
Like the rest of the Fools from the Skirts of the Town,
I trotted to gaze at his Chain and his Gown,
With Legs in a Kennel quite up to the middle
In Dirt; with a Stomach as sharp as a Needle,
I stood in the Cold clinging fast to a Stump,
To see the *Wiseacres* march by in their Pomp:
At last heard a Consort of Trumpets and Drums,
And the Mob crying out, *Here he comes, here he comes!* [1]

Then follows a description of the grand procession and the banquet.[2] The cynicism becomes diabolically amus-

[1] *Poems on State Affairs, 1640-1704*, III, 303, "O Raree Show! O Pretty Show! Or, The City-Feast."

[2] See F. W. Fairholt, *Lord Mayor's Pageants* (Percy Society, 1843), Part I, p. 124. The last lord mayor who rode on horseback at his mayoralty,

ing in a poem [1] called *The Court of Neptune Burlesqu'd.*
A Satyr upon the City (1700):

> Begin Diverting *Muse*, a Comick Strain,
> Of my L[ord] M[ayor] conducted o're the Main,
> Attended by the Hornèd City Train.

There is a dialogue between Mrs. Whiting and the
lord mayor, while poet Settle waits disconsolate on
the wharf:

> Sing how the Glassy *Thames* her Current mov'd
> In smoothest Streams, to show how much she Lov'd
> Her Yearly Patrons, whose Religious Care
> From filthy Receptacles kept her clear;
> And how each *Fish* arose with grateful Song,
> To greet the goodly *Court* that Row'd along.
>   On *Southwark* Coast an Ancient Port appears,
> To Market-Folks well known, call'd *Herring-Stairs*,
> Where the strong Tide when rough, hath Havock made
> Amongst the Steps and Posts with Age decay'd;
> There, on the Margin, Poet *Settle* stood,
> The *City's Genius*, Musing on the Flood,
> On a Joint-Stool, in Tatterr'd Robes Array'd,
> Which Poverty Proverbially display'd;
> *Poetick* Dulness dwelt upon his Meen,
> And want of Food had made his Visage Lean.

Hone informs us, was Sir Gilbert Heathcoat, in 1711. Cf. Thomas Jordan,
London's Glory, or the Lord Mayor's Show (1680).
  Cf. *Bagford Ballads*, I, 418, "London's Triumph: Or, The Magnificent
Glory at the head of Cheapside, on the Kings Birth Day, and the Fifth of
November, erected on a stately Structure, and splendidly set forth in lively
Figures. First, King Williams Landing with an Army to the relief of England.
Second, the Glorious Conquest of Ireland. Third, Lewis of France Murther-
ing his Protestant-Subjects. Fourth, The Gunpowder Plot and Faux with
his Dark-Lanthorn; With many other Beautiful Figures, appearing in the
aforesaid place both the Days, and each Night adorned with an innumerable
quantity of Candles lighted, which caused it to appear most Glorious to all
Spectators" (probably Nov., 1691).
  Cf. also John Tatham, *Dramatic Works* (1879), p. 293, "London's Glory,
represented by Time, Truth, and Fame. An Entertainment arranged for
Charles II, on July 5th, 1660."
  [1] By John Hughes.

While thus the *Genius* hover'd o're the *Thames*,
And with Suspicious Looks Survey'd the Streams.

Next to the Lord Mayor's Show in the estimation of
the crowd was Guy Fawkes Day, the 5th of November.
Then the rabble rejoiced in their favorite sport of burn-
ing effigies, especially that of the Pope. Soame Jenyns
with his usual perspicacity thinks little of their religious
enthusiasms and divides the masses into two lots:

> These to the church they fight for, strangers,
> Have faith in nothing but her dangers;
> While those, a more believing people,
> Can swallow all things — but a steeple.[1]

Ned Ward describes this performance also in *Hudi-
bras Redivivus* (Part VII, volume II, Canto VII):

> 'T was then, about the Hour of six,
> When Boys were stealing Tubs and Sticks,
> And lustier Mob, to please their Maggots,
> Were begging Pence to purchase Faggots.

All the houses are lighted as brilliantly as candles will do
it. The mob, gradually increasing, roars along through
the streets. Presently they come to an unlighted house.

> This House, I'm sure, without a Light,
> Belongs to some damn'd *Jacobite*.

Fortunately the doors are stout and the windows shut-
tered,[2] and the crowd passes on, baffled, leaving the poet

---

[1] *An Epistle from S. J., Esq. in the Country, to the Rt. Hon. the Lord Love-
lace in Town* (1735).
[2] Cf. "The Battle of the Busts," from *Parodies on Gay* (*ca.* 1810). The
bust of Addison is about to act as peacemaker in a dispute over precedence,
when an accident occurs which settles everything:

> "It should be known to all men, that
> The master was a Democrat;
> And on the night of this disputing,
> A mob came rioting and hooting,

to find out that the people in the house are really Quakers.

> At length I met a frantick Crowd,
> Roaring in Triumph very loud,
> Rattling their Clubs above their Noddles,
> And kicking Dirt from miry Puddles,
> To disoblige each other's Rags,
> That hung in Tatters and in Jags;
> I' th' Front sat mounted on a Bier,
> A Pope for Children to admire,
> Condemn'd, as I suppose, to th' Fire.[1]

The effigy is followed by a throng of small boys clad as cardinals — a good way, their mothers hope, to indoctrinate them with Protestant principles. Hogarth's illustration for Butler's *Hudibras*,[2] "The Burning of the Rumps at Temple Bar, 1726," will give a good idea of those riots, as will also Ward's description in his *Vulgus Britannicus, or the British Hudibras* (1710), though this is more forceful than elegant:

> 'T was then the very *Dregs* or *Arse*
> Of all the *Jarring Universe*,
> Spew'd out of *Alleys*, *Jayls*, and *Garrets*,
> Grown sturdy with *Neckbeef* and *Carrots*;
> Some liquor'd well with *Foggy Ale*,
> Others with Glorious *Mild* and *Stale*;

> In honor of a vict'ry famous;
> (Pity their loyalty should shame us!)
> All halloo'd for his candles loudly;
> When answering perhaps too proudly,
> They snatch'd up sticks, and stones, and cinders,
> And sent a volley through the windows."

[1] Cf. Pope, *Moral Essays*, III, 212:

> "Last, for his Country's Love, he sells his Lands.
> To town he comes, completes the nation's hope,
> And heads the bold Train-bands, and burns a Pope."

[2] Part III, Canto II, p. 336 (ed. of 1775).

> *Informers, Lab'rors, Brothel-Keepers,*
> *Pimps, Panders, Thieves,* and *Chimney-Sweepers,*
> And all the rest oth' *Heath'nish Race,*
> That do our Grand *Processions* grace.

He calls them, aptly enough, "the *High-born Traitor's*
noisy Tools," and gives a vivid account of the street
council of war they hold, and the election of a 'prentice
lad as leader.

> These *Tuchinites,* our *Mighty Lords,*
> According to that *Sage's* Words . . .
> Presum'd to make a Street Convention . . .
> Near an old *Ditch,* their wise Divan;
> Where leaning o'er the *Rails* they stood,
> Consulting Ancle-deep in *Mud;*
> Where *Dung-boats* sail'd in *Dirty Streams,*
> Beneath their Noses, from the *Thames.*

Business finished, the ragged warriors start off toward
St. Dunstan's, where they meet a parson and make him
ride in triumph, and take him to his home in uneasy
state:

> So when a *Prince* has done great Feats,
> And rides in *Triumph* thro' the Streets;
> Tho' *Farthing Candles* please his Sight,
> And the loud Mob his *Ears* delight;
> He's glad, when all the *Pomp* is past,
> To find he's got safe *Home* at last.

The next canto stages a raid on the poor parson's church,
and a bonfire of the plunder; the fourth, the revels
around the blaze:

> The *Sacred Pile* b'ing now in *Flames,*
> To th' Grief of many *Pious Dames;*
> Who wept to see the *Rabble* use,
> Their Consecrated *Seats* and *Pews;*
> Like *Crazy Chairs* with broken Backs,
> And Bedsteads full of *Bugs* and *Cracks;*

Disabl'd by the sinful *Follies*,
Of *Common Strumpets* and their *Bullies;*
And from some *Brothel* torn away,
Upon an *Easter Holyday;* [1]
At such a Merry time to please,
The *Cropeared London* 'Prentices;
That they might learn when *Young* and *Bold*,
To Mob with *better Grace* when Old.

But the mob, always eager to down the Pope, turn tail
quickly when the dragoons appear.

Such riotous doings must have had their dangers,
though of course they never resulted in such bloodshed
as Sir Bevis was responsible for:

So manye men at onys were neuere seye ded,
For þe water off Tempse of blood wax red.
Fro seynte Marye bowe to Lundone ston
Þat ylke tyme was housyng non.[2]

We may wonder, however, whether some such picture
was not in the mind of Shakespeare when he wrote the
riot scene in *Julius Caesar* (1601). Tumultuous up-
roars in the London streets must have been fairly com-
mon. D'Urfey's Collin lands in the midst of one when
he visits Westminster with the major. The crowd gath-
ers around the Parliament buildings and is in a nasty
mood.

---

[1] Cf. Jonson, *The Silent Woman* (1609), I, 1: "Shrove-tuesday's riot-day
for prentices to do what they list."
Also cf. "Pasquil's Palinodia" (1619), *Bagford Ballads*, I, 500:
"When mad-brained 'Prentices, that no men feare,
O'er-throwe the dens of bawdie recreation."

Compare also a most interesting entry in Pepys, March 24, 1668; and two
ballads in the Bagford collection: "The Whores' Petition to the London
Prentices" (I, 503), and "The 'Prentices' Answer to the Whores' Petition"
(I, 508).

[2] *Sir Beues of Hamtoun*, E., p. 213, l. 187, Early English Text Society
(1885).

> Ignorant of this, the Senate sat,
> Within as snug as any cat. . . .
> Till noise like that of baiting bears
> Informed their legislative ears.

The Battle of the Wigs (1768), by Bonnell Thornton, M.B., announced as an additional canto to Dr. Garth's poem of *The Dispensary*, is merely a fanciful account of the quarrel between the Fellows and Licentiates of the College of Physicians. The Licentiates are demanding extra privileges. They gather together and direct their course

> To the *Fleet Market*, — whose stupendous ditch
> A lazy current rolls, as black as pitch.

With the aid of a blacksmith, Vulcan, they break through the gates and enter the Hall, causing general consternation among the grave elders.

This kind of mob spirit must always be reckoned with, whenever there are brains to do the reckoning and will to enforce decision. England had neither at the time of the Gordon Riots in 1780, which Dickens describes so vividly in *Barnaby Rudge*. This, the last of the great London uproars, forms the subject also of some lines in "Hurly Burly," a poem by Horace and James Smith:[1]

> Oh fatal and disastrous year!
>   When oyster-vending dames,
> Made London's train bands disappear,
>   And wrapp'd her walls in flames:
> The chimney sweep assail'd the shop,
> The 'prentice climb'd the chimney top,
>   Impunity made cowards bold:
> While Plutus in his last retreat,
> Stood trembling in *Threadneedle Street*,
>   And hugg'd his bags of gold.

[1] *Horace in London* (1813).

Then we find allusion to the wild scenes about the Parliament Houses and the escape of Sir Francis Burdett from the Tower:

> We saw the mob, like Ocean's flood,
> By howling tempests driven,
> Assail the King's dragoons with mud,
> And menace old St. Stephen.

For lesser crises than these in town life the watch [1] was supposed to be ready. Gay's yeoman gets into trouble with them and spends the night in the Roundhouse. [2] Collin and the major are thrust unceremoniously into a similar place, but the major knows the ways of the town and bribes the constable. D'Urfey's description of this individual is interesting:

> A Wight of Conduct great, and Powers,
> Especially at the Midnight hours,
> When in his Wooden Throne he sits,
> To judge without, of others Wits,
> To put the puzzling questions too,
> Of whence d' ee come, and where d' ee go:
> And when the minutes Twelve repeat,
> Profoundly tell us that 't is late;
> Then with his Guard in State retire,
> To Smoak and Tope by Sea-cole fire.

Robert Lloyd evidently knows him well, too:[3]

> So have you seen with dire affright,
> The petty monarch of the night,
> Seated aloft in elbow chair,
> Command the prisoners to appear,

[1] Cf. "Mark Noble's Frollick," in *Roxburghe Ballads*, VI, 510 (before 1668).

[2] The "Tun" on Cornhill stood in the middle of the road near what is now the Royal Exchange. It was built by Mayor Henry Wallice in 1283, and used as a temporary prison for night-walkers, etc. It was nicknamed the Roundhouse because of its shape, and stood until 1400, when it was replaced by a conduit. See Stow, *Survey of London* (Dent), p. 97.

[3] *Poems* (1762), p. 33.

Harangue an hour on watchmen's praise,
And on the dire effect of frays;
Then cry, "You'll suffer for your daring,
And d—n you, you shall pay for swearing."
Then turning tell th' astonish'd ring,
I sit to represent the King.[1]

The pillory was also a place for the mob to show their *esprit du corps.* Defoe sings its praises in "A Hymn to the Pillory" (1708):

Hail *Hi'roglyphick* State *Machin,*
    Contriv'd to punish Fancy in:
Men that are Men, in thee can feel no Pain,
    And all thy *Insignificants* Disdain.

Gay advises a quick retreat from such a neighborhood. In a ribald poem by Edward Ward, called "The Rambling Fuddle-Caps: or a Tavern Struggle for a Kiss" (1709), the beau who does his share of the struggling slips backward into an overturned and uncooked pudding:

The Curls of his Wig were so pasted and matted,
All over so daub'd, so beplumb'd and befatted;
So Eggy withal, that a Man would have sworn,
He had just in the Pill'ry been taking a Turn. . . .
He looks, by my Soul, from the Head to the Rump,
Like a Pick-pocket just run away from the Pump.

Poor Ned Ward ought to know what he is talking about. He had been on the pillory twice, once on that which stood before the Royal Exchange, and once on the more famous one in Charing Cross.[2]

[1] Cf. *Much Ado about Nothing,* IV, 2 (1599).
[2] See Francis Douce, *Illustrations of Shakspere* (1807), ed. of 1839, pp. 90–93. Cf. *Parodies on Gay,* p. 9, "The Sharper and the School-Boy" (*ca.* 1810):
    "Sometimes the stocks our legs embrace,
        Sometimes the pillory we grace;
    And vainly then the victim begs
        Relief from mud and rotten eggs;

Much might be written on the mob's reaction to the frequent executions.[1] On the whole, they seem to have regarded them as a necessity, and attended them merely as spectacles which, no doubt, added dignity to the British nation and importance to the individual Londoner. Sympathy or abhorrence might be manifested, but there was little thought of interfering with the arm of the law. There were eight regular hanging-days through the year, and thus plenty of chance to observe the humors of this national sport.[2] Swift himself writes some verses on "Clever Tom Clinch going to be Hanged" (1727):[3]

> As clever *Tom Clinch*, while the Rabble was bawling,
> Rode stately through *Holbourn* to die in his Calling;
> He stopt at the *George* for a Bottle of Sack,
> And promis'd to pay for it when he'd come back.
> His Waistcoat, and Stockings, and Breeches were white,
> His Cap had a new Cherry Ribbon to ty't;
> The Maids to the Doors and the Balconies ran,
> And said, lack-a-day! he's a proper young Man!

We must think, however, that Chaucer's description of a similar scene in "The Man of Law's Tale" (line 645) was more frequently true:

> For boys, and men of ev'ry age,
> In this *delightful sport* engage.
> How wretched! how relentless those,
> Deaf to a fellow-creature's woes!"

Mrs. Elizabeth Cellier, implicated in the Meal Tub Plot, was tried in June, 1680, and acquitted. She sat, however, in the pillory for publishing a "malicious libel," her defence, but was allowed a chair and a wooden shield to defend her from the ultra-protestants in the crowd. See Ebsworth, *Bagford Ballads*, II, 660. Cf. Peter Pindar, *Royal Poems* (attributed to C. F. Lawler), "Odes to the Pillory." These were probably written in 1806.

[1] *Trivia*, II, 44.

[2] Between 1701 and 1713 there were 242 persons hanged in London.

[3] *Poems* (Dublin, 1747), p. 190. Cf. John Byrom, *Miscellaneous Poems* (Manchester, 1773), p. 18, "A Letter to R. L. Esq.," which contains a description of Jonathan Wild's progress to the gallows, Newgate to Tyburn.

Have ye nat seyn som tyme a pale face,
Among a prees, of him that hath be lad
Toward his deeth, wher-as him gat no grace,
And swich a colour in his face hath had,
Men mighte knowe his face, that was bistad,
Amonges alle the faces in that route:
So stant Custance, and loketh hir aboute.

John Byrom wrote a brief poem describing the execution of the Scottish lords Kilmarnock and Balmerino in 1745.[1] Perhaps this is one of the hangings that Thomas Warton attended in his youth, for they say that he had a penchant for hangings as well as for ghosts.

One of the Whig pamphlets in the days of their seclusion is a parody on Dryden's *MacFlecknoe*, called *Charnock's Remains: or S[acheverell] his Coronation* (1713).[2] This poem is reminiscent of the sensational overturn at Magdalen College during the reign of James II, when all the Fellows and most of the Demys were turned out by the Bishop of Oxford, and Mr. Charnock, their vice-president, and various Roman Catholics were put in their places. Charnock was afterwards implicated in the Assassination Plot and hanged:

Fated to *Tyburn*, did at length debate
To settle the Succession of his State.

Sacheverell is chosen, for he never even deviates into knave. The ceremony of coronation at Tyburn is described, along with a long speech of eulogy from the retiring king, till "Squire Jack" gets impatient and swings him up. His cloak falls on Sacheverell's shoulders.

The most energetic among the champions of gallows rogues is perhaps Butler Swift, the author of *Tyburn to the Marine Society* (1759):

[1] *Poems* (Manchester, 1773), p. 177.
[2] Published in 1719 as by Thomas Brereton, and called *Charnock Junior: or, The Coronation*.

It has been, all examples show it,
The privilege of every poet,
From ancient down through modern time,
To bid dead matter live in rhyme;
To dignify, with sense and speech,
The post on which you rub your breech;
With wit inspire even wooden blocks;
Draw repartee from senseless rocks;
Make buzzards senators of note,
And rooks harangue, that geese may vote.

With some classes of society Tyburn Tree will have nothing to do:

No: what their numbers and their worth,
How these admire, while those hold forth,
From Hide-park on to Clerkenwell,
Let clubs, let coffee-houses tell;
Where England, through the world renown'd,
In all its wisdom may be found.

He has incidentally his fling at the Tory Tavern:

O Cocoa-Tree, for sense and reason
Fam'd, as for never talking treason!

But Tyburn is to harangue a throng far different from any usually found in such resorts:

Now these, of each degree and sort,
At *Wapping* dropp'd, perhaps at Court,
Bred up for me, to swear and lie,
To laugh at hell, and heaven defy;
These Tyburn's regimented train,
Who risk their necks to spread my reign,
When gin inflames, when hunger arms,
Fill town and country with alarms.

A change of circumstance may, however, defraud the gallows:

Exalt a scoundrel, that sells plums,
Or macaroons, for city-drums,

And seat him on the bench — his curship
Assumes at once the man of worship;
Looks down, as he would look you dead,
And prates of laws he never read:
While neighbouring grocers, that now fear him,
With inward envy pine to hear him.[1]

Things grow difficult for the men of the road:

Blind *Fielding* too — a mischief on him!
I wish my sons would meet and stone him!
Sends his black squadrons up and down,
Who drive my *best boys* back to town.
They find that travelling now abroad,
To ease rich rascals on the road,
Is grown a calling much unsafe.

They therefore become poets, or money-jobbers, or hie to the gaming-table.

The Reverend William Dodd, the author, in his youth, of a burlesque poem called "A Day in Vacation at College" (1751), came to a bad end and was executed for forgery on June 27, 1777, although his case excited almost universal compassion, and various petitions were circulated in his favor, one of them signed by 23,000 people.[2] Curiously enough, considering this fact, an utterly heartless ballad, called "A New Song," [3] was written about him and circulated while he was in Newgate. He himself was one of the earliest to write about the inhumanity of the Tyburn shows, and saw what is now realized by all, that, instead of acting as a salutary

---

[1] Garth sometimes shows a similar vein of satire:

"Not far from that most celebrated Place,
Where angry Justice shews her awful Face;
Where little Villains must submit to Fate,
That great Ones may enjoy the World in state."
The Dispensary (2d ed., 1699), Canto I, l. 7.

[2] Dr. Johnson was much interested in this case.

[3] *Roxburghe Ballads*, VIII, 322.

lesson against crime, they served only to harden people into a capacity for vice which otherwise might never develop:

> We, too, with Europe humaniz'd, shall drop
> The barbarous severity of death,
> Example's bane, not profit . . .
> Teach the well-order'd sufferer to depart
> With each impression serious; nor insult
> With clamorous crowds and exultations base,
> A soul, a fellow soul, which stands prepar'd
> On time's dread verge to take its wonderous flight,
> To realms of immortality! Yes, the day
> — I joy in the idea, — will arrive,
> When Britons philanthropic shall reject
> The cruel custom, to the sufferer cruel,
> Useless and baneful to the gaping crowd! [1]

It does not take much imagination to realize how terrible his experience in Newgate must have been:

> Hear how those veterans clank, — ev'n jovial clank
> — Such is obduracy and vice, — their chains!

In 1716 there was published a little volume of *Poems of Love and Gallantry. Written in the Marshalsea and Newgate, by several of the Prisoners taken at Preston.* These were political prisoners, not the ordinary sort that inhabited Newgate. Their brave cheerfulness in such circumstances is worth commemoration. W. Tunstale in the Marshalsea writes to C. Wogan in Newgate:

> Now I this Tale to Thee have told,
>   (And Nothing can be worse)
> That I this Gaol, must *Have* and *Hold*
>   For *Better* and for *Worse;*
> Judge then, how bravely I shall quit
>   This Marriage *Noose* for *Tyburn Twitt.*
>   With a fa, la, la . . .

[1] *Thoughts in Prison*, in five parts (Bath, 1796), p. 60.

Wogan is not in so cheerful a mood in his answer "To
W. T. upon his Song to Clio":

> Halter'd and pinion'd astride the *Barnet* Steed,
> In Triumph thro' the City to the Prison led,
> The Noise of Chains within the Iron Gate,
> The pale-fac'd Image of poor *Robin's* Fate;
> And riding thence again in *Tyburn* State.
> These are the Subjects of my Muse and Mind,
> No Thoughts of *Mopsa*, or of Womankind,
> Can now prevail, or force my Muse to Sing.

But he soon gets back his gaiety in another song, "The
Preston Prisoners to the Ladies about Court and
Town":

> Meanwhile, within these Walls immur'd,
>   Think not our Spirit's lost,
> The vilest Ale our Gaol afford
>   Is *Nectar* with a Toast:
> And if some Wine creep in by Stealth,
> It has its Relish from your Health.

Tunstale expresses surprise at his friend's quick re-
covery:[1]

> Amidst the Noise of *Chains* and *Keys*,
>   Thou can'st of *Cupid* sing,
> The *Warders* their hoarse Bawling cease,
>   And *Drawers* watch thy String.
> So Storms t' *Arion* lent their Ears,
> And *Orpheus* play'd 'midst *Wolfs* and *Bears*.

His sixty years are staunch against Love's artillery:

> Thus jolly *Thames*, that us'd to bear
>   Upon his Curled Breast,
> The charming Burthens of the *Fair*,
>   Who seldom gave him rest;
> Now, indolent, and free from Vice,
> Sleeps undisturb'd in his own *Ice*.

---

[1] Page 13 (2d part), "From W. T. to C. W."

The repentances, last words, and so on, of criminals were published and no doubt read with that sort of hectic curiosity which finds sale for similar stuff to-day. In 1634 a certain John Clavell, who had, we fear, good family connections, was pardoned, and wrote as a sign of his gratitude an odd *Recantation Of An Ill Led Life: or, a Discoverie of the High-way Law. With Vehement Disswasions to all (in that kind) Offenders. As also, Many cautelous Admonitions and full Instructions, how to know, shunne, and apprehend a Thiefe: Most necessary for all honest Travellers to peruse, observe, and practise.* This gentleman, as he styles himself, is, at any rate, modest:

> For though I oft have seene *Gadd's-hill*, and those
> *Red* tops of *Mountaines*, where good people lose,
> Their ill kept purses, I did never climbe
> *Parnassus* Hill.

He goes on to tell how the judges must beware, for they are specially marked:

> There needs no cunning Settor to betray
> To his Companions, when, nor yet which way
> You are to ride, nor need the Theeves be told
> What store of Coyne you carry; they all hold
> You to be rich, and certaine prize; beside
> They know when from, when to, the Terme you ride.

The old story of collusion with the inn servants is retold:

> Oft in your Clothiers and your Grasiers Inne,
> You shall have Chamberlaines, that there have bin
> Plac'd purposely by theeves.

The street ballads sometimes served the same purpose as the sensational newspaper of modern times, for they found in the executions the pabulum for many a song. They often reflect a fiendish delight in the capture of traitors, which seems extraordinary to us, accustomed as we are to the exhibition of a different type of mob psychology. In the days of Queen Elizabeth, for example, there were several ballads produced on the death of Babington and Ballard and others for complicity in an attempt to aid the Queen of Scots, which seems on the whole rather a laudable enterprise at this distance. The London populace thought quite differently, however, and their reaction is plain enough in a ballad called "The Substance of all the late entended Treasons," by Thomas Nelson.[1]

Their treasons once discovered, then were the Traytors sought.
Some of them fled into a wood, where after they were caught,
And, being brought unto the Tower, for joye the belles did
    ring,
And throughout London bonfires made, where people psalmes
    did sing. . . .
And set their tables in the streates with meates of every
    kinde;
There was preparde all signes of joye that could be had in
    minde,
And praisde the Lord most hartely, that with his mightie
    hand,
He had preserved our gracious Queene, and people of this
    land.

Thomas Deloney's ballad on the same subject is reprinted in Collier's *Broadside Black-letter Ballads* (page 36). This "ballading silk-weaver" rejoices in long catalogues and gruesome details, yet even his dull verses cannot conceal all the pity and terror of the scene:

The first of them was Salsburie,
    and next to him was Dun,

[1] J. P. Collier, *Book of Roxburghe Ballads*, p. 189. See also *Fugitive Tracts* . . . First Series, 1493–1600 (1875), nos. XXV and XXVIII.

> Who did complaine most earnestly
> of proud yong Babington.

Others also were anxious to shuffle off some of the bur-
den of guilt to the shoulders of this young man. They
complain of his pride and of his lewdness "before the
time he died." Babington had been before this — be
it remembered — hanged and quartered, and his heart
cast into the fire. Some of his confederates pray unto
the holy saints. Some of them are terror-stricken.

> And in like maner Travers then
> did suffer in that place,
> And fearfully he left his life
> with crossing breast and face.
> Then Gage was stripped in his shirt,
> who vp the lather went,
> And sought for to excuse himselfe
> of treasons falce intent.
> *O praise the Lord with hart and minde* . . .

In another ballad (page 57) on the same evidently popu-
lar topic, we read of a young Felton, who with his old
father upheld the Pope, a desperate business at that time.
There was also a woman executed along with these for
aiding a priest to escape:

> One Margaret Ward there died that daye,
> For from Bridewell she did conuay
> A traiterous preest with ropes away,
> that sought to trouble our England:
> This wicked woman, voide of grace,
> Would not repent in any case,
> But desperatly even at that place,
> she died as a foe to England.

The Queen mercifully remits the quartering in this case.
   On the spot where the Marble Arch now stands was
a stone on which deserters from the army were shot.

Two sergeants met their fate here in 1751, and Draper[1] thus describes the shooting:

> Avaunt *Silenus!* thy lewd revels vile!
> Cold *Russia's* troops, in a more Northern clime,
> Are disciplined far better than to waste
> Their strength in fev'rish *Gin;* is this the scene
> Of execution military? more
> It seems *Silenus'* banquet. Ah! 't is done,
> No mercy meets the wretch; it is not due
> If *George* can give it not, whose royal breast
> Glows with forgiveness.

The writer had apparently seen the messenger returning from the King at Kensington.

Another horrid picture is that which Mrs. Aphra Behn recalls of the orgy of blood which succeeded the Popish Plot excitement:

> At *Golgatha,* they glut the'r Insatiate *Eyes*
> With *Scenes* of *Blood,* and *Humane Sacrifice,*
> *Men Consecrate* to *Heav'n,* were *piece-meal* hew'd
> For Sport and Pastime, to the brutal Crowd.
> The *World* ran *Mad,* and each distemper'd *Brain,*
> Did *strange* and *different Frenzies* entertain:
> Here *Politick Mischiefs,* there Ambition sway'd;
> The Credulous *Rest,* were *Fool* and *Coward-Mad.*
> The Wiser *few,* who did th' *Infection* shun,
> Were *those* most lyable to be *undone:*
> *Honour,* as *Breach* of *Priviledge,* was detected;
> And *Common Sense,* was *Popishly affected.*[2]

These lines commemorate one of the most frightful breakdowns in the history of English law; but the suborning or intimidation of witnesses is an old and a

---

[1] Quoted by Ashton, *Hyde-Park from Domesday-Book to Date,* p. 122, from Roque's *Survey,* May, 1741–45.
[2] From "A Poem to Sir Roger L'Estrange on his third Part of the History of the Times, Relating to the Death of Sir Edmund Bury-Godfrey" (1688).

long story by no means confined to the Titus Oates horrors.[1]

Since we have been busy photographing the London crowd in its more picturesque attitudes, it may be as well for us to inquire carefully at once into the character of this mass of humanity that peopled the city streets, to think of them now as individuals. Many writers complain that, owing to the general extravagance in dress, it was impossible to tell the hangman from the Duke of Plaza Toro; but for us it is really much easier to make that important distinction for early eighteenth-century society than for to-day, when, according to old-fashioned standards, society is standing on its head. Caste will, of course, never disappear any more than other things that are solidly grounded in human nature; but as any particular age recedes from view, we can see the telegraph poles in perspective one after the other in precise gradation, not like a grove of trees with little and big mixed together. So it happens that in Gay's picture, which is the centre of our gallery, it is not at all difficult to separate beggars and rogues from the various kinds of street workers, hawkers from shopmen, and these in turn from the pompous and very superior tradesmen, and to trace out his numerous references to professional men, ladies, fops, drummers, peasants, boys, zealots, and so on.

The English merchant of that time was lazy, accord-

---

[1] Cf.Oldham, "The Thirteenth Satire of Juvenal Imitated" (1682), *Works*, p. 287:

> " If *Temple-Walks*, or *Smithfield* never fail
> Of plying Rogues, that set their Souls for sale
> To the first Passenger that bids a price,
> And make their livelihood of Perjuries."

Cf. also Arthur Murphy, *Seventeen Hundred and Ninety-One, in Imitation of the Thirteenth Satire of Juvenal:*

> " Go, seek the courts, to Westminster retire,
> Where Jews give bail and evidence for hire."

ing to Sorbière.[1] The taverns were popular, and the
shopkeeper found his way into them too frequently.
He was always there in the evening, "et comme il en
revient souvent fort tard, ou à demy saoul, il ne se remet
guère au travail, et n'ouvre sa boutique, mesme en esté
qu' après sept heures du matin." The English were
quite unenterprising in their efforts to compete with the
Dutch in the herring fishery. They were not slow, how-
ever, to complain of the bad times, as one of the tracts
in Mr. Hazlitt's collection shows.[2] In his second volume
there are some verses called "The Citizens Complaint
for want of Trade, or the Trades-mans Outcry for lack
of Money," by G. M. (1663):[3]

> *Trading is dead*, is every mans complaint;
> The Shop keepers themselves begin to faint
> For want of Trade; And as for my own part,
> The want thereof doth pierce my very heart:
> My Trade's my life; for what I got thereby
> Would once maintain my self and family;
> But now, alas, the Times are grown so dead,
> That by my Trade I scarcely can get bread . . .
> My Alewives now begin to whet their Teeth;
> The Butcher cries, Now pay me for my Beef;
> The Baker swears; what though the Times are dead,
> He will be paid; for do you think his Bread
> Did cost him nothing; y' faith if I 'le not do 't,
> He knows a way whereby to force me to 't . . .
> (Were I to chuse my Prison, it should be
> Either of these, before the *Marshalsee*;
> God keep me thence; the Keepers may be well
> Compar'd to Devils, and their Prison Hell.)

---

[1] Samuel Sorbière, *Relation d'un Voyage en Angleterre* (1667), pp. 107–109.
Cf. *Trivia*: I, 161, 165; II, 29, 30, 40, 42, 57, 69, 71, 249, 251, 284, 349, 355,
542, 551, 565; III, 62.

[2] *Fugitive Tracts* (1875).

[3] Cf. *Roxburghe Ballads*, VII, 4, "The Tradesman's Complaint, Upon the
Hardness of the Times, Deadness of Trade, and Scarcity of Money" (*ca.*
1682).

The law students of Lincoln's Inn had suffered from their wiles, if we may judge from the character which John Stephens gives them in his *Satyrical Essayes, Characters and Others:* [1]

> They haue a tricke to whisper once or twise
> And leaue their voice when they abate the price,
> Seeming to tell you they haue bargaind so,
> As they abhor to let the neighbours know;
> When stuffe and price doe lesse in worth agree
> Then place and meritts where sweet minions bee. . . .
>   They doe discharge
> All their Professions faculty at large,
> If they can walke about their wealthy shopps,
> In sober gownes and very hansome slopps,
> Now looking on their Wiues, then on the ware,
> Casting about betimes how to prepare
> A place of worship for his infant Sonne . . .
> Or if they thinke how they may busie bee,
> They doe reuolue their sin-full booke, and see
> Where they may best amend the figures weight,
> And turne a twenty-sixe to twenty-eight.

While this is going on, their wives sit outside the doors "decked out in fine clothes, in order to see and be seen by passers-by." And this leads to further trouble, which does not escape Marston's quick eye: [2]

> Who would not chuck to see such pleasing sport —
> To see such troopes of gallants still resort
> Unto Cornutos shop? What other cause
> But chast Brownetta, Sporo thether drawes?

Some of these merchants are so miserly that, though they may invite the poet to dinner, they expect him to be extremely moderate in his consumption of food. Hall[3] gives an amusing picture of the grieved host, and incidentally a hint or two about table-manners in the days of the great Queen:

---

[1] 1615. P. 4.   [2] *Satires*, I (1598).   [3] *Satires*, V, 2 (1597).

And if but one exceed the common size,
And make an hillock in thy cheeke arise,
Or if perchance thou shouldest, ere thou wist,
Hold thy knife upright in thy griped fist,
Or sittest double on thy backward seat,
Or with thine elbow shad'st thy shared meat,
He laughs thee, in his fellow's ear to scorne,
And asks aloud, where Trebius was borne?

Free-lance traders must have been favored in some households, and in the poet's imagination at any rate they might be of either sex. Michael Drayton has a pretty account of Venus going up and down as a peddler:[1]

Nay then my dainty Girles, I make no doubt
But I my selfe as strangely found her out
As either of you both; in Field and Towne,
When like a Pedlar she went vp and downe:
For she had got a pretty handsome Packe,
Which she had fardled neatly at her backe:
And opening it, she had the perfect cry,
Come my faire Girles, let's see, what will you buy?
Here be fine night Maskes, plastred well within,
To supple wrinckles, and to smooth the skin:
Heer's Christall, Corall, Bugle, Iet, in Beads,
Cornelian Bracelets, for my dainty Maids:
Then Periwigs and Searcloth-Gloues doth show,
To make their hands as white as Swan or Snow:
Then takes she forth a curious gilded boxe,
Which was not opened but by double locks;
Takes them aside, and doth a Paper spred,
In which was painting both for white and red:
And next a piece of Silke, wherein there lyes
For the decay'd, false Breasts, false Teeth, false Eyes:
And all the while shee's opening of her Packe,
Cupid with's wings bound close downe to his backe:
Playing the Tumbler on a Table gets,
And shewes the Ladies many pretty feats.[2]

[1] *Muses Elizium* (1630), 7th Nymphal.
[2] Cf. "The Joviall Pedler," *Roxburghe Ballads*, VII, 49. A version of this appeared also in *Wit and Drollery* (ed. 1661).

The *Three Ladies of London*,[1] a comedy written by R. W. in 1592, contains a beggars' song and one for peddlers:

> New broomes, greene broomes, will you buy any;
> Come maidens, come quickly, let me take a penny.
> My broomes are not steeped
> But very well bound,
> My broomes be not crooked
> But smooth cut and round;
> I wish it should please you
> To buy of my broome,
> Then would it well ease me
> If market were done.
>
> Have you any old bootes
> Or any old shoes,
> Pouch, rings, or bussins,
> To cope for new broomes?
> If so you have maydens,
> I pray you bring hither,
> That you and I friendly
> May bargen together.

The most curious tract concerning trades and wares in Elizabethan times is one reprinted in *Fugitive Tracts* and called *A booke in Englysh metre, of the great Marchaunt man called Diues Pragmaticus, very preaty for children to rede: whereby they may the better, and more readyer, rede and wryte wares and Implementes, in this world contayned*, published originally by the author, Thomas Newbury, in 1563. The names of the trades and implements are introduced in the following way; surely these rhymes were just the thing for young 'prentices to spell through on Sundays:

> What lacke ye sir, what seke you, what wyll you bye?
> Come hether to mee, looke what you can spye:
> I have to sell of all thynges under the Skye,

[1] Cf. Rev. William Beloe, *Anecdotes of Literature and Scarce Books* (1812), II, 23.

What lacke you my masters? Come hether to me. . . .
I have to sell bookes, for men of Deuyne,
And bookes of all lawes, most pleasaunt and fyne.

The peddler was a popular figure with the street sing-
ers. In "The Pedlar's Lamentation"[1] he complains
that trading is dead:

> Then, maidens and men, come see what you lack,
> And buy the fine toys that I have in my pack!

He has points for men and pins for maids, garters,
cotton, bodkins, coifs, hoods, bandstrings, lace, gloves,
perfumes, powder for hair, songs, merry books.

The equipment of "The Italian Peddlar" in J. W.
Ebsworth's *Westminster Drolleries*[2] consists of love-
charms, gloves, bands, handkerchiefs, laces, knots, roses,
posies, masks, bodkins, jewels, toothpaste, powder for
hair, *et al.*

Another ballad, by Lawrence Price, called "Here's
Jack in a Box, that will conjure the Fox, or a new list of
the new Fashions now used in London,"[3] offers little
new. Indeed, the stock-in-trade of the itinerant mer-
chant was much the same then that it is to-day.

> Here's black Bags, Ribons, Copper Laces,
> Paintings, and beauty spots for faces?
> Masques, and Fans you here may have,
> Taffity Gownes and Scarfes most brave,
> Curled haire, and crisped Locks.
> Aprons white, and Holland Smocks:
> All sorts of powders here are sold
> To please all People young and old.
> Then come my Customers touch and try,
> Behold and see, draw forth and buy.

---

[1] Collier, *A Book of Roxburghe Ballads*, p. 304.
[2] Part II, p. 92 (1671–72).
[3] Quoted in Ashton, *Humour, Wit, and Satire in the 17th Century*, p. 199.

The ladies probably outnumbered the men as patrons of the smart shops:

> Strait then I'll dress, and take my wonted range
> Through India shops, to Motteux's, or the Change,
> Where the tall jar erects its stately pride,
> With antic shapes in China's azure dy'd;
> There careless lies a rich brocade unroll'd,
> Here shines a cabinet with burnish'd gold.[1]

But even the men could not escape the temptations of the New Exchange, as Ward amusingly suggests in a song "On the Wares at the New Exchange":

> *Fine* Lace *or* Linnen, *Sir*,
> *Good* Gloves *or* Ribbons *here;*
> *What is't you please to Buy, Sir?*
> Pray what d'ye ask for this?
> *Ten Shillings is the Price*,
> It Cost me, Sir, no less,
> *I scorn to tell a Lye, Sir.*[2]

Steele had also felt the attraction of this lively place:

> Did you buy anything? Some bawbles. But my choice was so distracted among the pretty merchants and their dealers, I knew not where to run first. One little lisping rogue, ribbandths, gloveths, tippeths. Sir, cries another, will you buy a fine Sword-knot; then a third, pretty voice and curtsey, Does not your lady want hoods, scarfs, fine green silk stockings. I went by as if I had been in a Seraglio, a living gallery of beauties — staring from side to side, I bowing, they laughing; so made my escape.

And Hillaria, the wise lady of Baker's *Tunbridge-Walks*, remarks apropos of Maiden, the fop, "The greatest Beaux we have about Town now, are Milliners, Mercers, Lawyers Clerks, and 't is such upstart fellows that ruin so many poor tradesmen; for amongst 'em all, you'll

---

[1] Lady Mary Wortley-Montagu, *Six Town Eclogues*, "The Toilette," in Dodsley, I, 97. Pirated by Hills in 1716.
[2] *The London Spy* (ed. by Ralph Straus, 1924), Part IX, p. 215.

scarce find a Periwig that's paid for." Later, in the general *débâcle* at the end of the play, Maiden confesses his plebian origin: "What a Pox, must I go the Change agen, and sell Gloves and Ribbons?"

The apprentices were by no means unimportant people about the streets. Their general character and their doings had been graphically described by Chaucer years before the time in which we are interested:

> He loved bet the tavern than the shoppe.
> For whan ther any ryding was in Chepe,
> Out of the shoppe thider wolde he lepe . . .[1]

There is a curious old street song among the *Roxburghe Ballads*,[2] called "The Time's Abuses," about an odd character of the streets whom the wags about town had nicknamed "Mull'd-Sack." His complaints are voiced in the ballad, one verse of which draws the apprentice to the life: [3]

The jeering fleering coxcombe, with hands behind his backe,
All day, which stands from morn till night, to cry "What doe you lacke?"
With scoffing and with taunting, will by the sleeve me pull;
"What is 't you'l buy?" he'l to me cry, yet, like a brainlesse gull,
He'l cast on me a scorneful looke, though harm I doe him none:
Cannot he looke to his shop-booke, and let Muld-Sacke alone?

For the desperate poor, Gay has, like Ward, sincere compassion, and doubtless distributed his pence, when he had any, more generously than most men. He did not, however, overlook the fact that in addition to the

[1] "The Cokes Tale" (ed. Skeat), p. 474.
[2] Vol. II, p. 575. Time of James I and Charles I.
[3] Henri Misson, *Mémoires et Observations* (1698), p. 8: "Un Aprentif est une espèce d'Esclave, qui n'a jamais ni chapeau ni bonnet sur sa tête: qui ne peut se marier, ni faire aucun négoce pour son propre compte. Tout ce qu'il gagne est au profit de son maître."

blind, the aged, and the helpless, there were always
many who made a trade of beggary and who labored to
improve themselves in "the canting art."

The ballad of "The Cunning Northerne Beggar" tells
the story well enough.[1]   This clever old sinner boasts
of his deceits. Sometimes he appears as a soldier—

> Although I nere was further
> Then Kentish street in Southwarke.

And sometimes as a sailor, or a cripple:

> My flesh I so can temper
> That it shall seeme to feister,
>   And looke all or'e
>   Like a raw sore,
> Whereon I sticke a plaister.

He can feign the falling sickness, or, as a blind man, be
led around by a boy or dog. One of his favorite devices
is to take a doxy and a child with him and go about cry-
ing, "My house and goods are burned." True, he some-
times gets the lash, but every profession has its disad-
vantages.

The training of "The Jovial Crew" is outlined in a
ballad of that name in the Bagford collection.[2]

> When Boyes do come to us,
>   And that their intent is
> to follow our Calling, we nere bind them Prentice:
>   Soon as they come too't,
>   We teach them to doo't,
> and give them a staff, and a Wallet to boo't;
> We teach them their Lingua, to crave and to Cant,
> The devil is in them, if then they can want.
>   *If any are here, that Beggers will bee,*
>   *We without Indentures will make them free.* . . .

---

[1] *Roxburghe Ballads*, I, 137.
[2] *Bagford Ballads*, II, 878 (not later than 1679); and I, 195 (written
between Oct., 1660, and the end of 1663).

> But if when we begg, Men will not draw their Purses,
> We charge and give fire, with a vally of curses:
> *The Devil confound your good Worship, we cry,*
> *And such a bold brazen-fac'd Begger am I.*[1]

The early nineteenth-century writer, probably Tom Dibdin, who produced the *Vocal and rhetorical imitations of Beggars and Ballad-singers*, takes his cue promptly from these very balladmongers. Like Proteus, the beggar changes his shape:

> Then a Sailor from the Wars, cover'd over with scars,
>   And from all, great and small, do I beg;
> My knuckles I hold flat, and in t' other arm my hat,
>   And thus I contract up my leg . . .
>
> In another disguise, I appear to want eyes,
>   But eyes very soon I can find;
> Led by my little dog, through the villages I jog,
>   And no one suspects but I'm blind . . .
>
> With a hump on my back, People's charity I sack,
>   And in that I'm at home to a T;
> With a snuffle in my nose, I their feelings discompose,
>   And in this way contract up my knee . . .
>
> Then there's Dolly and I, when our ballads we cry,
>   On a couple of stools take our stand;
> The people all crowd, while she bawls aloud,
>   And I takes my fiddle in hand.

Conditions must really have been rather terrible in the early eighteenth century. Beggars are numerous enough to-day in London streets, and their miserable appearance is sufficient strain on the sympathies of the sentimental; but Gay talks about the public squares,

---

[1] Samuel Rowlands wrote a ballad on "The Beggars Roguery discover'd," which details the conversation between two beggars by a hedge. See *Doctor Merry-Man: or Nothing but Mirth* (1616), p. 3.

THE BALLAD SINGERS

> Where, all beside the rail, ranged beggars lie,
> And from each other catch the doleful cry.[1]

One recalls that King James I of glorious memory, hearing that Camden, the learned author of *Britannia*, was in distress and poverty-stricken in his old age, issued for his benefit, with much preamble about services to the state — a license to beg. With or without license many distinguished men were brought to it during the seventeenth century, though in Queen Anne's day their position was appreciably better, and, in any case, they did not usually join the ranks beside the rail. The sympathy that Gay and other writers show for the blind and helpless, like his resentment against cruelty to dumb animals, is symptomatic of an essential change in manners, an emergence of compassion, a quality not conspicuous in the temperament of the Elizabethan. One can find it in those lines by Pope in which he satirizes the common attitude of the prosperous.[2] He was writing in 1730, just after the Parliamentary inquiry into the scandal of the Charitable Corporation, an organization which had been formed to lend money to the deserving poor on pledges.

> Perhaps you think the Poor might have their part?
> Bond damns the Poor, and hates them from his heart:
> The grave Sir Gilbert holds it for a rule
> That ev'ry man in want is knave or fool:
> "God cannot love (says Blunt, with tearless eyes)
> "The wretch he starves" — and piously denies:
> But the good Bishop, with a meeker air,
> Admits, and leaves them, Providence's care.

[1] Cf. *Bagford Ballads*, I, 209, "The Beggars Chorus" from R. Brome's *The Jovial Crew*, IV, 2 (acted 1641). See Dodsley's *Old Plays* (1744), VI, 372. This ballad did not appear in the first (1652) edition of *The Jovial Crew*.
[2] *Moral Essays*, III, "Of the Use of Riches."

This is great poetry. It does not disturb the sympathetic emotions like Shakespeare's splendid lines in *Lear*, but it cuts clean through the rind of intellectual selfishness and makes quite as strong an appeal to show the heavens more just. It is doubtful whether the most hard-hearted of rakes in Pope's time would have found it convenient to act like Quintus in Sir John Harington's Epigram: [1]

> When *Quintus* walketh out into the streete,
> As soone as with some beggar he doth meete,
> Ere that poore soule to aske his almes hath leasure,
> He first doth chase and sweare beyond all measure,
> And for the Beadle all about he sends,
> To beare him to *Bridewell*, so he pretends,
> The beggar quickly out of sight doth goe,
> Full glad in heart he hath escaped so.
> Then *Quintus* laughes, and thinks it is lesse charges,
> To sweare an oath or two, then giue a larges.

And the laws against the beggars and vagabonds, sturdy or otherwise, had relaxed considerably since Nicholas Breton wrote the following lines:

> Look but on beggars going to the stockes,
> How master constable can march before them,
> And while the beadle maketh fast the lockes,
> How brauely he can knaue them, and be-whore them. [2]

For, after all, there is a fairly large credit side in this account with the beggars. We find, for example, an unusually pleasant expression of the sturdy independence of some of the poor given in a street ballad:

> I am a poore man, God knowes,
>   And all my neighbours can tell,
> I want both money and clothes,
>   And yet I live wondrous well:

[1] Sir John Harington, *Epigrams* (1633), Book IV, Epigram 18.
[2] Nicholas Breton, *Pasquils Mad-cappe* (1626).

I have a contented mind,
  And a heart to bear out all,
Though Fortune (being unkind)
  Hath given me substance small.
Then hang up sorrow and care,
  It never shall make me rue;
What though my backe goes bare,
  I'me ragged, and torne, and true.

Ile be no knight of the post,
  To sell my soule for a bribe. . . .

A boote of Spanish leather
  I have seene set fast in the stockes,
Exposed to wind and weather,
  And foule reproach and mocks. . . .

I have seene a gallant goe by
  With all his wealth on his backe,
He lookt as loftily
  As one that did nothing lacke . . .

Some do themselves maintaine
  With playing at cardes and dice . . .
I have seene some gallants brave
  Up Holborne ride in a cart . . .

The pick-pockets in a throng,
  At a market or a faire,
Will try whose purse is strong,
  That they may the money share. . . .

'T is good to be honest and just,
  Though a man be never so poore;
False dealers are still in mistrust,
  Th' are afraid of the officer's doore:
Their conscience doth them accuse,
  And they quake at the noise of a bush,
While he that doth no man abuse
  For the law needs not care a rush.
Then wel fare the man that can say,
  I pay every man his due:

Although I go poore in aray,
I'me ragged, and torne, and true.[1]

And a still brighter picture is given us by Philip
Ayres [2] (1687) in his short lyric, "On a Fair Beggar,"
which I quote with pleasure because of its real beauty:

Barefoot and ragged, with neglected hair,
She whom the Heavens at once made poor and fair,
    With humble voice and moving words did stay,
    To beg an alms of all who pass'd that way.

But thousands viewing her became her prize,
Willingly yielding to her conquering eyes,
    And caught by her bright hairs, whilst careless she
    Makes them pay homage to her poverty.

So mean a boon, said I, what can extort
From that fair mouth, where wanton Love to sport
    Amidst the pearls and rubies we behold?
Nature on thee has all her treasures spread,
Do but incline thy rich and precious head,
    And those fair locks shall pour down showers of gold.

Blindly groping, the poor were even then seeking a
remedy for the injustices that were thrust upon them
by society. One of the *Roxburghe Ballads* expresses very
well this feeling. It has a refrain which reflects genuine
social unrest.

The rich men in the tavernes rore,
    But poore men pay for all. . . .
Me thought I saw a courtier proud,
    Goe swaggering along,
That unto any scarce allow'd
    The office of his tongue. . . .
Me thought I saw most stately wives
    Goe jetting on the way.[3]

---

[1] "Ragged, and Torne, and True," *Roxburghe Ballads*, II, 409 (*ca.* 1600).
[2] See *Minor Caroline Poets* (ed. Saintsbury), II, 279.
[3] "The Poore Man Payes for all," *Roxburghe Ballads*, II, 334.

The blind beggar with his dog was a much too familiar sight. Pompey the Little, in Francis Coventry's book (1751), has among his many adventures this task to do, and escapes from it only on the death of his master. Conditions were, however, better in England than on the Continent, for visitors frequently express surprise at the absence of poverty. Sorbière says, for example, "You will meet with no Faces there that move Pity, nor no Habit that denotes Misery." [1] The Englishman regarded wooden shoes and grinding poverty as characteristic of the Continent, especially of France. It seems strange to find a Frenchman of that time saying that "the *English* may be easily brought to anything, provided you fill their Bellies, let them have Freedom of Speech, and do not bear too hard upon their lazy Temper." His provisos are perhaps more important than one notices at first glance.

Gay knows also that the beggar often concealed the rogue. Like the linkman, he may turn thief on occasion and at night murderously wield the crutch that gained him sympathy by day:

> Thus all the day long he beg'd for relief,
> And late in the night he plai'd the false theefe.[2]

Cocke Lorell and his crew of rogues did it in Henry VIII's time, and Martin Mark-all, Beadle of Bridewell,[3] a celebrity of old times whose deeds are recorded in a curious tract in the British Museum:

After him succeeded by the Generall Councell, one Cocke Lorrell, the most notorious knave that euer liued: by trade he was a Tinker, often carrying a panne and a hammer for a shew: but when he came to a good booty, he would cast his

---

[1] Sorbière's book was translated in 1709.
[2] Cf. "The Stout Cripple of Cornwall," *Roxburghe Ballads*, II, 532.
[3] *Martin Mark-all*, by Samuel Rowlands (1610). Also in Harvard Library.

profession in a ditch, and play the padder and then would away, and as hee past through the towne, would crie, Ha you any worke for a Tinker. To write of his knaueries, it would aske a long time: I referre you to the old manuscript, remayning on record in Maunders Hall.

Cocke Lorell ruled the rogues till 1533.

For rogues and the organization of crime — probably a simple matter compared with the complications of the bandit and "rum-running" gangs of to-day — one had best go to *The Beggar's Opera* (1728) and *Jonathan Wild* (1743). *Trivia* merely shows us lawlessness in action on the streets. There the bewildered stranger is frequently the foredoomed victim, while anyone who allows himself to loiter in crowds is apt to find his pockets lighter by the weight of watch, snuff-box, or handkerchief:

> Let not the ballad-singer's shrilling strain
> Amid the swarm thy list'ning ear detain:
> Guard well thy pocket; for these Sirens stand,
> To aid the labours of the diving hand;
> Confed'rate in the cheat, they draw the throng,
> And cambric handkerchiefs reward the song.[1]

This must have been the common experience, for we find an early seventeenth-century ballad (after 1616) in which the ballad-singer disclaims this partnership. It is called "A Caveat for Cutpurses":[2]

> It hath been upbraided to men of my trade,
> That oftentimes we are the cause of this crime.

But even in Westminster Hall, under the eyes of the judges themselves, the nefarious business goes on:

> At playes, and at sermons, and at the Sessions,
>   'T is daily their practice such booty to make;
> Yes, under the gallows, at executions,
>   They stick not the stare-abouts' purses to take.

[1] *Trivia*, III, 77.
[2] *Roxburghe Ballads*, III, 491 (before the Civil Wars).

At Court one may find them, and especially at the
fairs:

> The players do tell you in Bartholmew Faire,
> What secret consumptions and rascals you are.

But the best of all preys is the booby from the country:

> The plain countryman that comes staring to London,
> If once you come near him he quickly is undone;
> For when he amazedly gazeth about,
> One treads on his toes, and the other puls 't out.

The poor serving-maid on her way to the market loses
her cash through the nimble fingers of these rascals.
The only advice that the ballad-singer can think of to
help his auditors is given in his last stanza:

> But now to my hearers this counsel I give,
> And pray, friends, remember it as long as you live,
> Bring out no more cash in purse, pocket, or wallet,
> Than one single penny to pay for this ballet.

The sword might go, Gay tells us, and, stranger still,
even the wig was not secure,[1] for

> High on the shoulder in a basket borne
> Lurks the sly boy; whose hand to rapine bred,
> Plucks off the curling honours of thy head.[2]

Of coney-catching devices Gay mentions two spe-
cifically, "the thimble's cheats"[3] and the "guinea-

---

[1] *Trivia*, III, 56.

[2] Cf. "A Satire," *Poems on Affairs of State, 1640–1704*, III, 133:

> "Upon the lofty Walls of *Lincolns-Inn*,
> Coming from *Holbourn*, I have often seen
> A Tongs, which closely lay at the Command
> Of this our Hero's most unerring Hand:
> And when a flutt'ring Spark did walk that way,
> It did its Master tenderly obey,
> And snap the Hat and Perriwig for a Prey."

[3] Cf. Borrow, *Lavengro*, chap. 53.

dropper's bait." In addition, there were the ordinary jugglers' tricks with dice and cards. The jugglers[1] seem to have been an especial attraction to Drunken Barnaby, for he gets into trouble at least twice with them:[2]

> Thence to *Islington*, at *Lyon*,
> Where a juggling I did 'spy one
> Nimble with his Mates consorting,
> Mixing Cheating with his Sporting;
>
> Thence to *Hoddesden*, where stood watching
> Cheats who liv'd by Coney-catching:[3]
> False Cards brought me, with them play'd I,
> Dear for their Acquaintance paid I.
> 'Fore a Justice they appeared,
> Them he praised, me he jeered.

Rowlands also gives us a good picture of the coney-catcher. This refers to the time of Elizabeth, but the general features of his character remained much the same a hundred years later:

> Speake Gentlemen, what shall we do today?
> Drinke some braue health upon the Dutch carouse?
> Or shall we go to the *Globe* and see a Play?
> Or visit *Shorditch*, for a bawdie house?
> Lets call for Cardes or Dice, and haue a Game,
> To sit thus idle, is both sinne and shame.
> Thus speakes *Sir Reuell*, furnisht out with Fashion,
> From dish-crown'd Hat, vnto th' Shooes square toe,
> That haunts a Whore-house but for recreation,
> Playes but at Dice to connycatch, or so.
> Drinkes drunke in kindnes, for good fellowship:
> Or to the Play goes but some Purse to nip.[4]

---

[1] Cf. Gay's Fable on "The Jugglers," *Poems* (ed. Underhill), II, 120.

[2] Richard Braithwaite, *Drunken Barnaby's Four Journeys to the North of England* (3d ed., 1723), pp. 61, 75.

[3] John Taylor, *Works* (1630), "The Water Cormorant his Complaint" contains some verses on "A Figure-flinger, or a couz'ning Cunning-man."

[4] Rowlands, *The Letting of Humours Blood* (1600).

Chapter IV

THE RAKE

THE rake, within sight of whom we have drifted in the preceding chapter, is a very interesting person, and has a gallery of picture-poems to his credit. He combines the characteristics of several noisome varieties, among them libertine, bully, fop, and bore. The rake was a fact in Queen Anne's London as he was in Nero's Rome. The account which Juvenal gives of him is often supposed to be exaggerated, but, as M. Widal has pointed out, the poet is everywhere supported by the historians and merely makes the dry facts of the chronicles vivid in our minds.[1] Nero did run about the streets disguised as a slave, and gay young men followed his example, committing the same sort of excesses that so much disturbed Londoners in the first decade of the eighteenth century.

The task of isolating the rake from all the strange environments in which he finds himself in the literature of our period would be interminable. We must, however, call attention to some of those poems in which he is the central figure, for he is a part of the streets, the God in Carfax.

We may be serious, if we like, and introduce him in the words of the preceptor John Dalton, in *An Epistle to a Young Nobleman*, a poem of seventeen pages addressed in 1736 to the young Viscount Beauchamp:

[1] See Widal, chap. 2; Tacitus, *Annals*, XIII, 25; Suetonius, *Nero*, 26; Dion Cassius, LXI, c. 9.

What, tho' their Hands ne'er hold *Britannia's* Reins,
Nor Swords e'er seek her Foes on crimson Plains?
Yet *Blount* shall own they drive six Horses well,
And *Hockley's* Heroes of their Bravery tell.
Their Name with *Mordaunt's Pope* disdains to sing,
Yet with their Triumphs does *Newmarket* ring,
Yet in her Annals is Life's glorious Course
Immortaliz'd — by some immortal Horse.
What tho', ye fair! they break thro' Honour's Laws?
Yet thence they gain a modish World's Applause:
Receiv'd, repuls'd, their Boast is still the same,
And still they triumph o'er each injur'd Name.
Their Vote, we know, ne'er rais'd the drooping State,
But rescu'd Operas from impending Fate.
Their Bounty never bids Affliction smile,
But pampers Fidlers with the Tradesman's Spoil;
And in one luscious Sauce is often drown'd,
What might have chear'd their beggar'd Tenants round.
No *Goth* to Learning e'er was Foe so fell,
Yet oft their Praises Dedications swell;
Yet *White's* allows them, in a Length of Years,
The first of Sharpers, tho' the last of Peers.

Or, we can introduce him in Pindarics and frivolously
by following Richard Ames, who published *The Rake:
or, the Libertines Religion* in 1693. A levee of the rake is
first described; friends arrive, and with them he adjourns
to a nearby tavern to plan some daring action. The
metre, by the way, has got down to ordinary heroics by
this time:

A Deed, which shall with Terrour make,
The *Sons of Midnight*, wrapt in Flannel, quake.
Frightning of Cullies, and *Bumbasting Whores*,
Wringing off Knockers, and from *Posts and Doors*,
Rubbing out Milk-Maids, and some other *Scores*,
Scowring the Watch, or *Roaring in the Streets*,
Lamp-blacking Signs, with divers other Feats,
Are low Mechanick Actions, most unfit
For Us, the *Sons of Fancy*, *Sense* and *Wit*.

In the meantime what is to be done? Study?

> For since I read my *Primmer* o're,
> *Thinking's* the thing I most abhor.

The Park's too common:

> If to the *Park* I go, there's nothing there
> That's *Tempting*, *Beautiful*, and *Fair*;
> Since *Ladies* must abhor a place,
> Which by lewd Custom now is grown,
> The *Rendezvous* of half the *Mob* in Town,
> Where *Footmen*, with the Greasie *Cook-Maids* walk,
> And *Low-priz'd Cracks* in *Masks*, with *Cullies* talk;
> 'T is these have brought the *Mell* in such Disgrace.

The Inns of Court walks are just as bad. With little originality he finally decides on the playhouse, where he starts the usual round, which ends, as it frequently must have done, in *ayenbite of inwit*.

The Circus: or British Olympicks; A Satyr on the Ring in Hide-Park is an anonymous poem published in 1709, and contains a rake who went to the Park and not to the playhouse. The preface is amusing in spots and gives some account of the things expected of a gentleman in the good old days. Modern parallels are too obvious to need remark. "I wonder anybody will demean themselves so much as to converse with dirty People that walk on Foot. A Gentleman should never be seen in the Street out of a Chair or a Coach." Gentlemen must also choose their company with care:

> Sometimes to prove their Conversation bright,
> They bring with them a Gamester, Rake, or Wit;
> Then decently deride the beauteous *Ring*,
> And bawdy Jests around the Circle fling.
> With bouncing *Bell* a lusheous Chat they hold,
> Squabble with *Mall*, or Orange *Betty* scold,
> Then laugh immoderately, vain, and loud,
> To raise the Wonder of th' attentive Crowd;

> At last to finish here their Puppy-Show,
> The Bawd's dispatch'd to serve a Billet-deux.

The *Satire against Man* (Anonymous, 1710) outlines the rake in three characteristic poses, as fop, bully, and gamester. The lines sound much like a revival of Hall and Marston:

> What Gaudy thing from *China* or *Japan*,
> Is this appears? — it cannot sure be Man,
> And yet it talks, and looks, and walks like one,
> Of those we call the modish Sparks o' th' Town.[1]

This curious person wears a dozen farms upon his back, and when one sees him in the Park,

> With formal steps he traverses the Grass.[2]

He meets a friend who has just returned from the Continent:

> What News from *Paris*? Are the *Ladies* fine?
> Shall we at *Locket's* Ordinary Dine?

---

[1] Cf. *The Rake of Taste* (Dublin, n.d.):
> "See in the Streets his gilded Chariot glares
> With Lackeys loaded, drawn by Flanders Mares;
> Envy'd by Fools, he, careless, sweeps along,
> Like a bright Comet, thro' th' admiring Throng."

Also,
> "Look round the Park, to kill the tedious Hours,
> You'll find variety of walking Flow'rs."

[2] Cf. Ward, *Hudibras Redivivus*, Part VI, vol. II, Canto VI:
> "So have I seen the gaudy Fop,
> Fit only for a Lady's Lap,
> Dance cross a Street with so much Pride,
> As if, at ev'ry Bound and Stride,
> He scorn'd his dirty Grannum Earth,
> From whence old *Adam* had his Birth,
> Yet has his proud fantastick Grace
> Fall'n down at last i' th' nasty'st Place."

Also Thomas Nevile, *Imitations of Horace* (1758), *Satires*, I, 3:
> "All whimsies in this man conspir'd to meet;
> Breathless sometimes he'd flutter down the street;
> Now with the pace of one, who bears a pall,
> He stalks a staring statue in the mall."

The picture of the bully is very effective:

> Like *Tom a Bedlam* he invades the Streets,
> And Quarrels, Huffs, and Fights with all he meets.
> But if that one whose Valour seems to stoop,
> To Noise and Nonsense, take the Villain up;
> And satisfaction for the Affront demand,
> Sir *Fright-All* lowers his *Top-sail* to your hand.
> Your Pardon Sir, says he, I must request,
> By G—, I thought you'd understood a Jest.[1]

We see the young spendthrift's passage through White's to Ludgate Prison. No warning is of any use.

> Consider, Lord! 't would make his Head grow giddy,
> He says he is not yet for *Bedlam* ready:
> But the next time that you thro' *Ludgate* pass,
> Through Grates you'll see the loving *Spend-All's* Face:
> And 't will some Pleasure be the *Wretch* to view,
> *Angling for single Money in a Shoe.*

The rake has little to do with the virtuoso. He disdains him. The travelled gentleman leaves that plebian interest to his tutor. This attitude comes out very clearly in a Sheldonian poem by the Reverend Tipping Silvester, a translation, called *The Beau and Academick* (1733):

> How unpolite! as if your well-bred Squire
> Could finger Rubbish, sav'd from *Corinth's* Fire!
> No; that's the dismal Task of him that knows
> His Tutor, counts his Money as it goes;
> Lays little out in Wine, and less in Cloaths.
> I saw some nicish Statues, carv'd of late;
> My Taste runs after Things of modern Date.
> But your old Pots of Ashes, broken Jars,
> And Statues, lopt like Vet'ran from the Wars,

---

[1] Cf. John Durant Breval, *The Confederates* (1717):

> "Not far from hence, there is a noted Lane,
> Where *Darby Captains* ev'ry Night abound
> For Want of Valour, and of Pence renown'd."

> Your dirty Medals, precious, trifling Ware,
> The musty Virtuoso's poring Care,
> I hate to think of: Once indeed, by chance,
> A noseless *Caesar*, arm'd with half a Lance,
> Came in my way; his Master's chiefest Pride,
> For squalid Face, and time-devoured Side:
> Rot me! 't was such a nasty Piece of Work,
> I'd not have touch'd it with a Pitching-Fork.

The general attitude toward the virtuoso was very different from that of to-day, as one may see from Oldham's lines in "The 8th Satire of M. Boileau Imitated" (1682).[1] Man is the greatest fool in nature, he says. Which of the brutes have universities?

> No, questionless; nor did we ever read,
> Of Quacks with them, that were Licentiates made,
> By Patent to profess the pois'ning Trade:
> No Doctors in the Desk there held dispute
> About Black-pudding, while the wond'ring Rout
> Listen to hear the knotty Truth made out:
> Nor Virtuoso's teach deep mysteries
> Of Arts for pumping Air, and smothering Flies.[2]

These antiquaries and scientists often allowed their enthusiasm to carry them to ridiculous extremes, and no doubt they were frequently imposed upon. An anonymous poet gives the following advice ("To Sir Herbert Powell, Bart., Upon his going to Travel"):[3]

> Nor doat on antique Pieces, nor despise:
> Oft view, but seldom purchase Rarities.

---

[1] *Works*, p. 277.

[2] Cf. Paul Whitehead, *Manners* (1738):

> "Without their influence, Palaces are cells;
> *Crane-Court*, a magazine of Cockle-shells."

The Royal Society left Gresham College in 1705, and was established at Crane Court, Fleet Street, by Nov. 8, 1710. Cf. the *Tatler*, Nos. 34, 216, and Shadwell, *The Virtuoso* (1676).

[3] *Miscellaneous Poems by Several Hands* (publ. by David Lewis, 1726), p. 137.

Trust not their Medals lately dug from Dust,
With modern Soil, and imitated Rust.
Your *Virtuoso* travels with Design
To heap up Treasures of uncurrent Coin:
Doats on the Letters round a *Graecian* Head,
Half-raz'd; which, were they plain, he could not read.
Pays Weight for Weight, new Gold for antient Stone:
And for an *Otho's* Head would give his own.

This advice to the "wonder-gaping" boys, and satire on the vain virtuosi, is all pertinent enough. It is rather surprising to find ideas of the same sort thrown into Spenserian form by Gilbert West as early as 1739. This curious document is styled *A Canto of the Fairy Queen, written by Spenser, Never before Published,* and in the advertisement is the statement: "A Friend of mine who lives in *Ireland,* having communicated to me the following Poem, which he said was given him by a Descendant of that great Poet, whose Name it bears." Archimago persuades the Red Cross Knight to visit foreign lands, where his companions are too apt to be Sensuality, Pride, and pompous Pedantry.

There in the middest of a ruin'd Pile,
There seem'd a Theatre of Circuit vast,
Where Thousands might be seated, he e'erwhile
Discovered hath an uncouth Trophy plac'd;
Seem'd a huge Heap of Stones together cast
In nice Disorder and wild Symmetry,
Urns, broken Freezes, Statues half defac'd,
And Cornices with antique Imagery
Embost, and Pillars huge of costly Porphyry.

Then follows an account of the great days of old, great soldiers, great poets, great governors. Rome and the grandeur of her past are enthusiastically described:

But sithence she declin'd from Wisdom's Lore,
They left her to display her pompous Toys
To Virtuosi vain and wonder-gaping Boys.

And with the proud city reduced to this, must enter next the usual curses of the tourist-ridden.

> For-thy to Her a numerous Train doth long
> Of Ushers in her Court well practised,
> Who aye about the monied Stranger throng,
> Off'ring with Shews of courteous Bountihed,
> Him through the rich Apartments all to lead,
> And shew him all the Wonders of her State,
> Whose Names and Price they wisely can areed,
> And tell of Coins of old and modern Date,
> And Pictures false and true right well discriminate.

The Fairy Knight rebukes them in good eighteenth-century philippics.

Whether the poet is concerned with ruling passions or mere affectations, the antiquarian humor is sure to get plenty of attention. *Human Passions, a Satyr, to which is added an Ode to Impudence* (1726) contains an amusing passage that is apropos:

> That is a Critic most divinely taught
> In what the ancient classics wrought and taught,
> And where they wrote amiss can mend the fault.
> Now would you see this learned Rabbi fret,
> Say you believe his AC should be ET,
> He stares, foams at the mouth, and calls you fool,
> Swears you deserve the lash again at school;
> Then turns a thousand musty volumes o'er,
> Which but confirm what he had said before:
> If unconvinced you yet remain, he flies
> To Cotton's, or the Bodleian Treasuries;
> Nay, tho' a Protestant beyond dispute,
> The Vatican he'll search but he'll confute.

The poem ends with a clever retelling of the story of Haman, and altogether is vigorous and readable.

James Miller, the author of *Harlequin-Horace*, is very good at tracing out the rake's idiosyncrasies. In 1738 he published a satire called *Of Politeness*. Where does one find the truly polite? among those who affect dress, gaiety, delicate food, learning, travel, music, rakishness, atheism, lasciviousness?

> Sir *John* comes next with Bow and Fiddle grac'd,
> *Fiddling* he thinks the very Cream of Taste;
> Then fiddles on with such incessant Care,
> You'd think his Soul breath'd only at his Ear.
> Yet all the while (Sir *John* must own 'tis true)
> He's doing what he least would wish to do.
> Not less *Spadillia Shakespear* understands,
> Yet runs each Night, and stares, and claps her Hands.
> Not *Tattle* less delights to hold his Tongue,
> Yet sits four Hours to hear an Op'ra sung;
> Not less Uneasiness does *Embrio* feel
> In Whalebone Stays — yet bids the next be Steel.
> For 'tis not what they like, or what they know,
> But as the *Fashion* drives the Fop must go.

The author then goes on to describe the usual rake's progress:

> To *Eaton* sent, o'er ev'ry Form you leapt,
> No studious Eves, no toilsome Mattins kept;
> Thence *Christ's Quadrangle* took you for its own;
> Had *Alma Mater* e'er so true a Son!
> *Half seven Years* spent in Billiards, Cards, and Tippling,
> And growing ev'ry Day a lovelier Stripling;
> With *half* a College Education got,
> Half Clown, half Prig, half Pedant, and half Sot;
> Having done all that ought to be undone,
> *Finish'd* those *Studies* which were ne'er *begun;*
> To foreign Climes my Lord must take his Flight,
> Only to be more foreign still to Right;
> Like Trav'lers, who when once they've miss'd their Way,
> The more they walk the more they go astray.

With a tutor he goes to Paris and to Rome:

> 'Tis done — Once more by *Goths* poor *Rome* is spoil'd,
> High! Mountain high! the pretious Plunder's pil'd.

Coins so antique, so very rusty grown,
That neither Stamp, nor Metal could be known;
Such curious Manuscripts as ne'er were seen,
You could not guess what Language they were in;
Bustoes that each a Nose or Chin had lost,
And Paintings of much Worth, for — much they cost.

With this cargo he returns, and to show his taste builds a new house, empties his purse on its magnificence, then marries a city bride to recuperate.

My-Lady dubb'd, she needs polite must turn,
Her Needle quit, her ill-bred Bible burn;
Old Friends with her *old Cloaths* cast quite aside,
The awkward City Mien and Dress deride,
And loath the nauseous Smell of sad *Cheapside*.
Inspir'd by dear *St. James's* magick Air
Eager she drinks in all the Follies there;
At each Assembly she's the first to play,
At ev'ry Masque the last to go away;
All Ear at Opera, and at Church all Tongue,
How came she here? — How! Why, an Anthem's sung.
To *Cock* at ev'ry Auction lends her Face,
What wants she there? — What! To out-bid *Her Grace*;
Who'll vie with her in China, Pearls, or Plate?
Who like her bask in Luxury and State?

But I am quoting too freely! the end of her story keeps pace with his, and can be seen from afar:

In Gallantry at last the Fair embarks,
And as you keep your Punks, she keeps her Sparks.

The various kinds of fool are hinted at in the opening lines of *Newmarket, a Satire* (1751), and among them the man who thinks himself an antiquary:

Some 'Squires, to *Gallia's* cooks most dainty dupes,
Melt manors in ragouts, or drown in soups.
This coxcomb doats on fiddlers, till he sees
His mortgag'd mountains destitute of trees;

Convinc'd too late, that modern strains can move,
With mightier force than those of *Greece*, the grove.
In headless statues rich, and useless urns,
Marmoreo from the classic tour returns;
So poor the wretch of current coin, you'd laugh —
He cares not — if his *Caesars* be but safe.
Some tread the slippery paths of love's delights,
These deal in cards, or shake the box at *White's*.
To different pleasures different tastes incline,
Nor the same *sea* receives the rushing *swine*.

In the same year, 1751, the ingenious Richard Owen
Cambridge published a very clever poem in six books,
which he called *The Scribleriad*, parts of which (Books
II and IV), containing an account of a submarine and
of an aerial race between a Briton and a German, have
been reprinted so late as 1918 by the Chiswick Press.
This extraordinary evidence of his prophetic soul must
not detain us here, nor should I stop to sample any of
his deliciously amusing similes in the mock-heroic style.
Here is one, however. The hero (Book III) is just re-
turning to his friends, who think him dead:

Soon as the morn dispens'd her earliest ray,
Strait to the shore I urg'd my speedy way.
Dissolv'd in tears my anxious friends I found,
The untouch'd cates neglected on the ground.
As when some ass (hir'd haply to repair
The riot-wasted rake or love-sick fair)
From her fond young, the tedious morning strays,
Driv'n thro' some pop'lous city's crouded ways;
Her absence, pent in dismal cots, they mourn:
But wild with rapture, at her blest return,
They leap, they bound, their braying fills the plain,
And the glad hills repeat th' harmonious strain.

Are we to suppose that our forbears read that without
laughter? — But the virtuoso is fast disappearing. Let
us clutch at him then as he comes to the surface in

Book V of this poem. The sage here prophesies a great future ahead of the scribbler:

> Be yours the task, industrious, to recal
> The lost inscription to the ruin'd wall;
> Each Celtic character explain; or shew
> How Britons ate a thousand years ago:
> On laws of jousts and tournaments declaim,
> Or shine the rivals of the herald's fame.
> But chief the Saxon wisdom be your care,
> Preserve their idols and their fanes repair;
> The cold devotion of the moderns warm
> With Friga's fair hermaphroditic form:
> And may their deep mythology be shown
> By Seater's wheel and Thor's tremendous throne.

Gay's *Three Hours after Marriage* probably attracted more public notice than any other early satire on the antiquary. This was generally reprobated. The public can usually be depended upon to distinguish the serious investigator from the frivolous dilettante. Charles Beckingham, in *The Lyre* (1726), may taunt our friend Fossile in the old style:

> Shall *Woodward* o'er important Trifles *plume*,
> And of the Urn of *Horace* pillage *Rome?*

But somehow people respected Woodward's intention, and the satirist must go off disgruntled and find a mere ape of learning to tease.

James Bramston's "Man of Taste" (1733) travelled early and saw through all religions before he was twenty-two; he knows the town, and because of his foreign education has very superior ideas of the fine arts, especially architecture:[1]

[1] Cf. John Armstrong, "Taste; an Epistle to a Young Critic" (1753), *Poetical Works* (1807), p. 88:

> "Range from Tow'r-hill all London to the Fleet,
> Thence round the Temple t' utmost Grosvenor-street,

Sure wretched *Wren* was taught by bungling *Jones*,
To murder mortar, and disfigure stones!
Who in *Whitehall* can symmetry discern?
I reckon *Covent-Garden* Church a *Barn*.
Nor hate I less thy vile Cathedral, *Paul!*
The choir's too big, the cupola's too small:
Substantial walls and heavy roofs I like,
'T is *Vanbrug's*[1] structures that my fancy strike.

He scorns the masquerade, since the masses favor it:

Thou, Heideggre! the *English* taste has found,
And rul'st the mob of quality with sound.
In *Lent*, if Masquerades displease the town,
Call 'em *Ridotto's*, and they still go down:
Go on, Prince *Phyz!* to please the British nation,
Call thy next *Masquerade* a *Convocation*.

Food is, of course, an important matter and must be delicate,[2] Frenchified, to show one's good breeding:

Sir Loins and rumps of beef offend my eyes,
Pleas'd with frogs fricasseed, and coxcomb-pies:
Dishes I chuse though little, yet genteel,
Snails the first course, and *Peepers* crown the meal.

Take in your route both Gray's and Lincoln's Inn,
Miss not be sure my Lords and Gentlemen,
You'll hardly raise, as I with Petty guess,
Above twelve thousand men of taste, unless
In desp'rate times a Connoisseur may pass."
Petty was the author of *The Political Arithmetic* (1691).

[1] Cf. Swift, "The History of Vanbrugh's House" (1708), *Works*, I, 73:
"And so he did; for, in a while,
He built up such a monstrous pile,
That no two chairmen could be found
Able to lift it from the ground.
Still at Whitehall it stands in view,
Just in the place where first it grew."

[2] Cf. Mrs. Centlivre, Prologue to *Love's Contrivance* (1703):
"At *Locket's*, *Brown's*, and at *Pontack's* enquire,
What modish Kick-shaws the nice Beaus desire,
What fam'd Ragoust, what new invented Salate
Has best Pretensions to regale the Palate."

Fashions in food are described in *A Panegyric on a Court*, a twenty-two-page pamphlet written by the author of the *World Unmasked*, a supporter of Walpole, in 1739:

> In foreign vests the gaudy Fops may shine,
> And on dissected frogs politely dine.

Later, Pope sketched the affectations of the man of taste with a finer pencil:

> 'T is strange, the Miser should his Cares employ
> To gain those Riches he can ne'er enjoy:
> Is it less strange, the Prodigal should waste
> His wealth, to purchase what he ne'er can taste?
> Not for himself he sees, or hears, or eats;
> Artists must chuse his Pictures, Music, Meats:
> He buys for Topham, Drawings and Designs,
> For Pembroke, Statues, dirty Gods, and Coins;
> Rare monkish Manuscripts for Hearne alone,
> And Books for Mead, and Butterflies for Sloane.[1]

The translators and imitators of Horace, *Satires*, II, 7, had an excellent opportunity to gibe the follies of the connoisseur:

> Pray Sir, when you so many hours lie lazing,
> On some rare piece of Painting vainly gazing,
> Wherefore are you more innocent than I,
> When on a *Battel* I do cast mine eye,
> With *Char-coal* or *Red-Oaker* rudely done,
> And see the *Fencers* nimbly strike and shun
> Each others blows, in various postures, so
> As if the Fight were real, not a Show:
> I must be call'd a loytering Rogue, but you
> In antient Painting for a Critick go.[2]

Compare also the following extract from the *Dialogue*

---

[1] *Moral Essays*, IV, ll. 1–10.
[2] [Alexander Brome], *The Poems of Horace*, etc. (1680).

between a Man of Fashion and his Valet, by Sir Nicholas
Nemo (1752):

> A *Guido* strikes with Rapture and Surprize;
> The well-drawn Figure charms your wond'ring Eyes;
> I like the Sign that hangs at *Broughton's* Door,
> And spy fresh Beauties, unobserv'd before;
> The Bruiser there in mimic Action stands,
> And seems to threaten with his uprais'd Hands:
> Yet I'm an ignorant and idle Fool,
> And you a *Connoisseur,* who judge by rule.

In the same year appeared an adaptation of this satire
by Richard Owen Cambridge which is certainly the
most powerful of the group. He calls it "A Dialogue
between an M.P. and his Servant."

> Like gamblers, half mankind
> Persist in constant vice combin'd.
> In races, routs, the stews, and White's,
> Pass all their days and all their nights.
> Others again, like Lady Prue,
> Who gives the morning church its due,
> At noon is painted, drest, and curl'd,
> And one amongst the wicked world:
> Keeps her account exactly even,
> As thus: Prue Creditor to Heaven;
> To Sermons heard on Extra-days.
> Debtor: To masquerades and plays.
> Item: To Whitfield, half an hour:
> Per Contra, To the Colonel, Four. . . .
> From *Mandeville* you take your Morals:
> Your Faith from Controversial quarrels;
> But ever lean to those who scribble
> Their crudities against the Bible . . .
> Shall you be struck with Titian's tints,
> And may n't I stop to stare at prints?
> Dispos'd along th' extensive glass
> They catch and hold me ere I pass.

Where Slack is made to box with Broughton,
I see the very stage they fought on:
The Bruisers live, and move, and bleed,
As if they fought in very deed.
Yet I'm a loit'rer, to be sure,
You a great Judge and Connoisseur.
  Shall you prolong the midnight ball
With costly banquet at Vaux-hall,
And yet prohibit earlier suppers
At Kilbourn, Sadlers-wells, or Cuper's?
Are these less innocent in fact,
Or only made so by the Act?
  Those who contribute to the tax
On tea and chocolate and wax,
With high ragouts their blood inflame,
And nauseate what they eat for fame.
Of these the Houses take no knowledge,
But leave them fairly to the College.
Oh! ever prosper their endeavours
To aid your Dropsies, Gouts and Fevers.
  Can it be deemed a shame or sin
To pawn my livery for gin,
While Bonds and Mortgages at White's
Shall raise your fame with Arthur's Knights?
Those worthies seem to see no shame in,
Nor strive to pass a slur on Gaming;
But rather to devise each Session
Some law in honor o' th' profession.
Lest sordid hands or vulgar place
The noble myst'ry should debase;
Lest ragged scoundrels in an alehouse,
Should chalk their cheatings on the bellows;
Or boys the sacred rites profane
With orange barrows in a lane.[1]

Cambridge wrote before and more freely than Nemo.

---

[1] *The Gamester's Petition to the House of Commons against the Bill for the better preventing of excessive and deceitful gaming.* A 5-page verse pamphlet. Bibl. Bodl., G. P. 1278 (*ca.* 1711).

It is of some such person as this that Young is think-
ing, too — the fop of learning:

> Thy books are furniture. Methinks 't is hard
> That science should be purchas'd by the yard;
> And Tonson, turn'd upholsterer, send home
> The gilded leather to fit up thy room.[1]

Pope also was very familiar with this surprising product
of the grand tour:

> Scarce was I enter'd, when behold! there came
> A Thing which *Adam* had been pos'd to name;
> *Noah* had refus'd it lodging in his Ark,
> Where all the Race of *Reptiles* might embark.

This is the travelled fop:

> I blest my Stars! but still afraid to see
> All the Court fill'd with stranger Things than he,
> Run out as fast, as one that pays his Bail,
> And dreads more Actions, hurries from a Jail.[2]

But the best description of this phenomenon is in *The
Modern Fine Gentleman*, by Soame Jenyns (1746). It is
a masterpiece of satiric extravaganza:

> Just broke from school, pert, impudent, and raw,
> Expert in Latin, more expert in taw,
> His honour posts o'er Italy and France,
> Measures St. Peter's dome, and learns to dance.
> Thence, having quick thro' various countries flown,
> Glean'd all their follies, and expos'd his own,
> He back returns, a thing so strange all o'er,
> As never ages past produc'd before:
> A monster of such complicated worth,
> As no one single clime could e'er bring forth:
> Half atheist, papist, gamester, bubble, rook,
> Half fiddler, coachman, dancer, groom, and cook.

[1] "Love of Fame," *Poems*, II, 70.
[2] *The Impertinent, or a Visit to the Court* (3d ed., 1737), printed as Pope's,
but compare Donne's Satire IV. See also John Byrom, *Poems* (Manchester,
1773), p. 37, "The Dissection of a Beau's Head." Cf. *Spectator*, No. 275.

Ben Jonson's communicative traveller keeps a diary:

> I went and paid a moccinigo
> For mending my silk stockings; by the way
> I cheapened sprats, and at St. Mark's I urined.
> Faith, these are politic notes!

The traveller in Jonson's day had really a bit of romance about him; he was more than the mere ape of fashion. In that great age of discovery he was a conspicuous figure in London streets and commanded considerable homage, at any rate from the curious and gullible. And no wonder, when one remembers the history of the time! He was always ready to tell "at the Barmodies how the Fishes fly," and to discourse on many other matters not so well vouched for by later investigation. He was a popular person on his arrival home, especially if his ventures had been successful. In Rowlands's *The Letting of Humours Blood* (1600),

> Polletique *Peeter* meetes his friend a shore,
> That came from Seas but newly tother day.[1]

But this friend is penniless, and Peter finds that he has other engagements. Many a big chance was taken cheerfully, as Hall [2] tells us:

> Ventrous Fortunio his farm hath sold,
> And gads to Guiane land to fish for gold.

Scepticism over the stories brought home soon succeeded the faith of an earlier age, and embarrassing questions were sometimes asked. The gallant about whom Rowlands tells in *Humours Looking-Glass* (1608) had evidently not chosen his audience carefully:

> Come my braue gallant come, uncase, uncase,
> Nere shall obliuion your great actes deface.

---

[1] Epigram XI.   [2] *Satires*, IV, 3.

He has been there where neuer man came yet,
An vnknowne countrie, I, ile warrant it,
Whence he could Ballace a good ship in holde,
With Rubies, Saphiers, Diamonds, and golde,
Great Orient Pearles esteem'd no more then moates,
Sould by the pecke, as chandlers mesure oates;
I meruaile then, we haue no trade from thence:
O tis too farre, it will not beare expence.
T 'were far indeede, a good way from our mayne,
If charges eate vp such excessiue gaine . . .
I heard him sweare that hee (twas in his mirth)
Had been in all the corners of the earth;
Let all his wonders be together stitcht,
He threw the barre that great *Alcides* pitcht:
But he that saw the Oceans farthest strands,
You pose him if you aske where Douer stands.

The other type of traveller, the grand-tour man, was also familiar at that time. Donne, who had himself travelled widely enough to spend a small fortune, sees his vagaries as well as any stay-at-home:

But Oh, God strengthen thee, why stoop'st thou so?
Why? he hath travayld; Long? No; but to me
(Which understand none) he doth seeme to be
Perfect French, and Italian; I replyed,
So is the Poxe.[1]

The bully and the boasting soldier may be considered as one type. The uniform was popular with the ladies [2]

[1] *Satires*, I (1593).
[2] Cf. Edward Ward, *The Delights of the Bottle* (1720), p. 31:
"From whence 't 'as been observ'd, that Women
Are caught like *Maycril* by our Seamen,
Bait but your Hook with Scarlet Cloth,
And you may eas'ly take 'em both."
Cf. also Thomas Baker, *Tunbridge-Walks* (1703), II, 1: "*Squib:* Scarlet's grown so common now-a-days, one hardly knows a Colonel from a *Coster-monger*"; and *St. James's Park: a Satyr* (1708):
"Inglorious Mortals! such, that go about
To kill the Fair with Powder, without Shot,
'Cause Death lies lurking in a Scarlet Coat."

and made intimidation easier with the men; hence it was sometimes assumed by the rake, and along with it any particular rank that suited his fancy. Such a personage has so completely disappeared from society to-day that it requires an effort to realize that he was ever more than one of the many balls which literary jugglers manage to keep in the air. He has such a long and, one might al-most say, honorable record in literature that it is pain-ful to think of his day as done. Horace introduces him in the Eighteenth Epistle of the First Book, imitated in English by Thomas Nevile (1756), so that here we may see the "Captain" in an eighteenth-century *mise en scène:*

> See, big with oaths, the Captain![1] you would swear
> A batt'ry were just bursting on your ear:
> With lips all trembling, and with starting eye,
> "Hell! Furies! shall I tamely take the lye?
> My honour question'd! sooner than forsake
> This point, I'd perish piecemeal on the rack."
> Whence could arise this storm? alas! from chat
> On trash; who speaks in this house, or in that;
> Who closets whom; or whether it be known,
> If C——'s complexion be her own.

Gay's treatment of him is particularly interesting, and does not in the least suggest that the author of

[1] Cf. "The Black-Smith," *Wit and Drollery* (1661), p. 10:
> "The Roring-Boy who everyone quailes
> And swaggers, and drinks, and sweares, and railes,
> Could yet never make the Smith eat his nailes.
> *Which nobody can deny.*"

Also *The Impertinent, or a Visit to the Court* (1733):
> "Nature made ev'ry Fop to plague his Brother,
> Just as one Beauty mortifies another.
> But here's the *Captain*, that will plague you both,
> Whose Air cries Arm! whose very Look's an Oath:
> What tho' his Soul be Bullet, Body Buff?
> Damn him, he's honest, Sir, — and that's enuff."

Trivia was a milksop. The lapdog type of man does not thrust the bully into the kennel so energetically. Gay's lines picture a scene very much like that already quoted from *A Satire against Man:*

> But when the bully, with assuming pace,
> Cocks his broad hat, edged round with tarnish'd lace,
> Yield not the way; defy his strutting pride,
> And thrust him to the muddy kennel's side;
> He never turns again, nor dares oppose,
> But mutters coward curses as he goes.[1]

The same instincts show themselves in the tavern scene so cleverly described by Francis Coventry in *Pompey the Little* (1751). Here the bully tries to force his political and religious opinions on his companions. "'Zounds, old *Walpole* is behind the Curtain still, notwithstanding his Resignation," he cries, and for a time has everything his own way. A little firmness, however, on the part of a new arrival soon dissipates his credit, and he leaves to go home and domineer over his unfortunate family; for, says the author, "To say the Truth, I scarce know a Man, who is not a *Tyrant in miniature*, over the Circle of his own Dependents."

Sometimes one finds an ingenious combination of bully and man of taste, as in *The Modern Reasoners: an Epistle to a Friend:*[2]

---

[1] Cf. Goldsmith's Epilogue to *The Sister:*

> "Yon broad, bold, angry spark, I fix my eye on,
> Who seems t' have robb'd his vizor from the lion;
> Who frowns, and talks, and swears, with round parade,
> Looking, as who should say, dam' me! who's afraid?
> Strip but his vizor off, and sure I am
> You'll find his lionship a very lamb."

Also Thomas Baker, *Tunbridge-Walks* (1703), III, 1: "*Reynard:* Ha! Who art thou with that blustering Face like the North-Wind at the corner of an old Map?"

[2] 1734. P. 8.

What he asserts, if any disbelieve,
How Folks can be so dull he can't conceive.
He knows he's right, he knows his Judgment clear,
But Men are so perverse they will not hear.
Swift, *Bramston*, *Gay*, are stupid Rogues enough,
And *Pope*, thy Satires are but empty Stuff.
This to deny if any dare presume,
Fool, Coxcomb, Sot, and Puppy fill the Room.

William Whitehead [1] also has a word to say about this kind of blunderbuss critic:

But chief avoid the boist'rous roaring sparks,
The sons of fire! — you'll know them by their marks.
Fond to be heard, they always court a croud,
And, tho' 't is borrow'd nonsense, talk it loud.
One epithet supplies their constant chime,
Damn'd bad, *damn'd* good, *damn'd* low, and *damn'd* sublime!
But most in quick short repartee they shine
Of local humour; or from plays purloin
Each quaint stale scrap which every subject hits,
'Till fools almost imagine, they are wits.

The reckless extravagance which is always conspicuous in the life of a great city has this very pitiful effect, that it drives many otherwise sensible people to living beyond their means. The vain poverty that Juvenal talks about is a fact in human nature. The frog tries to imitate the ox, and bursts in the process. This general observation is equally true when we confine it to the world of rakes, as Horace and an English adapter of his works, Thomas Nevile, realized from their experience in the two great capitals.

But of all wrong-heads sure the first is he,
Who dares to mimic men of quality;
Who nightly visits with the roaring race
The stews, or pinks a drawer, like his Grace;
Intrigues with Countesses, or frantic sets
His lands paternal on two desp'rate bets.

[1] *A Charge to the Poets* (1762), II, 297.

Fool! not to know the Great with jealous eye
See the base vulgar with their betters vie.
As Philips, when the dirty deed was done,
Would preach on chastity like purest nun;
Just so his Lordship, in punctilio nice,
Yet deep, as Milo, in the sink of Vice,
Will sagely hint, "This course can never last;
'T is not for you, my friend, to have a taste:
Manners should suit with fortune, and with place;
In Nobles, folly has a sort of grace." [1]

The rake's course is remarkably uniform.[2] Women and sharpers seize him in their turns:

At White's he maddens, and at Needham's burns;
To routs, to levees, runs; or in the ring
Saunters, a staring, loit'ring, listless thing:
Last, stript of manors, lands, and country seat,
He flaunts with ragged ribband in the Fleet.

James Bramston, in *The Man of Taste* (1733), describes with considerable skill the kind that Austin Dobson calls "the connoisseur against nature." This fine gentleman always tries to do the proper thing at the proper time, that is, from the rake's point of view, and does it whether he really wants to or not.

To boon companions [3] I my time would give,
With players, pimps, and parasites I'd live.

[1] Thomas Nevile, *Imitations of Horace* (1758), *Epistles*, I, 18.
[2] Cf. William Hamilton of Bangour, *Poems* (1760), p. 227, "To a Gentleman going to Travel":
"But, ah! How vain the joys the beau can boast;
A while he shines in tavern, visit, dance,
Unrival'd, clad in rich refulgent garb
Lac'd or brocaded; till the merchant bold,
Of merc'less heart, throw him in dungeon deep
Recluse from ladies."
[3] Cf. Alexander Brome, *The Poems of Horace*, etc. (1680), *Satires*, I, 2:
"The *Players*, *Empiricks*, *Beggars*, and the noise
Of *Fidlers*, all the *roaring Dam-me* boys,

I would with *Jockeys* from *Newmarket* dine,
And to *Rough-riders* give my choicest wine.
I would caress some *Stableman* of note,
And imitate his language, and his *coat.*
My ev'nings all I would with *sharpers* spend,
And make the *Thief-catcher* my bosom friend.
In *Fig* the Prize-fighter by day delight,
And sup with *Colly Cibber* ev'ry night.
  Should I perchance be fashionably ill,
I'd send for *Misaubin*, and take his pill.
I should abhor, though in the utmost need,
Arbuthnot, Hollins, Wigan, Lee, or *Mead* . . .
  Thus would I live, with no dull *pedants* curs'd,
Sure, of all blockheads, *Scholars* are the worst.

A very similar definition we find in *The Rake of Taste:* [1]

Here, you will learn that Study's loss of Time,
And Poets need not Sense, t' embellish Rhime.
That who drinks most, is most the Man of Merit,
And the gay Atheist shews, alone, true Spirit.
Who damns the Clergy, and frequents the Stews,
Dines at *Le Bec's*, does Mother H[e]y[woo]d's use;
Swears with good grace, calls Decency a Jest,
Talks without meaning, modishly is dress'd;
Sings luscious Songs, and laughs beyond all measure,
You'll find set down among the Men of Pleasure.

This rake and his friends lead a hard life:

Now view a sett of Youths, reverse of these,
One seem to Study, one to fly their Ease;
The latter Noise, and Mid-night broils delight,
To scour the Watch, or modest Matrons fright;

"And all that sort of *cattel* do appear
  Extremely *sad*, and much concern'd to hear
  Their friend *Tigellius* is diceas'd; For he
  Did *treat* them with great *liberality*."

[1] Anonymous (173-?). By the same writer as *The Female Rake, or Modern Fine Lady* (1735?) and *Folly* (1737).

To hurl a Flask, or some poor Drawer beat,
And make, at Night, an uproar in the Street:
These boldly into publick Places rush,
And glory, when they make the Modest blush;
They swear big Oaths, look big, but really are,
If brought to Tryal, timid as a Hare,
Avoided and abhorr'd where e're they come,
They've gain'd from all, the Appellation *Drum*.

Gay mentions the rakes and their characteristic attempts to dodge "the draper's everlasting dun,"[1] but his most famous lines in this connection are those describing the night escapades of these disturbers of the peace.[2] He mentions three different kinds of revellers, the Nickers, the Scowrers, and the Mohocks. Tope, in Shadwell's *The Scowrers,* seems to have been familiar with several earlier varieties of the same species:

I knew the *Hectors,* and before them the *Muns* and the *Tityre Tu's;* they were brave Fellows indeed. In those Days a Man could not go from the *Rose Tavern* to the *Piazza* once, but he must venture his Life twice, my dear Sir *Willy.*

The Scowrers made an early appearance. Shadwell's play was acted in 1691. They may conceivably have been at first a voluntary organization to help the watch preserve order. The word is frequently used as a verb, meaning to clear the streets. At any rate, they soon degenerated into clubs of drunken rake-hells amusing themselves at the expense of harmless people. The

[1] *Trivia,* II, 283; III, 313. Also Richard Ames, *Fatal Friendship; or the Drunkard's Misery* (1693):

"But how's Estate declines, he never thinks,
Till Duns on ev'ry side attack him so,
He must for safety to *Alsatia* go;
Where, while his Money lasts he shall not want,
Companions who will with him *Drink* and *Rant.*"

[2] Cf. Milton on "Sons of Belial," *Spectator,* No. 324; and *Wentworth Papers, Lady Stafford's Letters,* March 11, 1712.

Mohocks appeared first in 1709, and were at their
strongest about 1712. Naturally they find a place in
the *Spectator* and other reviews, in letters, and in docu-
ments of various kinds. Budgell [1] doubts

whether indeed there were ever any such Society of Men.
The Terror which spread itself over the whole Nation some
Years since, on account of the *Irish*, is still fresh in most
People's Memories, tho' it afterwards appeared there was not
the least Ground for that general Consternation.

"They are all Whigs," writes Swift to Stella in March,
1712, and was nervously anxious to avoid their com-
pany; not at all like the sturdy Dr. Johnson, who later
kept four such desperadoes at bay with a club until the
watch came up. Norman Pearson reminds us of their
supposed political significance and quotes a curious
"Satirical Ballad, Plot upon Plot": [2]

> You wicked Whigs! What can you mean?
>   When will your plotting cease
> Against our most renowned Queen,
>   Her Ministry and peace . . .
> You sent your Mohocks next abroad,
>   With razors arm'd, and knives;
> Who on night-walkers make inroad,
>   And scared our maids and wives:
> They scoured the Watch, and windows broke,
>   But 't was their true intent,
> (As our wise Ministry did smoke),
>   T' o'erturn the Government.

Again and again, down through the century, one comes
upon references to them or their like. *The Libertine's
Choice, or the Mistaken Happiness of the Fool in Fashion*
(1709) shows us just about what was likely to happen
throughout the day to one of these fools of fashion.

[1] *Spectator*, No. 347.
[2] *Society Sketches in the Eighteenth Century* (1911), p. 15.

When thus well fraighted with the chearful Juice,
We'd sally forth and give ourselves a loose,
Break Brothel Windows, scour the crazy Watch,
And with fresh Mischiefs crown the Night's Debauch . . .
And rise refresh'd, as *Drury-Lane* begins.

Playhouse, brothel, gaming-house, church, all figure in
his peregrinations:

Like Quality the *Sunday* would I spend,
And duly *Covent-Garden* Church attend;
Religion would I modishly profess,
By Seven rise, and take three Hours to dress;
Then in my Chariot rattle thro' the Street,
To Church, where Hypocrites in Clusters meet,
Amongst the list'ning Crowd I'd squeeze for Room,
And with my Snush the Sweaty Air perfume.

The Rake Reformed (1718) has a similar description.
Here we have one of the nickers in action:

With giddy Brains and more uncertain Feet,
I left the *Rose* and sally'd in the Street;
O'ercharg'd with Bumpers, and discharg'd of Sense,
I shatter'd Windows with my scatter'd Pence;
Th' adjacent Signs from off their Hinges tore,
Th' acquired Spoils in fancy'd Triumph bore
While Tradesmen in the Morn their painted Loss deplore.

Garrick suggests a similar scene as late as 1774 in his
clever Prologue to *The Maid of the Oaks*. St. George's
Fields and the notorious Dog and Duck Tavern were
over the river beyond Southwark.

St. George's Fields, with taste and fashion struck,
Display Arcadia at the Dog and Duck!
And Drury Misses, — here in carmine pride,
Are there Pastoras by the fountain side!
To frouzy bow'rs they reel thro' midnight damps,
With Fawns half drunk, and Driads breaking lamps.[1]

---

[1] Cf. Pope, *Moral Essays*, Epistle II, ll. 7–8.

Rowdyism through the streets at night, attacks on the watch, in those days called "boxing the Charlies," went bravely on through the twenties of the last century, until, in 1829, Sir Robert Peel established an efficient police, and London rested quiet under the ministration of her marvellous "Bobbies."

The rakes of Gay's time differed from their early seventeenth-century progenitors in some important respects. For one thing, tobacco was a novelty in Jacobean days and got more attention. It is mentioned frequently in earlier documents, often with disapproval. James I would have none of it. In the rules of Chigwell School, founded in 1629, we notice the following directions regarding the choice of a master:

> The master must be a man of sound religion, neither Papist nor Puritan, of a grave behavior, and sober and honest conversation, no tippler, or haunter of alehouses, and no puffer of tobacco.

Sir John Harington sees the business virtues of the leaf: [1]

> When our good Irish neighbours make repaire,
> With Lenton stuffe unto Bridge-waters Faire,
> At every Boothe and Ale-house that they come,
> They call for Herring straight, they must have some.

There is another of his Epigrams which deals with a "Sicknes which grew with a Tobacco pipe" (III, 38). Donne goes along the street with his humorous friend,

> till one — which did excel
> Th' Indians in drinking his tobacco well —
> Met us.[2]

Even in the theatre smoking was popular, as a "Satyricall Epigram" by Henry Buttes shows: [3]

---

[1] *Epigrams* (1633), II, 38, "Why Paulus takes so much Tobacco."
[2] Donne, *Satires*, I.
[3] *Dyets Dry Dinner: Consisting of eight seuerall Courses* (1599), p. 106.

It chaunc'd me gazing at the Theatre,
To spie a Lock-Tabacco-Chevalier,
Clowding the loathing ayr with foggie fume
Of Dock-Tabacco, friendly foe to rume.

Tobacco was one of the necessary appurtenances of the gallant. His qualifications in general at this early time are admirably suggested in William Goddard's *Neaste of Waspes* (1615):

Wouldst thou turne Rorer boye? wouldst growe in fashon?
Learne this garbe then, shall gaine faire reputation.
Tobacco take; run in each mercers score,
Visit plaies, be seene to court thy whore,
Laughe at learning; call preachers sheepishe men
Schollers asses: stick not nowe and then
To censure deedes of Kinges. Naie gainst gods deytie
Be bold to belche forth broadest blasphemie.
Must keepe a cattalogue: must haue the name
Of euerye merchaunts wife which is of fame,
Must slaunder all; the fairest dames muste staine,
Must saie with countesses, with queenes thast laine,
Muste bee noe coward: thyselfe must proudlie carye,
Muste mouthe-it stoutelie in eache ordynarye,
Where, yf but of thy losses thy tongue walke
Muste of noe lesse a losse then hundreds talke,
Muste learne to lie; muste learne thy lie to face,
And lastelie howe to sweare *God dam thee* with a grace.
Learne these young boie, great man thou shalt be then.
Who doe these Ill thinges well must needes bee men.

The daily round of the Elizabethan gallant is sufficiently monotonous and frequently resembles the programme of his Mohock brother. Sir John Davies in his *Epigrams* [1] describes a lackadaisical variety:

First, he doth rise at ten; and at eleuen
He goes to Gyls, where he doth eate till one;
Then sees a Play till sixe; and sups at seven;
And, after supper, straight to bed is gone . . .

[1] *Works* (ed. Grosart), I, 341.

This round he runs without variety,
Saue that sometimes he comes not to the Play,
But falls into a whore-house by the way.

Similarly, Edward Guilpin in *Skialetheia* (1598):

My Lord most court-like, lyes in bed till noone,
Then, all high-stomackt riseth to his dinner,
Falls straight to Dice before his meate be downe,
Or to disgest, walks to some femall sinner.
Perhaps sore-tyrde he gets him to a play,
Comes home to supper, and then falls to dice,
There his deuotion wakes till it be day,
And so to bed, where until noone he lies.

Beside these slack gentlemen Hall's Gallio [1] seems almost a hero:

Gallio may pull me roses ere they fall,
Or in his net entrap the tennis-ball,
Or tend his spar-hawke mantling in her mew,
Or yelping beagles busy heales pursue,
Or watch a sinking corke upon the shore,
Or halter finches through a privy doore,
Or list he spend the time in sportful game,
In daily courting of his lovely dame.

The manners of the fop in Jacobean times were elaborate. The scholar, when he comes to town, is dumbfounded by their strange formalities, if we may believe George Wither: [2]

When any stoopt to me with conges trim,
All I could doe was stand and laugh at him.
Blesse me, thought I, what will this Coxcomb doo,
When I perceiu'd one reaching at my shoo.
But when I heard him speake, why I was fully
Possest, we learn'd but barbarisme in *Tully*.
There was nor street, nor lane, but had a Wench,
That at once coming could haue learn'd them French.

---

[1] *Satires*, IV, 4.
[2] *Juvenilia* (Spenser Society, 1871), I, 36.

Grecians had little there to doe (poore soules,)
Unlesse to talke with begger-men in *Pauls*. . . .
There, I saw Guls that haue no braine at all,
And certaine Monsters which they Gallants call;
New broods of Centaures that were onely proud
Of hauing their beginning from a Cloud.

These pretty gallants are continually referred to.
They fear the satirist more than the Devil; nor is that
surprising, for the cynics of that time had a quick eye
and a sharp tongue. In a "Morall Satyre," by Henry
Fitzgeffrey, printed in *Certain Elegies* (1620), there is a
curious description of this "humour":

Beshrow mee (Sirs) if I dare strout in street,
Winke at a *Window:* a *God-dam-me* greet:
Usher a *Lady:* but salute her *Gloue:*
Or *Kisse* a Maide for manners more than *Loue:*
Cringe to a *Scriuener:* be conuersing seene
In *Ludgate*, with a broken *Citizen:*
Turne oft in *Pauls:* call for a stoole o' th' *Stage:*
Or walke atended with my *Hackney* Page:
Pace *Turnball, Shorditch, Long-lane,* or *Pickt-hatch,*
Least I be taken by this heedful watch,
These pickthanke Pesants; that with *Lynceus* eye
Inspect men's Actions too Iniuriously.

And once again, in a satire by Nicholas Breton, called
*Pasquils Mad-Cappe, Thrown at the Corruptions of these
Times* (1626), there is more than a hint at the possibil-
ities of the time:

He that walkes wanton with his head aside,
And knowes not well how he may see his feete;
And she that minceth like a maiden bride,
And like a shadow slideth through the streete . . .
She that hath a round table at her breech,
And like a puppet in her 'parrell dight;
He that is all formalitie in speech,
And like a rabbet that is set vpright . . .

He that with fat goes wallowing like a beare,
And puffes and blowes, and gapes to gather ayre;
She that all day sittes curling of her hayre,
And paints her face to make the fowle seeme faire.

George Wither notices the gallant as affected lover: [1]

And then to note (as I have seen) an ass
That by her window whom he loves must pass,
With what a feigned pace the woodcock stalks,
How scurvily he fleareth as he walks:
And if he ride, how he rebounds and trots,
As if the horse were troubled with the bots.

He who would be past master in the school of gallantry
had an elaborate series of courses to get through. Some
of the grades are indicated in *Skialetheia* (1598):

I prethee *Clodius*, tell me whats the reason,
Thou doost expect I should salute thee first,
I haue sized in Cambridge, and my friends a season
Some exhibition for me there disburst:
Since that, I haue been in Goad his weekly role,
And beene acquaint with *Mounsieur Littleton*,
I haue walk'd in Poules, and duly din'd at noone,
And sometimes visited the dauncing schoole.

Their congés alone must have required considerable
practice. Marston speaks of them in Satyre I:

Yet can I beare with Curios nimble feete,
Saluting me with capers in the streete.

And Richard Braithwaite, in *A Strappado for the Diuell*,[2]
describes their antics as follows:

And haue obseru'd thee, galloping thy round,
Making low Congees, till thou kisse the ground
With lip of thy humility, and then
Putting thy foot in stirrop once againe,

---

[1] *Abuses Stript and Whipt* (1622), p. 19.
[2] Written *ca.* 1588; publ. in 1615. Ed. of Rev. J. W. Ebsworth (Boston,
Lincolnshire, 1878), p. 69.

Mounted thy barbed steed, then with thy hand,
Straking thy horses crest to make him stand.

Drunkenness is always the "without which nothing"
of the breed,[1] and in Gay's time, one might almost say,
it was the business of all classes. These Scowrers and
Mohocks of the early eighteenth century were from the
higher grades of society, often of the highest rank. But
drunken folly was by no means confined to them, and the
glories of wine were sung by bricklayers as well as by
aristocrats. Robert Tattersal takes us down among the
lower sort in his *Humours of the Club of Bacchus* (1735):

> After a civil hug or two,
> Asking each other how they do,
> How fare their dames, and all at home,
> With one consent they sit them down;
> And thus agreeing, some combine
> To call for beer, and some for wine,
> Tobacco, pipes, and also fire,
> To raise their spirits somewhat higher.[2]

[1] Cf. Persius, Satire V:
> "an rem patriam rumore sinistro
> Limen ad obscoenum frangam, dum Chrysidis udas
> Ebrius ante fores extincta cum face canto?"

Cf. Alexander Brome, *Poems of Horace, etc.* (1680), *Satires*, I, 4:
> "And being *drunk*, walks in the open day
> With a *Torch* flaming in a scandalous way."

Cf. Edward Ward, *The Delights of the Bottle* (1720), p. 28:
> "I say, when these young callow Blades,
> Hugg'd by their Mothers and their Maids,
> At Tavern meet, to sing and roar,
> The Song of black-ey'd *Susan* o'er."

Cf. *Tatler*, No. 2, "The Medicine."

[2] Cf. "Mark Noble's Frollick; who being Stopp'd by the Constable near
the Tower, was examin'd where he had been; whither he was going; and his
Name and Place where he dwelt: to which he answered, 'where the Con-
stable would have been glad to have been'; and where he was going 'he dare
not go for his Ears,' as likewise his Name, which he called Twenty Shillings,
with an Account of what followed, and how he came off" (*Roxburghe Ballads*,
VI, 510; printed before 1668).

Curiously enough, this bastard son of the Muse makes his verse advertise his trade, and celebrates his abilities as bricklayer and teacher of writing, arithmetic, geometry, dialling, and so forth, on the fly-leaf of his *Miscellany*. Moreover, "N. B. He may be heard of at any time, by sending word to Mr. William Tetersal, Writing-Master of Kingston-on-Thames, who takes in boarders at very reasonable rates."

But, to come back from bricks to the bottle, there is an occasional hint of remonstrance, which, when we find it in such a poem as Ward's *The Delights of the Bottle*,[1] gives us pause to remember that the poets were at this time almost all on the side of the revellers, and that the great mass of reasonably sober citizens probably had ideas on the subject but no spokesman.[2] The following is from Ward:

> Our Teachers too, who would dethrone
> The God of Wine and pull him down,
> And, by their Doctrine, make us think,
> 'T is almost Popery to drink.

The good old days when a man could carry his wine are often the subject of tender allusion. Aaron Hill, for example, wrote a bright account in verse of an old servant in Trinity College, Cambridge, who laments the passing of the drink-hards. It was called "On the Death of Vulcan, of sordid memory," and was published along with other poems in a collection called *Original Poems and Translations*, in 1714. It is possible, then, that con-

---

[1] J. O. Halliwell in his *Catalogue of an Unique Collection of Ancient English Broadside Ballads* mentions "The Delights of the Bottle [LXXI] or the Town-Gallants Declaration for Women and Wine, being a perfect Description of a Town-bred Gentleman, with all his Intrigues, Pleasure, Company, Humor, and Conversation."

[2] Cf. *Poems on State Affairs, 1640–1704*, IV, 268 [Rev. Charles Darby], "Bacchanalia: Or a Description of a Drunken Club" (1683); and IV, 345, "A Satyr against Brandy. Written by Jo. Hains, as he saith himself" (1683).

ditions had improved since Elizabethan times, for the
writers of that period look upon the drunkard quite
frankly as an institution, though even here one must
qualify statements. George Gascoigne as early as 1576
wrote his *Delicate Diet, for daintie mouthde Droonkards.*
Wherein the fowle abuse of common Carowsing, and Quaf-
ing with hartie draughtes, is honestlie admonished. This
does not seem to have been specially popular, however,
for George Steevens's copy was the only one known to
exist in 1789, when the pamphlet was reprinted in Wal-
dron's *Literary Museum.* Hall and Rowlands tell the
usual story of merry English habits in those days:

> Nor drunken Dennis doth, by breake of day,
> Stumble into blind taverns by the way,
> And reel me homeward at the ev'ning starre,
> Or ride more eas'ly in his neighbour's chayre.[1]

Rowlands knows his man, or he could not describe him
so well.[2]

> Bid me go sleepe? I scorne it with my heeles,
> I know myselfe as good a man as thee.
> Let goe mine Arme I say, lead him that reeles,
> I am a right good fellow; dost thou see?
> I know what longes to drinking, and I can
> Abuse myselfe as well as any man.
> I care no more for twentie hunderd pound,
> (Before the Lord) then for a very straw.
> Ile fight with any hee aboue the ground.
> Tut, tell not mee whats what; I know the law.
> Rapier and Dagger: hey, a kingly fight.
> Ile now try falles with any, by this light.[3]

---

[1] Hall, *Satires*, VI, 1.   [2] Epigram 25, *The Letting of Humours Blood* (1600).
[3] Cf. *Ibid.*, p. 78:

> "For all exploytes it doth a man inable,
> T'out leape mens heades, and caper ore the table.
> To buroe Sacke with a candle til he reeles,
> And then to trip-vp his companions heeles,
> To sing like the great Organ pipe in *Paules*,
> And censure all men vnder his controules."

This fellow was far more lucky than the one Rowlands describes in his *Quips upon Questions* (1600). The latter picks up friends on his way, who relieve him of all his valuables:

> My friend was pleasant, drinking all the day,
> With huftie-tuftie, let us all be merrie,
> Forgetting how the time did passe away:
> Such is man's folly, making himself wearie.
> But now attend, and I will tell the rest,
> How my friends follie he could scarce digest.
> When he was beaten with a Brewers washing bittle,
> Or had indeed almost quite burst his thombe,
> Or had behelde the Diuell, where he did tipple,
> Or (the old word) was drunke, marke what did come.
>   Thus it fell out, as he himselfe did say,
>   He to the Curtain went, to see a Play.
> His friends went with him, and as wise as hee,
> Yet wiser as it chaunst, for he went reeling;
> A tottering world it was, God wott, to see,
> My friend disguisde thus without sense or feeling.
>   Here a fell downe, and up againe, God wott,
>   Backward and forward staggring like a sott.
> A soberer man than he, or girle or boy,
> I know not who — for he himselfe not knowes —
> Begins to looke into this goodly toy,
> And, to teach him wit, this deed at pleasure shows:
>   Into his pockets diues, and being alone,
>   Purse, hat, cloake, from my drunken friend was gone.

Most of the rogues and the failures in early eighteenth-century society, as now, may be tagged under the captions, wine, women, and the gaming-table. "Drabs, dice, and drinke are all his onely ioyes." [1] The cataloguing is rather a melancholy business, especially as the superiority of our own age is not always evident. We have already noticed the doings of the drunken

[1] Taylor, "The Water Cormorant His Complaint," *Works* (ed. of 1630), p. 6.

rakes. Their revels too often ended in a brothel, an institution which rivalled the playhouse and the bear-gardens in popularity. References to social vice are numerous; indeed they are multiplied *ad nauseam*. Altogether too many writers, like the poets to whom Robert Lloyd refers, seem to

> have sought the filthy stews
> To find a dirty slip-shod Muse.
> Their groping genius, while it rakes
> The bogs, the common-sew'rs, and jakes,
> Ordure and filth in rhyme exposes,
> Disgustful to our eyes and noses.[1]

Gay gives a good, clean-cut description of the whore and her methods in his last book, and localizes the tribe for the most part around Drury Lane. The Drury misses, however, as in Fielding, become *Pastoras* over in the larger liberties of St. George's Fields, or perhaps *Penelopes* in Tunbridge Wells.[2] They are ubiquitous, apparently. The Malt-Worms find them in Shoe-lane:

> *Shoe-lane*, howe'er disgrac'd by *Nooks* and *Alleys*,
> Wherein well-natur'd *Matrons* harbour *Salleys*.[3]

The roisterers of Cuper's Gardens will find them there, as Welsted tells us in his *Epistle of False Fame* (1732):

> For Cuper's Bowers, she hires the willing scull . . .
> While, here, a 'prentice; there, a captain bites.

Not long before the Restoration, Lawrence Price wrote a ballad called "The Merry Man's Resolution," [4] which gives a formidable list of the questionable resorts of London. In consideration for his new sweetheart the

---

[1] *Poems* (1762), p. 24.
[2] Thomas Baker, *Tunbridge-Walks* (1703).
[3] *A Vade Mecum for Malt-Worms*, p. 43.
[4] Collier, *A Book of Roxburghe Ballads* (1847), p. 317.

Merry Man says a long farewell to St. Giles, Turnbul
Street, the Grey-hound, the Bell, Long-Acre near the
Mews, Drury Lane, Sodom and all her painted drabs,
Bloomsbury, Crosse-lane, Common-garden, Westmin-
ster, Strand, Bank-side, Blackmans-street, Kent-street,
Horsly-down, Redriff town, Wapping, Black-wall, Rat-
clife High-way, Rosemary-lane, Shore-ditch, More-
fields, White-crosse-street, Golden-lane, every street
twixt that and Clarken-well, Cow-crosse, Smith-field,
Exchange, Cheap-side, and all the country girls.

In *The Folly of Love* [1] Richard Ames refers to Posture
Mall, "the Lady *Abbess* of the *Fleetstreet Nuns*," and
notes Gray's Inn Walks, Lincoln's Inn Walks, the Park,
and the Playhouse, as rendezvous.

In "The Canting Bawd: or Covetous Whore," a bal-
lad of the early seventeenth century, Samuel Rowlands
describes the luxuries of the prostitute, how she gives
keepsakes to her lovers.

> Thus fit I Fools in Humour still,
>   That come to me for Game,
> I punish them for Venery,
>   Leaving their Purses lame.
> In Newgate some take Lodging up,
>   Till they to Tyburn ride;
> And others walk to Woodstreet with
>   A Serjeant by their Side:
> Some go to Houndsditch with their Cloaths
>   To pawn for Money lending,
> And some I send to Surgeons Shops,
>   Because they lack some Mending:
> Others pass ragged up and down,
>   All tatter'd, rent, and torn;
> But being in that scurvy Case,
>   Their Companies I scorn. [2]

[1] (Second ed., 1693), pp. 12–13.
[2] *Doctor Merryman: or Nothing but Mirth* (1616), p. 19.

The parks and amusement gardens, along with the theatres, were the favorite stalking grounds.[1] John Dennis even sends her to church.

> But hark the *Bell*, the Parsons Trumpet,
> Sounds a Charge to a Ghostly Combat;
> Warns Sporting Female to arise
> T' a sadder Mornings Exercise.[2]

Her "baby" face, as people might call it in those days, appeared frequently among Duke Humphrey's guests at the Abbey.

> Next day came tripping in a light-heel'd Girl,
> Adorn'd with Ribbons, Paints, and Bastard-Pearl.
> We need not speak of either Feet or Legs,
> Her face seem'd 'nointed with the yolk of Eggs.
> Slily into the company she slid,
> A colour having got for what she did.
> Some blam'd her, saying, *Sinners us'd to Paint:*
> Others reply, *But she's a seeming Saint.*
> Nor was there want of Pocket-Pickers there,
> Nor Lifters of the careful Tradesmans Ware.[3]

In Elizabethan days the brothels were more numerous on the Bankside.

> Who, cumming from the Curtaine sneaketh in,
> To some odd garden noted house of sinne.[4]

And in both times vice brought its usual rewards. The barbers professed skill in medicine, though Hall makes fun of them:

> O Esculape! how rife is physick made,
> When each brasse-bason can professe the trade

[1] See John Cleland, *The Singular Life and Adventures of Fanny Hill.* The 3d edition of this in the Bodleian is bound with other chap-books into one volume of luscious biographies of whores and hermaphrodites.
[2] "A Days Ramble in Covent-Garden," *Poems in Burlesque* (1692).
[3] Samuel Speed, "The Legend of Duke Humphrey," *Fragmenta Carceris* (1675).
[4] Guilpin, *Skialetheia* (1598).

> Of ridding pocky wretches from their paine,
> And do the beastly cure for ten groats gaine? [1]

On occasion the law took notice of them, and the poorer sort might be flogged through the streets by the beadle, or sent to Bridewell to work out a penance at beating hemp. Fielding comments on the effectiveness of these methods in *Tom Thumb*.[2]

> So, when some wench to Tothill Bridewell's sent
> With beating hemp and flogging she's content;
> She hopes in time to ease her present pain,[3]
> At length is free, and walks the streets again.

The Reverend John Trusler, in his edition of the *Works* of Hogarth moralized, brings a much graver charge than inefficiency against the law, and in some lines labelled "A Woman Swearing her Child to a Grave Citizen" shows Justice with the scales sadly awry.[4]

> Here Justice triumphs in his elbow chair,
> And makes his market of the trading fair;
> His office-shelves with parish laws are grac'd,
> But spelling-books and guides between 'em plac'd.
> Here pregnant madam screens the real sire,
> And falsely swears her bastard child for hire
> Upon a rich old letcher; who denies
> The fact, and vows the naughty Hussif lies;
> His wife enrag'd, exclaims against her spouse,
> And swears she'll be reveng'd upon his brows;
> The jade, the justice, and churchward'ns agree,
> And force him to provide security.[5]

---

[1] *Satires*, IV, 1.
[2] *Works* (ed. G. H. Maynadier, New York, 1905), XII, 73.
[3] Cf. Ward, *The London Spy* (1704–06), Part VI.
[4] Quoted also in Nichols, *Biog. Anec. of Hogarth* (3d ed., 1785), p. 432. Written before 1735.
[5] The child was the last thing to worry about, though even the street poets could write beautiful lines occasionally about children. One bit brings Greene or Blake to mind:
> "Come, little babe, come, silly soul!
> Thy father's shame and mother's grief."
>   *Roxburghe Ballads*, II, 525.

Prostitution as a trade found initiates among the men as well as the women. With the one-sided modesty of modern times, one hates to come upon this sort of thing in literature and still more to read any comment on it. We remember with unwillingness its appearance in *Tom Jones* (1749), and the gorge rises at the thought of such horrors as actually found their way into print in poems like Breval's *MacDermot* (1717).[1]

Sometimes even actors found means to rival gallants in display. Thomas Randolph calls our attention to this portent of the town in his poem *In Lesbiam, et Histrionem* (1638):

> Keepe his Race-nags, and in Hide-parke be seen
> Briske as the best (as if the stage had been
> Growne the Court's Rivall) can to *Brackly* goe,
> To *Lincolne* Race, and to *New-Market* too;
> At each of these his hundred pounds has vie'd
> On *Peggabrigs*, or *Shotten-herrings* side;
> And looses without swearing. . . . *Histrio* may
> At *Maw*, or *Gleeke*, or at *Primero* play.
> Still Madam goes to stake, *Histrio* knows
> Her worth, and therefore dices too; and goes
> As deepe, the Caster, as the only Sonne
> Of a dead Alderman, come to twenty one
> A whole weeke since.

Times have changed and manners with them somewhat. Manners were changing then very rapidly, and, although the literary traditions of the Restoration were, like their royal patron, an unconscionable time a-dying, they were dying, and largely owing to the influence of Steele and Addison,[2] nobler standards of life and literature were about to emerge. Virtue might soon be fash-

---

[1] Cf. Juvenal, *Satires*, VI.
[2] Pope's *Horace: Epistles*, II, 1 (1737):
> "He, from the taste obscene reclaims our youth,
> And sets the Passions on the side of Truth."

ionable. The fact that this change could take place in literature with such comparative rapidity shows, I think, too, that obscenity was to a large extent a convention not based on any widespread corruption in morals. One has no business, certainly, to wander about in despair, ready to throw away the candle.

Gambling seems to have been a universal passion, from the boys who, according to Gay, in orange time "trust their copper fortunes to the dice," to Francis Charteris, who wins three thousand pounds from the Duchess of Queensberry by using a mirror which shows her cards. Venice alone could compete with London as a gambling centre. The State Lottery, established in 1709, was tremendously popular and was not abolished until 1828, at a loss to government of a quarter of a million pounds. All kinds of insurance schemes were rife, most of them unsound, and not a few entirely bogus. Wagering on the lives of eminent men was a favorite sport. "Running lives" they called it. The South Sea disaster of 1720 was merely the notorious effervescence of reacting elements long prepared in the mentality of the people. Rich and poor, men and women, were all touched, and fed the flame in one way or another. Of the gaming-houses White's was the best known among the upper classes. This was the place of which Swift says, that

The late Earl of Oxford, in the time of his Ministry, never pass'd by White's Chocolate-House (the common rendezvous of infamous Sharpers and noble Cullies) without bestowing a curse upon that famous Academy, as the bane of half the English Nobility.[1]

References to it are numerous. Paul Whitehead in his satire called *Manners* (1739) gives it the right name:

---

[1] See footnote on p. 30 of the *Poems* of Paul Whitehead (1777).

What Courts are sacred, when I tell your Grace,
Manners alone must sanctify the place?
Hence only each its proper name receives;
Haywood's a brothel; *White's* a den of thieves.

The "Man of Taste" [1] is quite convinced of its eminent
respectability.

Had I whole Counties, I to *White's* would go,
And set lands, woods, and rivers, at a throw.[2]

But for social as well as physical reasons all the world
could not go to White's, so we find one rake at least who
is satisfied with other resorts. This is the one who ap-
pears in *The Rake Reformed* (1718), and who comes to
a very virtuous end in the country after being scared
into repentance by the death of a friend. He recounts
his old experiences, another case of "fond memory":

---

[1] Bramston (1733).

[2] Cf. Paul Whitehead, *Honour, A Satire* (1747):

"'Load, load the Pallet, Boy!' hark! Hogarth cries,
'Fast as I paint, fresh swarms of Fools arise!' . . .
Vice levels all, however high or low;
And all the diff'rence but consists in show.
Who asks an alms, or supplicates a Place,
Alike is beggar, tho' in rags or lace:
Alike his Country's scandal and its curse;
Who vends a Vote, or who purloins a purse;
Thy Gamblers, *Bridewell*, and *St. James's* Bites,
The Rooks at *Mordington's*, and Sharks at *White's*."

Cf. Addison, Prologue to *The Tender Husband* (1705):

"Our modern wits are forced to pick and cull,
And here and there by chance glean up a fool:
Long ere they find the necessary spark,
They search the Town, and beat about the Park;
To all his most frequented haunts resort,
Oft dog him to the Ring, and off to Court,
As love of pleasure or of place invites;
And sometimes catch him taking snuff at *White's*."

Cf. Thos. Nevile, *The 17th Epistle of the 1st Book of Horace Imitated* (1756):

"Say, art thou one, who shuns the tinsel'd sights
Of liv'ry'd lords, or frantic fools at *White's*?"

Cf. Gay, *Trivia*, II, 335.

To *Bradbury's* at five I did repair,
Whose chief Frequenters Cheats and Bubbles are;
Where butter'd 'Squires, mercenary grown,
Too late repent the luckless Mains they've thrown.

A Satire against Man, a poem written in answer to a
similar diatribe against women,[1] after some clever lines
describing the beau, the travelled fop, and the bully,
contains the following rather suggestive hint about the
gambling-house:

Would you my *Muse* of *Hell* the Picture view,
And what distracted Looks the *Damned* shew;
Go to some Gaming-Ordinary where,
Shamwell and *Cheatly* and such Rooks repair,
To sharp the City Prigg or Country-*Heir*.[2]

The references to this vice are so numerous that it is
hard to choose the most interesting among them for
mention.[3] Young has an excellent description of a gam-
bling hell in his "Love of Fame, the Universal Passion."[4]
A similar resort makes its appearance also in Breval's
"MacDermot: or the Irish Fortune-Hunter" (1717).
Later on in the century, Butler Swift, in his poem called
"Tyburn to the Marine Society" (1759), rails at the
vogue of dice:

---

[1] *Love given over: or a Satyr against the pride, lust, inconstancy &c of
Woman.* With *Sylvia's Revenge, or a Satyr against Man*, Henry Hills (1709).
[2] Cf. Edward Moore, *The Gamester, A Tragedy* (1753), Prologue:
"Our Quixote Bard sets forth a Monster-taming,
Arm'd at all Points, to fight that Hydra — Gaming."
[3] Turner, *Horace's Epistles*, I, 1 (1738):
"Some rob at *Hounslow*, others rob at *White's*."
Cf. Pope, *The Impertinent, or A Visit to the Court* (1733).
"And now the *British* Youth, engaged no more
At *Fig's* or *White's*, with *Felons*, or a *Whore*,
Pay their last Duty to the *Court*, and come
All fresh and fragrant, to the *Drawing-Room*."
[4] *Poems* (ed. of 1852), II, 129.

'T is only Arthur's Knights I mean —
Not those of old renown'd in fable,
Nor of the *round*, but *gaming* table;
Who, every night, the waiters say,
Break every law they make by day;
Plunge deep our youth in all the vice
Attendant upon drink and dice,
And, mixing in nocturnal battles,
Devour each other's goods and chattels;
While from the mouth of magic box,
With curses dire and dreadful knocks,
They fling whole tenements away,
Fling time, health, fame — yet call it play!

Some lines from a poem called "Taylor's Motto" give
a curious list of the games popular in the seventeenth
century.[1]

The Prodigalls estate, like to a flux,
The Mercer, Draper, and the Silk-man sucks:
The Taylor, Millainer, Dogs, Drabs and Dice,
Trey-trip or Passage, or the most at Thrice;
At Irish, Tick-tacke, Doublets, Draughts or Chesse,
He flings his money free with carelessenesse:
At Nouum, Mumchance, mischance (chuse ye which)
At One and thirty, or at Poore and rich,
Ruffe, flam, Trump, noddy, whisk, hole, Sant, New-cut,
Unto the keeping of foure Knaues he'l put
His whole estate, at Loadum, or at Gleeke,
At Tickle-me quickly, he's a merry Greeke,
At Primefisto, Post and payre, Primero,
Maw, Whip-her-ginny, he's a lib'rall Hero;
At My-sow-pigg'd: and (Reader neuer doubt ye,
He's skill'd in all games, except) Looke about ye.
Bowles, shoue-groate, tennis, no game comes amiss,
His purse a nurse for anybody is.

Arthur's is also mentioned by Jenner in the second of his
Town Eclogues (1772).

[1] *John Taylor's Works* (1630), p. 54.

> It matters little where their sports begin,
> Whether at *Arthur's*, or the *Bowl and Pin*;
> Whether they tread the gay *Pantheon's* round,
> Or play at skittles at St. *Giles's* pound.

In his third Eclogue the same writer tells of the education of the fine lady: how

> Many a maiden flutters through her prime,
> Nor thinks on love, because she has not time.

Now she marries unhappily:

> Scarce one short week had bless'd him with her charms,
> Before *Newmarket* call'd him from her arms.

They quarrel, and the bored husband

> vents his discontent in many a curse,
> And flies to *Arthur's* to recruit his purse.

Arthur Murphy refers to this famous house in his satire, *Seventeen Hundred and Ninety-One*. He compares the good old days of King Alfred with modern times:

> To clubs at Bootle's, Arthur's, none could roam;
> Each hospitable baron liv'd at home.

Nor were the men the only sinners in this regard. The ladies followed suit. Richard Seymour's book of rules is advertised as written for the use of young princesses. It is called *The Compleat Gamester*, and reached a fifth edition by 1734. Half-a-crown was little enough to pay for full instructions on ombre, quadrille, quintille, picquet, basset, faro, chess, whist, all-fours, cribbage, put, lue, brag, and billiards. Pope's description of the game of cards in *The Rape of the Lock* (1712) is the best in the language.[1] "The Basset Table," printed by Dodsley as the Thursday poem in the *Six Town Eclogues*, by the Rt. Hon. L. M. W. M., is also interesting, but more satirical.

[1] Pope, *Works* (ed. Warton), II, 326.

A Lover lost, is but a common care:
And prudent Nymphs against the change prepare:
The Knave of Clubs thrice lost! Oh! who could guess
This fatal Stroke, this unforeseen Distress?

The allurements of basset are described with enthusiasm:

At the *Groom-Porter's* batter'd Bullies play,
Some Dukes at *Mary-Bone* bowl Time away.
But who the Bowl, or ratt'ling Dice compares
To *Basset's* heavenly Joys, and pleasing Cares?

And a little later the mood grows lyric:

But of what marble must that breast be form'd,
To gaze on *Basset*,[1] and remain unwarm'd?
When *Kings, Queens, Knaves*, are set in decent rank;
Expos'd in glorious heaps the tempting Bank,
Guineas, Half-Guineas, all the shining train;
The Winner's pleasure, and the Loser's pain:
In bright confusion open *Rouleaus* lie,
They strike the Soul, and glitter in the eye.
Fir'd by the sight, all Reason I disdain;
My Passions rise, and will not bear the rein.

The authorship of this poem, "The Basset Table," was questioned from the first. All six *Town Eclogues* were piratically published by Curll in 1716. Three *Court Poems*, that is, "The Basset Table," "The Drawing-Room," and "The Toilet," were "published faithfully, as they were found in a pocket book taken up in Westminster Hall, the last day of Lord Winton's Tryal," by J. Roberts and misdated MDCCVI. These were read in St. James's Coffee House and attributed by general voice to be productions of a Lady of Quality. At Button's, all insisted that Mr. Gay was the man. The foreman compared them with his *Pastorals* and found the style and turn of thought to be evidently the

---

[1] Cf. Mrs. Centlivre, *The Basset Table* (1706), Act IV.

same. The publisher called in an umpire who lived not far from Chelsea, — a gentleman of distinguished merit, — and he said, "Sir, depend upon it, these lines could come from no other hand than the judicious translator of Homer." Warton says that "The Basset Table" and "Roxana" are by Pope, and the other four by Lady Mary Wortley-Montagu.

In the *Mundus Muliebris, or the Ladies Dressing Room Unlocked, and her Toilette Spread,*[1] we get an early example of the sort of thing that Gay and Pope both delighted in.

> To play at ombre, or basset,
> She a rich purvil purse must get,
> With guineas fill'd, on cards to lay,
> With which she fancies most to play:
> Nor is she troubled at ill fortune,
> For should the bank be so importune,
> To rob her of her glittering store,
> The amorous fop will furnish more.
> Pensive and mute, behind her shoulder
> He stands, till by her loss grown bolder,
> Into her lap rouleau[2] conveys,
> The softest thing a lover says:
> She grasps it in her greedy hands,
> Then best his passion understands;
> When tedious languishing has fail'd,
> Rouleau has constantly prevail'd.

Though willing to throw away money at cards, the ladies were no more particular, apparently, about paying their bills than the gentlemen, and when fortune frowned, the tradesmen suffered.

> Tell how *Rufina* dines: She dines in State,
> The Side-Board loaded with the massy Plate,
> And Fifty unpaid Tradesmen at her Gate.

[1] (Quarto, 1690.) Reprinted in Fairholt, *Satirical Songs and Poems on Costume*, written by Sir John Evelyn and his daughter Mary.
[2] Forty-nine guineas.

Each Quadrille Lady trembles far and near,
From *Hyde-Park Corner* down to *Temple-Bar*.[1]

Pope, when he deals with the foibles of the ladies, is usually facetious. That was still the correct tone to assume.[2] Many references to this gambling vice were not at all trifling and remind us sometimes of the passionate climax portrayed in Hogarth's engraving. Debts of honor must be paid.

> This itch for play has likewise fatal been,
> And more than Cupid draws the Ladies in,
> A thousand guineas for Basset prevails,
> A bait when cash runs low, that seldom fails;
> And when the fair one can't the debt defray
> In sterling coin, does sterling beauty pay.

The female rake was the ever-present complement of the beau, though her opinion of his merits might not always be high. Hillaria, in *Tunbridge-Walks*, expresses the modish attitude. A friend is surprised at her familiarity with these beaux when she always speaks so disparagingly of them. Hillaria's answer is cool and cynical: "They give one Snuff, lose their money at cards, and pay Coach-hire."

The most powerful satire on women in the period under consideration was done by Edward Young in "Love of Fame, The Universal Passion."[3]

[1] "The Satirist" (Horace, *Satires*, I, 4), (Dublin, 1733).
[2] Cf. *Miscellaneous Poems by Several Hands* (published by David Lewis, 1726): "Melissa," p. 211.

> "She ne'er is found in Crowds unclean
> Entred Mysteries obscene,
> Nor seeks in Mask and antick Dress
> Unconfin'd Lasciviousness.
> Nor pale, and angry, gaming high
> Rattles the unlucky Die."

Cf. Gay, "Epistle to Pulteney" (ed. Underhill), I, 192, ll. 73 ff. Also, *Female Taste, a Satire*, by a Barrister of the Middle Temple (1755).
[3] *Poems* (2 vols., 1852), II, 96, 82, 122, 103.

> Britannia's daughters . . .
> As unreserv'd, and beauteous, as the sun,
> Through every sign of vanity they run;
> Assemblies, parks, coarse feasts in city-halls,
> Lectures, and trials, plays, committees, balls,
> Wells, bedlams, executions, Smithfield scenes,
> And fortune-tellers' caves, and lions' dens,
> Taverns, exchanges, bridewells, drawing-rooms,
> Installments, pillories, coronations, tombs,
> Tumblers, and funerals, puppet-shows, reviews,
> Sales, races, rabbits, (and still stranger!) pews.

He hits the petty fads of the fashionable in many an apt phrase.

> Sometimes, thro' pride, the sexes change their airs;
> My lord has vapours, and my lady swears.

The sport and the blue-stocking, the scientific female, the religious variety, the languid lady, and the masculine type, "a swearing lady, not a grenadier," the she-atheist, are sharply outlined. All are malicious in their gossip.

> "Daphnis," says Clio, "has a charming eye:
> What pity 't is her shoulder is awry!" . . .
> Owns her in person, wit, fame, virtue, bright:
> But how comes this to pass? — She died last night.

He prefers the country girl, and his lines about her prelude the phrasing so familiar in Gray's *Elegy:*

> In distant wilds, by human eyes unseen,
> She rears her flowers, and spreads her velvet green:
> Pure gurgling rills the lonely desart trace,
> And waste their music on the savage race.

Charles Jenner, too, later in the century,[1] thinks that

> Love flies from cities; tell me, ye who know,
> Is genuine love the produce of *Soho?*

---

[1] *Town Eclogues* (1772), III, 16.

Can *Almack's* boast such tender, constant swains
As weep in tufted groves, or sigh on plains?

His description of the fine lady's activities is interesting:

In one continued hurry roll'd her days,
At routs, assemblies, auctions, op'ras, plays,
Subscription balls, and visits without end,
And poor *Cornelys* own'd no better friend.
From loo she rises with the rising sun,
And *Christie* sees her aking head at one.[1]

The most common of complaints against the women
is extravagance. This is reflected in street ballads as
well as in the more dignified satire. One very good
example of these is called "The Invincible Pride of
Women; or the London Tradesman's Lamentation for
the Prodigality of his Wife, which doth daily pillage
his Purse." [2]

I have a Wife, the more's my care, who like a gaudy peacock
goes,
In top-knots, patches, powder'd hair, besides she is the worst
of shrows;
This fills my heart with grief and care
To think I must this burthen bear.
It is her forecast to contrive to rise about the hour of Noon,
And if she's trimm'd and rigg'd by five, why this I count is
very soon;

[1] Cf. Swift, *Poems* (ed. Bohn), I, 172, "The Journal of a Modern Lady"
(1728), and "The Auction, a Town Eclogue," by the Hon. Mr. —— (2d
ed., 1778). Cf. *Spectator*, No. 323. Cf. Pope, *Moral Essays*, II, "Of the
Characters of Women," ll. 53-56:

"Narcissa's nature, tolerably mild,
To make a wash, would hardly stew a child;
Has ev'n been prov'd to grant a Lover's pray'r,
And paid a Tradesman once to make him stare."

Cf. also *A Satyr against Marriage* (1700). Series of tales of misfortune.
*The Woman of Taste, in a 2nd Epistle from Clelia in the Town to Sappho in
the Country* (1733).
Matrimony, pro and con: or, the Resolve (1745).
[2] *Roxburghe Ballads*, VII, 20 (written *ca.* 1686-88).

> Then goes she to a Ball or Play,
> To pass the pleasant night away.

Frequently she returns with the bully Spark, proud in her exalted Topknot, in debt everywhere, but with long tongue invincible.

All varieties make their bow in verse. The old story of country girl in town, seduction, folly, and the rest, was as popular then as it is now. Futility was served with different sauces then — verse instead of prose for one thing, brothels and Irishmen and Indian Queens instead of cabarets and the throng of ineffective and inefficient, but unfortunately wealthy, youth. *A Genuine Epistle written sometime since to the late famous Mother Lodge* is a good example of the eighteenth-century way of doing it. This is complete autobiography — servant, 'prentice, whore, kept mistress, thief and deserter, dupe and derelict, emigrant and nabobess, final failure.

> To Wapping I retir'd, and ply'd
> Behind a Bar on Thames's side,
> And with my small Remains essay'd
> To drive a scanty, pedling trade,
> Rum, Brandy, Punch, a Wapping Queen,
> Measuring out to sailors keen.
>   Here still; but fat with ease, and ale,
> Known by Black Sarah of the Whale,
> Belov'd I live, drink more than eat,
> Renown'd thro' all the British fleet,
> Jaundice and dropsy all I fear,
> Just ent'ring on my fiftieth year.

With rakes of both sexes so numerous and speculation highly popular, the stock-jobbers and brokers naturally did a roaring business. One met them at Jonathan's in Exchange Alley.[1] The irate Yeoman of Kent in *Tun-*

---

[1] Cf. *Discontent, the Universal Misery* (1734):
     "See how that crowd of Knaves and Fools resort,
     Where Fortune keeps her variable Court!
     Change-Ally."

bridge-Walks declares: "Before I'de have a Wit inherit
my Estate, I'de Stockjobb it away at *Jonathans*."[1]
Woe to the young men who fell into the hands of these
very grasping gentlemen! Soame Jenyns's "Modern
Fine Gentleman" (1746), for instance, passes through
all the stages of travelled rake, independent Member of
Parliament,

> Though shallow, muddy; brisk, though mighty dull;
> Fierce without strength; o'erflowing, though not full,

venal courtier, aristocratic sharper, and finally, in the
utmost degradation,

> Hunts out young heirs, who have their fortunes spent,
> And lends them ready cash at cent per cent.

Gay knows well enough how very successful, in one
sense of the word, the "tricking gamester" or the "grip-
ing broker" may be. He sees him pass by frequently in
his gorgeous equipage,

> With Loves and Graces on his chariot's sides.

He is quick to notice him, too, when less pleasantly en-
gaged, slinking about the back alleys, "bent on some
mortgage."[2]

Thomas Nevile, in *The First Satire of the First Book of
Horace Imitated* (1755), provides us with a very satis-
factory sketch of this type:

> Weak as this doctrine seems to you and me,
> Yet not one flaw can Lombard's Sages see:
> Secure each pilfers on without controul,
> Lucre's soft nectar trickling on his soul.
> See! thro' the street, a rable at his heels,
> Shov'd, hooted, pointed at, Patritio steals:

---

[1] Thomas Baker, *Tunbridge-Walks* (1703), p. 23.
[2] Cf. Thomas Nevile, *Imitations of Horace* (1755), *Satires*, Book I:

> "From Lombard's Sages hear a soothing song:
> 'The man, who gets, is never in the wrong.'"

In vain, scoffs, curses, jests provoke his spleen;
He shrugs, and finds a comforter within.
Chin-deep in water, and stark mad with thirst,
Poor Tantalus for want of drink is curst —
You smile — ah Sir! change but a word or two,
Methinks the story might be told of You.
You, struck with awe, half stupid with amaze,
On consecrated gold devoutly gaze;
Like the fond zealot, who his All forsook
To doat on Whitfield with ecstatic look,
Or as some shelf grave connoisseurs behold,
Where men and monkeys grin in Indian mold.[1]

But the broker's big *coup* in Gay's time was the Bubble. This was the grand "fruit-basket exchange" for the wealth of the nation, and society was alternately shocked and amused by the appearance of what Ward chose to call "Southeans."

Among this merry motly Race,
The Bubble Upstarts claim a place,
Grown Rich by fictious Stocks and Funds,
As Asses thrive on barren Grounds.[2]

Swift writes a poem on "The South-Sea Project:"[3]

Subscribers here by thousands float,
And jostle one another down;
Each paddling in his leaky boat,
And here they fish for gold, and drown.

Thomas D'Urfey[4] wrote a musical farce which he called *The Two Queens of Brentford*, a sequel to Buckingham's *Rehearsal*. In this Bayes reads a comical Prologue to the two friends, which shows one disastrous consequence of the common madness.

[1] Cf. John Durant Breval, *Mac-Dermot: or the Irish Fortune-Hunter* (1717), p. 24. Description of Monmouth Street and the pawnbrokers.
[2] *The Delights of the Bottle* (1720).
[3] *Poems*, I, 120.
[4] *New Operas, with Comical Stories and Poems on Several Occasions* (1721).

Yet 't is a Farce, and by Stock-jobbers plaid,
Shopkeepers mourn, no Debts are to be paid;
Garters and Lords of Rank won't pay their Dues;
They can't be trusted for a Pair of Shoes;
If Dun crys out — my Lord, I shall be broke;
No help, crys he, my Money's all i' th' stock;
I 've scarce enough at this next Bubble-meeting
To pay my Friends, the Brokers, for their Sweating.

In the *Pills to Purge Melancholy* [1] there is a ballad on
"The South Sea Whim," beginning

> To you, fair Ladies, now ashore,
> We *South-Sea Cullies* write.

Joseph Mitchell addressed a poem on the subject "To
the Right Hon. James Craggs, Esq." in the hope of get-
ting some "inside" information:

> I too wou'd fain my Fortune try,
> Since *you've a Finger in the Pye.*
> 'T is plain, there is some *Charm*, or other,
> Else *wise* Folks wou'd not make a Pother
> About *Subscriptions*, great and small,
> And, in the crowded *Ally* bawl,
> Like *Brokers* with no Brains at all.

Other stocks, like York-buildings, Chelsea-water, River
Douglas, Indian, African, seem to have been popular
also, and he hesitates:

> Sometimes, I like the *South-Sea* best;
> Sometimes, believe it all a Jest.
> To-day, *Welsh-Copper's* my Delight;
> To-morrow, it appears a Bite. [2]

Mitchell seems to have been a sufficiently cautious in-
dividual. He warns his friends against the insidious
dangers of gambling:

[1] Ed. of 1714, VII, 93.   [2] Joseph Mitchell, *Poems*, I, 216.

> Chiefly, dear Youth, beware of snaring *Game*,
> Nor risque too far thy *Fortune*, and thy *Fame*.
> What tho' Success has thy *Adventures* crown'd,
> 'T is difficult to *stand on slipp'ry Ground*.[1]

And yet, on occasion, he is willing to have his friends take a chance on his account:

> Does M—— rate his *Game* so high,
> To grudge a *Chance* for such as I?
> No sure — altho' 't were but in Jest,
> Win *fifty* Pounds for *Me*, at least.[2]

He tells us in his poetical epistle "To Sir Richard Steele" (I, 313), among much other autobiographical detail, that he is Scotch, had been trained for the ministry, and came to London just

> When Store, long treasur'd, or improv'd in Trade,
> The *Lottery of Avarice* was made!

He suffered too from South Sea fever, but still more from the poetic itch, which incites him to nauseous effusions designed to further his schemes for preferment.

> 'T will cost you but a Word, to send me *North*,
> T' inspect *Tobacco*, *Brandy* — and so forth.

In one of these (I, 350), "An Anacreontique, to the Right Honourable John Earl of Stair" (1727), he begs robes for the Coronation.

> Tho' the Rascal-Rabble swears,
> That 't is *Collier's* Coat he wears;
> Or he 'as hir'd, from *Monmouth-street*,
> *Birth-Day* Cloaths, and made them meet.

He recommends the creation of a special Order for poets, "of Rainbow's various hue."

[1] "To Mr. M——," *Poems*, I, 281.
[2] "To Mr. M——l," *Ibid.*, 284.

Lord! how *Young* and *Gay* wou'd strut?
What a Figure *Hill* wou'd cut?
Little *Pope* improve his Size
Inches nearer to the Skies?

In a poem called "The South-Sea Project" Swift satirizes the gambling frenzy of the women:

Undone at play, the female troops
    Come here their losses to retrieve;
Ride o'er the waves in spacious hoops,
    Like Lapland witches in a sieve. . . .
There is a gulf, where thousands fell,
    Here all the bold adventurers came,
A narrow sound, though deep as Hell —
    'Change Alley is the dreadful name.[1]

Ward also has his eye on the ladies. In *A South Sea Ballad, or Merry Remarks upon Exchange-Alley Bubbles*,[2] he tells us about their enthusiasm:

Our greatest Ladies hither come,
    And ply in chariots daily;
Oft pawn their jewels for a sum,
    To venture 't in the Alley.[3]

Gay writes one of his very cleverest fables around a moral drawn from the manners of the *nouveaux riches* whom the South Sea threw up, "The Barley-Mow and the Dunghill." [4]

How many saucy airs we meet
From Temple Bar to Aldgate Street!
Proud rogues, who shared the South Sea prey,
And sprung like mushrooms in a day!
They think it mean to condescend
To know a brother or a friend;

---

[1] *Poems* (ed. Bohn), I, 120. Cf. Gay, "Epistle to Mr. Thomas Snow" (ed. Underhill), I, 214.
[2] Printed with *The Delights of the Bottle* (1720).
[3] *Roxburghe Ballads*, VIII, 258. Printed here, as by the Author of *The Cavalcade*, that is, Ned Ward.   [4] Ed. Underhill, II, 109.

They blush to hear their mother's name,
And by their pride expose their shame.

South Sea became a metaphor for anything variable, al-
most as familiar as *Fortune* herself. Among the attrac-
tions of Moorfields, for instance, there are flying horses,
which speed up to fifty miles an hour, but

> As for the pregnant Wife, or tim'rous Maid,
> Who fear, perhaps, to mount so swift a Pad,
> Here's a true South Sea Coach, that sporting flies
> Between the humbler Earth and lofty Skyes,
> Manag'd to rise and fall with little Pains,
> Like that uncertain Stock that turns our Brains.[1]

Gay has all the scorn of the old English country gen-
try for the climber, whether by South Sea or other
means. He devotes the last twenty lines of his second
Book to cataloguing the varieties of this social phe-
nomenon. Pope, however, in his *Moral Essays* (III,
385), gives perhaps the most elaborate account of this
Snob's Progress:[2]

> A Nymph of Quality admires our Knight;
> He marries, bows at Court, and grows polite:
> Leaves the dull Cits, and joins (to please the fair)
> The well-bred cuckolds in St. James's air:
> First, for his Son a gay Commission buys,
> Who drinks, whores, fights, and in a duel dies:
> His Daughter flaunts a Viscount's tawdry wife;
> She bears a Coronet and P-x for life.
> In Britain's Senate he a seat obtains,
> And one more Pensioner St. Stephen gains.
> My Lady falls to play; so bad her chance,
> He must repair it; takes a bribe from France;
> The House impeach him; Coningsby harangues;
> The Court forsake him, and Sir Balaam hangs:

---

[1] *A Vade Mecum for Malt-Worms*, n. d. (*ca.* 1712), pp. 2, 8.
[2] How much like Hogarth's *Marriage à la Mode!*

Wife, son, and daughter, Satan! are thy own,
His wealth, yet dearer, forfeit to the Crown:
The Devil and the King divide the Prize,
And sad Sir Balaam curses God and dies.

According to Butler Swift,[1] Tyburn is particularly in-
terested in the brokers and the climbers and regrets the
security which they generally enjoy.

> O search this sinful town with care:
> What numbers, duly mine, are there!
> The full-fed herd of money-jobbers,
> Jews, Christians, rogues alike and robbers![2]
> Who riot on the poor man's toils,
> And fatten by a nation's spoils!
> The crowd of little knaves in place,
> Our age's envy and disgrace.
> Secret and snug, by daily stealth,
> The busy vermine pick up wealth;
> Then, without birth, control the great!
> Then, without talents, rule the state!

The poet of the street corners has his eyes open, too,
and sees this variety of the rake, the upstart, along with
the "cheap sports" and the "rorers."[3]

> There be many Vpstarts,
>   that spring from the Cart,
> Who, gotten to th' Court,
>   play the Gentleman's part . . .

> There be many Gallants
>   that goe in gay rayment
> For which the Taylor
>   did neuer receiue payment;

---

[1] *Tyburn to the Marine Society* (1759).
[2] Cf. Arthur Murphy, *Seventeen Hundred and Ninety-One, in Imitation of the Thirteenth Satire of Juvenal* (1791), p. 7:
> "Go, preach at Jonathan's your musty rule;
> Each broker there will hiss you for a fool;
> A fool to think, when lucre is in view,
> That sacred truth can avarice subdue."
[3] *Roxburghe Ballads*, I, 116, "I know what I know."

They ruffle it out
    with a gorgeous show;
Some take them for Knights,
    but I know what I know.

There be many Rorers,
    that swagger and rore
As though they in th' warres had b[een]
    seuen yeeres and more;
And yet they neuer lookt
    in the face of a foe;
They seeme gallant sparkes,
    but I know what I know.

There's many rich Trades-men
    who liue by deceit,
And in Weight and Measure
    the poore they doe cheat.

Chapter V

AMUSEMENTS

A MAN'S laugh reveals his character more drastically, sometimes, than his dreams, and the way he goes about having a good time is at least one index of his imaginative power. What, then, are we to say about the character and imaginative power of these London citizens of Gay's time?

Some hints have already been thrown out in connection with the discussion of other topics. We have, for instance, noticed the Englishman's love of pageantry, still aboundingly alive in the time of Gay, though his instinctive passion for it reaches back through the Middle Ages.[1] He still loved his Lord Mayor's Day celebrations, his burning of the Pope on Guy Fawkes Day. The May Day festivities survived even in the city. He welcomed any occasion for a good time, and the gang spirit was strong within him. There was a certain hard side about his nature in this respect, and the mob psychology of the time showed little trace of sentimentality. If no

---

[1] See pp. 179–191 above. Cf. also Collier, *Broad-side Black-Letter Ballads*, p. 112, "The Honor of the Inns of Court Gentlemen, or a briefe recitall of the Magnificent and Matchlesse Show, that passed from Hatton and Ely house in Holborne to Whitehall, on Monday night being the third of February, and the next day after Candlemas." This procession took place between 7 and 9 o'clock in the evening. It presented "A various crew of anticks all, which seuerall humors in shape did represent." Then followed "A hundred sweet yong gentlemen," mounted gallantly, and clad in white cloth of tissue, red and white feathers — two by two, four by four, with drums and trumpets. At the last were six chariots, each drawn by four horses, and carrying maskers. This procession was for Shirley's Masque, *The Triumph of Peace*, performed at Whitehall, Feb. 3, 1633. The ballad was written by Martin Parker.

better opportunity for riot offered, the funerals of unpopular persons might serve, like that of Francis Charteris in 1731. The unwholesome sport around the pillory, and the attitude of the populace toward the tragedies of Tyburn showed a callousness to pain that was remarkable. Indeed, the main actors in these Tyburn affairs faced death in most cases with a bold indifference which was considered the proper style on such occasions, astonishing to foreign visitors. Hanging-days were looked forward to as holidays by the mass of the people; and the victims who provided the show, since what must be must be, were the last to wish to defraud their audience of a conventionally correct entertainment.

We have noticed also, in following the rake's progress, some of the pastimes of the upper classes. His pursuit of excitement in tavern, brothel, and gaming-house was a will-o'-the-wisp type of merriment and very close to tears and bitter regrets, but he chased his phantom feverishly and thought he was merry. We have seen in another chapter how fond the Englishman of Gay's time was, as he is to-day, of the long walking excursion or week-end party. It was the open air that called him, and he showed a happy facility for making his own fun.

In this chapter we shall be concerned with a general survey of the kinds of sport and entertainment that amused Londoners in the early eighteenth century, confining our attention to those features which throw light on life as it was in the town.

The visitor to-day is astonished and delighted with the enthusiasm that English people show for games of all kinds. As a rule they are not very much interested in the vicarious exercises of the grand stand; they want to be doing the thing themselves. This is by no means a new development. Gay preaches the gospel of exercise

persistently throughout his poem. He recommends the
strong cane for use and not for show.

> Rosy-complexion'd health thy steps attends,
> And exercise thy lasting youth defends.

In the old days before the arrival of coaches, the proud
lady had to trip about town with her petticoats tucked
up; her cheeks were rosy from distant visits, and exer-
cise bestowed unartful charms. And now, the sempstres-
ses in the Change play shuttlecock over the counters on
the frosty mornings, while outside, escaped from their
servitude, the apprentices love to play that low game of
football.

> The 'prentice quits his shop, to join the crew,
> Increasing crowds the flying game pursue.
> Thus, as you roll the ball o'er snowy ground,
> The gath'ring globe augments with every round.
> But whither shall I run? the throng draws nigh,
> The ball now skims the street, now soars on high;
> The dext'rous glazier strong returns the bound,
> And jingling sashes on the pent-house sound.

According to Misson, who visited England in 1698, foot-
ball was the popular game in the winter. His comment is
delightfully polite and supercilious at the same time:

> En Hyver le *Foot-ball* est un exercice utile et charmant:
> C'est un balon de cuir gros comme la tête et rempli de vent:
> cela se balotte avec le pied dans les rües, par celui qui le peut
> attraper: il n'y a point d'autre Science.

If anyone doubts the Frenchman's powers of observa-
tion and thinks there might be some art in it, I would
refer him to Matthew Concanen's poem "A Match at
Football," in three cantos.[1] There he will find a detailed
description of the game as it was played in the early

[1] Matthew Concanen, *Miscellaneous Poems*, etc. (1724), p. 24.

eighteenth century. Misson probably just saw the young fellows playing with the ball in the streets.

James Dance sings the joys of cricket in an "heroic poem" of that name.[1] His first canto compares cricket with billiards, bowls, and tennis, and eulogizes the game; in the second, Kent challenges all the other counties, the match is determined, and place and players described in turn; in the last canto the game itself is pictured with the victory assigned to Kent.

The characteristic which is always thrusting itself on the view of anyone who reads the literature of the time is the joyous and immediate response which the call to sport always gets with commons and gentility alike. In the Miscellany just referred to there is a poem by the Rev. Mr. James Ward, evidently an Irish parson, which describes "The Smock-Race at Finglas" with considerable spirit. Everyone who hears about the coming race hurries off to take part in it or to watch it:

> The *Dublin*-Prentice, at the welcome Call,
> In Hurry rises from his Cakes and Ale.

The butcher's wife wins the laurels, and in the exaltation of the moment almost forgets her plebian duties:

> Yet (hapless Wretch) the servile Thirst of Gain,
> Shall force her to her stinking *Stall* again.[2]

The river has always been a source of joy to the Londoner. Those who like Dickens's *Great Expectations* will remember how Pip made use of it first for sculling, then as a means to get his foster-father out of the country. It was even more a place for pleasure in the seventeenth and eighteenth centuries. The Water-poet was the pet

---

[1] Edinburgh, 1754, p. 1.
[2] Cf. *Roxburghe Ballads*, VII, 84, "The Virgin Race; or York-shire's Glory" (*ca.* 1672).

of London in those days, certainly not altogether be-
cause of the quality of his verses, which are rude enough,
but because all loved the river and were proud of anyone
who exalted its glories. Thomas Dekker prefixed some
verses to the 1630 edition of Taylor's *Poems*, which
show this spirit very well.

> Row on (good *Water-man*) and looke back still,
> (Thus as thou dost) upon the *Muses Hill*,
> To guide thee in thy course: Thy *Boate's* a sphere
> Where thine *Urania* moues *diuinely-cleare*.
> *Well* has thou *pli'd* and '(with thy *learned Oare*)
> Cut through a Riuer, to a nobler *shore*,
> Than euer any *landed-at*. Thy *saile*,
> (Made all of *clowdes*) swels with a prosp'rous *gale*.
> Some say, there is a *Ferriman of Hell*,
> The *Ferriman of Heau'n*, I now know well,
> And that's thyselfe, transporting *soules* to *Blisse*.
> *Urania* sits at *Helme* and *Pilot* is;
>   For *Thames*, thou hast the *lactea via* found,
>   Be thou with *baies* (as that with *stars* is) crownd.

The river was the most lively and diverting quarter of
the town, and it is no wonder that Tom Brown [1] takes
his Indian visitor to view its humors. Their experience
illustrates another feature of the Londoner's tempera-
ment.

> The next diverting Scene that the River afforded us, was a
> very warm Engagement between a Western Barge and a Boat
> full of *Lambeth* Gardeners, by whom *Billinsgate* was much
> outdone in stupendious Obscenity, tonitrous Verbosity, and
> malicious Scurrility, as if one side had been *Daniel D[e]f[oe]'s*
> Party, and the other the *Observator's*.

Fishing, hunting,[2] and fowling have to do with the
country and may be largely overlooked here. The de-

---

[1] Tom Brown, *Works* (1715), III, 328.
[2] See Ebsworth's notes on fox-hunting in literature, and the ballads which
follow on that subject, dating from 1660 to 1783, in *Roxburghe Ballads*, VII,
86.

light that people of all classes took in them at that time
is sufficiently attested by the large number of poems
about one or the other of these sports. Gay's early poem
on *Rural Sports* (1713) gives rather pleasing descrip-
tions of these diversions of the country. Tickell wrote
a poem on the same subject.[1] The idea is an old one.
As early as 1575, George Turberville produced some
curious verses which he called *The Noble Art of Venerie
or Hvnting*. In this we find a rather interesting picture
of Elizabeth with the huntsman kneeling to present the
"fewmets," or droppings of the deer:

> Before the Queen, I come report to make,
> Then husht and peace, for noble *Tristrame's* sake.
> From out my horne, my fewmets first I drawe,
> And then present, on leaues, by hunters lawe:
> And thus I say: my Liege, behold and see
> An Hart of tenne, I hope he harbored bee.
> For if you marke his fewmets euery poynt,
> You shall them find, long, round, and well annoynt,
> Knottie and great, without prickes or eares,
> The moystnesse shewes, what venison he beares.

Somerville's poem on *The Chace* (1735)[2] was perhaps
the most popular work on hunting in Gay's time.
Charles Dunster tells us, in *St. James's Street* (1790),
that by his time even the ladies had learned to hunt.
Budgell writes an essay about the sport in the *Spectator*,
No. 116.

[1] Steele, *Poetical Miscellanies* (1714). See also *King Satan, or the Hunting
of the Senator, a Newmarket Tale told by an old Fox-Hunter, and addressed to
all true Sportsmen* (1724).
[2] See also his *Field Sports* (1742). Both of these poems are written in
blank verse, about which, as thus applied, Dr. Johnson was censorious: "If
blank verse be not tumid and gorgeous, it is crippled prose; and familiar
images in labored language have nothing to recommend them but absurd
novelty; which, wanting the attractions of Nature, cannot please long. One
excellence of *The Splendid Shilling* is, that it is short. Disguise can gratify no
longer than it deceives." Johnson, *Lives of the Poets* (ed. by Cunningham,
1854), II, 338.

The Englishmen of Queen Anne's time were thick-skinned, and rather rough, or even cruel, sports seemed to amuse them most. Mildest among these were wrestling,[1] boxing, cudgelling,[2] and sword-play. To be able to defend oneself on occasion was necessary then. Fights in the streets were by no means uncommon, and parting the combatants was the last thing to enter the mind of the crowd. Nor was this fierce delight in the test of strength confined to the rabble. A gentleman must be fit to fight, though the occasion might be nothing more than a dispute over fares with his cabby. But this sort of thing was merely accidental. The mob delighted in the arranged fight, the wrestling match, or boxing, and particularly in the combat with cudgels. They made heroes of the victors with all the enthusiasm of modern fans. One of these popular cudgellers, a certain "John Parkes or Sparkes was buried at Coventry, and on his tombstone was inscribed, *inter alia*, that he was a man of mild disposition, a gladiator by profession, who fought 350 battles in different parts of Europe, when he retired. He died in 1733." [3] Possibly the most elaborate account of such a battle in the poetry of the time is Dr. Byrom's "Extempore Verses upon a Trial of Skill between the two great masters of Defence, Messieurs Figg and Sutton." [4] At this exhibition there is a prelude of cudgels by minor lights of the pugilistic world. Then the two heroes appear and show their skill with sword-play until both have been slightly scratched. At last, when the

---

[1] Cf. Nicholas James, *Poems* (1742), "Wrestling."
[2] Cf. *Vade Mecum for Malt-Worms*, n. d. (*ca.* 1712), II, 8:
"In Moor's most pleasant Field, where Northern Lads
With Western Youths, contend for broken Heads."
[3] Ashton, *Social Life*, p. 241.
[4] Dodsley, VI, 344. Figg died in 1734 (Nichols, *Biog. Anec.*, p. 210). Cf. Capt. John Godfrey's *Treatise on the Useful Science of Defence* (1747); J. Mitchell, "The Cudgel," *Poems* (2 vols., 1729), I, 67.

enthusiasm of the audience has reached its proper
height, they take up the quarter-staff and fight it out,
till Figg hits Sutton on the knee and disables him.

Readers more interested in boxing than in the cudgels
may examine Paul Whitehead's *The Gymnasiad, or Box-
ing Match.*[1] This is an elaborate poem in three Books,
the first of which describes the assembly:

> Shoals press on Shoals, from Palace and from Cell,
> Lords yield the *Court*, and Butchers *Clerkenwell*.
> *St. Giles's* Natives, never known to fail,
> All who have haply 'scap'd th' obdurate Jail;
> There many a martial Son of *Tott'nham* lies,
> Bound in *Deveilian* Bands, a Sacrifice
> To angry Justice, nor must view the Prize.

Some introductory rounds by little-known pugilists
start the entertainment, *hors d'oeuvres* to the main
course. First, the "infant progeny of Mars" fight, then,

> To these, the hardy iron Race succeed,
> All sons of *Hockley* and fierce *Brickstreet* breed.

The second Book describes the champions — Stephen-
son, a simple "charioteer" in ordinary life, and Brough-
ton, a waterman, who seems to be a general favorite:

> Soon as the Ring their ancient Warrior view'd,
> Joy fill'd the Hearts, and thund'ring Shouts ensu'd;
> Loud as when o'er *Thamesis'* gentle Flood,
> Superior with the *Triton* Youths he row'd;
> While far a-head his winged Wherry flew,
> Touch'd the glad Shore, and claim'd the *Badge* its Due.

They strip for action, and, with the third Book, fight it
through to a Broughton victory.

In that highly amusing book of burlesques by Horace
and James Smith called *Horace in London* (Boston,
1813), the eighth Ode is addressed "To Huntingdon the

---

[1] *Satires*, 1760. Written about twenty years earlier.

Preacher," and is a complaint against that distinguished gentleman for spoiling the author's servant. This young man had once been a favorite among the sports until he got religion.

> From young Hal, the tavern waiter,
> Oft the boxing prize he'd carry;
> Now the pious gladiator,
> Wrestles only with Old Harry.

> Potent once at quoits and cricket,
> Head erect and heart elate,
> Now, alas! he heeds no wicket,
> Save John Bunyan's wicket gate.

We have already noticed the ordinary human interest in the chance to win something for nothing, as developed to an extraordinary degree around the year 1720. This is evident, of course, from the grand fiasco of the South Sea Bubble; but that is by no means an isolated phenomenon. The same eagerness to take a chance appears, as it always does, in the realm of sport, sometimes in so humble a form as wagers on "stunts," sometimes in bets on the performances of cocks, dogs, and horses. The curious interest that the public to-day take in unusual athletic feats of any kind is no new thing. To one such performance there is a reference in *The Bow-Street Opera*, a rare and undated work written on the plan of *The Beggar's Opera*. In this, when the talk turns on pickpockets, the Governor says, "While Jemmy is *hopping* [to Brentford], his associates are always *diving*." [1]

---

[1] Horace Walpole's copy gives the date October, 1773, in his autograph. Cf. John Taylor, "The Pennilesse Pilgrimage," *Works* (1630), p. 122:

> "Away t'ward *Hockley* in the hole, we make,
> When straight a Horsman did me ouer-take,
> Who knew me, & would faine have giuen me Coine.
> I said, my Bonds did me from Coyne inioyne,
> I thank'd and prayd him to put vp his Chinke,
> And willingly I wisht it drownd in drinke."

The sports that one always associates with the earlier days of old England are cock-fighting,[1] baiting of bears and bulls, and, to a less extent, horse-racing. These were still popular in John Gay's time, the last increasingly so. Such things were the common subjects for talk when men got together, just as motor-cars form a safe topic in most groups to-day, or the theatre with a crowd of college men. Some were bored, no doubt, and complained, like Wildish in Thomas Shadwell's play:[2] "We talk'd of nothing but Cocks, Dogs and Horses." Later on in this play, he harks back again to his grievance: "And when you think you have a choice Company, in rushes some loud obstreperous Hunter, Hawker or Jocky, good for nothing else, and roars about Dogs, Kites, and Horses; and spoils that Meeting." Cock-fighting was falling on evil days. Hogarth's extraordinary print must have had wide influence, and the interest it aroused shows a growing tenderness in the public conscience with regard to such sports. Hogarth got his subject from a suggestion in some lines from the *Gentleman's Magazine* for 1747[3] (p. 292):

> Come, *Hogarth*, thou whose art can best declare
> What forms, what features, human passions wear,
> Come with a painter's philosophic sight,
> Survey the circling judges of the fight.
> Touch'd with the sport of death, while every heart
> Springs to the changing face, exert thy art;
> Mix with the smiles of Cruelty at pain
> Whate'er looks anxious in the lust of gain;
> And say, can aught that's generous, just, or kind,
> Beneath this aspect, lurk within the mind.[4]

[1] Cf. "A Match at Cock-Fighting," *Wit and Drollery* (1661), p. 110. Cf. W. Woty, "On the Beauty and Utility of Cock-Fighting," *Fugitive and Original Poems* (1786), p. 24.
[2] *Bury Fair* (acted 1689), I, 1; and III, 1.
[3] Quoted by John Nichols, in *Biog. Anec. of Hogarth* (1785), p. 368.
[4] Cf. Pepys, *Diary*, Dec. 21, 1663.

Pope refers to the increasing interest the people were taking in horse-racing, in his imitation of the first Epistle of Horace's second Book. He is thinking here of Charles II's reign.

> Then Peers grew proud in Horsemanship t' excell,
> Newmarket's glory rose, as Britain's fell.

Chappell [1] quotes from the *Travels of Cosmo*, third Grand Duke of Tuscany: "Newmarket has in the present day (1669) been brought into repute by the King, who frequents it on account of the horse-races; having been before celebrated only for the market for victuals, which was held there, and was a very abundant one." The most interesting song about the life at Newmarket is from Tom D'Urfey's *Several New Songs; and 120 Loyal Songs* (1684).[2] It is the usual type of street ballad, and was sung to the King at Newmarket. The author sends his servant to saddle Ball. "I'll to Newmarket scour." [3]

> Let's be to each other a Prey; to be cheated be ev'ryone's Lot!
> Or chous'd any sort of a way, but by another's damn'd Plot.
> Let Cullies that lose at the *Race*, go venture at *Hazard* and win;
> And he that is bubbl'd at *Dice*, recover't at *Cocking* again . . .
> Each corner of the Town rings with perpetual noise,
> The "Oyster"-bawling Clown joyns with "Hot Pudding-Pyes!"
> And both in consort keep, to vend their stinking ware;
> The drowzy God of Sleep hath no dominion there.
> "Hey, boys!" the Jockeys roar, "if the Mare and the Gelding run,
> I'll 'bet you five Guineys to four, he beats her, and gives half a stone."

---

[1] *Popular Music of the Olden Time.*

[2] *Roxburghe Ballads*, V, 144.

[3] Compare another song by D'Urfey, "The Call to the Races at New-Market" (*ca.* 1685), *Bagford Ballads*, I, 80; and Eustace Budgell, *A Poem upon H. M.'s late Journey to Cambridge and Newmarket* (1728).

"Ged dimme!" quoth Bully, "'t is done, or else I'm the son
of a (Sc)ore;
And fain would I meet with the man would offer it, would
offer it once more."
See, see the damn'd Fate of the Town! a Fop that was starv-
ing of late,
And scarcely could borrow a Crown, puts in to run for the
Plate.
Another makes chousing a Trade, and dreams of his Projects
to come,
And many a Crimp-match has made, by bribing another
man's Groom.
The Town's-men are *Whiggish*, G. rot 'em! their hearts are
but Loyal by fits;
For, should you search to the bottom, they're as nasty as
their streets.

The last stanza of this rude poem describes the throng
of ladies, beauty shining in the distance, their hats and
feathers like those of the men.

There were three Bear-gardens in the time of Queen
Anne, one in Hockley, Clerkenwell, one in Marry-
bone Fields at the back of Soho Square, and one in
Tuttle (Tothill) Fields, Westminster. This was a sport of
long-standing popularity among Englishmen. Everyone
remembers references to it in Elizabethan and Jacobean
literature. Then old Jack of Paris Garden was the hero
of the town, and even such distinguished people as law
students did not hesitate to get their stockings splashed
with mud in their eagerness to patronize his sports.
Davies has an Epigram (1590) on the subject:[1]

> Publius [a] student at the Common-law,
> Oft leaves his Bookes, and for his recreation,
> To Paris-garden doth himselfe withdrawe;
> Where he is rauisht with such delectation,
> As downe among the beares and dogges he goes.

[1] Sir John Davies, *Poems* (ed. Grosart), p. 343.

Some men thought the sport vicious, and even as early
as Henry VIII's time Robert Crowley had inveighed
against it. One of Jonson's thoughtful young men gets
a bear-ward with the dogs of some four parishes to cry
his games under master Morose's window,[1] and in an-
other place he speaks of the gentry watching the bear-
baiting in St. James's Park at Easter and Whitsuntide
from the banqueting-house window, when Ned Whiting
or George Stone was at the stake.[2] Hudibras has a des-
perate adventure with the bears.

> And round about the Pole does make
> A Circle like a Bear at Stake,
> That at the Chain's End wheels about,
> And overturns the Rabble-Rout.
> For after solemn Proclamation
> In the Bear's Name (as is the Fashion
> According to the Law of Arms,
> To keep Men from inglorious Harms)
> That none presume to come so near
> As forty Foot of Stake of Bear;
> If any yet be so fool-hardy,
> T' expose themselves to vain Jeopardy;
> If they come wounded off, and lame,
> No Honour's got by such a Maim.[3]

In *Trivia* (II, 405) Gay recounts some of the things that
enable Londoners to know the days of the week without
the calendar:

> Experienced men, inured to city ways,
> Need not the Calendar to count their days.
> When through the town with slow and solemn air,
> Led by the nostril, walks the muzzled bear;
> Behind him moves majestically dull,
> The pride of Hockley-hole, the surly bull;

[1] *The Silent Woman* (1609), I, 1.
[2] (Ed. by Gifford and Cunningham), III, 382. Cf. *Merry Wives of Windsor*, I, 1.
[3] Butler, *Hudibras* (1775), Part I, Canto I, ll. 685–698.

Learn hence the periods of the week to name,
Mondays and Thursdays are the days of game.

One fancies that Gay must have been an interested spec-
tator at some of these events, his eye for the essential
points of description is so keen. This is true particu-
larly of his Fable IX, "The Bull and the Mastiff." It is
curious enough to remember that this fable, along with
the others, was addressed by Gay and an ironic Fate to
the young Duke of Cumberland.

One of the features of London life in Gay's time which
is apt to shock us with its blatant callousness, is the at-
titude of the people, all the people apparently, toward
the insane. Conditions in hospitals for those suffering
from this disease leave much to be desired even in our
own time, but one trembles to think about the fate of
such unfortunates two hundred years ago. The word
"insane" covers many types and conditions, among
which there was at that time absolutely no discrimi-
nation. All whose nervous organism was in any way
abnormal were thrust into the horrors of Bedlam. And
Bedlam was one of the sights of the city! It continued
to be a favorite promenade until 1770, at which time
the revenue was four hundred pounds a year "from the
indiscriminate admission of visitors." Steele, good-
natured and tender-hearted as he was, used to go some-
times, as he tells us in the *Tatler* (No. 30): "I took three
lads, who are under my guardianship, a rambling, in a
hackney coach, to show them the town; as the lions, the
tombs,[1] Bedlam." Poems were written about it, one of
the most elaborate of which was published by David

---

[1] Compare in *Roxburghe Ballads*, VII, 268, a curious ballad by J. Phillips,
the nephew of Milton, on "The Tombs in Westminster Abbey." (The
verger shows the tombs.) Printed also in J. Phillips's *Sportive Wit*, p. 90,
and in *Wit and Drollery* (1682 ed. only), p. 47.

Lewis in *Miscellaneous Poems by Several Hands* [1] (1726), page 8. The authors of these pieces are not named. Bedlam was situated away to the north of the city, beyond Bishopsgate. [2]

> Where proud *Augusta*, blest with long Repose,
> Her ancient Wall and ruin'd Bulwark shows;
> Close by a verdant Plain, with graceful Height
> A stately Fabric rises to the Sight. . . .
> From this, from that, from ev'ry Quarter rise
> Loud Shouts, and sullen Groans, and doleful Cries;
> Heart-soft'ning Plaints demand the pitying Tear,
> And Peals of hideous Laughter shock the Ear.

The poet then goes on to describe various cases, the man who thinks himself a king, [3] the lovesick maid, the miser, the sage whose invention has been stolen from him and who is probably not insane at all, the fopling, the poet, the religious enthusiast. [4]

More wholesome as a pastime than laughing at the vagaries of these poor insane folk was the Londoner's inveterate craze for rarities. This trait in his character is neither new nor old; it is very human, and one with

[1] Cf. Thomas Fitzgerald, *Poems on Several Occasions* (1733), p. 1, and Hildebrand Jacob, *Bedlam, A Poem* (1723).

[2] Near what is now the Liverpool St. Station. Thomas Pennant, *The Antiquities of London* (2d ed., 1818), p. 43: "Between Bishopsgate and Moorfields, stood the hospital of St. Mary of Bethlehem, founded by Simon Fitz-Mary, sheriff of London in 1247." Figures of raving and melancholy madness were the work of Caius Gabriel Cibber, "the father of the admirable wit and comedian Colley Cibber."

[3] Paul Whitehead, *Manners* (1739):

> "Well — of all Plagues which make Mankind their Sport,
> Guard me, Ye Heav'ns! from that worst Plague — a Court.
> 'Midst the mad Mansions of *Moorfields*, I'd be
> A Straw-crown'd Monarch, in mock Majesty;
> Rather than Sov'reign rule *Britannia's* Fate,
> Curs'd with the Follies and the Farce of State."

[4] Cf. Gay, "Epistle to Mr. Thomas Snow" (ed. Underhill), I, 216, ll. 42 ff. Also Henri Misson, *Mémoires et Observations* (1698), p. 29: "Tous les Fous de Londres ne sont pas là-dedans."

which all circus-lovers can sympathize. There are many interesting references to it in the literature of the early seventeenth century. In 1621, Henry Farley, who was working to secure funds for necessary repairs for old St. Paul's, wrote a brief pamphlet, part verse, part prose, called *St. Paules-Church, her Bill for the Parliament*, in which he soundly berates the London populace for their readiness to spend their money in such foolish ways, when many important works remain undone for want of means. His enthusiasm is at times quite eloquent.

> To see a strange out-landish Fowle,
> A quaint Baboon, an Ape, an Owle,
> A dancing Beare, a Gyant's bone,
> A foolish Ingin moue alone,
> A Morris-dance, a Puppit play,
> Mad *Tom* to sing a Roundelay,
> A Woman dancing on a Rope;
> Bull-baiting also at the *Hope;*
> A Rimers Iests, a Iugler's cheats,
> A Tumbler shewing cunning feats,
> Or Players acting on the Stage,
> There goes the bounty of our Age:
> But vnto any pious motion,
> There's little coine, and lesse deuotion.

Of the Londoner's delight in strange sights and exhibitions we have no better expression than Trinculo's words: [1]

A strange fish! Were I in England now, as once I was, and had but this fish painted, not a holiday fool there but would give a piece of silver: there would this monster make a man; any strange beast there makes a man: when they will not give a doit to relieve a lame beggar, they will lay out ten to see a dead Indian. [2]

---

[1] *The Tempest*, II, 2.
[2] Cf. "The Savage; occasion'd by the bringing to Court a wild Youth, taken in the Woods in Germany, in the Year 1725," Lewis, *Miscellany* (1726), p. 305.

Henry Peacham, author of *The Compleat Gentleman*, has prefixed to Coryat's *Crudities* (1611) an account of the curiosities on show in England in the time of James I. He speaks of the unicorn's horn at Windsor, which was supposed to be an antidote for poison; of Drake's ship at Deptford, the *Golden Hind*, from remnants of which, by the way, one of the old chairs in the Bodleian was made; of the Perpetual Motion machine, which Cornelius Drebbel, the famous chemist and mechanician, exhibited in Eltham Park. Perhaps the most famous of the sights was Banks's trained horse, called Morocco. This surprising animal is continually turning up in the poetry of the time. Hall refers to him in one of his Satires (IV, 2):

> More than who vies his pence to view some trick
> Of strange Moroco's dumb arithmetick.

Rowlands, who may not write great poetry, but who knew the town, gives a summary of the sights in *Humors Looking Glasse* (1608):

> He shew'd his Maister sights to him most strange,
> Great tall Pauls Steeple and the Royall-Exchange:
> The Bosse at *Billings-gate* and *London-stone*
> And at *White-Hall* the monstrous great Whales bone,
> Brought him to the banck-side where Beares do dwell
> And vnto *Shor-ditch* where the whores keepe hell,
> Shew'd him the Lyons, Gyants in Guild-Hall,[1]
> King *Lud* at *Lud-gate*, the *Babounes* and all,
> At length his man, on all he had did pray,
> Shew'd him a theeuish trick and ran away,
> The Traueller turnd home exceeding ciuill,
> And swore in London he had seene the Deuill.

[1] The Gog and Magog of Guildhall were made in 1708 by Richard Saunders, a captain of trained bands and carver in King Street, Cheapside, to replace giants of pasteboard and wickerwork which had been carried in City processions. Philip Norman, *London Signs and Inscriptions* (1893), p. 17.

It is a curious kink in man's make-up, this interest in monstrosities, but it is evidently one that was put there to stay. Butler's picture of Fame in *Hudibras* [1] shows that he also noticed this weakness among his fellows.

> About her Neck a Pacquet-Male,
> Fraught with Advice, some fresh, some stale,
> Of Men that walk'd when they were dead,
> And Cows of Monsters brought to Bed;
> Of Hail-Stones big as Pullets Eggs,
> And Puppies whelp'd with twice two Legs;
> A Blazing-Star seen in the West,
> By six or seven Men at least.

Great excitement was caused in 1726 by the rumors about Mary Tofts, the rabbit-woman; the interest and credit with which the story was received is astonishing.[2] References to her appear occasionally in contemporary verse. Joseph Mitchell wrote a poem, for example, called "Peter, an Heroi-Comical Poem in Six Cantos," [3] only one canto of which fortunately was completed, and in that the following lines occur:

> Peter (whose Story puzzled all the *Town*,
> Ere *Gulliver* and *Mary Tofts* were known).[4]

Such credulity was naturally turned to financial advantage whenever possible. A doctor certifies the truth of the report about Mary, and forthwith she receives visitors for a consideration. Dr. Maningham wrote a pamphlet in defence of this story.

The David Lewis *Miscellany* contains "An excellent new Ballad on the South-Sea Dog-Fish, that was shewn on the River Thames, in July 1725:" [5]

---

[1] Part II, Canto I.   [2] John Nichols, *Biog. Anec. of Hogarth* (1785), p. 23.
[3] *Poems on Several Occasions* (2 vols., 1729), I, 373.
[4] Cf. "A Song on Tofts the Rabbit-Woman," in *The Honey-Suckle* (1734), p. 204. See also, *The Discovery, or, the Squire turned Ferret* (1727).
[5] Cf. *Bagford Ballads* (ed. by J. W. Ebsworth, 1878), I, 59, "A Most Strange, but True Account of a Very Large Sea-Monster." Prose. The mon-

This Dog-Fish he was young and tame,
And eke a Beauty rare,
As e'er was shew'd at *Bart'lemew*,
Ay or at *Southwark* Fair. . . .

From far and near, this Dog to see,
Came Skullers and came Oars;
Cits, Cuckolds, Cuckold-makers, Beaux;
Wives, Widows, Maids and Wh——.

Came thick and threefold *Wappineers*,
All thro' Bridge Ho! so jolly;
Came Shoals from *Battersea*, tho' cut
For Simples, to the *Folly*.

For at the *Folly*, you must know,
His wise Directors plac'd him;
And, like my Lord Mayor in his Barge,
With Flag and Trumpet grac'd him.

To see him, all their Testers gave;
And some gave all they had;
And so our Dog he bit 'em all:
'T is well he was not mad.

Unfortunately they forgot to feed the fish and he died.
The *Folly*, by the way, was a disreputable pleasure-
barge anchored pretty well up the river opposite West-
minster.[1]

By the time that Horace comes to London in the per-
sons of the humorists Horace and James Smith, nearly
a century later, the popular sights are of rather a differ-
ent sort. The populace is not so easily amused. Their
third Ode[2] is called "The Baronet's Yacht." The

ster was exhibited at the Black Swan Ale-house. It figures in Partridge's
Almanac for 1704. Partridge, the famous butt of one of Swift's practical
jokes, was the successor of William Lilly as favorite soothsayer with London
cullies.

[1] "A true and full account of a late Conference between the wonderful
speaking Head, and Father Godwyn, as 'twas related by the Head's own
Mouth to Dr. Frazier" (by Sir Fleet Shepherd), *Poems on State Affairs 1640–
1704*, III, 121.

[2] *Horace in London* (1813).

ᵔcrash of shells, the tunnel under Highgate Hill, the
brilliance of illuminating gas, the parachute (with Gar-
nerin), all are new and startling things. Life is almost
too fast for the quiet man.

> Great Jupiter! for mercy's sake,
> Me to a cooler planet take,
> For at this rate we soon shall make
> The world too hot to hold us!

There were three celebrated London fairs, Bartholo-
mew, May Fair, and Southwark.[1] They had all started
as market-places for the encouragement of trade, but
had far outgrown this early pious intention. Bartholo-
mew, for instance,[2] had entered upon its famous history
as a modest mart for cloth. The riotous doings of a
later time naturally scandalized the sober among Lon-
don citizens, and attempts were made first to shorten
the time of the fair, and then to suppress it altogether.
May Fair fell in November, 1708, never to rise.[3]

It was at these fairs that London life appeared in its
highest colors. Swift's "Description of the Legion
Club"[4] (1736) would lose at least some of its sardonic
exaggeration and get closer to a plain statement of fact,
if applied to the fairs and the giddy throngs that fre-
quented them.

> How I want thee, humorous Hogarth!
> Thou, I hear, a pleasant rogue art.

[1] See Gay, Fable XL, "The Two Monkeys."

[2] How intimate a part of a Londoner's life this Smithfield show was is
evident from the fact that a man like Theobald draws his comparisons thence.
In a letter about Pope's criticisms, while discussing the line "*Nought but
himself can be his Parallel*," he remarks: "This, he hints, may seem borrowed
from the Thought of that Master of a *Show* in *Smithfield*, who writ in large
Letters over the Picture of his Elephant, *This is the* greatest *Elephant in the
World except* himself." (*Twickenham Hotch-Potch* [1728], p. 32.)

[3] Cf. *Tatler*, No. 20.

[4] *Poems* (ed. Bohn), II, 264. Cf. *Bartholomew-Fair: or, a Ramble to Smith-
field. A Poem in Imitation of Milton* (1729).

> Were but you and I acquainted,
> Every monster should be painted:
> You should try your graving tools
> On this odious group of fools;
> Draw the beasts as I describe them:
> Form their features while I gibe them;
> Draw them like; for I assure you,
> You will need no *car'catura;*
> Draw them so that we may trace
> All the soul in every face.

The most lively description of their gaieties is in Ned Ward's *Hudibras Redivivus.*[1] The author makes his way through Newgate, and enters Smithfield [2] by way of Gilt-Spur Street, heavy with the odor of fried pork.

> At last I came into the Fair,
> Where Crowds in such Confusion were,
> Acting as if bereft of Wits,
> Like so many loose *Bedlamites;*
> Some squeezing in amidst the Rout,
> And others elbowing to get out.

A lively description of the people he sees follows; then of the noises that assault his ears:

> All sorts of Noises blended were,
> T' improve the Musick of the Fair.
> Drums ratling, Lott'ry-Trumpets farting,
> And croaking Fools their Lungs exerting.

[1] (1708), Part V, vol. II, Canto III.

[2] In his attempts to get some attention paid to the needs of St. Paul's, Henry Farley had naturally contrasted the amounts spent on other public improvements with the pittance granted to the old cathedral. The great market of Smithfield had been completely renewed a short time before he wrote his *Complaint of Paules* (1616):

> "From thence to Smithfield, if thou chance to hit,
> Tell me what costs they have bestowed on it;
> It was before a filthy, noisome place,
> And to the Citie verie much disgrace,
> Yet now some say it may with best compare,
> Of market places that in England are."

> Young Flat-caps, with extended Throats,
> Crying their Damsons, Pears, and Nuts.
> Boys with their penny Cat-calls tooting.
> The Mob at *Merry Andrew* shouting.
> The Actors brawling to the Rabble,
> A Riot here, and there a Squabble.

He wanders off to see the rope-dancers, then to a puppet show. In one of the booths he witnesses a terrific fight between a giant and a centaur. Suddenly he comes upon the merry-go-rounds and the flying coaches:

> I rambl'd round into the Rear,
> To see the hair-brain'd Doings there,
> Where a young Fry of Mob I found
> In Boats and Coaches, flying round
> Between the Heavens and the Ground.[1]

There are music booths also, and a cabaret with dancers and acrobats. Off in another part of the field one may see harlequins and rope-walking artists.

> Thus, as I elbow'd too and fro,
> Like Country Hob at Lord May'rs Show,
> Viewing the Shops on ev'ry side,
> Where Lasses in their utmost Pride,
> Sate dizen'd up, to please the Sight.[2]

The soldier is there, too; he leads the way to the gaming-house, where butcher and beau rub elbows over the tables, in utter disregard of the social distinctions which would certainly stiffen as soon as the hall door was passed.

Another good description of the doings at the fair is in Sir William Davenant's poem, "The Long Vacation in London." [3]

---

[1] Part IV.
[2] Part V, vol. II, Canto V.
[3] Chalmers's *English Poets*(1810), VI, 433. Also published in *Wit and Drollery* (1661), p. 87.

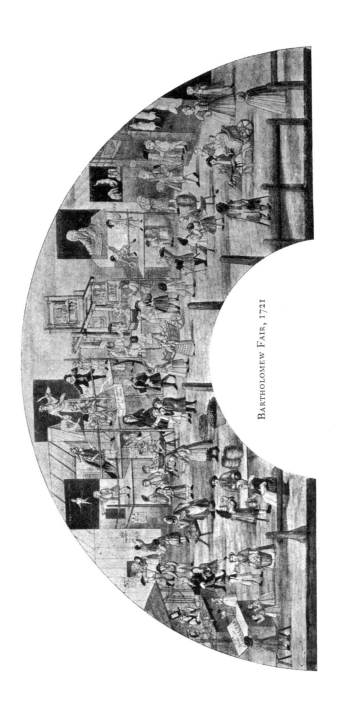

Bartholomew Fair, 1721

Now vaulter good, and dancing lass,
On rope, and man that cryes "Hey, pass,"
And tumbler young that needs but stoop,
Lay head to heel to creep through hoope;
And man in chimney hid to dress,
Puppit that acts our old queen Bess,
And man that whilst the puppits play,
Through nose expoundeth what they say,
And man that does in chest include,
Old Sodom and Gomorrah lewd:
And white oate-eater that does dwell
In stable small, at sign of Bell:
That lifts up hoofe to show the prancks,
Taught by magitian, stiled Bankes; [1]
And ape, led captive still in chaine,
Till he renounce the pope and Spaine.
All these on hoof now trudge from town,
To cheat poor turnep-eating clown.

There are two "Bartholomew Fair Songs" in Playford's *Pleasant Musical Companion* (1701), one of which comes from Charles II's time, and contains a reference to a famous rope-dancer.

Here's *Jacob Hall* that can jump it, jump it.[2]

"The Second Part of Bartholomew Fair" lists the rarities:

Here are the rarities of the whole fair!
Pimperle-Pimp, and the wise *Dancing Mare;*
Here's valiant *St. George and the Dragon*, a farce,
A girl of fifteen with strange moles on, *etc.*
Here is *Vienna Besieg'd*,[3] a most delicate thing,
And here is *Punchinello*, shown thrice to the King.

---

[1] For references to Banks's famous horse, see Donne, *Satires*, I; *Love's Labour's Lost*, I, 2; *Every Man out of His Humour*, IV, 4; Jonson, *Epigrams*, 133 (ed. Gifford); Taylor, *Cast over the Water*, p. 159, *The Description of naturall English Poetry*, p. 249; Sir Kenelm Digby, *Of Bodies*, ch. 37, para. 3; Hall, *Satires*, IV, 2. [2] *Bagford Ballads*, I, 125.

[3] The Turks and Hungarians besieged Vienna in 1683. It was later relieved by Sobieski, King of Poland. Lotteries were prohibited in 1687, raffling in 1688. The song was printed in 1688.

Ladies mask'd to the Cloysters repair,
But there will be no raffling, — a pox take the Mayor.

The merry-andrew was a familiar figure both in the
streets and at these fairs. He is frequently associated
with the quack. He gathered the crowd and thus gave
the doctor a chance to vend his wares. Ned Ward tells
about one such combination in *Hudibras Redivivus*.[1]
The gaping Zany turns fool, and presently his audience
surrounds him and he has an opportunity to lecture on
his pill.

> The bouncing Quack's alluring Babble
> Prevailing with the list'ning Rabble,
> Old coughing Fools, and crazy Nurses,
> Began apace to draw their Purses,
> Hoping that now they should be freed
> From Corns, and Coughs, and aching Head,
> And all the Plagues that wait each Day
> On Age, hard Labour, and Decay,
> Believing, as the Doctor said,
> They now should be immortal made.

Meanwhile, the merry-andrew, not to waste his time,
sells charms and beauty washes. There was a famous
merry-andrew who acted for Pinkethman, and who was
at other times a horse doctor.[2] His fame we find echoed
in lines from the Harleian MS. (5931, 251):

> That used to visit Smithfield or May Fair,
> To pertake of the lewdness that is acted there;
> T' oblige the mobb, that did some pastime lack,
> He'd Merry Andrew turn; and name of Quack
> Forsake a fortnight, then that time expired
> The name of Doctor was again acquired.

Mr. Addison dignified these popular diversions by actu-
ally writing a brief Latin poem about them. This is

[1] Part I, vol. II, Cantos I and II.
[2] Cf. Thomas Brown, *The Life of the Famous Comedian, Jo. Hayns* (1701),
pp. 35–40.

translated as "The Puppet-Shew," and finds a place in
the Lewis *Miscellany* (page 100):[1]

> Where the throng'd Street resounds with Laughter loud,
> And *Andrew* drolling charms the gaping Crowd,
> Within (whom Mirth and Novelty invite
> To humble Sport, and innocent Delight)
> In a small Theatre an Audience meets,
> And fills, but unpromiscuous fills, the Seats.

There is a tragic hero among the puppets, a King and
his court, and a bloody battle.

The fortune-teller also, of whatever stripe, had here
his opportunity:

> In which might easily be seen
> The Drift of all contain'd within;
> As *Moor-fields* Conjurers can see,
> By th' Art of Phisiognomy.[2]

Their pretensions were rather more formidable than
they are to-day.

> Men who foretold whats'ever was
> By consequence to come to pass;
> As death of great men, alterations,
> Diseases, battles, inundations;
> Or search'd a planet's house to know,
> Who broke and robb'd a house below,
> Examin'd Venus and the moon
> To find who stole a silver spoon.[3]

But like the Delphic oracle, their limitations were acute.

> For as those men that trade with Stars,
> And foretel Famines, Plagues, and Wars,
> In doubtful terms their thoughts express,
> To save their Credits if they miss.[4]

---

[1] Translated by Thomas Fitzgerald, *Poems on Several Occasions* (1733),
p. 17.

[2] Ward, *Hudibras Redivivus* (4th ed., 1708), Part II, p. 5.

[3] Butler, *Hudibras*, Part II.

[4] Thomas D'Urfey, *Collin's Walk through London and Westminster* (1690),
p. 110.

A ballad about a really imaginative fortune-teller was printed "with allowance, Ro. L'Estrange" (1663–85). This was *Poor Robin's Prophesie, or The Merry Conceited Fortune-teller*. Robin tells of a golden age coming, when gallants will pay the shopkeepers, the lawyer neglect his fees, the usurer open his coffers, the physician strive to keep men alive, "Nor Mountebank-Bills in the streets you shall find." Ladies of pleasure will live like nuns, bullies leave off gaming, Hecks and Padders find a new trade. Newgate will be empty; the tradesmen will help each other.

> The Tapsters no more shall their Ticklers froth,
> No Coffee-men blind us with their Ninny-broth . . .
> Those men who of late with *Duke Humphrey* have dined,
> *With plenty shall flow — when the Devil is blind* . . .
> Then Poets in both pockets *Guinneys* shall find,
> *And purchase estates — when the Devil is blind.*[1]

The star quacks of the earlier time were, however, the alchemists, though no doubt some of these, like Cornelius Drebbel, were making honest investigations and seeking scientific truth. Rowlands finds a place for the pretenders in his catalogue of sinners:

> You base Quacksaluer in a Common wealth,
> That practize Phisicke out of olde wiues tales,
> You that can make them sicke which haue their health
> And learne by Almanackes, to pare your Nayles.
> You that can tell what signe is best affected
> To picke ones Teeth, or haue his Beard corrected.
>   Ile Stabbe yee.[2]

In his Satire III the same writer brings the alchemist out on the street:[3]

---

[1] *Roxburghe Ballads*, VIII ², 78. Guineas were first coined in 1663. The African Company had the right to stamp a picture of an elephant on the coin.

[2] "Looke to it" (1604).

[3] *The Letting of Humours Blood*, p. 59.

And note him wheresoeuer that he goes,
His Booke of Characters is in his hose.
His dinner he will not presume to take,
Ere he aske counsell of an Almanacke. . . .
Alcumie in his braines so sure doth settle,
He can make golde of any copper kettle;
Within a three weekes space or such a thing,
Riches vpon the whole worlde he could bring,
But in his owne purse one shall hardly spie it,
Witnesse his Hostesse, for a twelue-moneths diet.

Apparently, the acrobatic sports, especially the dancing on the tight rope, were favorite exhibitions with the crowd.[1] Dryden says impatiently in one of his prologues,[2]

Go back to your dear Dancing on the Rope,
Or see what's worse, the Devil and the Pope!

There were even songs composed in honor of these artists of the tight rope, one of which is to be found in John Cotgrave's *Wits Interpreter, the English Parnassus,* etc., etc. (1655, page 317). It is called "A new Song on the Turkish Artist which is lately come into England, which danceth on a Rope eight and thirty foot from the ground."

He towers like a Falcon over the people,
Before he coms down he's as high as Pauls steeple.

They really did thrilling feats.

Then a speech is made in a heathenish tongue,
Even of his own accord;
To say what he sayes I should doe you wrong,
For I understand never a word.

---

[1] Davenant, "The Long Vacation," in *Wit and Drollery* (1661), p. 87. Here the Mayor rides to Bartholomew Fair, while the aldermen play quoits. Others go to Finsbury to practise archery. At the fair may be seen as usual the vaulters, the girls dancing on ropes, the tumblers, and various sideshows.

[2] *Miscellany Poems* (3d ed., 1702), I, 209.

> He quits his pole and his thumbs,
> He wipes his face, and he picks his gums,
> He dons his doublet, and down he comes,
>   And there's an end of the Turk.[1]

The idea of actually flying is as old, no doubt, as the desire of the first man to imitate the bird. The *Philosophical Transactions to the End of Year 1700*[2] contain an illustration and description of the flying machine of Sieur Besnier, and Richard Owen Cambridge has a very good description of an air-race between a Briton and a German in Book IV of his *Scribleriad* (1751). The setting for his race seems rather Greek than English, and the result involves an incident which hardly suits our ideas of clean sport.

> Soon as Aurora's beams disperse the gloom,
> The pious crowd surround th' Acrostick's tomb:
>
> .   .   .   .
>
> Yon sloping hill's umbrageous side commands
> The spacious ocean and the level sands:
> The living marble there shall yield a seat,
> While solemn games the hallow'd rites compleat.
> Thither the prizes bring ordain'd to grace
> The rapid victor in th' aerial race.

The chief prize is a great ox, which moves the hero to excited speech. Nothing can restrain him from competing but the memory of his loss. For him this is a day of mourning; let brisker youths prepare their light silken wings and skim the buxom air.

> Mov'd by my words, two youths of equal fire
> Spring from the croud, and to the prize aspire.
> The one a German of distinguish'd fame:
> His rival from projecting Britain came.

---

[1] The poem states that this man stood on his head on the pinnacle of Bowe. Cf. Nichols, *Biog. Anec.*, p. 183. Cadman flies from St. Martin's steeple.

[2] Ed. by John Lowthorp (2d ed., 1716), 3 vols.

They spread their wings, and with a rising bound,
Swift at the word together quit the ground.
The Briton's rapid flight outstrips the wind:
The lab'ring German urges close behind.
As some light bark, pursu'd by ships of force,
Stretches each sail to swell her swifter course,
The nimble Briton from his rival flies,
And soars on bolder pinions to the skies.
Sudden the string, which bound his plumage, broke;
His naked arms in yielding air he shook:
His naked arms no more support his weight,
But fail him sinking from his airy height.
Yet as he falls, so chance or fate decreed,
His rival near him urg'd his winged speed,
Not unobserv'd (despair suggests a thought)
Fast by the foot the heedless youth he caught,
And drew th' insulting victor to the ground:
While rocks and woods with loud applause resound.

Consolation prizes — yon damsel and a statue of
Icarus — are offered to this quick-witted youth, and the
day ends happily for both. It is perhaps worth noticing
that Britain is here styled "projecting Britain"; the
author himself experimented in various types of light
sailing craft and had ideas on the development of water-
power. He was much interested in the possibilities of air-
craft and under-water vessels. He brings submarines
into the story of this poem and reminds his readers in a
footnote that "Cornelius Drebell made a vessel for
James I to be row'd under water with twelve rowers.
It was try'd on the Thames." Bishop Wilkins (John),
in *Mathematical Magic*, Book II, chapter 5, comments on
the advantages of under-sea vessels.

The temper of the people and their *joie de vivre* is per-
haps best shown when something out of the ordinary
routine of life occurs, which gives them opportunity to
test their spirit and the historian a chance to observe it.

Such opportunities were furnished by the great frosts which about once in a generation bound the Thames solid for two or three months. The one to which Gay refers occurred in 1709–10. The varied uses which the populace found for this new source of amusement should put to shame their modern descendants, who for the most part are too self-conscious to show any originality in their pleasures, and too stupid often to see either joke or insult in the appointment of supervisors for children's games. Gay's lines deserve quotation:

> O roving Muse, recall that wond'rous year,
> When winter reign'd in bleak Britannia's air;
> When hoary Thames, with frosted osiers crown'd,
> Was three long moons in icy fetters bound.
> The waterman, forlorn along the shore,
> Pensive reclines upon his useless oar,
> Sees harness'd steeds desert the stony town,
> And wander roads unstable, not their own:
> Wheels o'er the harden'd waters smoothly glide,
> And rase with whiten'd tracks the slipp'ry tide.
> Here the fat cook piles high the blazing fire,
> And scarce the spit can turn the steer entire.
> Booths sudden hide the Thames, long streets appear,
> And num'rous games proclaim the crowded fair.
> So when a general bids the martial train
> Spread their encampment o'er the spacious plain;
> Thick rising tents a canvas city build,
> And the loud dice resound thro' all the field.

There are numerous old ballads on the same subject, and the descriptions of what took place, especially during the extraordinary winter of 1683–84, on the frozen surface of the Thames are very interesting. The *Roxburghe Ballads* contain several of these. One is called "London's Wonder: The Great Frost, 1683–84." [1]

---

[1] *Roxburghe Ballads*, V, 457.

Come, listen a while (tho' the weather be cold),
In your pockets and plackets your hands you may hold:
I 'll tell you a story, as true as 't is rare,
Of a River turn'd into a *Bartholomew*-Fair:
   Since Old *Christmas* last,
   There has been such a Frost,
That the *Thames* has by half the whole Nation been crost.
   Oh! Scullers, I pity your Fate of extreames,
   Each Land-man has now become free of the *Thames*.

The ballad has its own political implications. Indeed, the blame for the unusual severity of the weather was always laid on the shoulders of the Whigs.

'T is some *Lapland* acquaintance of Conjurer *Oates*,
That has tied up your hands, and imprison'd your Boats;
You know he was never a friend to the crew
Of all those that to Admiral *James* have been true.
   Where Sculls once did row
   Men walk to and fro,
But e're four months are ended 't will hardly be so;
   Should your hopes of a *Thaw* by this weather be crost,
   Your Fortune will soon be as hard as the Frost.
In Roast-Beef and Brandy much money is spent,
And Booths made of *Blankets*, that pay no ground-rent;
With old-fashion'd Chimneys the Rooms are secur'd,
And the Houses from danger from Fire are ensur'd.
   The chief place you meet
   Is call'd *Temple-Street*,
If you do not believe me, then you may go see't;
   From the *Temple* the Students do thither resort,
   Who are always great patrons of revels and sport.

The hard heart of the Whigs is made responsible for the frost, and Titus Oates figures unfavorably in many of the verses. A reference to his remarks serves as an introduction to "Freezeland Fair; or The Icy Bear-Garden": [1]

---

[1] *Roxburghe Ballads*, V, 458.

He said that the *Pope*
(Pray mind, 't is a *Trope*)
Wou'd send us his *Bulls* by the way of the Hope;
  And tho' for the *Sign* we have all along been waiting,
  I t'other day saw on the *Ice* a *Bull-baiting!*

It is the spontaneity and enthusiasm with which these
novel amusements were hailed that is the remarkable
thing. Everyone goes in for a good time.

Cooks' Shops with roast Victuals, and Taverns with Wine,
Already are seen on the River with plenty,
Which are fill'd ev'ry morning before you can dine,
By two's and by three's, I may truly say twenty;
        Jack, Tom, Will, and *Harry,*
        Nan, Sue, Doll, and *Mary,*
Come there to devour plum-cakes and Canary:
And if with their Dancing and Wine they be tir'd,
For a Tester a-piece there's a Coach to be hir'd.[1]

Two broadsides about the frost may be found in the
British Museum, and another in the Ashmolean.[2] The
town moved out on the river, shop-keepers and all,

Where shop rents were so cheap, and goods so dear.

Coffee-houses appeared, games of football and ninepins,
bear-baiting and bull-baiting, small vessels under sail,
dancing on ropes, puppet plays, Dutch whimsies,

And some do say a giddy senseless ass
May on the Thames be furnished with a lass.

The watermen are idle naturally, and "the shoars no
longer sound with Westward hoe." One enterprising
person started a printing house on the Thames and pro-
duced *Thamasis's Advice to the Painter, from her frigid
zone, etc., printed by G. Croom, on the river of Thames:*

---

[1] "The Whigs Hard Heart for the Cause of the Hard Frost," *Roxburghe
Ballads,* V, 461.
[2] William Andrews, *Famous Frosts and Frost Fairs in Great Britain* (1887).

To the print-house go,
Where Men the art of Printing soon do know,
Where for a Teaster, you may have your name
Printed, hereafter for to show the same:
And sure, in former Ages, ne'er was found
A Press to print, where men so oft were droun'd.

An ox was roasted whole and some enthusiasts even in-
dulged in fox-hunting on the ice. The poor suffered, as
they always do at such times.

This frost lasted such a long time that many feared
London was doomed to some special visitation of the
wrath of the Almighty. Finally the end of it came, how-
ever, and deliverance from its rigors was hailed in an-
other street ballad, called this time "London's Wonder:
being a Description of God's Mercy and Goodness, in
the breaking of this late mighty Frost, which began
about the middle of December, 1683, and continued till
the 4th of February following." [1]

Then during the Frost there they followed their blows,
In Musick and Gaming, and acting of Shows;
On this mighty River they Roasted an Ox,
They Bated the Bull, and they Hunted the Fox:
But yet I was troubled those pleasures to see,
For fear that our Lord he should angry be. . . .

The Water-men now at all Stairs they shall ply,
"Next Oars" and "Next Sculler!" let this be their Cry:
For now you may see they have changed their notes,
They pull'd down their Tents, and they Row in their Boats.
'T was the works of the Lord, we may well understand,
He made mighty Rivers as firm as the Land.

This frost of 1683–84 seems to have been of all the
most famous. There were others, some of which occa-
sionally got honorable mention in verse of a higher type

---

[1] *Roxburghe Ballads*, V, 463.

than street ballads. For instance, George Wither writes
of one in his *Juvenilia*, "Abuses Stript and Whipt": [1]

> for th' other day,
> When the hard frost had stopt the Scullers way,
> And left fair *Thames* with Ice so strongly archt,
> That on the melting pauement people marcht.

This could not have been so severe, for he tells a story of
a man who gets adrift on a cake of ice and is finally
rescued by a rope thrown from the bridge.[2]

If people were capable of doing so much with an un-
inviting sheet of dirty ice, we may expect to find their
capacity for enjoyment more evident in the many parks
and gardens of which Queen Anne's London had reason
to boast. The livelier iris of spring should show still
more interesting scenes, since even dull winter is gay.

Hyde Park was perhaps the chief centre of the city
pleasures in the season. All classes of society fre-
quented it.

> Come all you noble, you that are neat ones.
> Hide-Park is now both fresh and green.[3]

So runs the old "Song called Hide-Park," which J. W.
Ebsworth prints in his *Westminster Drolleries*.[4] Come,
gallants!

> Come all you Courtiers in your neat fashions,
> Rich in your new unpaid-for silk.

You brave wenches, great ladies, drawn with six horses
at least! All from the Strand, from Westminster Hall,

---

[1] *Poems* (printed for the Spenser Society, 1871), Part I, p. 115. First
published in 1622.

[2] Cf. *Trivia*, II, 381.

[3] Cf. John Durant Breval, *The Confederates* (1717):

> "To Morrow to the *Park* my Course I steer,
> Where good Duke *Humphry's* Guests dine half the Year."

[4] Boston, Lincolnshire (1875), Part I, p. 73. The songs date about 1671-72.

merchants' wives that keep their coaches, country girls
who have bought out the Exchange, aldermen's daugh-
ters, all must come to the Park! Sunday was the favorite
day for crowds to gather:

> On that dull day which, ev'ry week, affords
> A glut of 'prentices, in bags and swords;
> When sober families resort to pray'r,
> And cits take in their weekly meal of air;
> While, eastward of St. Paul's, the well-dress'd spark
> Runs two long miles, to saunter in the park.[1]

The main attraction was, of course, to see and to be
seen. Pope strikes just the right note in his description
of the ordinary situation.[2]

> Rufa, whose eye quick-glancing o'er the Park,[3]
> Attracts each light gay meteor of a Spark,
> Agrees as ill with Rufa studying Locke,
> As Sappho's di'monds with her dirty smock.

There were no arranged amusements or sights here un-
til a later time. The exhibition of naval manoeuvres in
miniature on the Serpentine[4] just one hundred years
after the accession of George I created considerable
popular interest. Various skits were written about this
Naumachia, which John Ashton collects in *Hyde Park
from Domesday-Book to Date* (page 68).

> A simple Angler, throwing flies for trout,
> Hauled the main mast, and lugg'd a First Rate out.

---

[1] Charles Jenner, *Town Eclogues* (1772), II, 8.

[2] *Moral Essays*, II, "Of the Characters of Women." Cf. *The Mall: or, the Reigning Beauties, containing the various Intrigues of Miss Cloudy and her Governante Madam Agility* (1709), Bibl. Bodl., G. P. 1278.

[3] Cf. Shadwell, *A True Widow* (1679), I, 1: "Your Side-Glass let down hastily, when the Party goes by, is very passionate."

[4] Queen Caroline added the Serpentine to the beauty of the Park. The water came in those days from Hampstead Heath.

C. F. Lawler wrote verses about it. The transference of
the ships' barges overland from Woolwich was watched
with amusement.

Besides the great Park, however, there were several
pleasure resorts which in time became famous, especially
Vauxhall and, later, Ranelagh Gardens. From the first
there was an agreeable atmosphere of scandal about
these places, though none of the *élite* showed any dispo-
sition to shun them. There were plays to be seen.
George Ogle refers to one of these by Colley Cibber in
an adaptation he made of the Eighth Satire of the Sec-
ond Book of Horace, *The Miser's Feast*, *A Dialogue
between the Author and the Poet Laureate* (1737).

> One of his comedies! and worth them all!
> Better than that he acted at Vauxhall.

Vauxhall is here described in a foot-note as "A garden
of nightly pleasure, where clergymen of gallantry may
entertain ladies with church music, without the least
scandal to the cloth." The poem goes on to describe a
feast held there, the conversation indulged in, amusing
incidents, and so forth.

A note in one of Horace Walpole's letters gives a very
good idea of the catholicity of the crowds at Ranelagh:[1]

> Nobody goes anywhere else — everybody goes there. . . .
> You can't set your foot without treading on a Prince of Wales
> or Duke of Cumberland. The company is universal: there is
> from his Grace of Grafton down to children out of the Found-
> ling Hospital — from my Lady Townshend to the Kitten.

The Kitten may have been either Kitty Fisher, the cour-
tesan, or Kitty Clive, the actress; probably he meant
the former.

---

[1] To the Hon. Henry Seymour Conway, June 29, 1744. Cf. Horace Wal-
pole's account of Lady Caroline Petersham's party at Vauxhall, in his letter
to G. Montagu, June 23, 1750. See also, Walpole's letter to Sir Horace
Mann, May 26, 1742.

Sir Roger visited "Foxhall." Whether he stopped to see life as it was on the *Folly* is questionable, like the pleasures on that barge.

> When Drapers smug'd Prentices,
>   With *Exchange* Girls most jolly,
> After Shop was shut up,
>   Could Sail to the Folly.[1]

But the London youths in search of a good time were not confined to the Park and the pleasure gardens. Within easy reach of the city were several favorite watering-places.[2]

> Sweethearts with their sweethearts go
> To Islington or London Spaw;
> Some go but just to drink the water,
> Some for the ale which they like better.[3]

A poem by W. Woty, printed in the *London Chronicle*, 1760 (VII, 531), reproduces the spirit of the thing very well.

> Wish'd Sunday's come, mirth brightens ev'ry face,
> And paints the rose upon the housemaid's cheek,
> Harriot, or Moll, more ruddy. Now the heart
> Of 'prentice, resident in ample street,
> Or alley, kennel-wash'd, Cheapside, Cornhill,
> Or Cranbourne, thee for calcuments renown'd,
> With joy distends. His meal meridian o'er,
> With switch in hand, he to White Conduit House
> Hies merry-hearted. Human beings here
> In couples multitudinous assemble,

---

[1] "The Long Vacation," in D'Urfey's *Pills to Purge Melancholy* (4th ed., 1714, 7 vols.), III, 65.

[2] Cf. *From Caelia to Cloe* [by Richard West?], Dodsley, II, 348 (1765):
> "Now when the Mall's forlorn, the beaux and belles
> All for retirement crowd to Tunbridge-Wells;
> Say, will not Cloe for awhile withdraw
> From dear Vaux-hall and charming Ranelagh?"

[3] *Poor Robin's Almanack* (1733), quoted in Wroth, *Pleasure Gardens* (1896), p. 30.

Forming the drollest group that ever trod
Fair Islingtonian plains. Male after male,
Dog after dog succeeding, husbands, wives,
Fathers and mothers, brothers, sisters, friends,
And pretty little boys and girls. Around,
Across, along the gardens' shrubby maze
They walk, they sit, they stand. What crowds press on,
Eager to mount the stairs, eager to catch
First vacant bench, or chair in long room plac'd.
Here prig with prig holds conference polite,
And indiscriminate the gaudy beau
And sloven mix. Here he who all the week
Took bearded mortals by the nose, or sat
Weaving dead hairs, and whistling wretched strain,
And eke the sturdy youth, whose trade it is
Stout oxen to contund, with gold-bound hat
And silken stocking strut. The red-arm'd belle
Here shows her tasty gown, proud to be thought
The butterfly of fashion.[1]

The popularity of these outlying amusement places is
well attested by the large number of ephemeral verses
which were written about them. On the rise of Islington
to fame we have some lines in a poem called "May Day,
or the Origin of Garlands" (1720):[2]

> Now nine-pin alleys, and not skettles grace
> The late forlorn, sad, desolated place;
> Arbours of jasmine fragrant shades compose
> And numerous blended companies enclose.[3]

Better than this is a poem by George Bickham, called
"The Charms of Dishabille, or New Tunbridge Wells
at Islington,"[4] illustrated with a view of the gardens:

---

[1] Quoted in Wroth, p. 132.   [2] *Ibid.*, p. 30.
[3] Cf. Shadwell, *Virtuoso* (1676), Act V: "Your Glass-Coach will to *Hyde-Park* for Air; the Suburb-fools trudge to *Lambs-Conduit* or *Tottenham;* your sprucer sort of Citizens gallop to *Epsom;* your Mechanick gross Fellows, shewing much conjugal Affection, strut before their Wives, each with a Child in his Arms, to *Islington* or *Hogsden.*"
[4] Called also, "The Humours of the New Tunbridge Wells at Islington" (1734).

Behold the Walks, a chequer'd shade,
In the gay pride of green array'd;
How bright the sun! the air how still!
In wild confusion there we view
Red ribbons grouped with aprons blue;
Scrapes, curtsies, nods, winks, smiles, and frowns,
Lords, milkmaids, duchesses, and clowns,
In their all-various dishabille.

A somewhat quieter picture of such a place, this time Sadler's Wells, is given in " The New River," by William Garbott (*ca.* 1725):

There you may sit under the shady trees,
And drink and smoke fann'd by the gentle breeze.

Bagnigge Wells was also popular and continued so down to the time of Colman, who wrote a Prologue for Garrick's *Bon Ton* in 1775:

Bon Ton's the space 'twixt Saturday and Monday,
And riding in a one-horse chair o' Sunday!
'T is drinking tea on summer afternoons
At Bagnigge Wells, with China and gilt spoons!

A "Prentice Song" (*ca.* 1779), which must have amused a good many listeners and readers, refers to this, the most conveniently situated of London watering-places. The lovers have quarrelled and he tries to bribe her into good humor.

Come prithee make it up, Miss, and be as lovers be,
We'll go to Bagnigge Wells, Miss, and there we'll have some tea;
It's there you'll see the lady-birds perched on the stinging nettles,
The crystal water fountain, and the copper shining kettles.
It's there you'll see the fishes, more curious they than whales,
And they're made of gold and silver, Miss, and wags their little tails;
They wags their little tails, they wags their little tails.[1]

[1] Wroth, p. 62.

A little more original in his means of entertaining the crowds was James Howell, the so-called "Welsh Ambassador," at Belsize House. A poem about this place appeared in 1722, by a "serious person of quality." Just why this puritanic versifier should call the house a nuisance to the land is not clear in the poem, which mentions nothing but the most innocent amusements:

This house, which is a nuisance to the land,
Doth near a park and handsome garden stand,
Fronting the road, betwixt a range of trees
Which is perfumed with a Hampstead breeze.
The Welsh Ambassador has many ways
Fool's pence, while summer season holds, to raise.
For 't is not only chocolate and tea,
With ratafia, bring him company.
Nor is it claret, Rhenish wine or sack
The fond and rampant Lords and Ladies lack,
Or ven'son pasty for a certain dish
With several varieties of fish;
But hither they and other chubs resort
To see the Welsh Ambassador make sport,
Who in the art of hunting has the luck
To kill in fatal corner tired buck,
The which he roasts and stews and sometimes bakes,
Whereby His Excellency profit makes.
He also on another element
Doth give his choused customers content
With net and angling rod, to catch a dish
Of trouts or carp or other sorts of fish.

Such were the resorts of the eighteenth century. Each must meet competitors for popularity, and echoes of their rivalries come down to us in newspaper verses, prologues to plays, street ballads, and the like. Fashions changed, and the popular resorts of one generation were forgotten by the next.

Time was, when sattin waistcoats and scratch wigs,
Enough distinguish'd all the city prigs,

Whilst ev'ry sunshine Sunday saw them run
To club their sixpences, at *Islington;*
When graver citizens, in suits of brown,
Lin'd ev'ry dusty avenue to town,
Or led the children and the loving spouse,
To spend two shillings at *White-conduit-house:*
But now, the 'prentices, in suits of green,
At *Richmond,* or at *Windsor* may be seen;
Where in mad parties they run down to dine,
To play at gentlefolks, and drink bad wine:
Whilst neat post-chariots roll their masters down
To some snug box, a dozen miles from town.[1]

The Prologue to *The Orphan,* spoken by Mr. Gibson at
the New Theatre in Haymarket on the 31st of May,
1762, was printed in *Owen's Weekly Chronicle or Universal
Journal* for June 5 to 12, 1762, and suggests some of the
novelties which were introduced to draw the crowds:

How dull, methinks, look Robin, Sue and Nancy,
At Greenwich park did nothing strike your fancy;
Had you no cheese-cakes, cyder, shrimps or bun,
Saw no wild beastis, or no jack-ass run?
Blest Conduit House! what raptures does it yield;
And hail, thou wonder of a Chelsea field!
Yet Zucker still amazingly surpasses
Your Conduit-house, your pigmy, and your asses.[2]

The pigmy was a dwarf, Coan, who might be seen at
Dwarf's Tavern in Chelsea Fields.

The end of the perfect day brought the young men
and maidens back to some of the tea-drinking stands in
the city.

On Sabbath day who has not seen
In colours of the rainbow dizened,
The 'prentice beaux and belles, I ween,
Fatigued with heat, with dust half-poisoned,

---

[1] Charles Jenner, *Town Eclogues* (1772), II, 10.
[2] Quoted in Wroth, p. 146. Not reprinted in *The Babler* (1767).

To Dobney's strolling, or Pantheon,
Their tea to sip or else regale,
As on their way they shall agree on,
With syllabubs or bottled ale.[1]

The first of the places referred to here was in Exmouth Street, and the second on the southeast corner of Penton Street.

Many of the plays of the Restoration and later take one into the midst of these gay resorts of pleasure. Shadwell is particularly useful as a guide to the social life of his time. Bellamy, his malcontent in *Bury Fair* (acted 1689), has a poor opinion of both place and people: "So many pens of wild beasts upon two legs, undermining, lying in wait, preying upon, informing against, and hanging one another: a crowd of fools, knaves, whores, and hypocrites." Their conversation is dull and dangerous, because it runs into parties and government. The transformation of a French peruke-maker into a count occasions much of the business of the play; his delight in the high life of the place, the excitement of the flying horses, his pleasure in the performance of "a fellow that acts Tom of Bedlam to a miracle," as well as his adventures among the ladies, are all amusingly introduced. All turns out well at the last, and Oldwit, the patron of the group, is ready to make everybody happy: " Call all my servants; lay down all my meat to the fire; set all my hogsheads abroach; call in the fiddlers; let's revel for a month at least."

Even more illuminating than this is a play called *Tunbridge-Walks; or, the Yeoman of Kent.* This play was written by Thomas Baker, who knew the town and possessed some slight literary ability. His description

---

[1] *London Evening Post*, Aug., 1776. Quoted in Wroth, p. 143.

of the assembly at this ancient watering-place suggests
a most interesting variety:

Like most publick Assemblies, a Medly of all sorts, Fops
majestick and diminutive, from the long flaxen Wig with the
splendid Equipage, to the Merchant's Spruce Prentice that's
always mighty neat about the Legs; Squires come to Court
some fine Town-Lady, and Town-Sparks to pick up a Russet-
Gown; for the Women here are wild Country-Ladies, with
ruddy Cheeks like a *Sevil*-Orange, that gape, stare, scamper,
and are brought hither to be Disciplin'd; Fat City-Ladies
with tawdry Atlases, in Defiance of the Act of Parliament;
and slender Court-Ladies, with *French* Scarffs, *French* Aprons,
French Night-Cloaths, and *French* Complexions.[1]

All these places were the resorts of the holiday-maker.
For the ordinary loafer St. Paul's, the Exchange, and
the Abbey were popular.

If any single house or building might be regarded as
the centre of London life till the time of the Great Fire,
it certainly was St. Paul's Cathedral. Its glories, along
with the old building, had departed before Gay came to
write of London. But earlier, its popularity was im-
mense. All kinds of people made their way thither, for
business, for pleasure, for news, or to eat with Duke
Humphrey, who from his legendary tomb presided over
many a meatless meal, as the following ingatherings
from the poetry of the time will show. In Hall's *Sat-
ires* we notice these lines:

Seest thou how gayly my yong maister goes,
Vaunting himselfe upon his rising toes;
And pranks his hand upon his dagger's side;
And picks his glutted teeth since late noon-tide?
'T is Ruffio: Trow'st thou where he din'd today?
In sooth I saw him sit with Duke Humfray.[2]

[1] *Tunbridge-Walks* (1703), p. 2.   [2] Hall, *Satires* (1597), III, 7.

Robert Hayman, in *Quodlibets*,[1] "To Sir Pierce Penni-
lesse" (1628), also speaks of this habit of loafing in
Paul's when there was no money in pocket to pay for
a meal:

> Though little coin thy purseless pockets line,
> Yet with great company thou 'rt taken up;
> For often with Duke Humfray thou dost dine,
> And often with Sir Thomas Gresham sup.

Sir Thomas Gresham was the founder of the Royal Ex-
change just across the street, and the patron of similar
banquets. A later poem by Samuel Speed, called *Frag-
menta Carceris, or The Kings-Bench Scuffle* (1675), shows
that the tradition still lingered on, late in the century:

> Some on Devotion came to feed their Muse;
> Some came to sleep, or walk, or talk of News.
> For though they came to dine, they loathed Meat;
> For many had almost forgot to Eat. . . .
> Some came with jingling Spurs instead of Chink,
> For that was melted on their Mornings Drink:
> And drink they must; I never yet knew one
> Could quench his thirst with reading Dr. *Donne*.

Beggars, amorists, scholars, soldiers, are there, and they
are politely invited to come again.

> But ere that happy day was fully grown,
> A dreadful Fire consumes the Kitchin down:
> Which Fire began not in His Graces House,
> But thither came, and burnt both Rat and Mouse.
> On which the *Duke*, to shun a scorching doom,
> Perambulated to *Ben Johnson's* Tomb,
> Where *Shakespear*, *Spencer*, *Camden*, and the rest,
> Once rising Suns, are now set in the West:
> But still their lustres do so brightly shine,
> That they invite our Worthies there to dine.

---

[1] *Quodlibets, lately come over from New Britaniola, Old Newfoundland.*
Four books by Robert Hayman, the rest by James Owen.

The place was even used as a billboard to expose the
"want ads." The parson himself, out of a job, might
come looking for a benefice.

> Saw'st thou ever Siquis patch'd on Paul's church doore,
> To seeke some vacant vicarage before?
> Who wants a churchman that can service say,
> Read fast and faire his monthly homiley?
> And wed and bury, and make christen-soules?
> Come to the left-side alley of Saint Poules.[1]

There were evidently a few who disapproved of this
scandalous condition of affairs. In 1621, Henry Farley
wrote a brief poem called "St. Paules Church her Bill
for the Parliament," in which the following lines occur:

> And let those base, prophane, and idle Rout,
> That daily passe with burthens, in, and out . . .
> O whip them soundly that abuse thy Temple.

It is worth noting that St. Paul's had the only street
lamps in the city in that early time. Across the street
was the Royal Exchange, another popular news centre.
On the steeple of this building was a grasshopper, the
crest of the founder. We find the Exchange called by
this name sometimes as if by a sign. Thus in Hall's
Satires (IV, 6):

> And now he plies the newes-full grasshopper,
> Of voyages and ventures to enquire.

The Royal Exchange seems to have been also the best
place to go to hear the fabulous stories of travel so
greedily devoured in those days. Rowlands laughs at
this in his *Letting of Humours Blood* (1600), Satire I:

> Sometimes into the *Royall Exchange* he'll droppe,
> Clad in the ruines of some Brokers shoppe:
> And there his tongue runs byas on affaires,
> No talke but of comodities and wares . . .

---

[1] Hall, *Satires* (1597), II, 5.

> If newes be harkend for, then he preuailes,
> Setting his mynt aworke to coyne false tales. . . .
> Heele tell you of a tree that he doth know,
> Vpon the which Rapiers and Daggers grow,
> As good as any Fleetstreete hath in shoppe;
> Which being ripe, downe into scabbards droppe. . . .
> His wondrous trauels challenge such renowne,
> That *Sir John Maundeuille* is quite put downe.
> Men without heades, and *Pigmies* hand-bredth hie,
> Those with one legge that on their backes do lie,
> And doe the weathers iniurie disdaine,
> Making their legges a penthouse for the raine.

Besides Paul's and the Exchange, the Guildhall always attracted the attention of visitors to the city, chiefly on account of the grotesque Gog and Magog on its gates.

> And makes such faces that meseems I see
> Some foul Megaera in the tragedy,
> Threat'ning her twined snakes at Tantale's ghost;
> Or the grim visage of some frowning post
> The crabtree porter of the Guild-hall gates;
> While he his frightful beetle elevates. [1]

Two of the main social centres of the Londoner at all times have been mentioned but incidentally so far, the tavern [2] and the playhouse. The tavern appealed to both rich and poor, but to the poor it provided the centre for all their social contacts. It was club and opera alike to them. The playhouse, on the other hand, catered to a much smaller section of the public, and for that reason will not receive so much of our attention here. For us, both are to be viewed simply as amusement places, part of the London life of the time.

The coffee-houses developed early in Restoration times. They were at first in ill repute as springs of

[1] Hall, *Satires*, VI, 1.
[2] Gay, *Trivia*, I, 154; II, 190, 335; III, 116, 275.

Whiggish disaffection, and were at times under ban of government. Evidently closing them proved to be poor policy, for, as Woolnoth's little poem called *The Coffee Scuffle* [1] says in 1662,

> Where Loyalists brew there Fanaticks bake too,
> And the Good will be mix'd with the Bad.

They flourished in spite of frowning authorities, for they filled a real need in the Londoner's life. There he met those with similar views and interests, and discussed the questions of the day with an astonishing freedom.

The sort of gossip one might hear in such places is very well described by Thomas Jordan in a street ballad. [2]

> You that delight in Wit and Mirth, and long to hear such News,
> As comes from all parts of the Earth, *Dutch, Danes,* and *Turks* and *Jews,*
> I'le send you a Rendezvous, where it is smoaking new:
> Go hear it at a *Coffee-house,* — *it cannot but be true.*

There you will hear all about battles on land and sea, bloody plots of all kinds.

> Who last did cut *De Ruiter's* corns, amongst his jovial Crew,
> Or who first gave the Devil horns: *which cannot but be true.*
> A Fisherman did boldly tell, and strongly did avouch,
> He caught a shoal of Mackerel, that parley'd all in *Dutch;*
> And cry'd out *Yaw, yaw, yaw, Myn Here;* but, as the Draught they drew,
> They stunk for fear that *Monck* was there: *which cannot but be true.*

---

[1] *The Coffee Scuffle, occasioned by a contest between a learned Knight and a pitifull Pedagogue. With the character of a Coffee-House* (1662). Satirical verses said to have been made by Woolnoth on Sir J. Langham and Evans, a schoolmaster.

[2] "News from the Coffee-House," by Thomas Jordan (1667), *Roxburghe Ballads,* V, 177. Cf. "Spatter's Rambles," by Hugh Kelly, *Works* (1778), p. 474.

There, too, you will hear rumors of a French invasion,
what lady-ware is grown too light, what wise man falls
from favor, when trade shall flourish.

> They know all that is Good or Hurt, to damn ye, or to save ye;
> There is the Colledge and the Court, the Countrie, Camp and
>   Navie;
> So great a Universitie, I think, there ne'er was any:
> In which you may a Scholar be *for spending of a Penny*. . . .
> You shall know, there, what Fashions are; How Perrywiggs
>   are curl'd;
> And for a Penny you shall heare all Novells in the world;
> Both Old and Young, and Great and Small, and Rich and
>   Poore you'll see:
> Therefore let's to the *Coffee* all, Come all away with me.

They were by no means exclusive resorts. Admission
was but a penny, and the coffee was sold for twopence,
though at that time tea and coffee retailed for nearly
ten times the present price. In general, White's and
Almack's were favorites with persons of quality, Will's,[1]
Button's, and the Grecian, with poets and scholars.
Button's was in Covent Garden, Will's in the Strand,
and the Grecian in Devereux Court. Child's was the
resort of doctors and undertakers, an association for
mutual encouragement, apparently.[2] The Rose coffee-

---

[1] [John Dennis], "A Day's Ramble in Covent-Garden" (March 20, 1691),
Poems in Burlesque (1692):

> "To *Wills* I went, where Beau and Wit
> In mutual Contemplation sit;
> But which were Wits, and which were Beaus,
> The Devil sure's in him who Knows,
> For either may be which you please,
> These look'd like those, who talk'd like these:
> To make amends, there I saw *Dryden*,
> Whom *Pegasus* takes so much Pride in,
> He suffers few beside to ride him."

[2] See Paul Whitehead's lines (*Satires* [1760], p. 86):

> "Be mine, to stay some Friend's departing Breath,
> And *Child's* may take the Drudgery of Death."

Jonathan's was a stock-jobber's house in Exchange Alley.

house was in Temple Bar, not so famous an institution as its namesake the tavern in Covent Garden. Politics and foreign affairs were common topics in all the houses. That was what the authorities disliked about them. The fop in *Tunbridge-Walks*, for instance, proud of his own fastidious superiority, says, "Then we never read Gazzetts, nor talk of *Venlo* and *Vigo*, like you Coffee-House Fellows." The usual tone of the conversation in these resorts is rather well outlined in a poem by Joseph Mitchell, — though to say that this unhappy petitioner does anything well is perhaps a mistake, — an epistle in verse "To Aaron Hill, Esq." [1]

> How wou'd you wonder at my alter'd Case,
> Cou'd you behold me walk, with *Spanish Pace*,
> *Affected Gravity*, and *solemn Face?*
> In *Coffee-Houses*, wage a War with Wit!
> At *Church*, as formal, as the *Parson*, sit,
> With Eyes, new-disciplin'd precisely right,
> Both when to wink, and how to turn the *white!*
> While making Visits, quarrel with the Age!
> Lampoon the *Muses*, and the modern *Stage!*
> Declaim against new-fashion'd *Coats* and *Wigs!*
> And worry all the *Independent Whigs!*
> Still, thus restrain'd, had I but liv'd, and wrote,
> I had, long since, fair *Testimonials* got.

Many a curious session must have been held in such places. We know, for example, from the *Gentleman's Magazine* for 1736 (page 617), that the bonesetter, Mrs. Mapp,[2] used to come up from Epsom once a week and perform cures in the Grecian before the distinguished Hans Sloane.

It is very easy to see how the clubs grew out of these

---

[1] *Poems on Several Occasions* (2 vols., 1729), I, 303.
[2] This is the Mrs. Mapp who figures in some verses to quacks, Ward and Taylor, which Nichols prints (*Biog. Anec.*, pp. 240–243).

coffee-houses.[1] The best-known was the Kit-Cat, which was organized in 1701, under the patronage of Jacob Tonson, and lasted nearly thirty years. Whence the name arose is still unsettled. Christopher Cat made mutton pies (as Addison says); or maybe it was from Christopher at the Cat and Fiddle. Blackmore says in his long poem on the subject that the Club met at the Fountain in the Strand, in summer at the Flask in Hampstead. Forty-two members presented Tonson with portraits (36 × 28) painted by Kneller, for his house at Barn Elms. Arbuthnot refuses to dogmatize:

> Whence deathless *Kit-Cat* took its name,
>   Few critics can unriddle;
> Some say from pastry-cook it came,
>   And some from *Cat* and Fiddle.
> From no trim beaus its name it boasts,
>   Gray statesmen or green wits;
> But from its pell-mell pack of toasts
>   Of old *Cats* and young *Kits!* [2]

The groups that had gathered about Jonson and Dryden were less definitely organized. Any humble follower of the Muse might be welcomed. Such a place was Ben Jonson's Club-Room, about which the following verses from the Lewis *Miscellany* were written (page 71): "On Ben Johnson's Club-Room, call'd the Apollo; at the Devil-Tavern in Fleet-street."

> Once on a Time, as plac'd supream in State,
> Amidst his Sons old merry *Ben* was sate;
> At some rare Strain the jovial Bard essay'd,
> And call'd the Muse and *Phoebus* to his Aid:
> In vain; nor *Phoebus* nor the Muse obey'd.
> Nonplust at this, and in a strange Quandary,
> He fill'd a lusty Bumper of Canary.

---

[1] Ned Ward, "History of Clubs," in *The London Spy* (1704–06), Part IX.
[2] See [James Caulfield], *Memoirs of the Celebrated Persons composing the Kit-Cat Club* (1821).

Soon as this Nectar glided o'er his Tongue,
He rous'd, and tun'd his Lyre, and sweetly sung.
Then to the Room which the rich Juice supply'd,
Henceforth be thou *Apollo* call'd, he cry'd;
Apollo let thy Name forever be,
That lab'ring Bards, in Time to come, may see,
If they their Father *Ben's* Advice will take,
The best Inspirer is delicious Sack.

The Devil Tavern was on the site of the present No. 2 Fleet Street.

The fame of the great Tory club was satirized in *The Swan Tripe-Club: a Satyr on the High-Flyers in the Year 1705* (published. 1710):[1]

Near that Fam'd Place, where slender *Wights* resort,
And gay *Pulvilio* keeps his Scented Court;
Where *Exil'd Wit* ne'er shews its hated Face,
But happier *Nonsense* fills the Thoughtless Place;
Where *Sucking Beaux*, our *future Hopes*, are bred,
The *Sharping Gamester*, and the *Bully Red*,
O'er-stock'd with Fame, but indigent of Bread:
   There stands a Modern Dome, of vast Renown,
For a plump Cook, and plumper Reck'nings known . . .
Young *Doctors* of the *Gown* here shrewdly show,
How *Grace Divine* can ebb, and *Spleen* can flow;
The pious *Redcoat* most devoutly swears,
Drinks to the *Church*, but ticks on his Arrears;
The gentle *Beau* too joins in wise Debate,
Adjusts his Cravat, and Reforms the State.

It was a great age of conversation, an art in which Englishmen still take special delight. The coffee-houses and the taverns provided the arena for many a

---

[1] Possibly by Swift. Quoted from *A Collection of the Best English Poetry, by Several Hands* (1717), vol. II. Cf. Gay, Fable XLI, "The Owl and the Farmer":

    "So have I seen a man of news,
    Or 'Post-boy,' or 'Gazette,' peruse;
    Smoke, nod, and talk with voice profound,
    And fix the fate of Europe round."

spectacular tournament of words, fought with all the ardor which the fates of empires might command.

> We'll change the Scene, and with those Sages mix
> Who smoke a speculative Pipe at *Dick's;*
> The World's great Patriots! Here, in every Face,
> The Fates of Empires and of Kings we trace:
> The needy Tradesman, with Imperial Frowns,
> Guides distant Senates, and disposes Crowns.[1]

Ned Ward was the king of taverners. He played the genial host at a house, first, in Moorfields, and later, next Gray's Inn, probably the King's Head. To him we owe very much of our detailed knowledge about London at that time. His duties and those of anyone who attempted to run one of the popular taverns must have been anything but easy. One of the Roxburghe ballads, "The Industrious Smith," [2] tells the story of what might happen when an inexperienced man attempted the task. This ballad incidentally gives a rather elaborate account of the ordinary doings at a tavern from day to day.[3] The women were patrons as well as the men, and the story of Elinour Rummyng must have been frequently repeated. Hints of such crude jollity are to be found again and again in the street ballads, for instance in "The Jolly Welsh-Woman. Who drinking at the Sign of the Crown in London, found a Spring in her Mugg, for Joy of which hur Sung the praise of Old England, resolving never to return to Wales again." [4] The women

---

[1] *Discontent the Universal Misery. In an Epistle to a Friend* (Anon., 1734).

[2] Humfrey Crowch, 1635–42; *Roxburghe Ballads*, I, 469.

[3] Cf. Richard Ames, *A Farewell to Wine* (1693). This describes a scene in a tavern. No claret is to be had. The rake orders port, which proves bad. The boy offers to pierce a fresh hogshead, names other kinds, and finally brings some more from the same cask, which is declared worse than the first. Compare also Matthew Prior, "Down-Hall: a Ballad," *Poems* (ed. Austin Dobson, 1889), p. 93.

[4] *Roxburghe Ballads*, VII, 724. Soon after 1688.

were sometimes the owners and managers of such places.
Jenny Man, a strong Whig in principle, kept Old Man's
Coffee-House in Tilt-Yard, Whitehall. Her politics got
her into trouble with the Tory government of the time,
and she lost her license to sell wines, as is humorously
recorded in *The Flying Post* for November 6-7, 1712:

> Alas! alas! for Jenny Man,
> 'Cause she don't love the Warming Pan,
> High Church will all her actions scan
>   Since she was an inch long, Sirs;
> She is no friend to Right Divine,
> Therefore she must not sell French wine,
> But tea and coffee, very fine,
>   And sure that is no wrong, Sirs.

The warming-pan business shows how the Tories were
at this time flirting with St. Germain's, and how delicate
was the balance in which the political world of England
trembled in 1714.

Scenes from tavern life were favorite subjects with
the poets of the seventeenth and early eighteenth cen-
turies, as no doubt they deserved to be. Nichols [1] prints
a poem addressed to the ingenious Mrs. Hogarth and
called "The Bacchanalians; or a Midnight Modern
Conversation." The personnel of this particular con-
versation is sufficiently varied, and includes parson,
bully, lawyer, justice, patriot, tradesman, fop, soldier,
and doctor. Frequently the assemblies were more lively
than chaste, and sometimes these rowdy sessions got
recorded in verse. In that curious collection of poems
called *Wit and Drollery, Joviall Poems*, by Sir J[ohn]
M[ennes], Ja[mes] S[mith], Sir W[illiam] D[Avenant],
J[ohn] D[onne], and printed in 1661, there is a poem by
James Smith with the odd title, "The Preface to that

[1] *Biog. Anec.*, p. 204.

most elaborate piece of Poetry Entituled Penelope
Ulisses." The author regrets his mean employment:

> Nor was't my aime when I took pen in fingers,
> To take imployment for the Ballad singers.

His Muse runs away from him, but he finds her and re-
proaches her with her unfaithfulness:

> I'm very sure
> I have commended thee above ould *Chaucer;*
> And in a Tavern once I had a Sawcer
> Of Whit-wine Vinegar, dasht in my face,
> For saying thou deservest a better grace,
> Thou knowest that then I took a Sawsedge up,
> Upon the knaves face it gave such a clap,
> That he repented him that he had spoken
> Against thy fame.

A similar scene of revelry is recorded in "Good Ale for
my Money." [1]

> Your domineering, swaggering blades,
>   and Cavaliers that flashes, —
> That throw the Jugs against the walls,
>   and break in peeces glasses, —
>
> When Bacchus round cannot be found,
>   they will, in merriment,
> Drinke ale and beere, and cast off care,
>   and sing with one consent:
>
> *I cannot go home, nor I will not go home,*
>   *it's 'long of the oyle of Barly;*
> *Ile tarry all night for my delight,*
>   *and go home in the morning early.*

The wild carouses of the roarers in these taverns are
reflected as well as satirized in another Roxburghe
ballad,[2] "The Man in the Moon Drinks Claret." In

---

[1] By Lawrence Price, in Charles I's reign; *Roxburghe Ballads*, I, 412.
[2] Vol. II, Part II, p. 256.

ANACREONTICKS IN FULL SONG

this are mentioned the curious toasts that were popular among these lofty spirits. Some were drunk in "greasie flapdragons," namely, candle-ends floating in a cup of spirits and set on fire. Sometimes the liquor was tinged "with health tap'd in arms, upon naked knees." [1] The most vivid description of a tavern row is to be found in a poem by Robert Speed, called "The Counter Scuffle" (1647).[2] In one of the taverns conversation turns on the relative importance of the various professions. The lawyer has been harshly treated and defends his trade.

> *Noble*, and *Rich:* It doth subdue
> The *Souldier*, and his swaggering crue.
> But at that word the Captaine grew
> In choller.
> He lookt full grim, and at first word,
> Rapt out an Oath, that shooke the board,
> And strucke his fist, that the sound roar'd
> Like thunder.
> It made all skip, that stood him neare,
> The frighted *Custard* quak'd for feare,
> And those that heard it, stricken were
> With wonder.
> Nought did he now but frowne, and puffe,
> And hauing star'd, and swore enough,
> Thus he began in language rough . . .

His exceedingly provocative speech is followed by a battle royal over the table, which is described roughly but with considerable energy.

Pontack's was the most expensive ordinary in town. This is the one mentioned by Thomas Nevile in his imitation of Persius, Satire III (1769):

---

[1] See Nares's *Glossary* under "Candle-ends," "Flap-dragon," "Arms."

[2] "The *Counter-Scuffle* has more Wit and Art,
Than the stiff formal Stile of *Gondibert*."
Sir William Soames, *Translation of Boileau's Art of Poetry* (1710), Canto IV.

When in ill hour Quin's footman at the door:
A turtle at Pontack's precise at four —
He yields, some minutes with himself at strife.

The bills at any of these taverns might be at times
surprising, and were occasionally disputed. The Lewis
Miscellany (1726) contains a brief poem on this very
human situation, "A Taylor, on a Tavern Bill."

Let me see! — Bread and Beer — Tripe and Dressing —
   Hey Day!
And Wine, and Welsh Rabbet — Here's the Devil to pay!
And then, o' my Conscience, besides his long Bill,
Out of ev'ry poor Pint he has cabbag'd a Gill.
For all his fine Bows, and his Speeches, and Wheedle,
I swear that a Vintner's as sharp as a Needle.
The Vintner, in hearing, reply'd, 't is your Pleasure
'Gainst another Man's Bill to run out beyond Measure.
If we come to tax Reckonings, we all easily find
Many *Items* and *Items* not at all to our Mind:
There's your Silk, Twist, and Buckram; Materials and Mak-
   ing,
And a Remnant — But pardon the Freedom I'm taking.
Come, live and let live, without any repining:
I pay for my Doublet; pay You for your Lining.

When the man about town grew bored with the coffee-
house and the tavern, the theatre was always ready to
amuse him.[1] Five o'clock [2] was the time for plays, though
the ultra-fashionable usually planned a late arrival in
order to be conspicuous.[3] The rush from coffee-house to

---

[1] Gay, *Trivia*, III, 256.

[2] "How would your useless time, 'twixt five and eight,
   Have dragged its wings without this loved retreat;
   What other nameless place had been so fit
   For Pit to ogle Boxes, Boxes Pit."
Charles Shadwell, Prologue to "The Fair Quaker of Deal," *Works* (2 vols.,
1720).

[3] "Hillaria: There's the Play, Where I generally sidle in about the middle
of the Second Act." Thomas Baker, *Tunbridge-Walks* (1703), IV, 1.

theatre [1] is very well described by Lady Mary Wortley-Montagu in her Tuesday Eclogue:[2]

> The opera queens had finished half their faces,
> And city-dames already taken places;
> Fops of all kinds, to see the Lion, run;
> The beauties stay till the first act's begun,
> And beaux step home to put fresh linen on.
> No well-dress'd youth in coffee-house remain'd.

A very good description of the theatre of the time is to be found in a satire called "The Play-House," by T. G., Gent.:[3]

> Near to the *Rose* where *Punks* in numbers flock,
> To pick up Cullies to increase the Stock;
> A lofty Fabrick does the sight invade,
> And stretches round the Place a pompous Shade;
> Where sudden *Shouts* the Neighbourhood surprize,
> And *Thund'ring Claps*, and dreadful *Hissings* rise.

Then follows an account of the stage, the tiring-house, the various characters, their make-up, and so forth.

The connection of playhouses with the lewd elements of the town is frequently noticed in earlier satire. William Goddard in *A Neaste of Waspes* [4] is sufficiently emphatic:

> Goe to your plaie-howse you shall actors haue:
> Your baude, your gull, your whore, your pandar knave:
> Goe to your bawdie howse, y' aue actors too,
> As bawdes, and whores, and gulls: pandars also.
> Besides, in eyther howse (yf you enquire)
> A place there is for men themselues to tire.
> *Since th' are soe like, to choose there's not a pinn*
> *Whether bawdye-howse, or plaie-howse you goe in.*

---

[1] There were four theatres in Gay's time: Dorset Gardens, which grew disreputable and was disused about 1698; Lincoln's Inn Fields; Drury Lane; and the Queen's Theatre in Haymarket.

[2] "Six Town Eclogues," Dodsley, I, 97.

[3] *Poems on Affairs of State*, II, 374.

[4] (Dort, 1615), Epigram 64.

Marston, for a wonder, is not quite so disagreeable.[1]

> Then hence, lewd nags, away,
> Goe read each poast, view what is plaid today,
> Then to Priapus gardens.

The author probably got to the house more promptly than the fine ladies and gentlemen, if we may judge all of them by some lines in Robert Lloyd's *Poems* (1762):[2]

> The coach below, the clock gone five,
> Now to the theatre we drive:
> Peeping the curtain's eyelet through,
> Behold the house in dreadful view!

This writer seems to have been specially sensitive to the reaction of the critics:

> Critics, who like the scarecrows stand
> Upon the poet's common land,
> And with severity of sense,
> Drive all imagination thence.

His ordeal preliminary is suggested in Young's "Love of Fame":[3]

> Yon lady lolls! with what a tender air!
> Pale as a young dramatic author, when,
> O'er darling lines, fell Cibber waves his pen.

But the most amusing account of an author's pains may be found in an extraordinary farce by John Durant Breval, whose pen-name was Joseph Gay. The *Confederates* was written in 1717, to ridicule the failure of a stupid play by Pope, Arbuthnot, and Gay, called *Three Hours after Marriage*. Breval represents Gay as coming to the theatre to watch the fortunes of the play on the first night, and later telling his experience to Pope:

---

[1] *Works* (ed. Halliwell), III, 243.
[2] Pp. 91 and 96.
[3] *Poems*, II, 102.

Betimes, the better to conceal my Face,
In th' *Eighteen-Penny Row* I chose a Place;
Whence, unobserv'd, I might attend the *Play*,
And the loud Criticks in the *Pit* survey.
So vast a Throng took up the spacious Round,
Scarce for a Mouse, or You, had Room been found;
Heroes and Templers here were mix'd with Wits,
There Bawds and Strumpets, with a Group of Cits:
Rang'd in each Box were seen th' Angelick Fair,
Whose Footmen had since *Two* been posted there.
Round me I gaz'd with Wonder and Delight,
And wish'd that this had been the *Poet's Night*.

The brilliant potentialities of the moment, however, fail
to develop. Everything goes wrong.

Each smutty Phrase, and ev'ry cutting Line,
Was thrown away, and lost, like Pearls on Swine.

The play, as a matter of fact, was damned utterly and
deservedly. Its humor was flat, stale, and unprofitable,
and the audience had sense enough to know it. The
plays of the period were not particularly chaste, though
they were decidedly better than those of Rowley's glori-
ous reign. Jeremy Collier had dusted the boards at any
rate, had effected what Tom Brown called "a drowsie
reformation." Lady Mary, in her Monday Eclogue,
writes of leaving the opera and going to filthy plays:

Alas! how chang'd! — with the same sermon-mien
That once I pray'd, the *What-d'ye-call't* I've seen.

Sir William Soames, also, in his translation of Boileau's
Art of Poetry (1710), harshly censures the throng of
playwrights who take this miserable short cut to the
vulgar heart:

But for a tedious Droll, a Quibling Fool,
Who with low nauseous Baudry fills his Plays;
Let him begone and on two Tressels raise

Some *Smithfield* Stage, where he may act his Pranks,
And make *Jack Puddings* speak to Mountebanks.[1]

But the Puritan spirit, which smashed Cheapside Cross
and closed the theatres, which thought the fire a judg-
ment on the stage, and of which Collier was the spokes-
man, was gradually having its way in the theatres. The
extravagant outbursts which had discredited it in the
past were, after all, but the crest of the wave; the weight
was always in the gray mass below, — décent public
opinion, — and that swept onward to do its work and
subside. The *Three Hours after Marriage* was a Sunday
School entertainment compared with some of the Resto-
ration productions; and yet this play raised such an
astonishing flurry of satire from the frivolous and pro-
test from the serious, that Pope and Arbuthnot hurriedly
brushed all the dust they could from their skirts and
got in off the streets, while Gay good-naturedly acknow-
ledged the manifold sins and transgressions of the group
as his own. This is the play that Giles Jacob pokes fun
at in his preface to *The Rape of the Smock*,[2] a poem, by
the way, which needs more apology than he ever thought
of making:

But now I think on't, why should a poor *Author* be at the
Trouble of making an Apology for writing upon a *Smock*,
when the *Beauties* of this Age, look upon it as a Want of Good
Breeding, to Blush at a harmless *Double Entendre*; and I have
seen, not long since, a *Front-Box* sit so *Unconcern'd* at the
smuttiest Performance, that a *Stranger* would have been apt
to question, whether there were One *Natural Complexion*
among them All; and one would imagine, that Mother *Wy-
bourn* (like some *Potentates*, when they are put to't very
hard for *Men*) had Listed all the *Sex*, from *Sixteen* to *Sixty*.

In view of the part which Pope certainly took in the
composition of this silly farce, it scarcely becomes him to

----

[1] Canto III, 3. 32.   [2] Publ. in *The Ladies Miscellany* (1718).

be so supercilious with the monster of the pit, whose
appetite he had evidently catered to, but failed to
satisfy.

> There still remains to mortify a Wit
> The many-headed Monster of the Pit:
> A senseless, worthless, and unhonor'd crowd;
> Who, to disturb their betters mighty proud,
> Clatt'ring their sticks before ten lines are spoke,
> Call for the Farce, the Bear, or the Black-joke.[1]

The taste of the audience in regard to smut had certainly
changed for the better. Matthew Concanen reprints, in
his *Miscellaneous Poems* (1724), a Prologue to *The Con-
scious Lovers*, spoken by the Ghost of Sir Fopling Flut-
ter, on the occasion of its being played at the request of
the Young Gentlemen of the College, Dublin. In this
the following lines occur:

> Ladies, ye stare as if ye knew me not —
> What! can Sir *Fopling* be so soon forgot?
> There was a Time, when *Dorimant* and I
> Won ev'ry Heart, and reign'd in ev'ry Eye:
> 'Till this *new* Sot, this *moralizing* Fool,
> Has turn'd the *Theatre* into a *School.*

But it was not of this moralizing, or sentimentalizing, of
the drama, that the playwrights themselves complained.
It was the insane desire for spectacle that annoyed
them. The audience had jumped from filth to fireworks,
and one was as discouraging as the other. Dr. Johnson's
famous Prologue, spoken by Mr. Garrick at the opening
of the Theatre in Drury-Lane, 1747, is a history of the
drama in miniature.[2] He refers to Restoration tragedy,
in which

> Intrigue was plot, obscenity was wit.

[1] *Imitations of Horace, Epistles*, II, 1, l. 304 (1737).
[2] Printed in Dodsley, I, 231.

Then to the over-weighted classicism which culminated in Addison's *Cato* (1713):

> Then crush'd by rules, and weaken'd as refin'd,
> For years the pow'r of tragedy declin'd;
> From bard to bard, the frigid caution crept,
> 'Till declamation roar'd, while passion slept.[1]

New horrors of obscenity and spectacle may await us in the future. Vaudeville may supersede the drama.

> But who the coming changes can presage,
> And mark the future periods of the stage? —
> Perhaps if skill could distant climes explore,
> New Behns, new Durfeys, yet remain in store.
> Perhaps, where Lear has rav'd, and *Hamlet* dy'd,
> On flying cars new sorcerers may ride.
> Perhaps (for who can guess th' effects of chance?)
> Here Hunt may box, or Mahomet may dance.

He warns his audience of their responsibility, and expects them to get what they deserve.

> The drama's laws the drama's patrons give,
> For we that live to please, must please to live.

---

[1] Cf. Robert Lloyd, *Poems* (1762), p. 28, "Epistle to J. B. Esq." (1757):

> "Again I urge my old objection,
> That modern rules obstruct perfection,
> And the severity of Taste
> Has laid the walk of genius waste.
> Fancy's a flight we deal no more in,
> Our authors creep instead of soaring,
> And all the brave imagination
> Is dwindled into declamation."

Or Charles Churchill, *The Apology* (1761), p. 18:

> "In polish'd numbers, and majestic sound,
> Where shall thy rival, Pope, be ever found?
> But whilst each line with equal beauty flows,
> E'en excellence, unvary'd, tedious grows."

This poem of Churchill's contains also (p. 15) an early use of the rhetorical question device in the form which Scott made famous:

> "Is there a man, in vice and folly bred . . .
> If there be such a monster" . . .

The patrons of the theatre in the early years of the eighteenth century were evidently determined on getting sensation — if not one kind, then another. If we must not debauch our imaginations with Manly's love entanglements, by all means let us be astounded by gorgeousness of setting, noise, and display. As early as October, 1701, Steele complains of this demand:

> Nature's deserted, and dramatic art,
> To dazzle now the eye, has left the heart;
> Gay lights and dresses, long extended scenes,
> Demons [1] and angels moving in machines,
> All that can now, or please, or fright the fair,
> May be performed without a writer's care,
> And is the skill of carpenter, not player.[2]

After all, this is an old, old story with the playhouse. Shadwell produced *A True Widow* in 1679 with a prologue by Dryden. In the fourth act of this play, the first scene represents the interior of a theatre, with the orange-girls going about, the gentlemen entering on tick to see the play. Finally, it gives a sample of the pompous play of the time. "Gad, I love drums, and trumpets, and much ranting, roaring, hussing and fretting, and good store of noise in a Play." The ladies appear in masks; there is a grand fight; mock devils descend and fly up with the hero in their embrace; and two other characters are carried up in chairs and hang swaying in the air. This is the play which contains the wise remark, "What would become of the writing Coxcombs, if it were not for the reading Ones?"

---

[1] Dennis's thunder was famous. Thomas Cooke, in *The Battle of the Poets; or the Contention for the Laurel* (1731), humorously represents him as saying (p. 12), "I'll use my Interest to make him *Thunderer* at one of the Play-houses."

[2] Richard Steele, *Plays* (ed. by G. A. Aitken, 1894), Prologue to *The Funeral*. For stage properties, see *Tatler*, No. 42.

The most extraordinary account of one of Rich's pantomimes is offered for our consideration in a poem called *British Frenzy: or, the Mock-Apollo* (1745). The unknown author takes us right to the doors of the famous theatre of Lincoln's Inn Fields. We can see people crowding about the pit entrance:

> At *Orpheus'* Name, ye swarm like clust'ring Bees,
> And *Shakespeare, Dryden, Otway*, fail to please:
> The silly Bees are won with tinkling Brass,
> So *Tom the Tinker* gains on human Race.

Now we are inside:

> Mark! with what Humour *Drudge* comes stalking in!
> The Pot unbottom'd, blazing all within!
> The yawning Blund'rer stumbles on the Floor,
> The China rattles, — and the People roar!
> Like changing *Proteus, Harlequin* appears,
> A *Sailor's* Jacket, o'er the *Knave's*, he wears,
> The Witch, his Step-dame, strains him in her Arms,
> And mutters inwardly her hellish Charms;
> To ev'ry Danger hardned, by her Art,
> But Love's resistless and unerring Dart.

The hero falls in love, of course, with Columbine, and in various disguises as tinker, sweep, baker, dwarf, duenna, seeks to carry her off. Finally they get away, and then follows the essential pursuit:

> The Flight, more quick than *Helen's*, is betray'd,
> And *Pantaloon* pursues the ravish'd Maid;
> What Laughters rise, when stiffen'd as a Log,
> Slow *Drudge* behind him, mocks the turn-spit Dog!
> Or dares the Cook-maid fierce, in sturdy Battle,
> While Spits, Tongs, Pokers, in the Kitchen rattle!
> Or when, with *Columbine*, the Lads and Lasses
> For Melons pass, hid under Melon-glasses!
> How loud the Clap! when like a drowning Cub,
> The Clown sprawls headlong in the Water-tub!

Children and Fools admire the Changeling's Art,
Or in the *Sawyer's* or the *Gard'ner's* Part!
Is that huge Serpent shewn to entertain?
Hark! they encore the Clock-work back again!
More curious this, than that which did deceive,
In Paradise, the first-form'd Woman, *Eve!*

Next comes a tableau of hell itself, followed incongruously by a scene with a milk-white steed and cheated gibbets:

They groan'd for *R[ich]*, in earnest, long ago.

And then, to conclude the poem and possibly to give us a clue to its *raison d'être*, we find a satiric description of Rich refusing a play which he has not read.

A little later than this, James Dance wrote a satire which he called *The Stage*.[1] In this, he gives us some interesting sidelights on the tastes of the theatre-going public of that time:

At *four* conven'd, two tedious hours remain
Before the trembling poet can be slain.

He tells of some of the usual noises of the playhouse, the imitation of animal calls, and evidently thinks the audience incapable of receiving much intellectual stimulus.

To gay *Burletta's* painted charms repair,
Where sense shall never wound your tortur'd ear . . .
    Or hark — the *Pantomine* invites! behold
The *Sorcerer* his fairy scenes unfold!
Rich knows your taste . . .
    Flush'd with fresh vigour, *Harlequin* shall soar;
New *Devils* sweetly sing, new *Dragons* roar;
To lulling strains the *Gods* shall dance the hay,
And painted *Gewgaws* glitter Thought away:
Merit and *Wit* shall own themselves outdone,
And *Common Sense* shall yield to Mr. *Lun.*

[1] *Poems* (Edinburgh, 1754), p. 23.

Moreover, this same delight in spectacle was lively enough a hundred years later, and it is not unknown in our own day. Charles Jenner notes it in the first of his Eclogues.[1]

> Whilst prudent managers, who know wit scarce,
> From pillag'd *Molière* cull the flimsy farce;
> Or bid, the shortest and the easiest way,
> The Tailor and the Painter make a play.

As if this freshened enthusiasm for reviews were not enough to dishearten the playwrights, the Italian Opera made its way into England in 1704, and in spite of satire established itself in the esteem, if not the affection, of the people. It was considered the proper thing to hear and entertain the foreign singers. Not till the appearance of *The Beggar's Opera* (1728) [2] were these favorites even temporarily dislodged. No wonder, then, that Addison's *Cato* (1713), though for a time a prodigious success as a political play, soon lost its pristine charm, and completely failed to establish a new and vigorous tragic *genre*. As George Sewell says in his poem "Upon Mr. Addison's Cato": [3]

> Long had the *Tragic Muse* forgot to Weep,
> By modern *Operas* quite lull'd a-sleep:
> No Matter what the Lines, the Voice was clear,
> Thus Sense was sacrific'd to please the Ear.
> At last, *One Wit* stood up in our Defence,
> And dar'd (O Impudence!) to publish — Sense.

It is not so very long, however, before Joseph Warton writes, in *The Enthusiast, or the Lover of Nature*,[4]

---

[1] *Town Eclogues* (1772).

[2] John Ireland, *Hogarth Illustrated*, II, 328. The author relates that an Italian he knew concluded an harangue calculated to throw Gay's taste and talents into contempt with, "Saire, this simple signor did tri to pelt mi countrymen out of England with *Lumps of Pudding*" (one of the tunes used by Gay).

[3] *Poems on Several Occasions* (1719), p. 15.   [4] (1740), Dodsley, III, 115.

What are the lays of artful Addison,
Coldly correct, to Shakespear's warblings wild?

Having thus suggested some of the things that the
people were eager to see in the theatre in John Gay's
time, we may go on to notice a few features of their be-
havior which differ from our manners in the playhouse
at present, and are on that account interesting.

There was, in the first place, a disregard of the rights
of others which would not be tolerated now: a tendency
to noise and unnecessary movement, an apparent de-
light in making one's self conspicuous, which must have
been a severe trial to the players and those in the audi-
ence of more modest aspirations. John Dennis, in his
translation of the Fourth Satire of Boileau,[1] speaks of
the beau,

Who to the Park or Play rides jingling, where
By his loud nauseous Chat, and graceless Air,
He plagues the Sensible, and frights the Fair.

The little side-plays of the fop, carried through solely to
attract attention, must have been intensely irritating.
Such a performance is very well described in Thomas
Baker's play, *Tunbridge-Walks:* [2]

But the surprizing Joy when two Fops meet in the Side-
Box, tho' they parted but two Minutes before, at a *Chocolate-
House;* the Side-Bow, the Embrace; and the fulsome Trick
you Men have got of Kissing one another. Then down you
sit, and observe the Women— She's well enough — says one,
but they say she has been had—Mind how she Ogles us, says
t' other, when they are a couple of wretched hatchet Fac'd
things, that are Physical to look at 'em — Then, the Toss o'
the Head, the Airs o' the Snuff-Box, and the Leer at an Ac-
tress on the Stage; and all the ridiculous Actions of a Monkey,
or a Madman; but I think, they say most of you Beaux are

[1] *Miscellany Poems* (2d ed., 1697), p. 38.
[2] (1703), p. 16.

craz'd; for taking such a prodigious deal o'Snuff, it open'd
your Heads so much, the Wind got in, and quite turn'd your
Brains — And when any Expressions on the Stage are smart
upon the Side-Boxes, how you force a Grin, and wou'd fain
Laugh 'em off.

The manners of the people in the playhouse were thus
a fit subject for the reforming zeal of *The Spectator.*[1]
One disturbing element was the shameless habit of mak-
ing the theatre a general clearing-house for social en-
gagements. Steele notices this in the paper referred to
above:

> Now turn, and see where loaden with her freight,
> A Damsel stands, and Orange-wench is hight;
> See! how her charge hangs dangling by the rim,
> See! how the balls blush o'er the Basket-brim;
> But little those she minds, the cunning *Belle*
> Has other fish to fry, and other fruit to sell;
> See! how she whispers yonder youthful Peer,
> See! how he smiles, and lends a greedy ear.
> At length 't is done, the note o'er Orange wrapt
> Has reach'd the box, and lays in Lady's lap.

Fees from the aristocrats in the boxes were apparently
collected during the performance, and needy rakes
showed a tendency frequently to try to cheat the com-
pany.

> With Transport to th' half-acted Play I ruu,
> And there by changing Boxes sav'd my Crown.[2]

Even so distinguished a gentleman as the one described
in *The Fatigues of a Great Man* (Anon., 1734) might con-
sider it below his dignity to pay for admission:

> After a gentle Nap refresh'd he wakes;
> And now a little Tour to *White's* he takes,
> *Loiters about*, and *whiles* the Time away:
> At last his Fancy leads him to the *Play:*

[1] *Spectator*, Nos. 240, 361.   [2] *The Rake Reform'd* (1718).

The *Old House* likes him not, he seeks the *New;*
Ev'n there he tarries but an *Act* or two.
   The Box-Keepers approach with awful Bow,
While he receives 'em with a scornful Brow;
He feeds their Eyes, displays a silken Purse,
Goes out enrag'd, and pays 'em with a Curse:
And if it chance to be an Infant-Play,
Well may the wretched Author rue the Day!
My Lord is disoblig'd, and that's enough;
The Bard's an Ass, the Play is stupid Stuff.

The ladies at this time were getting increasingly delicate. It was quite the proper thing to be taken suddenly ill in a public place, and their extreme fragility must often have been the cause of disturbance in the theatre. Hillaria, in *Tunbridge-Walks*, after disclaiming authorship, gives some hints on etiquette to her less-experienced friends: "You must be very timorous, and fearful, skream at the Jolt of a Coach, or the Pop of a Pistol, Die away at the Sight of a Rat; all well-bred Ladies are frighted at ev'rything but a Man."

Up in the gallery the footmen still gave cause for uneasiness. Maiden, in the play just referred to, has some interesting things to say about them and the servant problem generally:

But I Love a Spring-Chariot mightily, and there's nothing we Beaux take more Pride in, than a Sett of Genteel Footmen; I never have any but what wear their own Hair, and I allow 'em a Crown a Week for Gloves and Powder; if one should n't, they'd Steal horridly to set themselves out, for now not one in ten is without a Watch, and a nice Snuff-Box with the best Orangerie, and the Liberty of the Upper-Gallery has made 'em so confoundedly pert, that as they wait behind one at Table, they'll either put in their Word, or Mimick a body, and People must bear with 'em, or else pay 'em their Wages.

This audience up among the gods had also its own ideas of what a play should be, and doubtless influenced to some extent the quality of those produced.

> There's not a Vizzard sweating in the Gallery,
> But likes a smart Intreague, a Rake, and Raillery.
> And were we to Consult our Friends above,
> A pert and witty Footman, 't is they love.
> And now and then such Language as their own,
> As Damn the Dog, you Lye, and knock him down.[1]

Of the performances by strollers that one might witness in the outlying villages there is a most interesting account in some verses called "A Lampoon on the Greenwich Strowlers," one of the curiosities which Richard Brome collected in his *Covent Garden Drollery* (1672).[2] Many grains of salt are doubtless needed to make this dish fit for imaginative consumption, but with that addition the flavor is excellent. The author represents himself as going down by river to Greenwich, and there finding a company of strollers ready to entertain the public in their stable-theatre. There is no play on Monday, but,

> On *Tuesday* at three a clock I was we'e 'em,
> I kist their doorkeeper and went in to see 'em,
> Being enter'd an Actor straight brought me a stool,
> Hee'd a held my cloak too, but I wa'nt such a fool.
>
> The first that appear'd when I was come in
> With her train to her ankles, was who but the Queen.
> She civilly made me a curtsy and straight
> Retired to sit on her Fagots of state.
>
> Then in came the King with a Murtherous mind,
> Gainst his new married Queen which when I did find;
> I call'd him aside, and whispering in 's Ear,
> Desired him to fetch me a Flagon of Beer.

---

[1] Charles Shadwell, *Works* (2 vols., 1720), Epilogue to *Irish Hospitality, or Virtue Rewarded*.

[2] See Thomas Brown, *The Life of the Famous Comedian, Jo Hayns* (1701), p. 26.

There's twelve pence, said I, take the rest for your pains,
Your Servant, said he, Sir, sweet Mr. *Haines.*
His Majesty, faith, I must needs say was civil,
For he took up his Heels, and ran for't like a Devil.

Meantime I address myself to his Bride,
And took her into the tireing House side;
A hay loft it was which at a dead lift,
Instead of a better serv'd then for a shift.

But mark the Fate of her Civility,
The Players did rant both at her and me:
And therefore because for fear she'd be lack'd,
I ordred the Drummer to beat a long Act.

He beat and he beat, but no Queen appear'd,
He beat till at length the house was all clear'd;
By my Troath a sad loss, but to make 'em amends,
I threw 'em a Crown, and we were all Friends:
And so this Renowned History ends.

I have said enough to show that the Englishman of
John Gay's time was decidedly liberal in his pleasures,
by no means inclined to admit the death's head at the
feast, eager for gaiety and color, and possibly capable of
getting more joy out of living than his modern counter-
part. His sense of personal dignity was not so acute, for
one thing, and he had not yet discovered that the course
of the world's history depends on his daily decisions.
The superman of to-day, of course, is the one who can
develop an attitude of mind superior to the confused
mass of our over-organized social fabric. Two hundred
years ago there was no need for such exertion. One
could laugh without expecting any part of the social
mechanism to crack. Moreover, Gay's contemporaries
seem to have largely forgotten that haunting fear of
death which disturbed the Elizabethans. Thoughts of
death and the grave were with Young and Blair [1] a kind

[1] Cf. Parnell, "A Nightpiece on Death," *Poems* (1770), p. 116.

of sentimental debauch. They thoroughly enjoyed their contemplation of sorrow, as some people still do, even in the very presence of death. Their reflections are merely a pleasurable indulgence, compared with the real melancholy of the lines:

> O, how shall summer's honey breath hold out
> Against the wreckful siege of battering days,
> When rocks impregnable are not so stout,
> Nor gates of steel so strong, but Time decays?

Nor would any street poet of the early eighteenth century think of portraying death as lurking among the various resorts of business and pleasure, as an unknown poet did in "Death's Dance"[1] shortly before 1581.

> If Death would come and shew his face,

at the Waterside, at the Royal Exchange,[2] in Paul's, or Westminster Hall, if he should become a "checkerman" in the Hall, into what fear would the townsmen be cast:

> If Death would keepe a tippling house
>   where Roysters do resort,
> And take the cup, and drinke, carowse,
>   when they are in their sport,
> And briefly say, "My Masters all,
>   Why stand you idle here?
> I bring to you Saint Giles his bowle!"[3]
>   't wold put them all in feare.
>
> If Death would make a step to dance
>   where lusty Gallants be,
> Or take [the] Dice and throw a chance
>   when he doth gamesters see,

---

[1] *Roxburghe Ballads*, I, 283.

[2] The Royal Exchange was opened in 1570.

[3] Stowe says that convicts on the way to execution through St. Giles in the Fields were presented with a bowl of ale at St. Giles's Hospital, which was called St. Giles's Bowl, "thereof to drink at their pleasure, as to be their last refreshing draught in this life." *Survey of London* (ed. Dent), p. 393.

And say, "My masters, Have at all!
   I warrant it will be mine!"
They'd too much in amazement fall
   to set him any Coyne.

He might appear among the crabbed wives, or the
landlords, the tradesmen, or the hucksters in the mar-
ket, among the gentlemen in their haunts of pleasure,
among the whores in their suburban dens. He was
always to be expected with the Elizabethans, and the
possibility of his appearance was a disturbing idea.
Timor mortis perturbat me. A hundred years later the
superficial pose was more frivolous. The child who
fears the dark had passed into the college sophomore:

Life is a jest, and all things show it;
I thought so once, and now I know it.

To-day, the Englishman, grown up, dons his frock-coat
and silk hat, looks at life and death alike seriously, and
expects the world to take him at his own estimate.

Chapter VI

VIGNETTES OF STREET AND RIVER

IN MOST of the poetry which we have passed in review so far, even in that which nominally satirizes the city and its ways, one feels the underlying fascination of the town, its kaleidoscopic variety, its brilliance and its squalor, its moody enthusiasms, and one knows that the city mouse is content with her heritage. The poets complain, they dip their pens in acid, but their voices would have returned to them with but a faint echo, had not the town furnished training ground, material, inspiration, and audience. "The cityë of London," says Chaucer, "that is to me so dere and sweete, in which I was forth growen; and more kindely love have I to that place than to any other in yerth." No wonder that the poets wrote of London from time to time in our history, sometimes in the tone of eulogy, often descriptions of special places and monuments, sometimes impressions of street, river, park, or shop, possibly in our later poetry with a touch of pathos in the thought of the masses swept under the tides, as in Shelley's lines:

> London; that great sea whose ebb and flow
> At once is deaf and loud, and on the shore
> Vomits its wrecks, and still howls on for more.
> Yet in its depths what treasures!

and again with that detailed, meticulous brushwork which makes *Trivia* so curiously interesting, things which, following the suggestion of Juvenal's poem, begin in English literature with the early seventeenth-century satirists and continue down to Robert Bridges's charming piece on "London Snow," or the latest ephemeral production in the anthologies.

Of those which are primarily eulogistic, Dunbar's poem, "The Flour of Cities All,"[1] is the earliest, and certainly one of the best. His description of the river and the bridge, the buildings and the people, is very good:

> Aboue all ryuers thy Ryuer hath renowne,
>   Whose beryall stremys, pleasaunt and preclare,
> Under thy lusty wallys renneth down,
>   Where many a swanne doth swymme with wyngis fare;
>   Where many a barge doth saile, and row with are,
> Where many a ship doth rest with toppe-royall.
>   O! towne of townes, patrone and not compare:
> London, thou art the floure of Cities all.
>
> Upon thy lusty Brigge of pylers white
>   Been merchauntis full royall to behold;
> Upon thy stretis goeth many a semely knyght
>   [All clad] in velvet gownes and cheynes of gold.
>   By Julyus Cesar thy Tour founded of old
> May be the hous of Mars victoryall,
>   Whos artillary with tonge may not be told:
> London, thou art the flour of Cities all.
>
> Strong be thy wallis that about thee standis;
>   Wise be the people that within thee dwellis;
> Fresh is thy ryver with his lusty strandis;
>   Blith be thy churches, wele sownyng be thy bellis;
>   Riche be thy merchauntis in substaunce that excellis;
> Fair be their wives, right lovesom, white and small;
>   Clere be thy virgyns, lusty under kellis:
> London, thow art the flour of Cities all.

George Peele, in an address to the Lord Mayor, in "A Pageant, 1585",[2] wrote some lines in praise of the city,

---

[1] William Dunbar, *Poems* (ed. by John Small; 3 vols., Scottish Text Society, 1884–85), II, 276.
[2] George Peele, *Works* (ed. by Alexander Dyce; 2d ed., 1829), II, 147.

which compare favorably with the productions of most "city poets." He sees her as a rich jewel entrusted to the hands of wise magistrates, who care for her welfare and her worthiness.

> Lo, lovely London, rich and fortunate,
> Fam'd through the world for peace and happiness,
> Is here advanc'd and set in highest seat,
> Beautified throughly as her state requires!

The franklin and the husbandman bring their sacks of corn to her as presents from the country. The Thames, "a sweet and dainty nymph," performs her part. The soldier and the sailor are ready to fight for her, while science also is vowed to honor London with her skill. Praise then be to God, the Queen, and a worthy Lord Mayor!

Spenser's stanza in the *Prothalamion* (1596) is partly eulogy and partly impressionism.

> At length they all to mery London came,
> To mery London, my most kyndly nurse,
> That to me gave this lifes first native sourse;
> Though from another place I take my name,
> An house of auncient fame.
> There when they came, whereas those bricky towres,
> The which on Themmes brode aged backe doe ryde,
> Where now the studious lawyers have their bowers,
> There whylome wont the Templer Knights to byde,
> Till they decayd through pride:
> Next whereunto there standes a stately place,
> Where oft I gayned giftes and goodly grace
> Of that great lord which therein wont to dwell,
> Whose want too well now feeles my freendles case:
> But ah! here fits not well
> Olde woes, but joyes to tell,
> Against the bridale daye, which is not long:
> Sweete Themmes, runne softly, till I end my song.

Among our older poets Herrick is perhaps the most sincere in his eulogy of the great city. Doomed to spend the most of his life in far-away Devon, he felt his banishment keenly, and writes of London with the enthusiasm of a lover:[1]

> From the dull confines of the drooping West,
> To see the day spring from the pregnant East,
> Ravisht in spirit, I come, nay more, I flie
> To thee, blest place of my Nativitie!
> Thus, thus with hallowed foot I touch the ground,
> With thousand blessings by thy Fortune crown'd.
> O fruitfull Genius! that bestowest here
> An everlasting plenty, yeere by yeere.
> O *Place!* O *People!* Manners! fram'd to please
> *All Nations, Customes, Kindreds, Languages!*
> I am a free-born *Roman;* suffer then,
> That I amongst you live a Citizen.
> London my home is: though by hard fate sent
> Into a long and irksome banishment;
> Yet since cal'd back; henceforward let me be,
> O native countrey, repossest by thee!
> For, rather then I'le to the West return,
> I'le beg of thee first here to have mine Urn.
> Weak I am grown, and must in short time fall;
> Give thou my sacred Reliques Buriall.

Many years later, we find Cowper writing of London with quite different feelings. For him the city breeds rank abundance, sloth and lust and wantonness. Vice is hidden with most ease there, or seen with least reproach. Yet for all that, he honors her as the nursery of the arts and the mother of sciences.

> With nice incision of her guided steel
> She ploughs a brazen field, and clothes a soil
> So sterile with what charms soe'er she will,
> The richest scenery and the loveliest forms.

[1] Herrick, *Poems* (ed. Grosart, 3 vols., 1876), II, 233. First published in 1648. See also Glover, *London, or the Progress of Commerce* (1739).

Where finds philosophy her eagle eye
With which she gazes at yon burning disk
Undazzled, and detects and counts his spots?
In London. Where her implements exact
With which she calculates, computes, and scans
All distance, motion, magnitude, and now
Measures an atom, and now girds a world?
In London. Where has commerce such a mart,
So rich, so thronged, so drained, and so supplied,
As London; opulent, enlarged, and still
Increasing London? Babylon of old
Not more the glory of the earth than she,
A more accomplished world's chief glory now.[1]

All these poets are willing, like Alfred Noyes's cuckoo in "A London Invitation," to sing a song for London. Sometimes they confine their praise to some special house or place in the town. Waller, for instance, writes a poem on "St. James's Park" in 1661, which has no great interest except that from it we learn that the King, Charles II, was very anxious to improve the park, and had already made several important changes. Cowley wrote on "Somerset House" in 1668 with the too obvious idea of pleasing the owner. Another poem on "St. James's Park," this time a satire and anonymous, was issued from the press of H. Hills (Gay's "pirate Hills") in 1708. The most interesting part of this production has to do with the various types that frequent the park. The inane but self-complacent rake, with a group of congenial companions, talks about nothing as the idle hours pass,

> Then loudly laughs at the insipid Jest,
> As rustick *Hob* does at a Country Feast;
> When eager Mastiff takes the Bull by th' Ear,
> Or *Roger's* overturned by the Bear.

The soldier is there, too, carrying death for the ladies lurking in his scarlet coat.

[1] "The Sofa," from *The Task* (1785).

Nor can the sober trading Cit forbear,
From coming to regale his Palate here,
With the fresh Breezes of *St. James's* Air.

Much better than this is the brief poem on "Holland House" by Thomas Tickell:

Thou Hill, whose brow the antique structures grace,
Rear'd by bold chiefs of *Warwick's* noble race,
Why, once so lov'd, when-e'er thy bower appears,
O'er my dim eye-balls glance the sudden tears!
How sweet were once thy prospects fresh and fair,
Thy sloping walks, and unpolluted air!
How sweet the gloomes beneath thy aged trees,
Thy noon-tide shadow, and thy evening breeze!
His image thy forsaken bowers restore;
Thy walks and airy prospects charm no more,
No more the summer in thy gloomes allay'd,
Thy evening breezes, and thy noon-day shade.
   From other ills, however fortune frown'd,
Some refuge in the muse's art I found:
Reluctant now I touch the trembling string,
Bereft of him, who taught me how to sing,
And these sad accents, murmur'd o'er his urn,
Betray that absence, they attempt to mourn.[1]

This is something far more than a mere vignette of Holland House. There is lyric sincerity in its expression of sorrow for the friend who is gone, a modest simplicity, which marks the genuineness of pain. Pope never could have done it. Tickell has also a poem on "Kensington Gardens,"[2] which may be compared with Matthew Arnold's verses on the same theme. Tickell is as much alive to the spring beauty of the trees and flowers as Arnold, but the scene would be incomplete, probably dull, for him, apart from the lovely ladies who wander

[1] Inserted in the Preface to *The Works of Joseph Addison* (ed. by Tickell, 4 vols., 1721).
[2] *Poems* (Boston, 1854), p. 130.

through the walks, and the Queen who is to charm a
people to her father's side.

> Where Kensington high o'er the neighbouring lands
> Midst greens and sweets a regal fabric stands,
> And sees each spring, luxuriant in her bowers,
> A snow of blossoms, and a wild of flowers,
> The dames of Britain oft in crowds repair
> To groves and lawns and unpolluted air.
> Here, while the town in damps and darkness lies,
> They walk in sunshine and see azure skies;
> Each walk, with robes of various dyes bespread,
> Seems from afar a moving tulip-bed,
> Where rich brocades and glossy damasks glow,
> And chintz, the rival of the showery bow.
> Here England's daughter, darling of the land,
> Sometimes, surrounded with her virgin band,
> Gleams through the shades. She, towering o'er the rest,
> Stands fairest of the fairer kind confessed,
> Formed to gain hearts, that Brunswick's cause denied,
> And charm a people to her father's side.

These lines show a treatment of nature which is not un-
known in recent poetry, a search for the word which will
suggest an exact and colorful image, an eye for the pic-
turesque possibilities of fabrics, along with the feeling
that background is not less important than form. In a
word, Tickell has the painter's attitude toward his sub-
ject. Arnold ("In Kensington Gardens") has perhaps
the painter's attitude, but he shows also that revulsion
from society which the poets of the early eighteenth
century would not have understood at all, that appre-
hension of nature as something apart from mankind, an
entity which may possibly comfort or exalt the wan-
derer from man's impious uproar, but which is entirely
independent of his uneasy strivings, and which carries
through its own purposes, driven by an urge that is all
its own.

In this lone open glade I lie,
    Screen'd by dark trees on either hand;
And at its head, to stay the eye,
    Those black-topped, red-boled pine-trees stand.

   ·   ·   ·   ·   ·   ·   ·   ·

Sometimes a child will cross the glade
    To take his nurse his broken toy:
Sometimes a thrush flit overhead
    Deep in her unknown day's employ.

Here at my feet what wonders pass,
    What endless active life is here!
What blowing daisies, fragrant grass!
    An air-stirr'd forest, fresh and clear.

   ·   ·   ·   ·   ·   ·   ·   ·

Calm Soul of all things! make it mine
    To feel, amid the city's jar,
That there abides a peace of thine,
    Man did not make, and cannot mar.

This attitude, the poet's re-creation of the universe under the spell of, or in revolt against, the mechanistic theory, is of course a comparatively new thing in literature. The older poets were, as one would expect, objective and impressionist. Take, for example, Michael Drayton's praise of the Thames:[1]

But now this mighty Flood, upon his voyage prest,
(That found how with his strength, his beauties still increast,
From where, brave *Windsor* stood on tip-toe to behold
The fair and goodly *Tames*, so far as ere he could,
With kingly houses crown'd, of more than earthly pride,
Upon his either banks, as he along doth glide)
With wonderful delight, doth his long course pursue,
Where *Otlands*, *Hampton-Court*, and *Richmond* he doth view,
Then *Westminster* the next great *Tames* doth entertain;
That vaunts her Palace large, and her most sumptuous Fane:

[1] *Polyolbion* (1612). See *Complete Works* (ed. Rev. Richard Hooper, 1876), II, 218.

The Land's Tribunal seat that challengeth for hers,
The Crowning of our Kings, their famous Sepulchres.
Then goes he on along by that more beauteous Strand,
Expressing both the wealth and brav'ry of the Land.
(So many sumptuous Bowers,[1] within so little space,
The all-beholding sun scarce sees in all his race.)
And on by *London* leads, which like a crescent lies,
Whose windows seem to mock the star-befreckled skies;
Beside her rising spires, so thick themselves that show,
As do the bristling reeds, within his banks that grow.
There sees his crowded wharfs, and people-pestred shores,
His bosom over-spread, with shoals of labouring oars:
With that most costly Bridge, that doth him most renown,
By which he clearly puts all other Rivers down.

This shows the pride of a rising people, their delight in imagining their river, their city, their bridge the most famous and remarkable in the world. The words pulsate with the astonishing virility of the Elizabethans, but there is more than that in them. They show, especially in the last lines, a remarkable sensitiveness in the choice of the right epithet, two of which at least are Homeric in form and packed with suggestion. And what could be fitter for its purpose than the metaphor of the "bristling reeds"? How much better than that in the modern poem which its author, James Thomson ("B. V."), calls "Sunday at Hampstead"![2]

> This is the Heath of Hampstead,
>   There is the dome of St. Paul's;
> Beneath, on the serried house-tops,
>   A chequered lustre falls:
>
> And the mighty city of London,
>   Under the clouds and the light
> Seems a low wet beach, half shingle,
>   With a few sharp rocks upright.

---

[1] Cf. Gay, *Trivia*, II, 492:
   "Arundel, Essex, Cecil, Bedford, Villiers, only
   Burlington remains."

[2] *Poems* (1895), I, 203.

An unknown author, quoted in John Thomas Smith's
The Streets of London (1861, page 286), finds a humorous
and not ineffective solution for the same problem:

> Lo, like a bishop upon dainties fed,
> St. Paul's lifts up his sacerdotal head;
> While his lean curates, slim and lank to view,
> Around him point their steeples to the blue.

Indeed, one has to go to Herrick [1] to find a rival for
Drayton's praise of the Thames, and here again there
is something different and additional. The note of per-
sonal emotion enters — no false sentiment, but a form of
hypochondria with which we are all familiar.

> I send, I send here my supremest kiss
> To thee, my *silver-footed Thamasis*.
> No more shall I reiterate thy Strand,
> Whereon so many Stately Structures stand:
> Nor in the summers sweeter evenings go,
> To bath in thee (as thousand others doe),
> No more shall I along thy christall glide,
> In Barge (with boughes and rushes beautifi'd)
> With soft-smooth Virgins (for our chast disport)
> To *Richmond*, *Kingstone*, and to *Hampton-Court:*
> Never againe shall I with Finnie-Ore
> Put from, or draw unto the faithfull shore:
> And Landing here, or safely Landing there,
> Make way to my *Belovéd Westminster:*
> Or to the Golden-cheap-side, where the earth
> Of *Julia Herrick* gave to me my Birth.
> May all clean *Nimphs* and curious water Dames,
> With Swan-like-state, flote up and down thy streams:
> No drought upon thy wanton waters fall
> To make them Leane, and languishing at all.
> No ruffling winds come hither to discease
> Thy pure, and *Silver-wristed Naides*.
> Keep up your state, ye streams; and as ye spring,
> Never make sick your Banks by surfeiting.

[1] Robert Herrick, *Poems* (ed. by Grosart, 3 vols., 1876), III, 56. First
published in 1648.

> Grow young with Tydes, and though I see ye never,
> Receive this vow, *so fare-ye-well for ever.*

The Thames as it flows through the city certainly caught the imagination of our poets, though they reacted to that stimulus in very different ways. The usual thing in Augustan literature is inspired by Denham's "Cooper's Hill" (1642), which is, except for the one famous quatrain, a rather dull poem.

> My Eye descending from the Hill, surveys,
> Where *Thames* among the wanton Vallies strays.
> *Thames!* the most lov'd of all the Oceans Sons,
> By his old Sire to his Embraces runs,
> Hasting to pay his Tribute to the Sea,
> Like Mortal Life to meet Eternity. . . .

And so on. A very minor poem by Charles Hopkins, called "The Court Prospect" (1699), is somewhat better than this, though not much. It begins,

> Above that Bridge,[1] which lofty Turrets crown,
> Joining two Cities; of itself a Town.
> As far as fair *Augusta's* Buildings reach,
> Bent, like a Bow along a Peaceful Beach.
> Her Gilded Spires the Royal Palace show,
> Tow'ring to Clouds, and fix'd in Floods below.
> The Silver *Thames* washes her Sacred sides,
> And pays her Prince her Tributary Tides.

Pope does the same sort of thing in "Windsor Forest" (1713). It is really a disease of the times.

> Thou, too, great father of the British floods!
> With joyful pride survey'st our lofty woods;
> Where tow'ring oaks their growing honours rear,
> And future navies on thy shores appear.
> Not Neptune's self from all her streams receives
> A wealthier tribute than to thine he gives.

[1] Cf. William Hinchliffe, "London Bridge," *Poems* (1718), p. 117. (A short descriptive poem of 14 lines.)

Paul Whitehead also makes the Thames meander in much the same way as Denham, but occasionally in his turnings one discovers a good line or two:

> Thames, made immortal, by her Denham's Strains,
> Meand'ring glides thro' Twick'nham's flow'ry Plains;
> While royal Richmond's Cloud-aspiring Wood,
> Pours all its pendant Pomp upon the Flood.[1]

The best that the age of Pope can do for the Thames is to be found in Thomson's Seasons, "Autumn":

> On either hand,
> Like a long wintry forest, groves of masts
> Shot up their spires; the bellying sheet between
> Possessed the breezy void; the sooty hulk
> Steered sluggish on; the splendid barge along
> Rowed regular to harmony; around,
> The boat light skimming stretched its oary wings.

The river meant so much more in the life of the town in Gay's time than it does now, that it is essential to keep it in mind as the picturesque background for many an old-world scene. The Londoner of those days was very proud of the great bridge.

> Let the whole world now all her wonders count,
> This bridge of wonders is the paramount.[2]

The seventeenth century had her Water-poet in John Taylor; and those who did not care to dodge the traffic in the narrow bridge might get him or his fellows to row them over. A noisy bunch they were, too! Taylor himself thinks it necessary to excuse their vociferousness by comparing them with the apprentices at the shop doors.[3]

---

[1] Satires (1760), p. 88.
[2] James Howell, Londinopolis (1657).
[3] Works (coll. ed., 1630), p. 267.

The Mercer, as you passe along the way,
Will aske you what d'e lacke? come neer I pray. . . .
So Watermen, that for a fare contends,
The fare once gone, the Watermen are friends.

He is himself a very independent gentleman.

Let Trencher-Poets scrape for such base vailes,
I'll take an Oare in hand when writing failes.[1]

The best description of that risky and, for that reason,
attractive escapade of "shooting" the bridge I find in a
burlesque of the early nineteenth century, called "The
Loves of the Triangles," by George Ellis and John
Hookham Frere.[2] This catches the style of the earlier
period so well that one might easily think it written by
some poet of Queen Anne's time.

So thy dark arches, London Bridge, bestride
Indignant Thames, and part his angry tide;
Where oft — returning from those green retreats,
Where fair Vauxhallia decks her sylvan seats; —
Where each spruce nymph, from city compters free,
Sips the frothed syllabub, or fragrant tea;
While with sliced ham, scraped beef, and burnt champagne,
Her 'prentice lover soothes his amorous pain;
—There oft, in well-trimmed wherry, glide along
Smart beaux and giggling belles, a glittering throng;
Smells the tarred rope — with undulation fine
Flaps the loose sail — the silken awnings shine;
"Shoot we the bridge!" — the venturous boatmen cry —
"Shoot we the bridge!" — the exulting fare reply.
— Down the steep fall the headlong waters go,
Curls the white foam, the breakers roar below.
— The veering helm the dexterous steersman stops,
Shifts the thin oar, the fluttering canvas drops;
Then with closed eyes, clenched hands, and quick-drawn
    breath,
Darts at the central arch, nor heeds the gulf beneath.

[1] "A Very Merry Wherry-Ferry Voyage," *Works* (ed. 1630), p. 13.
[2] *Parodies and other Burlesque Pieces* (ed. by Henry Morley, 1890), p. 262.

— Full 'gainst the pier the unsteady timbers knock,
The loose planks starting own the impetuous shock;
The shifted oar, dropped sail, and steadied helm,
With angry surge the closing waters whelm —
Laughs the glad Thames, and clasps each fair one's charms
That screams and scrambles in his oozy arms.
— Drenched each smart garb, and clogged each struggling limb,
Far o'er the stream the cockneys sink or swim:
While each badged boatman clinging to his oar,
Bounds o'er the buoyant wave, and climbs the applauding shore.

The river was an ever-present reality, an integral part of the city's life. The spendthrift Hoccleve loved it in days long past.[1]

> Wher was a gretter maistir eek than y,
> Or bet acqweyntid at Westmynstre yate,
> Among the tauerneres namely,
> And Cookes? whan I cam eerly or late?
> I pynchid nat at hem in myn acate,
> But paied hem as that they axe wolde;
> Wherfore I was the welcomere algate,
> And for 'a verray gentil man' y-holde.

> And if it happid on the Someres day
> That I thus at the tauerne hadde be,
> Whan I departe sholde, and go my way
> Hoom to the priuie seel so wowid me
> Heete and unlust and superfluitee
> To walke vn-to the brigge and take a boot
> That nat durste I contrarie hem all three,
> But dide all that they stired me god woot.

> And in the wintyr for the way was deep,
> Vn-to the brigge I dressid me also,
> And ther the bootmen took vp-on me keep,
> For they my riot kneewen fern ago:

[1] *La Male Regle de Hoccleue* (1406), ll. 177–208. See Hoccleve's *Works* (ed. Furnivall, Early English Text Society, 1892).

With hem was I I-tugged to and fro,
So wel was him that I with wolde fare;
For riot paieth largely eueremo;
He styntith neuere til his purs be bare.

Other than 'maistir' callid was I neuere,
Among this meynee, in myn audience.
Me thoghte I was y-maad a man for euere:
So tikelid me that nyce reuerence,
That it me made larger of despense
Than that I thoghte han been o flaterie!
The guyse of thy traiterous diligence
Is, folk to mescheef haasten and to hie.

In some districts the wash of the river was always in one's ears and the smell of it the solvent for less agreeable odors. We find this true in some of the street ballads and popular tales of the eighteenth century. There is one collection of comic tales called *The Muse in Good Humour*,[1] which contains "The Billingsgate Contest. A Piscatory London Eclogue. In Imitation of the Third Eclogue of Virgil." Here we have a dialogue between two fishwives, Oysteria and Welfleta, and later a song contest, with Maccarella as judge. The love of the sailor lad is their topic,[2] and the oily surface of the river is, no doubt, just behind them as they talk.

I'm with sweet *William* more in grace than you;
To me he swore at *Wapping* to be true:
Hoisting the sails, when he on deck did stand,
To me adieu he cry'd, and wav'd his faithful hand.

It is the same scene that we have in Gay's ballad "Sweet William's Farewell to Black-eyed Susan,"[3] with an echo even of its phrasing.

[1] (Two vols., 8th ed., 1785), II, 136.
[2] J. O. Halliwell in his *Catalogue of an Unique Collection of Ancient English Ballads* (1856) lists one (LVII) called "The Distressed Damsels, or a Doleful Ditty of a sorrowfull Assembly of young Maidens that were met together near Thames-Street, to bewail the Loss of their Loves which were lately press'd away to Sea."   [3] *Poems* (ed. Underhill), II, 261.

How old the "Ballad of London Bridge" [1] may be, it is difficult to determine.

> London Bridge is broken down,
>   Dance o'er my Lady Lee;
> London Bridge is broken down,
>   With a gay lady.
> How shall we build it up again?
>   Dance o'er my Lady Lee;
> How shall we build it up again?
>   With a gay lady.

Silver and gold will be stolen away; iron and steel will bend and bow; wood and clay will wash away; so,

> Build it up with stone so strong,
>   Dance o'er my Lady Lee;
> Huzza! 't will last for ages long,
>   With a gay lady.

The first bridge over the river at that point was finished in 1209, and collapsed in 1282.[2] Do the games of our childhood claim descent from so long an ancestry?

The more modern treatments of city life in poetry that come into one's mind are different from those we have already examined, and show strands of thought and idealism which may be typified in three poems, one by Wordsworth, one by Thomas Hood, and one by Walt Whitman. On the morning of September 3, 1802, Wordsworth was in London and got up early to see the city from Westminster Bridge. He remembered his impression in a later time of tranquillity, and wrote a very beautiful sonnet about it.

> Earth has not anything to shew more fair:
> Dull would he be of soul who could pass by

---

[1] *Gammer Gurton's Garland* (ed. by Joseph Ritson, 1810), p. 4.
[2] Richard Davey, *The Pageant of London* (2 vols., 1906), I, 97. See also Nicholas Hawksmoor, *A Short Historical Account of London-Bridge; with a Proposition for a new Stone-Bridge at Westminster* (1736).

A sight so touching in its majesty:
This City now doth like a garment wear
The beauty of the morning; silent, bare,
Ships, towers, domes, theatres, and temples lie
Open unto the fields, and to the sky;
All bright and glittering in the smokeless air.
Never did sun more beautifully steep
In his first splendor valley, rock, or hill;
Ne'er saw I, never felt, a calm so deep!
The river glideth at his own sweet will:
Dear God! the very houses seem asleep;
And all that mighty heart is lying still![1]

This is, after all, what we should expect Wordsworth to do when he touches the city. With London asleep he can enter into full sympathy. He can endow her with a motion and a spirit, that mysterious sense of personality, an apperception of the inevitability of natural law, in which his mind seemed to find rest like St. Augustine's *in sua voluntate*. But, with folks awake, he was disturbed. It may be that his memories of revolutionary Paris were too recent.

O Friend! I know not which way I must look
For comfort, being, as I am, opprest,
To think that now our Life is only drest
For shew; mean handy-work of craftsman, cook,
Or groom!

Wordsworth could also feel the tears of things as they touched human existence, and the little poem which he calls "The Reverie of Poor Susan" shows that he could combine the feeling for nature referred to above with a very delicate appreciation for contrasts in the fortunes of mankind.

Bright volumes of vapour through Lothbury glide,
And a river flows on through the vale of Cheapside.

[1] Wordsworth, *Poems in two Volumes* (1807; ed. Helen Darbishire, Oxford, 1914), pp. 126 and 147.

This is the second literary strand that I have to mention. It touches many a London vignette of the earlier nineteenth century. Since we have been thinking of the river and its fortunes among the poets, we may take Thomas Hood's "The Bridge of Sighs" [1] as our main illustration. Humanitarianism has come into full flower, the seed of which was scarcely broken in Gay's time. The new feeling toward the weak and unfortunate, so prominent in the literature of the last century, did not then exist, or, at any rate, was not often reflected in the poetry.[2] Cruelty to dogs and horses really claimed attention before the misfortunes of men and women. In Hood's poem, a girl has jumped from the bridge.

> Where the lamps quiver
> So far in the river,
> With many a light
> From window and casement,
> From garret to basement,
> She stood, with amazement,
> Houseless by night.
>
> The bleak wind of March
> Made her tremble and shiver;
> But not the dark arch,
> Or the black flowing river:

---

[1] *Poems* (1846).

[2] Notice, however, James Thomson's lines, written at the time of the investigation into conditions at the Fleet Prison (1728), *Poems* (Aldine ed.), II, 198:

> "Unpitied and unheard, where misery moans,
> Where sickness pines, where thirst and hunger burn,
> And poor misfortune feels the lash of vice;
> While in the land of liberty — the land
> Whose every street and public meeting glow
> With open freedom — little tyrants rag'd,
> Snatch'd the lean morsel from the starving mouth;
> Tore from cold wintry limbs the tatter'd weed,
> Even robb'd them of the last of comforts, sleep;
> The freeborn Briton to the dungeon chain'd,
> Or, as the lust of cruelty prevail'd,
> At pleasure mark'd him with inglorious stripes,
> And crush'd out lives, by secret, barbarous ways."

Mad from life's history,
Glad to death's mystery,
Swift to be hurl'd —
Anywhere, anywhere
Out of the world!

The third thread of interest in these modern pictures
of city life is suggested by Walt Whitman's reflections
from the rail of the ferry in East River, New York. He
has in one sense got beyond the romantic view of nature
and the humanitarian attitude as well, and sees himself
as a mere unit in the great stream of humanity from the
beginning of time and on into the future, one with all
that have been and that will be. The external world,
bridges, high-towered buildings, the glassy surface of the
river, masts, and smoke funnels, resume their proper
place in the pageantry of man. A day is as a thousand
years.

We have illustrated these differences and develop-
ments by the use of poems that have to do with the
river-front, but the same variations int aste and empha-
sis may be noticed-in sketches of any phase of city life
whatever. The city found a good many admirers among
the minor poets of the nineteenth century. Joanna
Baillie has some very good descriptive lines, which
should possibly have been noted along with Drayton's
general view of the city. This poet overlooks the town
from Hampstead Heath, thinks England's vast capital
a goodly sight through the clear air, when

St. Paul's high dome amidst the vassal bands
Of neighb'ring spires, a regal chieftain stands;

but when surveyed through the denser air, when mois-
tened winds prevail,

She is sublime. — She seems a curtain'd gloom
Connecting heaven and earth, — a threat'ning sign of doom.

With more than natural height, rear'd in the sky
'T is then St. Paul's arrests the wondering eye;
The lower parts in swathing mist conceal'd,
The higher through some half spent shower reveal'd,
So far from earth removed, that well, I trow,
Did not its form man's artful structure show,
It might some lofty alpine peak be deem'd,
The eagle's haunt, with cave and crevice seam'd.

The luminous canopy overhanging the city in the darkness also strikes the imagination of this poet, and the roar of many wheels as one approaches, the flood of human life in motion.

Horace and James Smith record the growth of the city on the south bank of the river in a poem called "New Buildings" (1813). This was the site of the Dog and Duck, a celebrated sporting tavern of the old days; the one, by the way, that Davenant talks about in his "Long Vacation in London,"[1] in which the merchant returns home to be told by his apprentice that his wife is off to Islington.

Ho, ho! to Islington! enough!
Fetch Job, my son, and our dog Ruffe!
For there in pond, through mire and muck,
We'l cry, "Hay, duck! there, Ruffe! hay, duck!"

And Garrick in his Prologue to Burgoyne's *The Maid of the Oaks* (1774), tells how

St. George's Fields, with taste and fashion struck,
Display Arcadia at the Dog and Duck!

Later, the Smith brothers give us the end of the story:

Saint George's Fields are fields no more,
The trowel supersedes the plough;
Huge inundated swamps of yore,
Are changed to civic villas now.

---

[1] Chalmers, *English Poets* (1810), VI, 433; *Wit and Drollery* (1661), p. 87. Davenant died in 1668.

The builder's plank, the mason's hod,
   Wide, and more wide extending still,
Usurp the violated sod,
   From *Lambeth Marsh* to *Balaam Hill.*

Pert poplars, yew trees, water tubs,
   No more at *Clapham* meet the eye,
But velvet lawns, Acacian shrubs,
   With perfume greet the passer by.[1]

Then comes a complaint about modern extravagance, and against the charity that begins and ends at home.

Blake and Browning both write about the city in its various moods, and people like Locker-Lampson (*London Lyrics*, 1857), Robert Buchanan (*London Poems*, 1866), and William Ernest Henley (*London Voluntaries*, 1888–92) have volumes of such sketches to their credit. The list of London vignettes by nineteenth-century poets is long, and need not be reproduced here. Reasonably good anthologies are available. Perhaps Lord Lytton's attempt to restore the *Poet-Shapes* of old time deserves special mention, while Matthew Arnold's "East London" and "West London," especially the latter, show keen observation and economy of expression. Arnold writes:

Crouch'd on the pavement close by Belgrave Square
   A tramp I saw, ill, moody, and tongue-tied;
   A babe was in her arms, and at her side
A girl; their clothes were rags, their feet were bare.
Some labouring men, whose work lay somewhere there,
   Pass'd opposite; she touch'd her girl, who hied
   Across, and begg'd, and came back satisfied.
The rich she had let pass with frozen stare.
Thought I: Above her state this spirit towers;
She will not ask of aliens, but of friends,
Of sharers in a common human fate.

[1] *Horace in London* (1813).

She turns from that cold succour, which attends
The unknown little from the unknowing great,
And points us to a better time than ours.

It would be absurd to suppose that all the poems cited
derive from Juvenal's Third Satire, though they doubt-
less bear some general relation to it. There is, however,
a group of poems which were certainly inspired by the
work of the old Roman. They are not merely vignettes
of street life; they are just the sort of vignettes that
Juvenal gives us. Even if a careful examination of the
documents leaves us still doubtful of origins, the fact
that such things appear in our literature in the work of
the first imitators of Juvenalian satire, at a time when
the enthusiasm for the classical writers, especially the
Roman, was at its height, should dissipate any hesita-
tion. To these satirists of the early seventeenth century
we have been referring from time to time for various
purposes. Here it is necessary only to illustrate this
very special *genre* from their work, and then to note
some of their later followers in the same style.

Donne wrote his First Satire in 1593.[1] In it he repre-
sents the poet as plagued by a youthful friend to leave
his books and come out with him to see the world.
Yielding against his better judgment, the poet follows
his friend into the streets. Here they meet various
people and have various experiences. The pictures are
clear, and of precisely the same type that we are already
familiar with in the work of the Roman poet.

Hall and Marston have scattered sketches of the same
kind, nothing, however, so carefully elaborated as this.
Edward Guilpin, on the other hand, repeatedly does

---

[1] Collier, in his *Poetical Decameron*, I, 155, states that there is in the
British Museum a MS. copy of the first three Satires of Donne (*Harl.* MS.
5110), entitled, *Ihon Dunne his Satires. Anno Domini 1593.*

this sort of thing in his *Skialetheia* (1598). Notice especially his Satire V:

> What more variety of pleasures can
> An idle Citty-walke affoord a man?
> More troublesome and tedious well I know
> 'T will be, into the peopled streets to goe:
> Witnes that hotch-potch of so many noyses,
> Black-saunts of so many seuerall voyces,
> That chaous of rude sounds, that harmony,
> And *Dyapason* of harsh *Barbary*,
> Compos'd of seuerall mouthes, and seuerall cries,
> Which to mens eares turne both their tongs and eies.
> There squeaks a cart-wheel, here a tumbrel rumbles,
> Heere scolds an old Bawd, there a Porter grumbles.
> Heere two tough Car-men combat for the way:
> There two for lookes begin a coward fray:
> Two swaggering Knaues heere brable for a whore:
> There brawls an Ale-Knight for his fat grown score.

The tradition of such fragments is fairly continuous down through the seventeenth century. Occasionally one finds a poem that contains practically nothing else but pencil drawings of crowds and streets. Such a work is Samuel Speed's *Fragmenta Carceris* (1675). We may notice particularly the poem in the same volume that deals with the legend of Duke Humphrey, as it refers to St. Paul's, and, after the fire, rather lamely to Westminster Abbey. The penniless must dine with Duke Humphrey, and the Duke was never without guests.

> Perhaps among the croud a Sword was seen,
> But rusty grown, in *Holland* it had been:
> And he that wore it, walk'd with such a grace,
> As who should say, My steps shall speak my race.
> A waggish Boy not yet discreetly grown,
> To understand the Virtues of the Town,
> Walk'd by, but kept at distance, as afeard,
> Still looking back, and as he look'd, he snear'd.

Captain, quoth he: The Captain turns about;
Whoop, Captain, quoth the Boy, and so runs out.
The Captain he pursues, as mov'd in wrath,
Makes strong attempts to draw his Weapon forth,
But all in vain: At which, the Captain curs't,
Whil'st standers by, with laughing almost burst.

No period in the history of our literature is more pro-
ductive of documents of one kind or another on the life
of the town than the early years of the eighteenth cen-
tury. Even before 1700 such writers as Ned Ward, Tom
Brown, and D'Urfey had shown some of the possibil-
ities which might attract men interested in street and
tavern scenes. Their work in prose was rugged, often
obscene or pornographic, amorphous certainly, but it
showed a virility which was later to blossom forth in the
polished essays of Steele, Addison, and Swift. These
Tatler and *Spectator* numbers on the town no doubt gave
fresh life to poetic effusions on the same type of subject.
The ninth number of the *Tatler*, April 30, 1709, contains
a brief poem by Swift on "Morning in Town."

Now hardly here and there an hackney-coach
Appearing, show'd the ruddy morn's approach.
Now Betty from her master's bed had flown,
And softly stole to discompose her own;
The slip-shod 'prentice from his master's door
Has pared the dirt, and sprinkled round the floor.
Now Moll has whirl'd her mop with dext'rous airs,
Prepared to scrub the entry and the stairs.
The youth with broomy stumps began to trace
The kennel's edge, where wheels had worn the place.
The small-coal man was heard with cadence deep,
Till drown'd in shriller notes of chimney-sweep:
Duns at his lordship's gate began to meet;
And brick-dust Moll had scream'd through half the street.
The turnkey now his flock returning sees,
Duely let out a-nights to steal for fees:

> The watchful bailiffs take their silent stands,
> And schoolboys lag with satchels in their hands.

This, along with another poem by the same author, called "The City Shower," [1] was the acknowledged model of Gay when he came to write *Trivia*. In the same year with these poems by Swift, came from the press of Henry Hills an anonymous production called *The Long Vacation, a Satyr, addressed to all disconsolate Traders*. There are several poems of this name in Augustan literature, and the popularity of such a subject shows how persistently the literary men, at any rate, thought in terms of the town.

> Bless us! how silent is the noisy Gown?
> How quiet are the *Temples*, *Park*, and Town?

Even the news-sheets are no longer scattered about:

> The weary Press, at Ease in Safety sleeps,
> No supple Oil the polish'd Iron keeps.
> The Hawkers now we very rarely meet,
> Faction and Treason venting in the Street.
> From *Will's* and *Tom's* the well-dress'd Youths are fled,
> And Silence there with Poppies binds her Head.
> To Country Seats the Men of Sense go down,
> And for their rural Joys neglect the Town.

Then follow references to the stage and its favorites, *Lear*, *Hamlet*, *Tamburlaine*, *Othello*, *Statira*, *The Man of Mode*, *Camilla*, *Arsinoe*. Most men of fashion and means are out at Hampton Court, or off to Bath, where atheists foregather with parsons, bawds with staid matrons, sharpers with spendthrift "cits." One of these last takes his wife to Epsom, where she soon succeeds in spending all his wealth.

> In the *Queen's-Bench* we shall her Husband meet,
> In *Ludgat* lock'd, or Pris'ner in the *Fleet*.

[1] Swift, *Poems* (2 vols., Bohn, 1910), I, 78 and 83.

Commission'd Harpies his Effects shall claim,
And the Gazette shall publish thrice his Name.

All the merchants are distressed for want of trade. The
vintners themselves are idle:

The Bankrupt Vintners starve for Want of Trade,
Few Payments now are to the Merchant made.
Score in the Bar, the Master seldom bawls,
Nor little Bell, the tardy Drawer calls.

The centre of London's business, the Royal Exchange,
is no longer popular, now that the hot weather is ap-
proaching:

The buzzing *Change*, and *Gresham's* Walks grow thin.
Catch-poles without, and Brokers sweat within.

And even the parks are deserted:

Late to the *Park* no whining Beaus repair,
And tell their Passion to the am'rous Fair:
No burning Flambeaux light the dolesome Shade,
Nor Waxen Beams strike thro' the verdant Glade.
The fierce Patroul, which march the Rounds by night,
Wild Ducks and Geese their sole Spectators fright.
Round the Canal no new-made Prints appear;
No cooing Lovers in the Grove we hear;
The waking Soldiers only guard the Deer.

The real spirit of the park in season is very well sug-
gested in the Canning burlesques:[1]

Such rich confusion charms the ravished sight,
When vernal Sabbaths to the Park invite.
Mounts the thick dust, the coaches crowd along,
Presses round Grosvenor Gate the impatient throng;
White-muslined misses and mammas are seen,
Linked with gay cockneys, glittering o'er the green:
The rising breeze unnumbered charms displays,
And the tight ankle strikes the astonished gaze.

[1] Ed. Morley, 1890, p. 247.

This is roguish imitation of an earlier style.[1] To get the real spirit of gaiety as it appeared in the late seventeenth century, we must go back to a ballad called "News from Hide-Park."[2]

> One evening, a little before it was dark,
>   Sing *tantara rara tan-tivee*,
> I call'd for my Gelding and rid to *Hide*-Park
>   On *tantara rara tan-tivee*.
> It was in the merry month of *May*,
> When meadows and fields were gaudy and gay,
> And flowers apparell'd as bright as the day,
>   *I got upon my tan-tivee.*
>
> The Park shone brighter than the skyes,
>   Sing *Tantara rara tan-tivee*,
> With jewels and gold and Ladies' eyes,
>   That sparkled and cry'd, "Come, see me!"
> Of all parts of *England*, *Hide*-Park hath the name
> For coaches and horses, and persons of fame;
> It look'd at first sight, like a field full of flame,
>   *Which made me ride up tan-tivee.*
>
> There hath not been seen such a sight since *Adam's*,
>   For perriwig, ribbon, and feather,
> *Hide*-Park may be term'd the market of Madams,
>   Or Lady-Fair, chuse you whether;
> Their gowns were a yard too long for their legs,
> They shew'd like a Rainbow cut into rags,
> A Garden of flowers, or a Navy of flags,
>   *When they all did mingle together.*
>
>   .   .   .   .
>
> We talkt away time until it grew dark,
>   The place did begin to grow privee;
> The Gallants began to draw out of the Park,
>   Till their Horses did gallop *tan-tivee*:

---

[1] Erasmus Darwin, *Loves of the Plants* (1789).
[2] *Circa* 1670–75. *Roxburghe Ballads*, VI, 496, or *Luttrell Collection*, II, 147.

> But finding my courage a little to come,
> I sent my Bay-Gelding away by my Groom,
> And proffer'd my service to wait on her home,
> *In her coach we went both tan-tivee.*

In the summer all this was transferred to the popular watering-places, and the same kind of scene made its appearance at Epsom, or Bristol, or Tunbridge, or Sadler's Wells. Someone wrote a "New Song on Sadler's Wells" in 1740,[1] and in it we find about the usual thing with perhaps a little more of the country flavor.

> These pleasant streams of Middleton
> In gentle murmurs glide along,
> In which the sporting fishes play
> To close each wearied Summer's day.
> And Musick's charms in lulling sounds
> Of mirth and harmony abounds;
> While nymphs and swains with beaux and belles
> All praise the joys of Sadler's Wells.
> The herds around o'er herbage green
> And bleating flocks are sporting seen,
> While Phoebus with its brightest rays
> The fertile soil doth seem to praise.

This gay life would not be congenial to the Visionary that Charles Jenner tells about in his sixth Eclogue.[2] For him, doubtless, the pleasantest time of the year would be the Long Vacation. In ordinary times he would avoid the mob.

> Oft have I seen him at the close of day,
> Shun the broad street, and steal his cautious way
> Through silent alleys to his lov'd resort
> In some dull garden of the inns-of-court.

Gay's poem on London streets is the most complete and interesting thing of its kind in English literature.

[1] Wroth, *Pleasure Gardens* (1896), p. 45.
[2] *Town Eclogues* (1772).

It is a series of sketches, full of accurate detail, an inval-
uable document in historical research altogether apart
from its literary value, which is high. Its material,
merits, and defects have been already considered. All
that we need to do here is to register its right to an
honored place in the Juvenalian succession.

To show that the *genre* did not die with Gay is a very
easy task. We have already mentioned some poems of
a later time, which might, without any great stretch of
critical judgment, be placed in this category. Perhaps
a little more assured of its parentage is a late eighteenth-
century poem by Charles Dunster, published pseudony-
mously in 1790. It is called *St. James's Street, a Poem in
Blank Verse, by Marmaduke Milton.* The claims of other
squares and streets are first examined and rejected; then
we learn that the spring and the height of the season
are to set the *tempo* for the poem. "Britannia's sportive
Sons" are just returning from country pleasures—the
hunt, and so on — to town, where they hope to spend
the vernal May in London's gay delights. Some sugges-
tions about the scenes of the early morning are quite in
the *Trivia* tradition. It is dawn, and quiet,

> Save when the three-hors'd stage or lumb'ring cart
> Rolls o'er thy sleepy stones in rumblings rude.

The gambler still sleeps and grasps in fancy many a rich
rouleau.

> A few short hours may pass; but soon he'll wake
> To sad realities: — for, if the morn
> Announce the opening fair of vernal May,
> The sable Scaler of his chimney's height,
> With all his troop, in motley dress array'd
> And bushy Perukes, once the outward sign
> Of solemn Science, tho' of late disdain'd,
> Save by the Legal Sage, of Pomp still fond,

Shall underneath his window deftly foot
The Moresque gay; and with the patt'ring Brush
To Shovel, rival of the sounding Shell,
Harmoniously applied, elicit sounds
That bid the drowsy God immediate fly
His willing Votaries; or else the song
Of *Mackarel Rare*, scream'd out by ceaseless lungs,
That thro' the jocund Spring no Sabbath know,
Shall rouse him to Reflection's joyless task.

It is noon now on vulgar streets, when the fashionable morning begins on St. James's. A groom leads a horse up and down, waiting for his master to appear at the door. Presently the gentleman comes down.

He mounts and trots impetuous up the street,
Or gallops furious thro' the *Embarràs*
Of Piccadilly, fill'd with many a Stage,
And tilted Waggon's vast unwieldy length,
To take his morning Saunter in Hyde Park,
And breathe the genial air of Rotten Row.[1]

The description of the Drawing Room which follows gives opportunity for a eulogy of the King and Queen. In the park outside the ladies pass, borne in chairs. Powdered footmen attend, with a sable youth at their head in a milk-white turban. The Fair have their hoops reverted, and sit in a very cramped position, with heads bent forward because of three feet of various ornament above. The poet expresses strong disapproval of the fashions of the day, especially the extraordinary head-gear, pomade, powder, puffs, the French *friseur*, and all his cosmetics. Youths high on well-built phaetons drive down the street through hackney-coaches, coal-carts, brewers' wagons. A four-in-hand passes, or a sporting conveyance with six high-bred grays. Girls also, reject-ing their native delicacy, mount these lofty cars, and

[1] Cf. Thomas Hood, "Miss Kilmansegg in London" (1846).

drive like Jehu through the street. Our author frowns on these athletic females, who learn not only to drive, but to hunt, and to shoot flying. Evidently the more languorous variety pleases him better, who,

> Seated in highly-varnish'd Vis-a-Vis
> Superbly painted, with silk Cushions lin'd,
> Come beauteous forth.

Youths stroll in the park. Even the Prince of Wales shows himself. The soldiers are there, too:

> The Sons of War, glitt'ring in Scarlet Pride
> Richly belac'd, nor wanting Hats fierce-cock'd,
> With Plumes erect, snow-white, or sanguine red,
> Or heavenly azure.

The parsons stroll about, sable-clad:

> The Rev'rend Tribe alike these regions seek,
> Not, as in days of yore, with Grizzle wigs
> Of size portentous, and with Beavers vast
> O'ershadowing, girt with intertwisted Snakes
> Of sable silk uniting in a rose.

The flower girl is popular, and the poet finds a song to honor her:

> At Boodle's Door 't is thine to stand,
> Thy well-stor'd basket in thy hand.

Presently the dinner hour arrives; the beaux and belles retire to eat at such places where they may be assured of every delicacy that can

> please
> The *Gourmand* Sage who scientific eats.

It really sounds as if the calories might be marked on the menu. By this time it is night. Indeed, the ancient curfew hour has long since passed.

> 'T is now the hour when sober Citizens,
> Sunk in the ignorance of Vulgar life,
> Betake them to their Beds.

Not so the sons of St. James's! They wander off to the gaming-houses and revel all night.

> Above the rest *Three* rise pre-eminent,
> With vaulted domes, and boast the well-known names
> Of *Boodle, Brookes*, and *White*.

They do not blush to borrow part of day itself for their protracted ceremonies, which the poet finds beyond the power of his description; he halts, unable to "sing the *Scene Ineffable*."

One naturally wonders what happened to the poetry of the streets in the early years of the nineteenth century, when poets were turning from society to nature,[1] from satire to enthusiasm, and often from the drab present to the romantic past. Strangely enough, one of the most vivid impressions of the town and its life comes from the pen of the apostle of the new movement, William Wordsworth. Though not a great enough poet to see virtue in vice in the Shakespearean sense, without confusion, he could see the color of the city, and it made the same kind of appeal to his imagination as that of the hills and lakes. The lines on London occur in "The Prelude,"[2] and begin,

> There was a time when whatsoe'er is feigned
> Of airy palaces, and gardens built
> By Genii of romance; or hath in grave
> Authentic history been set forth of Rome,

---

[1] How old are some of the new ideas! Young knew all about the sermons in stones. See "Love of Fame" (1728), *Poems*, II, 67:

> "On every thorn delightful wisdom grows;
> In every rill a sweet instruction flows."

[2] Wordsworth, *Poems* (ed. by Wm. Knight, Edin., 1883), III, 260–65.

> Alcairo, Babylon, or Persepolis;
> Or given upon report by pilgrim friars,
> Of golden cities ten months' journey deep
> Among Tartarian wilds — fell short, far short
> Of what my fond simplicity believed
> And thought of London — held me by a chain
> Less strong of wonder and obscure delight.

Then the poet tells of a schoolmate of his, a cripple from birth, who made the journey to London; how disappointed he was, on the friend's return, to find him unchanged by contact with the great city; the answers to his eager questions

> Fell flatter than a cagèd parrot's note,
> That answers unexpectedly awry,
> And mocks the prompter's listening.

Those long-past dreams of gorgeous spectacle in the town where next-door neighbors do not know each other's names have almost faded. Vauxhall and Ranelagh by night, the many other broad-day wonders!

> The River proudly bridged; the dizzy top
> And Whispering Gallery of St. Paul's; the tombs
> Of Westminster; the Giants of Guildhall;
> Bedlam, and those carved maniacs at the gates,
> Perpetually recumbent.

Statues, flowery gardens, vast squares, the Monument, the Tower packed with memorials of the past!

> Rise up, thou monstrous ant-hill on the plain
> Of a too busy world! Before me flow,
> Thou endless stream of men and moving things!
> Thy every-day appearance, as it strikes —
> With wonder heightened, or sublimed by awe —
> On strangers, of all ages; the quick dance
> Of colours, lights, and forms; the deafening din;
> The comers and the goers face to face,
> Face after face; the string of dazzling wares,

Shop after shop, with symbols, blazoned names,
And all the tradesman's honours overhead:
Here, fronts of houses, like a title-page,
With letters huge inscribed from top to toe,
Stationed above the door, like guardian saints;
There, allegoric shapes, female or male,
Or physiognomies of real men,
Land warriors, kings, or admirals of the sea,
Boyle, Shakespeare, Newton, or the attractive head
Of some quack-doctor, famous in his day.

This is the proper Wordsworthian attitude toward the city. It is an impression. The paint is dashed on thick. One has to stand well back to see it at·all. From the right angle, with the light just so, it is satisfying. This is not all, however. In the next section we find the poet handling the humors of the town in much the same way as the eighteenth-century writers. He can see detail, and represent it for us.

Meanwhile the roar continues, till at length,
Escaped as from an enemy, we turn
Abruptly into some sequestered nook,
Still as a sheltered place when winds blow loud!
At leisure, thence, through tracts of thin resort,
And sights and sounds that come at intervals,
We take our way. A raree-show is here,
With children gathered round; another street
Presents a company of dancing dogs,
Or dromedary, with an antic pair
Of monkeys on his back; a minstrel band
Of Savoyards; or, single and alone,
An English ballad-singer. Private courts,
Gloomy as coffins, and unsightly lanes
Thrilled by some female vendor's scream, belike
The very shrillest of all London cries,
May then entangle our impatient steps;
Conducted through those labyrinths, unawares,
To privileged regions and inviolate,
Where from their airy lodges studious lawyers
Look out on waters, walks, and gardens green.

After this little excursion into comparative solitude, the poet returns to the crowd. He notices the ballads dangling from dead walls. Giant advertisements stare him in the face. He passes the cripple, and the beggar with his chalked pictures on the pavement. The nurse is here,

> The Bachelor, that loves to sun himself,
> The military Idler, and the Dame,
> That field-ward takes her walk with decent steps.

All kinds of figures, selected no doubt for their picturesque quality, get his attention. He is noticeably not one with them, as the inferior poets with whom we have been associating for the most part in this investigation are one with the crowds they describe. He seems to move among these strange people as a superior being, possibly invisible.

> Now homeward through the thickening hubbub, where
> See, among less distinguishable shapes,
> The begging scavenger, with hat in hand;
> The Italian, as he thrids his way with care,
> Steadying, far-seen, a frame of images
> Upon his head; with basket at his breast
> The Jew; the stately and slow-moving Turk,
> With freight of slippers piled beneath his arm!
>   Enough; — the mighty concourse I surveyed
> With no unthinking mind, well pleased to note
> Among the crowd all specimens of man,
> Through all the colours which the sun bestows,
> And every character of form and face:
> The Swede, the Russian; from the genial south,
> The Frenchman and the Spaniard; from remote
> America, the Hunter-Indian; Moors,
> Malays, Lascars, the Tartar, the Chinese,
> And Negro Ladies in white muslin gowns.

That last line looks forward rather than backward, and might well be from the pen of Amy Lowell.

Having come thus far down through the years, it will be as well at this point to illustrate the kind of work that strictly modern writers do when they approach this topic. Richard Le Gallienne has written "A Ballad of London," which begins with a picture and ends with reflection.

> Ah, London! London! our delight,
> Great flower that opens but at night,
> Great City of the Midnight Sun,
> Whose day begins when day is done.
>
> Lamp after lamp against the sky
> Opens a sudden beaming eye,
> Leaping alight on either hand
> The iron lilies of the Strand.
>
> Like dragon flies, the hansoms hover,
> With jewelled eyes, to catch the lover;
> The streets are full of lights and loves,
> Soft gowns, and flutter of nocturnal doves.
>
> The human moths about the light
> Dash and cling close in dazed delight,
> And burn and laugh, the world and wife,
> For this is London, this is life!

He then goes on to speak of the world of weeping trodden things from whose corruption springs this bright flower, and ends conventionally enough by recalling the glories of the great cities of the past and imagining, through the dim mists of the future, the towers of London abased to the desert.

One of the finest impressions of this kind in all our literature has been done by the present poet-laureate. He calls it "London Snow." [1] It shows that marvellous sense for the right word which is more characteristic of

---

[1] Robert Bridges, *Shorter Poems*.

the earlier seventeenth-century lyrists than of the work of those who call themselves "imagists" in our day. Besides this, there is a freedom within bounds in the measures, an adaptation of the metrical effects to fit the thought, sound to sense, and an elasticity in the transitions from one group of images to another, which only a great poet can manage.

When men were all asleep the snow came flying,
In large white flakes falling on the city brown,
Stealthily and perpetually settling and loosely lying,
   Hushing the latest traffic of the drowsy town;
Deadening, muffling, stifling its murmurs failing;
Lazily and incessantly floating down and down:
   Silently sifting and veiling road, roof and railing;
Hiding difference, making unevenness even,
Into angles and crevices softly drifting and sailing.
   All night it fell, and when full inches seven
It lay in the depth of its uncompacted lightness,
The clouds blew off from a high and frosty heaven;
   And all woke earlier for the unaccustomed brightness
Of the winter dawning, the strange unheavenly glare:
The eye marvelled — marvelled at the dazzling whiteness;
   The ear hearkened to the stillness of the solemn air;
No sound of wheel rumbling nor of foot falling,
And the busy morning cries came thin and spare.
   Then boys I heard, as they went to school, calling,
They gathered up the crystal manna to freeze
Their tongues with tasting, their hands with snow-balling;
   Or rioted in a drift, plunging up to the knees;
Or peering up from under the white-mossed wonder,
"O look at the trees!" they cried, "O look at the trees!"
   With lessened load a few carts creak and blunder,
Following along the white deserted way,
A country company long dispersed asunder:
   When now already the sun, in pale display
Standing by Paul's high dome, spread forth below
His sparkling beams, and awoke the stir of the day.
   For now doors open, and war is waged with the snow;

And trains of sombre men, past tale of number,
Tread long brown paths, as toward their toil they go:
　But even for them awhile no cares encumber
Their minds diverted; the daily word is unspoken,
The daily thoughts of labour and sorrow slumber
At the sight of the beauty that greets them, for the charm
　they have broken.

Envoi

And has the promise of this book been fulfilled for any
but the writer? Its origin is probably obvious enough.
Quotations, as usual in such a work, have been numer-
ous and lengthy, and to omit them would destroy what
value the book may have, for I fear the head-links and
end-links have little enough interest here. Have these
quotations re-created the town in any sense? Have they
brought the reader any quickened feeling for values in
the verse of that period? Go, little book, and scatter
your bibliographies if you can do nothing else. And may
the one who is blessed bless us, if I may so profanely
apply the gracious old *benedictus benedicat*.

APPENDICES

Appendix A

COSTUME

WILLIAM MASON, in his poem called "The Birth of Fashion,"[1] has a clever adaptation of Pope's phrase which may be kept in mind during the reading of the following notes on costume:

> For I opine, 't is clear as light,
> *Whatever is* in dress *is right.*

The poets of Elizabeth's reign and the early seventeenth century were never tired of the literary exercise of jesting about the styles, though following them was usually out of the question. Curiously ambiguous reasons are given for quite unreasonable processes, like drinking whiskey to keep one warm in winter and cool in summer.

> Today hir owne haire best becomes which yellow is as gold,
> A perriwigs better for to-morrow, blacker to behold,
> To-day in pumps and cheverill gloves, to walke she will be bolde,
> To-morrow cuffes and countenance for feare of catching colde.
> Now is shee barefast to be seene straight on her muffler goes,
> Now shee is hufft up to the crowne, straight musled to the nose.[2]

The town was then overflowing with young men of leisure and wealth, whose travels had given them ideas about clothes, and whose brains were quite unequal to the task of assigning limits to fancy. These set the pace, but they ran their course by no means alone. All the ambitious youth of the town, whether rich or poor, learned or lewed, sought to follow their gay example, so that many time-honored distinctions between class and class, as far, at any rate, as externals were concerned, disappeared, and Thomas Weelkes, a gentleman of His Majesty's bedchamber, could write in 1608:[3]

---

[1] *Poems* (York, 1797), III, 83. Written in 1746.
[2] "The Cobbler's Prophesie" (1594), Davey, II, 78.
[3] *Ayres, or Phantasticke Spirites* (1608).

> Ha, ha, ha, ha! this world doth pass
> Most merrily I'll be sworn;
> For many an honest Indian Ass
> Goes for an Unicorn.[1]

Mistakes of the kind that Rowlands tells about in "A Paire of Spy-Knaves"[2] were inevitable.

> A Giddy gallant that beyond the seas
> Sought fashions out, his idle pate to please,
> In trauelling did meete vpon the way,
> A fellow that was suted richly gay,
> No lesse than Crimson Veluet did him grace,
> All garded and re-garded with gold Lace,
> His Hat was feather'd like a Ladies Fan,
> Which made the Gallant thinke him some great man,
> And vayl'd vnto him with a meeke salute,
> In reuerence of his gilded Veluet sute.
> Sir (quoth his man) your Worship doth not know
> What you haue done to wrong your credit so:
> This is the *Bewle* in Dutch, in English plaine
> The raskall Hangman, whom all men disdain,
> I saw him tother day on castell greene
> Hang foure as proper men as ere were seene.

The executioner may have been well able to pay for his clothes. With eight regular hanging-days and many extras, he was a busy man, and had, shall we say, a comfortable income. But all the young men who tried to keep up with the rapidly changing fashions were not so fortunate, and their brilliance was often short-lived. The sons of country gentlemen were continually arriving and were just as continually driven to desperate expedients in the struggle to keep their wardrobes properly replenished.

[1] In the good old days,
> "No gold nor silver parchment lace
> Was worn but by our Nobles . . .
> Now every gull's grown worshipful."
Even
> "The hangman now the fashion keeps,
> And swaggers like our gallants."
Collier, *Book of Roxburghe Ballads*, p. 49 (*ca.* 1600–10).
[2] Rowlands, *Works* (Hunterian Club), vol. II.

Unfortunately, sometimes all was spent on clothes. Marston tells of a young man of this sort in Satire III (1598):

> Now, after two yeers fast and earnest prayer,
> The fashion change not (lest he should dispaire
> Of ever hoording up more faire gay clothes),
> Behold at length in London streete he showes. . . .
> And all the band with feathers he doth fill,
> Which is the signe of a fantastick still,
> As sure as (some doe tell me) ever more
> A goate doth stand before a brothell dore.

Donne no doubt knew what he was talking of:

> As fresh, and sweet their apparrells be, as bee
> The fields they sold to buy them.[1]

And John Taylor is even more particular:

> To weare a Farm in shoo-strings, edg'd with gold,
> And spangled Garters worth a Coppy-hold;
> A hose and dublet, which a Lordship cost,
> A gawdy cloake (three Manours price almost),
> A Beaver Band and Feather for the head,
> Prized at the churches tythe, the poor man's bread.

Hall (*Satires*, V, 4) describes the young farmer's son selling his land to play the prodigal in London:

> Whiles one piece pays her idle waiting-man,
> Or buys an hoode, or silver-handled fanne,
> Or hires a Friezeland trotter, halfe yard deepe,
> To drag his tumbrell through the staring Cheape.

A resource for the soldier who wishes to dress well is suggested in Donne's First Satire:

> Not though a Captaine do come in thy way
> Bright parcell gilt, with forty dead mens pay.

This same writer goes on to express his despair over the swiftly changing fashions:

> And sooner may a gulling weather Spie
> By drawing forth heavens Scheme tell certainly
> What fashioned hats, or ruffes, or suits next yeare
> Our subtile-witted antique youths will weare.

---

[1] Satire IV (1593).

Certainly the Englishman of that time was oddly suited! King James, who was nervous of his health in the land of his adoption, set the fashion of the huge breeches:

> A gentleman called King James,
> In quilted doublet and great trunk breeches,
> Who held in abhorrence tobacco and witches.

According to Bulwer,[1] these were often stuffed with rags or bran, and many are the ridiculous stories told about them. The smallest hole might spell disaster. He tells about a man "in whose immense hose a small hole was torn by a nail of the chair he sat upon, so that, as he turned and bowed to pay his court to the ladies, the bran poured forth as from a mill that was grinding, without his perceiving it, till half his cargo was unladen on the floor."[2]

Rowlands in *More Knaves Yet* (*ca.* 1611) thus describes the prevailing styles:

> As now the honest Printer hath bin kinde,
> Bootes, and Stockins, to our Legs doth finde
> Garters, Polonia Heeles and Rose Shooe-strings,
> Which somewhat us two Knaues in fashion brings. . . .
> Well, other friends I hope we shall beseech
> For the great large abhominable breech
> Like brewers Hopsackes: yet since new they be
> Each knaue will haue them, and why should not wee?
> Some Laundresse we also will entreate,
> For Bands and Ruffes. . . .
> Scarffes we doe want to hange our weapons by . . .
>   . . . hats of the newest blocke.[3]

---

[1] *Artificial Changling* (1653), p. 542.

[2] Cf. Jonson, *The Silent Woman* (1609), Act IV, sc. 2: "If he could but victual himself for half a year in his breeches, he is sufficiently arm'd to over-run a country."

Cf. also Butler, *Hudibras* (1663–68), Part I, Canto I, ll. 309–350:

> "But a huge Pair of round Trunk-Hose:
> In which he carry'd as much Meat
> As he and all the Knights cou'd eat."

[3] Cf. *Doctor Merryman* (1616), p. 4:

> "A Money Monger choyce of Sureties had,
> A Country Fellow plain in Russet clad . . .
> The other Surety of another Stuff,
> His Neck environ'd with a double Ruff."

Ben Jonson, like Shakespeare, had noticed the travelled gen-
tleman's interest in fashions. In *The New Inn* (1629), Act II,
scene 2, he has a passage like the familiar one in *The Merchant
of Venice* (1596):

> I would put on
> The Savoy chain about my neck, the ruff
> And cuffs of Flanders, then the Naples hat,
> With the Rome hatband, and the Florentine agat,
> The Milan sword, the cloke of Genoa, set
> With Brabant buttons; all my given pieces,
> Except my gloves, the natives of Madrid.

The finished product must have been prodigious enough, and
it is not surprising to read astonished comments scattered
through the literature of the period. Jonson speaks of these
extravagant garments once more in his epigram,[1] "On the
New Motion":

> See you yond' Motion? not the old fa-ding,
> Nor captain Pod, nor yet the Eltham thing;
> But one more rare, and in the case so new:
> His cloak with orient velvet quite lined through;
> His rosy ties and garters so o'erblown,
> By his each glorious parcel to be known!

More detail of the costume is to be found in the following de-
scription from *Skialetheia:*[2]

> See you him yonder, who sits o're the stage,
> With the Tobacco-pipe now at his mouth?
> It is *Cornelius*, that braue gallant youth,
> Who is new printed to this fangled age:
> He weares a Jerkin cudgeld'with gold lace,
> A profound slop, a hat scarce pipkin high,
> For boots, a paire of dagge cases; his face,
> Furr'd with *Cads*-beard: his poynard on his thigh.

Cf. also "Christmas Lamentation" (*ca.* 1600), *Roxburghe Ballads*, I, 154:
"Since pride, that came vp with yellow starch."

[1] Entered in Stationers' Register, 1612. *Works* (ed. by Gifford and Cun-
ningham, 1875), VIII, 200.
[2] Epigram 53.

He wallows in his walk his slop to grace,
Sweares *by the Lord*, daines no salutation.[1]

Braithwaite, in *A Strappado for the Diuell*,[2] raises his protest almost to a shriek:

Now heauen preserue mine eyesight, what is here?
A man made vp in Wainscot? now I sweare,
I tooke him for some Colosse.

We can easily imagine the Water-poet getting the country gallant and his equipage properly stowed away in his boat for the trip up river.[3]

Drabs, dice, and drinke are all his onely joyes,
His pockets, and his spurs his gingling boyes,
A Squirels tayle hangs dangling at his eare,
A badge which many a gull is knowne to weare. . . .
With two shagg'd Ruffians and a pyde-coat Page,
Who beares his boxe, and his Tobacco fils,
With stopper, tongs, and other vtensils.

The gilded spurs were highly prized. Fungoso, in *Every Man out of His Humour*,[4] speaks of a very special variety: "I had spurs of mine own before, but they were not ginglers." In *Witts Recreations* [5] the same kind is mentioned.

Strotzo doth weare no ring upon his hand,
Although he be a man of great command;
But gilded spurres do jingle at his heeles
Whose rowels are as big as some coach-wheels,
He grac'd them well, for in the Netherlands,
His heels did him more service then his hands.

The trunk hose, as already noticed, were huge, and, by way of effective contrast, the waist was ridiculously confined by corsets. Hall [6] expresses this contrast well enough:

[1] Cf. Sir John Davies, *Works* (ed. Grosart), I, 326:
"He weares a hat of the flat-crowne block,
The treble ruffes, long cloake, and doublet French;
He takes tobacco, and doth weare a lock,
And wastes more time in dressing than a wench."
[2] 1615; ed. Ebsworth, p. 124.
[3] Taylor, *Works* (collected ed., 1630), "The Water-Cormorant," p. 6.
[4] Act II, sc. 2. Stationers' Register, 1600; acted 1601.
[5] 1640. Epigram 59.　　　　[6] *Satires*, III, 7.

> So slender waist with such an abbot's loyne,
> Did never sober nature sure conjoyne.

And Henry Fitzgeffrey in *Certain Elegies* (1617) shows the extremes of effeminacy to which the dandies at times descended:

> Yon Affecting *Asse*,
> That neuer walkes without his *Looking-Glasse*,
> In a *Tobacco* box, or *Diall* set,
> That he may priuately conferre with it.
> How his *Band* iumpeth with his *Peccadilly*,
> Whether his Band strings ballance equally:
> Which way his *Feather* wagg's: And (to say truth)
> What wordes in vtterance best become his mouth. . . .
> . . . . Hee'l haue an attractiue *Lace*,
> And *Whalebone-bodyes*, for the better grace.

The hair must have been a considerable worry to them also. Lodge mentions the time devoted to its care in his "A Fig for Momus": [1]

> Then in the presence of thy toward heire
> Beware to frisle, currle, and kembe thy haire,
> To spend three houres, in gazing in a glasse,
> Before thy wife and daughter goe to masse.

The lovelock was apparently essential, and continued fashionable through the century:

> From Barbors tyranny to save a locke,
> His mistris wanton fingers to provoke.[2]

> His haire, French like, stares on his frighted head,
> One lock amazon-like disheveled.[3]

The wig also was gaining in popularity. They were sometimes stolen, as in Gay, by youngsters carried in baskets or trays on

---

[1] 1595. Satyre III.
[2] Henry Fitzgeffrey, *Certain Elegies* (ed. 1620).
[3] Cf. Hall, *Satires* (1597), III, 7. Also Davenant, *Love and Honour* (1649), Act II, sc. 1:

> "A lock for the left side, so rarely hung
> With ribbanding of sundry colours, sir,
> Thou'lt take it for a rainbow newly crisp'd
> And trimm'd."

a man's shoulders; and with fair opportunity the wind also
naturally played havoc with them:

> Late travailing along in London way,
> Mee met, as seem'd by his disguis'd array,
> A lustie courtier, whose curled head
> With abron locks was fairely furnished.
> I him saluted in our lavish wise:
> He answeres my untimely courtesies.
> His bonnet vail'd, ere ever he could thinke,
> Th' unruly winde blowes off his periwinke.
> He lights and runs, and quickly hath him sped,
> To overtake his over-running head.
> The sportfull winde, to mocke the headlesse man,
> Tosses apace his pitch'd Rogerian:
> And straight it to a deeper ditch hath blowne;
> There must my yonker fetch his waxen crowne.
> I lookt and laught, whiles in his raging minde,
> *He curst all courtesie, and unruly winde.*[1]

Some features of the toilet which we consider essential were,
however, neglected.

> Oh, do but mark yon crisped Sir, you meet!
> How like a Pageant he doth stalk the street?
> See how his perfum'd head is powdred o're:
> 'T wu'd stink else, for it wanted salt before.[2]

The ladies, moreover, were quite as capable of extrava-
gance as the men. The sober statutes of the realm testify to
that. In 26 Elizabeth (1584) there are certain regulations
about the taxation necessary to carry out the orders regarding
the breeding of horses. In them this phrase, which tells its
own story, occurs: "If any person should be thought of ability
to be charged by reason of lands and goods, or by their wives'
apparell, they were to be so charged." The following rather
effective description of the lady of fashion is from Rowlands's
Looke to It:

> You with the Hood, the Falling-band, and Ruffe,
> The Moncky-wast, the breeching like a Beare:

---

[1] Hall, *Satires* (1597), III, 5.
[2] *Witts Recreations* (ed. of 1663), Epigram 693.

The Perriwig, the Maske, the Fanne, the Muffe,
The Bodkin, and the Bussard in your heare:
You Veluet-cambricke-silken-feather'd toy,
That with your pride, do all the world annoy.
Ile Stabbe yee.

This description, taken from its context, might, except for the hood and fan, suit either man or woman. Nor is this strange, for the smart thing in women's fashions at the time was an affectation of masculinity. Goddard tells us in the *Mastif Whelp* that the beauties of the day wore a long lock of hair upon one side, the hat with a feather at a rakish angle, the buttoned bodice with a skirt like a doublet. Now, if one takes away the mask which they affected, and the fan without which they were not properly dressed, they might pass for men in any place:

To see Morilla in her coach to ride,
With her long locke of hair upon one side;
With hat and feather, worn in swaggering guise;
With buttoned bodice, skirted doublet-wise;
Unmaskt, and sit i' the booth without a fan:
Speake, could you judge her less than be some man? [1]

Feathers were periodically popular, as to-day:

What feather'd fowle is this that doth approach
As if it were an *Estredge* in a Coach?
Three yards of feather round about her hat,
And in her hand a bable like to that:
As full of Birdes attire, as Owle, or Goose,
And like vnto her gowne, herselfe seemes loose.
Cri' ye mercie Ladie, lewdnes are you there?
Light feather'd stuffe befits you best to weare. [2]

The feathered fan figures also in Harington's clever bit of description. [3] His lines might well inspire an artist:

[1] Cf. Marston, Satire II:
"Ho, Lynceus! what's yonder brisk neat youth
Bout whom yon troupe of gallants flocken so,
And now together to Brownes Common goe?
. . . since strumpets breeches use."
[2] Rowlands, *Humours Looking Glasse* (1608).
[3] Book I, Epigram 70 (ed. of 1633).

> When *Galla* and myselfe do talk together,
> Her face she shrowds with fan of tawny Fether,
> And while my thought somewhat thereof deviseth,
> A double doubt within my mind ariseth:
> As first, her skin or fan which looketh brighter,
> And second, whether those her looks be lighter,
> Than that same Plume wherwith her looks were hidden,
> But if I cleer'd these doubts, I should be chidden.

Painting the face was the order of the day, and patches of the most unusual design made their appearance. John Hall wrote a small volume against long hair, and "the vanities and exorbitances of many women in painting, patching, spotting, and blotting themselves." These for him, at any rate, were "the badge of an harlot; rotten posts are painted, and gilded nutmegs are usually the worst." His writing and that of Bulwer (1653) is much in the tone of the New England manifesto, that it is "an impious custom and a shameful practice, for any man who has the least care for his soul to wear long hair."

Of the patches R. Smith, in his *A Wonders of Wonders . . .* (1662), has many unkind things to say.

> Pride is a Plague, sure these are the Sores,
> I will write *Lord have Mercy* on your doors.

To pass from the sartorial whimsicalities of the early seventeenth century to those of a hundred years later requires no readjustment of one's sense of values. All is vanity! For the satirist is not really interested in the sober citizen and his wife; they but provide the dull background for the scene. With him we slip from the very top to the bottom of the social ladder. Extremes are his delight, and when he discusses clothes, we may expect to revel in silks or shiver in rags.

Dress got considerable attention from the Augustan poets. Their work was to such a large extent satiric and social, rather than romantic and humanitarian, that this interest in externals is not to be wondered at. *Trivia* is packed with exact and interesting descriptions of the kind of clothing worn in 1716. Gay was a close observer of details. His notes about shoes, for instance, are illuminating:

Then let the prudent walker shoes provide,
Not of the Spanish or Morocco hide;
The wooden heel may raise the dancer's bound,
And with the scallop'd top his step be crown'd:
Let firm, well hammer'd soles protect thy feet
Thro' freezing snows, and rains, and soaking sleet.
Should the big last extend the shoe too wide,
Each stone will wrench th' unwary step aside:
The sudden turn may stretch the swelling vein,
Thy cracking joint unhinge, or ankle sprain;
And when too short the modish shoes are worn,
You'll judge the seasons by your shooting corn.

Then, as if this were not enough, later on he speaks of the fine lady with her foot bound in braided gold, and the fop who risks his red-heeled shoes to save coach hire, while the story of the bootblack and his origin is amusingly told in Book II.

Gay's long description of the proper kinds of material for the winter coat suggests an almost professional familiarity:

Nor should it prove the less important care,
To choose a proper coat for winter's wear.
Now in thy trunk thy D'oily habit fold,
The silken drugget ill can fence the cold;
The frieze's spongy nap is soak'd with rain,
And showers soon drench the camlet's cockled grain,
True Witney broad-cloth with its shag unshorn,
Unpierced is in the lasting tempest worn.

He notices the broad hat of the bully, edged round with tarnished lace, like the sons of war in Dunster's *St. James's Street* (1790). Wigs receive considerable attention from Gay. He advises the worst wig for rainy weather; he notices the fop,

Whose mantling peruke veils his empty head.

And lastly, he calls attention to the curiously bold practice of actually stealing wigs from the heads of their owners. Wigs were at this time at the height of their popularity. Raillery did not discourage the fashion, nor discomfort. The joke which Hillaria in *Tunbridge-Walks* indulges in at the fop's expense must have been gray-headed: "Nay really I have often accus'd the Tyranny of the Mode, in obliging you to wear those Great Wigs, 't is well you Beaus are not Inclin'd to be Hot-Headed." The business of manufacturing them was an industry of some importance. It formed a branch of every barber's work, and in addition there were many specialists. Shadwell's pseudo-French count in *Bury Fair* (1689) was a peruke-maker by trade, while *The London Spy* (1704–06) tells of coming "to the corner of a narrow Lane, where *Money for old Books* was writ upon some part or other of every Shop, as surely as *Money for live Hair* upon a *Barbers* Window."[1]

The fashion of the curl was not yet a thing of the past. In the Epilogue to Mrs. Centlivre's *Platonick Lady* (1707) there is a reference to this practice:

> Yet, tell me, Sirs, don't you as nice appear,
> With your false Calves, Bardash,[2] and Favrite's here?

Before this time and for a hundred years back this wanton curl had pleased the beaux. In this case also they were always ready to give a reason for their faith:

> Ask me no more why I do wear
> My Hair so far below my ear:
> For the first Man that e're was made
> Did never know the Barbers Trade.[3]

Dryden's lines in the Epilogue to *The Man of Mode* (1676) suggest a type of lovelock much like those in favor the day before yesterday:

> Another's diving Bow he did adore,
> Which with a shog casts all the Hair before;
> 'Till he with full *Decorum* brings it back,
> And rises with a Water-Spaniel shake.

Indeed, the barbers had, if we may believe a curious passage from *Midas*,[4] an exacting task:

How, sir, will you be trim'd? Will you have your beard like a spade, or a bodkin? A penthouse on your upper lip, or an ally on your chin? A low curle on your head like a bull, or dangling locke

---

[1] *The London Spy*, Part V, p. 115.   [2] Cravat.
[3] *Westminster Drolleries* (1671; ed. by Ebsworth, 1875), Part I, p. 77.
[4] John Lyly, *Midas* (1592), III, 2.

like a spaniell? your mustachoes sharpe at the ends, like shomakers aules, or hanging downe to your mouth like goates flakes? your love-lockes wreathed with a silken twist, or shaggie to fall on your shoulders?

After a hair-cut like this, one would be capable of anything. The men seemed to go on the general principle enunciated by *The Tatler*[1] that "a sincere Heart has not made half so many Conquests as an open Wastcoat."[2] Certainly, the gentleman who boasted the outfit described in *The Downfall of Dancing*[3] must have been irresistible:

> My gold-lac'd *Vest*, of green *Velour*,
> So wond'rous gay and nice;
> My silver *Snuff-box* figur'd o'er,
> And *Lid* of smart Device,
> My Chevron'd Clocks and silk-bound *Shoes*
> Are thrown aside, no more for Use.

Fashion sometimes showed an interest in politics. Vigo was captured in 1702, and at the time a huge amount of the best quality of snuff was taken. Immediately, that particular shade of brown became popular:

> The City 'Prentices, those upstart Beaus,
> In short spruce Puffs, and *Vigo-Colour* Cloaths.[4]

Clothes did not always mean gentility. Indeed, the more exotic and extravagant the costume, the more doubtful in general was the pedigree of the wearer. Defoe had often noticed this gradual transformation:

> With Clouted Iron Shooes and Sheep-skin Breeches,
> More Rags than Manners, and more Dirt than Riches:
> From driving Cows and Calves to *Layton*-Market,
> While of my Greatness there appear'd no Spark yet,
> Behold I come, to let you see the Pride
> With which Exalted Beggars always ride.[5]

---

[1] No. 151, March 28, 1710.
[2] See article by Budgell in *Spectator*, No. 319.
[3] *Foundling Hospital for Wit* (1749), II, 46.
[4] Epilogue to Mrs. Centlivre's *Love's Contrivance* (1703).
[5] Defoe, *The True-Born Englishman* (1708), Part II, p. 34.

The ladies are usually credited with more extravagant desires in fashion than the men. There were certainly some features of their dress in the early eighteenth century that seem odd enough to us now. The hoop-petticoat appeared in 1709, and this and the storied coiffure and the patches were all elements capable of the wildest exaggeration. Before the hoop arrived, however, *The London Spy* was complaining of extremes:

> At *Hackney*, *Stepney*, or at *Chelsea* bred,
> In Dancing Perfect, and in Plays well Read. . . .
> Impatient of Extreams, with Pride half Craz'd,
> Then must her Head a Story higher be rais'd:
> In her next Gaudy Gown, her Sweeping Train
> Is order'd to be made as long again;
> All things must vary from the common Road,
> And reach a Size beyond the Decent Mode:
> Thus Monstrously Adorn'd, to make a show,
> She walks in State, and Courtsies very low,
> And is a proper Mistress for the *Fool*, a Beau.[1]

One of the *Bagford Ballads* is called "The Vindication of Top-Knots and Commodes,"[2] and here there is much talk of "Our Towers, and Top-Knots, with Powdered Hair"; moreover,

> We'll wear our breasts bare, and curl up our hair,
> And shew our *Commodes* to the people.

In Tom D'Urfey's "De'il take the War, that hurry'd Willy from me,"[3] the girl tells of the devices she used to attract the men:

> I Wash'd and Patch'd to make me look provoking,
> Snares that they told me wou'd catch the Men;
> And on my Head a huge Commode sat cocking,
> Which made me shew as tall agen.

On the exposure of the bosom even Dante once had something to say,[4] and the Elizabethans were often very unpleasant in

---

[1] *The London Spy*, Part XVI, p. 396.
[2] *Bagford Ballads*, I, 122 (1691).
[3] Before 1705. Quoted in *Bagford Ballads*, I, 123.
[4] *Purgatorio*, Canto XXIII.

their remarks about it. Stephen Gosson, for example, in his *Pleasant Quippes for upstart new-fangled Gentlewomen* (1595), says:

> These Holland smockes, so white as snowe,
> and gorgets brave with drawne-worke wrought,
> A tempting ware they are, you know,
> wherewith (as nets) vaine youths are caught. . . .
> These perriwigges, ruffes armed with pinnes,
> these spangles, chaines and laces all;
> These naked paps, the Devils ginnes,
> to worke vaine gazers painefull thrall.

Gay amusingly infers that the ladies dress neither by instinct nor reason:

> Nor do less certain signs the town advise,
> Of milder weather, and serener skies.
> The ladies gaily dress'd, the Mall adorn
> With various dyes, and paint the sunny morn;
> The wanton fawns with frisking pleasure range,
> And chirping sparrows greet the welcome change:
> Not that their minds with greater skill are fraught,
> Endued by instinct, or by reason taught,
> The seasons operate on ev'ry breast;
> 'T is hence that fawns are brisk, and ladies dress'd.

His failure to call attention to the hoop-petticoat suggests that it was little worn at the time, though Francis Chute's poem on *The Petticoat*,[1] published shortly after *Trivia* (1716), may serve as evidence to the contrary. He explains in his introduction that he took a hint from Gay's poem on "The Fan" (December 8, 1713) and from the digression on the patten in *Trivia*:

> Ladies: The Invention of the Fan, and the Pattin, having gain'd your approbation, I hope this of the *Hoop-Petticoat*, as the Design is laudable, will come in for a small share of your Favour. Tho' I am no less than *Cousin-German* to the Author of those admir'd Productions: Yet, I, by no means, desire to Graft a Reputation upon his Stock.

---

[1] See Ralph Straus, *The Unspeakable Curll* (1927), p. 133.

His poem opens with a story of the Apollo–Daphne variety, which contains a curious description of a garden. The maiden's prayer, however, is this time unheard, and desperate expedients shortly become necessary. Thus the hoop-petticoat is invented and advertised to the society of sister nymphs, who approve its introduction:

> This Doctrine ev'ry prudent Nymph allow'd,
> And joint Applauses eccho'd from the Crowd:
> As when, the Glory of the Tragick Scene,
> The Manly *Booth*, in Majesty serene,
> Attracts the pleas'd Spectators ravish'd Ears,
> And seems to Be, the *Cato* he appears;
> At ev'ry Pause, resounding Shouts prevail,
> And often stop, and interrupt his Tale.

Breval humorously suggests later, in *The Art of Dress* (1717), that this extraordinary design for the petticoat was modelled on Wren's St. Paul's. This poem, like *The Art of Dancing* by Soame Jenyns (1730), has much to say about costume. Jenyns refers to the white gloves, and sword held by a silk guard, the powdered wigs, the elegant buckles on the shoes, the hoop's enormous size, the whalebone bondage of the slender waist, and the fan. As if that sort of thing were not already overdone, he discourses on the invention of the fan, with the conventional type of story, this time, of course, about Fanny and Aeolus. The whole poem is a carefully worked-out imitation of Gay's *Trivia*.[1]

The popularity of the wide skirts lasted through the century. They grew wider and wider until in 1770 a lady, in the attempt to avoid a sweep, got her skirt caught in a hook above a shop window, and thus became the heroine of a famous print, called "The Lady's Disaster."[2]

> A nymph in an unguarded hour,
> (Alas! who can be too secure?)
> Dire Fate has destin'd to be seen,
> Entangled in her wide Machine,
> Whilst carmen, clowns and gentlefolks,
> With satisfaction pass their jokes!

---

[1] On the fan, see *Spectator*, No. 102.
[2] Davey, *The Pageant of London* (2 vols., 1906), II, 375.

Gay is never inclined to grow giddy over feminine eccentricities. He is too much of a realist for that. He speaks, for instance, of exercise as bestowing unartful charms, but the only place where he mentions rouge is in the account of the whore:

> 'T is she who nightly strolls with saunt'ring pace,
> No stubborn stays her yielding shape embrace;
> Beneath the lamp her tawdry ribbons glare,
> The new-scower'd manteau, and the slattern air;
> High-draggled petticoats her travels show,
> And hollow cheeks with artful blushes glow.[1]

The powder which the men use in the wigs excites his contempt. The fop he likens to a miller, whom we must pass with caution,

> Lest from his shoulder clouds of powder fly.

And even the patches are mentioned very indirectly. Cloacina sees a mortal scavenger, and immediately falls in love with him.

> The muddy spots that dried upon his face,
> Like female patches,[2] heighten'd ev'ry grace.

This is noticeably more restrained than the remarks about such matters in R. Smith's *Wonder of Wonders* (1662), or in

---

[1] Cf. Pope, "The Basset Table" (ed. Warton), II, 326, publ. piratically by Hills in 1716, misdated 1706:

> "She owes to me the very charms she wears,
> An aukward Thing, when first she came to Town;
> Her shape unfashion'd, and her Face unknown:
> She was my friend, I taught her first to spread
> Upon her sallow cheeks enliv'ning red:
> I introduc'd her to the Park and Plays;
> And by my int'rest, *Cozens* made her Stays.
> Ungrateful wretch, with mimick arts grown pert,
> She dares to steal my Fav'rite Lover's heart."

[2] Cf. *Spectator*, No. 81. Cf. *Bagford Ballads*, II, 548. Before 1707 John Weldon set to music the following song:

> "That little Patch upon your Face
> Would seem a Foil on one less fair,
> On you it hides a charming Grace,
> And you in pity plac'd it there."

the early street ballad "Upon the Naked Bedlams and spotted beasts in Covin Garden," from John Cotgrave's *Wits Interpreter* (1655), page 131.

The patches were cut at times in the most curious shapes and must have been distracting.

> And yet the figures emblematick are,
> Which our She-wantons so delight to wear;
> The Coach and Horses, with the hurrying wheels,
> Shew both their giddy brains and gadding heals;
> The Crosse and Croslets in your face combin'd,
> Demonstrate the crosse humours of their mind.[1]

The importance of a patch, however, was fully recognized in Gay's time. The cynic in *Tunbridge-Walks* knows this: "Then there's more Policy and Consultation us'd in placing your Patches to Advantage, than at a Council of War, in the disposing a whole Army." A little later, Thomas Cooke descants on the same subject in his "Love and Old Age":[2]

> Thus rav'd *Canidia*, as the lovely Fair
> Made the Position of a Patch her Care.
> No sooner had the Nymph just step'd aside,
> But from the Box, her Magazine of Pride,
> A thousand Implements the Table spread,
> Teeth, Eyes, the Perfume, and the liquid Red.[3]

Charles Dunster, the author of *St. James's Street* (1790), disapproves of all cosmetics, rouge, pomade, powder, and puffs, then so favored by the ladies.[4] He tells about the diffi-

---

[1] R. Smith, *A Wonder of Wonders . . .* (1662).
[2] *Original Poems with Imitations and Translations* (1742), p. 141.
[3] Cf. Jonson, *The Silent Woman* (1609), Act IV, sc. 1: "*Otter:* All her teeth were made in the Black-friars, both her eye-brows in the Strand, and her hair in Silverstreet. Every part of the town owns a piece of her."
[4] Richard Ames, *The Folly of Love* (2d ed., 1693), p. 7:
> "How Mother *Shipton* Looks drest up in Point,
> Who, tho her Face with Paint she so anoint,
> That like a Joynted Baby she appears,
> So *sleek*, so *plump*, so *ruddy*, and so clear,
> Yet *all* can never hide her *Threescore Years*."

culties of managing the hoop in a sedan-chair, and frowns even more on the absurd headgear, and the French *friseur* that it necessitates. D'Urfey calls it

> That Steeple geer upon your Brow;
> Which, to my Judgment, makes you seem
> Just like a Fore-horse of a Team.[1]

Masks were coming into fashion with the ladies about 1700. The country squire whose exploit is recounted in *The London Spy* would no doubt have the sympathy of the crowd who watched him. Incidentally, the fact that a frog was handy on that London street tells its own additional story:

> An Arch *Country Bumpkin* having pick'd up a Frog in some of the Adjacent Ditches, peeping into the Coach, as he pass'd by, and being very much Affronted that they hid their Faces with their Masks, *Adsblood*, says he, *you look as Ugly in those black Vizards as my Toad here; e'en get you all together*, tossing it into the Coach: At which the fright'ned *Lady Birds* Squeak'd out, open'd the Coach Doors, and leap'd out amongst the Throng to shun the loathsome Companion.[2]

Gay mentions the riding-hood as a sensible covering for the head, and worn by all classes from prostitute to citizen's wife:

> Good housewives all the winter's rage despise,
> Defended by the riding-hood's disguise:
> Or underneath th' umbrella's oily shed,
> Safe thro' the wet on clinking pattens tread.
> Let Persian dames th' umbrella's ribs display,
> To guard their beauties from the sunny ray;
> Or sweating slaves support the shady load,
> When eastern Monarchs show their state abroad;
> Britain in winter only knows its aid,
> To guard from chilly showers the walking maid.

Umbrellas had been known in England as early as Ben Jonson's time, but they did not come into fashion much before 1700, and were then used almost altogether by women. Swift considered them as fit only for the ladies, though how the frail beauties were to be expected to carry these great

---

[1] *Collin's Walk through London and Westminster* (1690), p. 119.
[2] *The London Spy* (1704–06; ed. Straus), Part VII, p. 174.

machines does not seem to have bothered him. An umbrella of this early period has been preserved in the South Kensington Museum and weighs six pounds. *The Female Tatler* for December 12, 1709, contains an amusing advertisement about a lost umbrella. They seemed doomed to community service from the start.

The Young Gentleman belonging to the *Custom-House*, that for fear of Rain, borrow'd the Umbrella at *Will's Coffee-House* in *Cornhil*, last Friday Night of the Mistress; is hereby Advertised, that to be dry from Head to Foot on the like occasion, he shall be welcome to the Maids Pattens.[1]

Gay's "Epistle to the Right Honourable William Pulteney, Esq.," written on the occasion of his visit to Aix-la-Chapelle with that gentleman in the summer of 1717,[2] contains more interesting material on dress.[3] He seems to have felt freer to talk about the frivolities of the French ladies than he did about those of their English cousins.

> Shall he (who late Britannia's city trod,
> And led a draggled Muse, with pattens shod,
> Through dirty lanes, and alley's doubtful ways)
> Refuse to write, when Paris asks his lays?

After all, the styles came from Paris, and the beaux and belles of the two great cities will be at least first cousins.

> How happy lives the man, how sure to charm,
> Whose knot embroider'd flutters down his arm!
> On him the ladies cast the yielding glance,
> Sigh in his songs, and languish in his dance;
> While wretched is the wit, contemn'd, forlorn,
> Whose gummy hat no scarlet plumes adorn;
> No broider'd flowers his worsted ankle grace,
> Nor cane emboss'd with gold directs his pace;
> No lady's favour on his sword is hung.
> What, though Apollo dictate from his tongue,

[1] Cf. *Notes and Queries*, Ser. 1, vol. II, p. 25 (June 8, 1850). See *Trivia*, I, 211.
[2] *Suffolk Letters*, I, 32. Possibly written during the 1719 visit.
[3] *Poems* (ed. Underhill), I, 192.

His wit is spiritless and void of grace,
Who wants th' assurance of brocade and lace.
While the gay fop genteelly talks of weather,
The fair in raptures dote upon his feather;
Like a court lady though he write and spell,
His minuet step was fashion'd by Marcell;
He dresses, fences. What avails to know?
For women choose their men, like silks, for show.
Is this the thing, you cry, that Paris boasts?
Is this the thing renown'd among our toasts?
For such a flutt'ring sight we need not roam;
Our own assemblies shine with these at home.

The lady's toilet was a favorite subject with Gay and his friends.[1] The sort of poem that pleased them is to be found as early as 1690 in the *Mundus Muliebris, or the Ladies Dressing Room Unlocked, and her Toilette Spread.*[2] I may quote the description of the room itself as particularly interesting:

The chimney furniture of plate,
(For iron's now quite out of date):

---

[1] Cf. Swift, *Poems* (2 vols., Bohn, 1910), I, 193, "The Lady's Dressing Room" and Richard Ames, *The Folly of Love* (2d ed., 1693). Cf. also Edward Young, *Poems* (2 vols., 1852), II, 115:
"Acquainted with the world, and quite well bred,
Drusa receives her visitants in bed."
and II, 120:
"For her own breakfast she'll project a scheme,
Nor take her tea without a strategem."
Also Anon., *Fashion, a Satire* (Dodsley, 1765, III, 314):
"With him the fair, enraptur'd with a rattle,
Of Vauxhall, Garrick, or Pamela prattle:
This self-pleas'd king of emptiness permit
At the dear toilette harmlessly to sit . . .
Muscalia dreams of last night's ball 'till ten,
Drinks chocolate, stroaks Fop, and sleeps agen;
Perhaps at twelve dares ope her drowsy eyes,
Asks Lucy if 'tis late enough to rise;
By three each curl and feature justly set,
She dines, talks scandal, visits, plays piquette:
Meanwhile her babes with some foul nurse remain,
For modern dames a mother's cares disdain."
Cf. Sir Charles Hanbury Williams, *Poems* (3 vols., 1822), I, 72, "Isabella, or The Morning,"; and Pope, *The Rape of the Lock.*
[2] Quarto (1690). Reprinted in Fairholt, *Satirical Songs and Poems on Costume.*

Tea-table, skreens, trunks, and stand,
Large looking-glass richly japan'd,
An hanging shelf, to which belongs
Romances, plays, and amorous songs;
Repeating clocks, the hour to show
When to the play 't is time to go,
In pompous coach, or else sedan'd
With equipage along the Strand,
And with her new beau foppling mann'd.

The main business of the place Gay gives us in his "Epistle to Pulteney":

But let me not forget the toilette's cares,
Where art each morn the languid cheek repairs:
This red's too pale, nor gives a distant grace;
Madame to-day puts on her Opera face;
From this we scarce extract the milkmaid's bloom,
Bring the deep dye that warms across the room;
Now flames her cheek, so strong her charms prevail,
That on her gown the silken rose looks pale!
Not but that France some native beauty boasts,
Clermont and Charleroi might grace our toasts.

Appendix B

EARLY EDITIONS OF *TRIVIA*

TRIVIA was first published on the 26th of January, 1716, in an octavo volume of 96 pages. The ordinary edition was sold to the public at one-and-sixpence, while a number of large-paper copies were subscribed for by the poet's friends and patrons at a guinea apiece. The large-paper edition bears the imprint of Lintot, the Cross Keys, on the title-page. Above the opening lines of the poem is an engraving of a street scene, showing a woman with an umbrella, a coach, watchman, scavengers, pedestrians. The lines are not numbered, but the book contains the little side-headings. It was first advertised for sale in the *Daily Courant* of January 26, 1716: "This day is published, '*Trivia: or the Art of Walking the Streets of London.*' By Mr. Gay. Printed for Bernard Lintot between the Temple Gates." Copies of this edition sold for forty dollars in 1901. The decorative inserts in the ordinary copy are different.

The title-page of the second edition is the same as that of the large-paper copy of the first, except that after the motto occur the words "The Second Edition," and in place of the imprint of the Cross Keys occurs the engraving of the street scene used before at the head of Book I. It is unlined, and indexed by pages like the first edition. It bears no date, but must have been issued between January 26, 1716, and January 21, 1717, when *Three Hours after Marriage* was published, for that contains at the end of the Epilogue an advertisement of the second edition of *Trivia* among the "Books printed for Bernard Lintott." And J. Nichols's *Literary Anecdotes* (1812-15), I, 118–121, has the following item:

1716. In this year, Mr. Bowyer's accompt-book begins with regular entries . . . the following articles deserve to be cursorily mentioned: . . . "*Trivia, or the Art of Walking the Streets of London,* Second Edition, 8vo."

In addition to these, there appeared what is apparently a pirated edition, undated, published by Mrs. Newcomb, at the Naked Boy, near Temple Bar. The price was one shilling and six-pence. The lines in the copy are not numbered, the paragraph captions are printed between the lines, not at the side, and the Cloacina episode does not appear. The price is the same as the other early editions. All these circumstances point to a date not later than 1720, and probably at least two years earlier.

Following the collected *Poems on Several Occasions* (1720) there was a Dublin edition of *Trivia*, printed along with *Rural Sports* and inscribed to Mr. Pope. It was printed by S. Powell, for George Risk, at the Corner of Castle-lane, opposite the Horse-guard, in Dame's-street, and dated 1727. This is a very small copy and has the index immediately after the advertisement instead of at the end as in the others.

The third regular edition appeared in 1730, with title-page and decorative inserts practically the same as in the large-paper copies of the first edition. The lines, however, are numbered. This edition was advertised three times in the *Craftsman*, March 21 and 28, and April 4, 1730:

This day is Published, the Third Edition of Mr. Gay's *Trivia: or, the Art of Walking the Streets of London*. A Poem ... With Additions, Corrections, and a compleat Index to the Whole, by the Author. Price 1*s* ... Printed for B. Lintot. ...

Two later editions may be noticed, one printed for T. Gay, Esq. Kensington, and sold at the Circulating Library, Shoe Lane, at six-pence. This bears on its title-page Dr. Johnson's endorsement from his *Life of Gay*: "To *Trivia* may be allowed all that it claims; it is *sprightly, various*, and *pleasant*." Facing the title-page is a print of a young man in a doubtful frame of mind, with insert "Pub. as Act directs May. 1795," and below, the lines:

> O! may my virtue, guide me through the roads
> Of Drury's mazy courts, and dark abodes,
> The Harlot's guileful paths, who nightly stand,
> Where Catherine Street descends into the Strand.

The title-page of this edition is embellished with a portrait of Gay.

In 1807, an edition of *Trivia* was published along with Dr. Johnson's *London*. It was printed by Ballantine and Law, Duke-street, Adelphi, and sold by Effingham Wilson, Paternoster-Row, and all other booksellers. Facing the title-page is a print of a street scene, showing a girl with a mop, an uneasy beau with white breeches and hose, with cane under arm in the forbidden position, a sweep dangerously close, a bursting wine-cask spraying the beau's new hat, and what appears to be the portico of St. Paul's Church, Covent Garden, in the background.

BIBLIOGRAPHY

BIBLIOGRAPHY

NOTE: *Unless otherwise stated, the books listed below were published in London*

POETRY

Addison, Joseph. Works. Ed. Richard Hurd. 1856.

Akenside, Mark. Collected Poems. 1772.

[Allison, John.] Upon the Late Lamentable Fire in London. By J. A. of King's College in Cambridge Fellow. 1667.

Ames, Richard. The Pleasures of Love and Marriage. 1691.

The Jacobite Conventicle. 1692.

The Bacchanalian Sessions: or the Contention of Liquors: with A Farewell to Wine. 1693.

The Search after Claret; or a Visitation of the Vintners. 2 Cantos. 2d ed. 1691.

A Farther Search after Claret. 1691.

The Last Search after Claret in Southwark. 1691.

The Mineral Wells at Islington, near London, describing the company who resorted to them. Ed. J. O. Halliwell, 1861. This is a reprint of Islington Wells, or the Threepenny Academy, 1691.

The Folly of Love. A new Satyr against Women. 2d ed. 1693

Fatal Friendship; or the Drunkard's Misery: being a Satyr against Hard Drinking. 1693.

The Long Vacation. 1691.

A Dialogue between Claret and Darby-Ale. 1692.

The Rake: or, the Libertine's Religion. 1693.

Amhurst, Nicholas [Caleb D'Anvers]. A Collection of Poems on Several Occasions. 1731.

The Twickenham Hotch-Potch. 1728.

Armstrong, John. Poetical Works. 1807.

The Art of Preserving Health. 1768.

Arwaker, Edmund. Fons Perennis. A Poem on the Excellent and Useful Invention of Making Sea-Water Fresh. 1686.

Ayres, Philip. Lyric Poems, made in Imitation of the Italians. 1687.

Baker, Daniel. Poems upon Several Occasions. 1697.

[Barber, Mrs. Mary.] Poems on Several Occasions. 1734.

Beckingham, Charles. The Lyre. 1726.

Behn, Aphra. Works. Ed. Montague Summers. 6 vols. 1915.
A Poem to Sir Roger L'Estrange on his third Part of the History of the Times, Relating to the Death of Sir Edmund Bury-Godfrey. 1688.
Blackmore, Sir Richard. A Collection of Poems on Various Subjects. 1718.
A Satyr against Wit. 3d ed. 1700.
[Boyse, Samuel.] The Satirist: In Imitation of the fourth Satire of The First Book of Horace. Dublin, 1733.
Bramston, James. The Woman of Taste. 3d ed. Dublin repr., 1733.
The Man of Taste. London pr.; Dublin repr., 1733.
The Art of Politicks. 1729.
Braithwaite, Richard. Barnabee's Journal. Ed. Joseph Haslewood. Revised by W. C. Hazlitt. 1876.
Drunken Barnaby's Four Journeys to the North of England. Repr. York, 1852.
Natures Embassie, Divine and Moral Satires, etc. Repr. Boston, England, 1877.
A Strappado for the Devil. Ed. J. W. Ebsworth. Boston, Lincolnshire, 1878.
Brereton, Thomas. Charnock Junior: or, The Coronation. 1719.
Breton, Nicholas. Works. Ed. A. B. Grosart. Edinburgh, 1875-79.
Breval, John Durant. Mac-Dermot: or the Irish Fortune-Hunter, in 6 Cantos. 1717.
The Art of Dress. 1717.
The Church-Scuffle, or News from St. Andrews, a Ballad, to the tune of A-begging we will go. 1719.
The Confederates. 1717.
[Brome, Alexander.] The Poems of Horace, Consisting of Odes, Satyres, and Epistles. Rendred in English Verse by Several Persons. 1666.
Songs and other Poems. 1664.
Brown, John. The Stage. 1819.
Patronage, A Poem: an Imitation of the Seventh Satire of Juvenal. By Mandanis. 1820.
Butler, Samuel. Hudibras. Adorned with Cutts, designed and engraved by Mr. Hogarth. 1775.
Hudibras. Ed. Henry Morley. 1885.
Buttes, Henry. Dyets Dry Dinner consisting of eight severall courses and a Satyricall Epigram. 1659.
Byrom, John. Miscellaneous Poems. Manchester,1773.
Cambridge, Richard Owen. The Scribleriad, an Heroic Poem. 6 Books. 1751.
Works. Ed. by his son. 1803.

Canning, George — Ellis, George — Frere, John Hookham. Parodies and other Burlesque Pieces. Ed. Henry Morley. 1890.

Carter, Elizabeth. Poems. 1762.

Caulfield, J. The Manners of Paphos; or the Triumph of Love. 1774.

Chamberlaine, James. A Sacred Poem, wherein the Birth, Miracles, Death, Resurrection, and Ascension of the Most Holy Jesus are Delineated. 1680.

Chatterton, Thomas. Miscellanies in Prose and Verse. 1778.

Chaucer, Geoffrey. Works. Ed. Skeat.

Chudleigh, Lady Mary. Poems on Several Occasions. 3d ed. 1722.

Churchill, Charles. An Epistle to William Hogarth. 1763.
  The Apology. 1761.

[Chute, Francis.] The Petticoat: an heroi-comical poem in two books, by Mr. Gay. 2d ed. 1716.

Clavell, John. A Recantation of an ill led life: etc. 3d ed. with addition. 1634.

Cleveland, John. Works. 1687.

Cobb, Samuel. The Mouse Trap, a Poem, written in Latin by E. Holdsworth of Magd. Coll. Oxon. made English by Samuel Cobb, M. A., late of Trinity College, Cambridge. 1712.

Congreve, William. Complete Works. Ed. Montague Summers. 4 vols. 1923.

[Cooke, Thomas.] The Battle of the Poets; or the Contention for the Laurel. 1731.
  Original Poems with Imitations and Translations. 1742.

[Cooper, J. G.] Poems on Several Subjects. 1764.

[Cotgrave, John.] Wits Interpreter, the English Parnassus. 1655.

Cotton, Charles. Poems. Ed. John Beresford. 1923.

Cowley, Abraham. The Puritan and the Papist, a Satire. 1643.
  Works. 2 vols. 1707.

Creech, Thomas. The Odes, Satyrs, and Epistles of Horace. 5th ed. 1730.

C[rouch?], H. London Vacation and the Countries Tearme. 1637.

[Crowe, William.] Lewesdon Hill. Oxford, 1788.

[Dalton, John.] An Epistle to a Young Nobleman from his Praeceptor. 1736.

[Dance, James.] Poems on Several Occasions. By James Love, Comedian. Edinburgh, 1754.

Darby, Rev. Charles. Bacchanalia, or A Description of a Drunken Club; a Poem. 1680.

D'Assigny, F. Poems on Several Occasions, etc. 1730.

Davenant, Sir William. Poems. In Chalmers' English Poets. 1810. London. 1648.

Davies, Sir John. Poems. Ed. A. B. Grosart. 1869.
[Defoe, Daniel.] The True-Born Englishman. 1708.
A Hymn to the Pillory. 1708.
Dekker, Thomas. Verses prefixed to Taylor's Works. Coll. ed.
1630.
Deloney, Thomas. Strange Histories. 1607. Repr. Percy Society,
vol. I. 1841.
Denham, Sir John. Cooper's Hill, etc. 2d ed. 1650.
Dennis, John. Poems in Burlesque. 1692.
Miscellany Poems. 2d ed. 1697.
Dodd, Rev. William. Thoughts in Prison. Bath, 1796.
A Day in Vacation at College. 1751.
Dodsley, Robert. An Epistle to Pope. 1734.
The Art of Preaching. 1738.
Donne, John. Poems. Ed. Grierson, H. J. C. 2 vols. Oxford, 1912.
Drayton, Michael. Works. With annotations of the learned Sel-
den. 1753.
The Muses Elizium, lately discouered, by a new way over Par-
nassus, etc. 1630. Repr. Spenser Society, Manchester, 1892.
Duck, Stephen. Poems on Several Subjects. 7th ed. 1730.
[Duer, John.] The Third Satire of Juvenal, translated, etc. 1806.
Dunbar, William. Poems. Ed. John Small. 3 vols. Scottish Text
Society. [1884–85.]
[Dunster, Charles.] St. James's Street, a Poem in Blank Verse, by
Marmaduke Milton. 1790.
D'Urfey, Thomas. Butler's Ghost: or Hudibras. 4th Part. 1682.
New Poems, Consisting of Satyrs, Elegies, and Odes, etc. 1690.
Collin's Walk through London and Westminster. 1690.
New Operas, with Comical Stories, and Poems on Several Occa-
sions. 1721.
Dutton, Thomas. The Literary Census. 1798.
Egerton, Mrs. Sarah Fyge. Poems on Several Occasions. n. d.
[Evans, A.] The Apparition. 1710.
[Evelyn, Sir John.] Mundus Muliebris. 1690.
Farley, Henry. St. Paules Church, her Bill for the Parliament.
1621.
[Fenton, Elijah.] Poems on Several Occasions. 1717.
[Fitzgeffrey, Henry.] Certain Elegies, done by sundrie excellent
wits with Satyrs and Epigrams. 1620.
The Third Book of Humours: intituled Notes from Black-Fryers.
[Fitzgerald, Thomas.] Poems on Several Occasions. 1733.
Flecknoe, Richard. A Collection of the Choicest Epigrams and
Characters of —. 1673.
Ford, Simon. The Conflagration of London. 1667.

Garth, Samuel. The Dispensary. 2d ed. 1699.
    Works. Dublin, 1769.
Gascoyne, George. Delicate Diet for daintie mouthde Droonkardes.
    1576.
Gay, John. Poems on Several Occasions. 1720.
    Poems. Ed. John Underhill. 2 vols. 1893.
    Trivia: or, the Art of Walking the Streets of London. 1716. (see
        Appendix B.)
    Trivia. Ed. W. H. Williams. 1922.
Gerard. An Epistle to the Egregious Mr. Pope in which the beauties
    of his mind and body are amply displayed. 1734.
Glover, Richard. London: or the Progress of Commerce. 1739.
[Goddard, William.] A Satyrical Dialogue. 1615. Ed. J. S. Farmer.
    1897.
    A Neaste of Waspes. Dort, 1615. Ed. C. H. Wilkinson. Oxford.
Goldsmith, Oliver. Poems. Muses Library.
[Gould, Robert.] Love given over: or a Satyr against the Pride,
    Lust, and Inconstancy of Woman. 1710.
    Poems Chiefly Consisting of Satyrs and Satyrical Epistles. 1689.
Granville, George (1st Baron Lansdowne). Poems upon Several
    Occasions. 1712.
[Griffith, Rev. Mr.] An Answer to the Satyr against Mankind.
    [1675]
[Guilpin, Edward.] Skialetheia, or A Shadow of Truth in Certaine
    Epigrams and Satyres. 1598.
Hall, John. Poems. Cambridge, 1646.
Hall, Joseph. Satires. 1753.
Hamilton, William, of Bangour. Poems on Several Occasions.
    Edinburgh, 1760.
    Poems on Several Occasions. 1st ed. Glasgow, 1748.
Harington, Sir John. Orlando Furioso in English Heroical Verse,
    with the addition of the Author's Epigrams. 1634.
Hayman. Quodlibets. 1628.
Heard, William. A Sentimental Journey to Bath, Bristol, and their
    environs, a descriptive poem; to which are added miscellaneous
    pieces. . . . 1778.
Herrick, Robert. Hesperides. Ed. W. C. Hazlitt, 2 vols. 1869.
    Poems. Ed. A. B. Grosart, 3 vols. 1876.
    Poetical Works. Ed. F. W. Moorman. Oxford, 1915.
[Hervey, Lord John.] An Epistle from a Nobleman to a Doctor of
    Divinity. 1733.
Heywood, James. Poems and Letters on Several Subjects. 1724.
Higden, Henry. A Modern Essay on the Tenth Satyr of Juvenal.
    1687.

Higgins, Bevill. A Poem on Nature. 1736.

[Hill, Aaron.] The Fanciad. 6 cantos. 1743.

Original Poems and Translations. 1714.

[Hinchliffe, William.] Poems, Amorous, Moral, and Divine. 1718.

Holland, Lord. Imitations. [1798–99?]

Hopkins, Charles. Epistolary Poems on Several Occasions, etc. 1694.

The Court-Prospect. 1699.

Hopkins, John. Amasia, or the Works of the Muses, 3 vols. 1700.

Hughes, John. Poems on Several Occasions. Ed. William Duncombe. 1735.

The Court of Neptune. 1700.

[Jacob, Giles.] The Rape of the Smock, an heroi-comical poem, in two books. . . . 1717.

Jacob, Hildebrand. Bedlam, a Poem. 1723.

James, Nicholas. Poems on Several Occasions. Truro, 1742.

Jenner, Charles. Town Eclogues. 1772.

[Jenyns, Soame.] Poems. 1752.

Johnson, Samuel. Poems. Muses Library.

Jonson, Ben. Works. Ed. Gifford and Cunningham. 9 vols. 1875.

Jordan, Thomas. London's Glory, or the Lord Mayor's Show: performed Friday, Oct. 29, 1680. 1680.

Kelly, Hugh. Works. 1778.

Kenrick, William. Love in the Suds. 4th ed. 1772.

[Killigrew, H.] Epigrams of Martial Englished, with some other pieces, Ancient and Modern. 1695.

King, William. Poetical Works. 2 vols. Edinburgh, 1781.

Miscellanies in Prose and Verse. n. d.

Lawler, C. F. (Peter Pindar). Royal Poems. n. d.

[Lennox, Mrs. Charlotte Ramsay.] Poems on Several Occasions. 1747.

Lewkenor, John. Metellus His Dialogues. The First Part, Containing a Relation of a Journey to Tunbridge-Wells. 1693.

Lloyd, Robert. Poems. 1762.

L[odge], T[homas]. A Fig for Momus. 1595.

Works. Hunterian Club. 4 vols. 1875–83.

Madan, M. Translation of Juvenal and Persius. 2 vols. 1829.

Mallet, David. Of Verbal Criticism, an epistle to Mr. Pope occasioned by Theobald's Shakespear and Bentley's Milton. 1733.

Poetical Works. Edinburgh, 1780.

[Manning.] Poems written at different Times on Several Occasions by a Gentleman who resided many Years abroad in the Two last Reigns with a Publick Character. 1752.

Marston, John. Works. Ed. J. O. Halliwell. 3 vols. 1856.

Marvell, Andrew. The Poems and Some Satires. Ed. E. Wright. 1904.

Mason, William. Poems. 3 vols. York, 1797.

The Dean and the Squire, a political Eclogue. 3d ed. 1783.

Mathias, T. J. The Pursuits of Literature. 1794.

[Miller, James.] Harlequin-Horace: or the Art of Modern Poetry. 1731.

Of Politeness. 1738.

The Art of Life. In Imitation of Horace's Art of Poetry. 1739.

Miscellaneous Works in Verse and Prose. 1741.

[Mitchell, Joseph.] The Promotion and the Alternative. 1726.

Poems on Several Occasions. 2 vols. 1729.

Murphy, Arthur. An Ode to the Naiads of Fleet-Ditch. 1761.

Seventeen Hundred and Ninety-One, in Imitation of the Thirteenth Satire of Juvenal. 1791.

The Examiner, in reply to Murphiad and other attacks. 1761.

Works. 7 vols. 1786.

Nemo, Sir Nicholas. Dialogue between a Man of Fashion and his Valet. Horace, Sat. 7, Bk. II, 1752.

Nevile, Thomas. Imitations of Horace, Juvenal, Persius. 1785.

Newbery, Francis. Verses on Several Occasions. 1815.

Newcomb, [Thomas]. An Ode sacred to the memory of that truly pious and honourable lady, the Countess of Berkeley. 1717.

Occleve, Thomas. Works. Ed. F. J. Furnivall. E. E. T. S. 1892-97.

Ogle, George. The Miser's Feast. A Dialogue between the Author and the Poet Laureate. Sat. 8, Bk. II, 1737.

Oldham, John. Works. 6th ed. 1703.

Ozell. La Secchia Rapita, the Trophy-Bucket, a mock-heroic, poem, the first of its kind, by Signior Allessandro Tassoni. . . . Done from the Italian into English Rhime, by Mr. Ozell. 1710.

Parker, Samuel. Homer in a Nutshell: or his War between the Frogs and Mice, paraphrastically translated. 3 cantos. 1700.

Parnell, Thomas. Poems on Several Occasions, with Goldsmith's Life of Parnell. 1770.

Homer's Battle of the Frogs and Mice. 1717.

[Philips, Mrs. Katherine.] Poems. By the Incomparable Mrs. K. P. 1664.

Pope, Alexander. Works. Ed. Joseph Warton. 9 vols. 1797.

Prior, Matthew. Poems on Several Occasions. Ed. A. R. Waller. Cambridge, 1905.

Radcliffe, Alexander. Ovid Travestie, a Burlesque upon Ovid's Epistles. 2d ed. 1681.

The Ramble: an anti-heroick Poem, together with some Terrestrial Hymns and Carnal Ejaculations. 1682.

Randolph, Thomas. Poems. 5th ed. 1668.
The Poems and Amyntas of Thomas Randolph. Ed. J. J. Parry. New Haven, 1917.
Rochester and Roscommon, Earls of. Works. To which is added A Collection of Miscellaneous Poems. 3d ed. 1709.
[Rowe, Mrs. E. S.] Poems on Several Occasions. 1st ed. 1696.
Rowe, Nicholas. Poetical Works. 1733.
Rowlands, Samuel. Complete Works. Hunterian Club. 1872–80.
Doctor Merry-Man: or Nothing but Mirth. [1616.]
Greenes Ghost Haunting Cony-Catchers. 1602.
Martin Mark-all, Beadle of Bridewell. 1610.
Savage, Richard, Miscellaneous Poems and Translations. 1726.
The Wanderer: a Poem. 5 cantos. 1729.
Sewell, (G). Poems on Several Occasions. 1719.
Shadwell, Charles. The Tenth Satire of Juvenal. With illustrations upon it. English and Latin. 1687.
Silvester, Rev. Tipping. Original Poems and Translations. 1733.
[Smedley, Jonathan.] Poems on Several Occasions. 1721.
Smith, Horace and James. Horace in London. Boston, 1813.
Smith, James. Memoirs, Letters, and Comic Miscellanies in Prose and Verse. 2 vols. 1840.
[Smith, James, of Tewkesbury.] The Art of Living in London. 1768.
Smith, R. A Wonder of Wonders: or A Metamorphosis of fair faces voluntarily transformed into foul Visages, etc. 1662.
Smollett, Tobias. Poems. Ed. Thomas Park. 1807.
Soames, Sir William. Translation of Boileau's Art of Poetry, revised by Dryden. 1710.
Somervile, William. Poetical Works. 2 vols. 1807.
S[peed], R. The Counter-scuffle. Whereunto is added, the Counter-Ratt. [ca. 1647.]
Speed, Samuel. Fragmenta Carceris, or The Kings-Bench Scuffle, with the Humors of the Common-Side. The Kings-Bench Litany and the Legend of Duke Humphrey. 1675.
Spenser, Edmund. Poetical Works. Ed. J. C. Smith and E. de Selincourt. Oxford, 1912.
Stephens, John. Satyrical Essayes Characters and Others. 1615.
Suckling, Sir John. Poems. Ed. A. H. Thompson. 1910.
Swift, Butler. Tyburn to the Marine Society. 1759.
Swift, Jonathan. Poems. Ed. W. E. Browning. 2 vols. 1910.
Tattersal, Robert. The Bricklayer's Miscellany. 1735.
Taylor, John. Works. Collected ed. 1630.
Works. Spenser Society. 1870.
[Theobald, J.] Poems on Several Occasions. 1719.

[Thomas, Elizabeth.] The Metamorphosis of the Town, or the View of the Present Fashions. 1730.

Thomson, James. The Seasons. 1730.

Thornton, Bonnell. The Battle of the Wigs. 1768.

Thurston, Joseph. Poems on Several Occasions. 1729.

Tickell, Richard. The Wreath of Fashion, or The Art of Sentimental Poetry. 2d ed. 1778.

Tickell, Thomas. Poetical Works. Boston, 1854.

Epistle from a Lady in England to a Gentleman in Avignon. 1717.

Turberville, George. The Noble Art of Venerie or Hunting. 1575.

Turner. Horace, Ep. 1, Bk. I. 1738.

Ward, Edward. The Poet's Ramble after Riches. 1710.

The Republican Procession; or the Tumultuous Cavalcade. 2d ed. 1714.

A Vade Mecum for Malt-Worms. ca. 1712.

The Libertine's Choice, or The Mistaken Happiness of the Fool in Fashion. 1704.

Hudibras Redivivus, or a Burlesque Poem on the Times . . . 4th ed. to which is now added the Rambling Fuddle-Caps: Or a Tavern Strugle for a Kiss. n. d.

Vulgus Britannicus, or the British Hudibras. 1710.

The Delights of the Bottle, to which is added A South Sea Song upon the late Bubbles. 1720.

A Journey to Hell. 2d ed. 1700.

The Field-Spy: or, the Walking Observator. 1714.

Watson, William. Poems. 1899.

[Wells, Jeremiah.] Poems upon Divers Occasions. With a Character of a London Scrivener. 1667.

Welsted, Leonard. Works. Ed. Nichols. 1787.

Palaemon to Caelia at Bath, or The Triumvirate. 1717.

Welsted, Leonard, and Moore-Smythe, James. One Epistle to Mr. A. Pope, occasioned by Two Epistles lately published. 1730.

[West, Gilbert.] A Canto of the Fairy Queen. Written by Spenser. Never before Published. 1739.

Whitehead, Paul. Satires. 1760.

Manners, a Satire. 1738.

The State Dunces, inscribed to Mr. Pope. 1733.

Whitehead, William. Plays and Poems. 1774.

An Essay on Ridicule. 1743.

The Danger of Writing Verse. 1741.

[Wild, Dr. Robert.] Iter Boreale, attempting something upon the successful and matchless march of the Lord Gen. George Monck from Scotland to London. 1660.

Williams, Sir Charles Hanbury. Poems . . . with notes by Horace Walpole, Earl of Orford. 3 vols. 1822.
Winchilsea, Countess of. [Anne K. Finch.] Miscellany Poems on Several Occasions, written by a Lady. 1713.
Wither, George. Abuses Stript and Whipt, or Satirical Essays, divided into two books. 1613.
Juvenilia, a Collection of Poems. 2 vols. 1622.
Woolnoth. The Coffee Scuffle. 1662.
Wortley, F. Mercurius Britannicus his Welcome to Hell. 1647.
Wortley-Montagu, Lady Mary. To the Imitator of the Satire of the Second Book of Horace. 1733.
Woty, W. Fugitive and Original Poems. 1786.
The Shrubs of Parnassus. 1760.
Campanalogia, a Poem in Praise of Ringing. 1761.
Young, Edward. Poems. 2 vols. 1852.

ANONYMOUS

An accurate . . . encomium on the most illustrious persons whose monuments are erected in Westminster Abbey, an heroic poem in Latin and English . . . by a Gentleman late of Baliol College, Oxford. 1749.
The Art of Beauty. 1719.
The Art of Poetry. 1741.
The Art of Stock-Jobbing. 1746. [7th ed., 1820. B. M. 8226, cc.]
The Auction, a Town Eclogue. By the Hon. Mr. — . 2d ed. 1778.
Authors of the Town. 1725.
The Ballad of The King shall enjoy his own again: with learned Comment thereupon, at the request of Capt. Silk, dedicated to Jenny Man. 1711.
The Banished Beauty; or, a Fair Face in Disgrace. 1729.
Bartholomew-fair: or, a Ramble to Smithfield. A Poem in Imitation of Milton. 1729.
The Beau-Thief Detected: a Poem, inscribed to the Fair Maids of Honor. By J. W., Westminster, 1729.
Beauty, or the Art of Charming. 1735.
British Frenzy: or, the Mock-Apollo. 1745.
Brooke and Hellier. 1712.
The Causidicade, etc., on the Strange Resignation and Stranger Promotion. 1743.
The Character of a Trimmer. 1683.
Churchill Dissected. 1764.
The Church Yard, a Satirical Poem. 1739.
The Circus: or British Olympicks. A Satyr on the Ring in Hide-Park. 1709.

The Court of Neptune Burlesqu'd. A Satyr upon the City. 1700.
A Description of Mr. D–n's Funeral. 1700. [By T. Browne?]
Discontent the Universal Misery. In an Epistle to a Friend. 1734.
An Epistle from Matt of the Mint, lately deceased to Captain Macheath. 1729.
An Epistle to Sir J–r–y S–b–k. 1735.
The Fatigues of a Great Man. 1734.
The Female Faction: or, the Gay Subscribers. 1729. [MS. notes.]
The Female Rake, or Modern Fine Lady. Dublin pr., London repr., n. d.
Female Taste: A Satire. By a Barrister of the Middle-Temple. 1755.
Folly. A Poem. Written by the Author of the Female Rake, and the Rake of Taste. 1737.
A Genuine Epistle written sometime since to the late famous Mother Lodge. n. d.
Human Passions, a Satyr, to which is added an Ode to Impudence. 1726.
The Humours of the New Tunbridge Wells at Islington. 1734.
The Junto. 1712.
Juvenal and Persius. The State of Rome under Nero and Domitian: a Satire. 1739.
The London Address: or Magistrates against the Muses. 1730.
The Long Vacation, a Satyr, addressed to all disconsolate Traders. 1709.
The Modern Reasoners: an Epistle to a Friend. 1734.
New-Market, a Satire. 1751.
New Song on Sadler's Wells. 1740.
A New Tale of an Old Tub. 1752.
An Ode to Mr. Pulteney. 1739.
A Panegyric on a Court. By the author of The World Unmasked. 1739.
Parodies on Gay, to which is added The Battle of the Busts. 1810.
A Poem on the Civil-Wars of the Old-Baily, Occasion'd by a Late Dispute, between the Sheriffs and Students of the Law. 1713.
A Poem on a Voyage of Discovery. 1792.
Rake Reformed, a Poem in a Letter to the Rakes of the Town. By A. G. — Gent. 1718.
The Rake of Taste, a Poem. Dedicated to Alex. Pope, Esq. Dublin, n. d.
A Ramble of Fancy through the Land of Electioneering. 1768.
Raven and Owl: a politico-polemico-sarcastico-historical dialogue. By Neuter Neither-side of No-land, Esq. 1739.
A Ride and Walk through Stourhead. 1780.

The Rival Wives, or, the Greeting of Clarissa to Skirra in the Elysian Shades. 1738.
The Rival Wives Answer'd: or, Skirra to Clarissa. 1738.
St. James's Park: a Satyr. 1708.
A Satyr against Man. 1710.
Scandalizade. By Porcupinus Pelagius, Author of the Causidicade. 1750.
Scarborough, a Poem in Imitation of Mr. Gay's Journey to Exeter, in The Scarborough Miscellany. 1734.
The Swan Tripe-Club: a Satyr on the High-Flyers in the Year 1705. 1710. [Ascribed by some to Jonathan Swift.]
The Thimble, an Heroi-comical Poem. 1743.
A Trip lately to Scotland with a true Character of the Country and People. 1705.
A Trip to Nottingham, with a Character of Mareschal Tallard and the French Generals. 1705.
The Voice of Liberty; or a British Philippic. 1738.
A Walk from St. James's to Convent Garden, the back-way through the Meuse: in imitation of Mr. Gay's Journey to Exeter, in a letter to a friend. 1717.

COLLECTED

Arbuthnot, Pope, and Gay. Miscellanies. Vol. III, 1742.
Ashton, John. Humour, Wit, and Satire of the Seventeenth Century. 1883.
Bagford Ballads. Ed. J. W. Ebsworth. 1876–77.
B[rome], R[ichard]. Covent Garden Drollery. Collected by R. B. 1672.
A Collection of the most remarkable Poems published in the Reign of King George III.
Collection of Poems. [10487.75 (14) Harvard.]
A Collection of the Best English Poetry, by Several Hands. 2 vols. 1717. [15476.60 Harvard.]
A Collection of Merry Poems, etc. from Oldham, Brown, Prior, Swift, and other eminent Poets. 2d ed. 1736.
A Collection of Poetical Pamphlets, beginning with The Pleasures of a Single Life. 1709. [15476.37* Harvard.]
Collier, J. P. A Book of Roxburghe Ballads. 1847.
Illustrations of Early English Popular Literature. 2 vols. 1863.
Concanen, [Matthew]. Miscellaneous Poems, Original and Translated by Several Hands, viz. Dean Swift, Parnell, Delany, Brown, Ward, Sterling, Concanen, and others. 1724.
Cooper, Elizabeth. The Muses Library, or a Series of English Poetry from the Saxons to the Reign of King Charles II. 1737.

Cotgrave, J. Wit's Interpreter, the English Parnassus. 3d ed. 1671.

Dennis, John. Miscellany Poems. With Select Translations of Horace, Juvenal, Boileau, Aesop, etc. 2d ed. 1697.

[Dodsley, Robert.] A Collection of Poems in Six Volumes. 1765.

Dryden, John. Miscellany Poems. 3d ed. 1702.

D'Urfey, Thomas. Wit and Mirth, or Pills to Purge Melancholy. 4th ed. 7 vols. 1714.

Ebsworth, J. W. Choyce Drollery: Songs and Sonnets, reprinted from edition of 1656. Boston, England, 1876.

Fairholt, F. W. Satirical Songs and Poems on Costume. Percy Society, vol. xvii, 1849.

Poems and Songs relating to George Villiers, Duke of Buckingham, and his assassination by John Felton, Aug. 23, 1628. Percy Society, vol. xxix, 1850.

Lord Mayors' Pageants. Percy Society, 1843.

The Foundling Hospital for Wit. 1743.

The Fugitive Miscellany, being a Collection of such Fugitive Pieces in Prose and Verse. 1774-75.

Gammer Gurton's Garland: or, the Nursery Parnassus. Ed. Joseph Ritson. 1810.

Hazlitt, W. C. Fugitive Tracts. 2 vols. 1875.

Hindley, Charles. The Old Book Collector's Miscellany. 1873.

The Honey-Suckle. 1734.

Hyatt, A. H. The Charm of London. n. d.

Lewis, David. Miscellaneous Poems by Several Hands. 1726.

The Ladies Miscellany. 1718.

Miscellaneous Poems, 1739-68. [15476.53 Harvard.]

The Muse in Good Humour: a Collection of Comic Tales. By Several Hands. 2 vols. 8th ed. 1785.

Nichols, J. A Select Collection of Poems with Notes Biographical and Historical. 1781.

The Norfolk Poetical Miscellany, to which are added some select essays and letters in prose . . . by the author of The Progress of Physick. 1744.

Poems on Affairs of State, 1620-1707. 1716.

Poems by Eminent Ladies. 1755.

Poems of Love and Gallantry. Written in the Marshalsea and Newgate, by several of the Prisoners taken at Preston. 1716.

Poems. Vol. 19. [10487.75 Harvard.]

Poems by Several Gentlemen of Oxford. 1757.

Rimbault, E. F. Old Ballads illustrating the great Frost of 1683-4, and the Fair on the River Thames. Percy Society, vol. ix, 1844.

[Rowlands, Samuel.] Doctor Merry-Man: or, Nothing but Mirth. 1616.

Roxburghe Ballads. Ed. William Chappell and E. B. Ebsworth. 1871.

Saintsbury, George. Minor Poets of the Caroline Period. 3 vols. Oxford, 1906.

Savage, Richard. Miscellaneous Poems and Translations by several hands published by Richard Savage, son of the late Earl Rivers. 1726.

Southey, Robert. Specimens of the Later English Poets. Vol. III. 1807.

Steele, Richard. Poetical Miscellanies, Consisting of Original Poems and Translations. By the best Hands. 1714.

Taubman, Matthew. Loyal Poems and Satyrs upon the Times, etc. 1685.

Various Poetical Tracts. 1729–31.

Waldron, F. G. The Literary Museum. 1792.

Whitten, Wilfred. London in Song. 1898.

Wit and Drollery, Joviall Poems. 1661.

Witts Recreations. 1640.

PROSE

Anonymous

The Art of Living in London. 2d ed. 1793.

The Country Gentleman's Vade Mecum. 1699.

Hickelty-Pickelty: or, a Medley of Characters. 1708.

Low-Life, or One half of the World knows not how the other half live . . . with an address to Mr. Hogarth. 3d ed. 1764.

A Trip through London. 1728.

Assigned

Brown, Thomas. Works. 4 vols. 4th ed. 1715.

The Life of the Late Famous Comedian, Jo. Hayns. 1701.

Bulwer, John. Anthropometamorphosis: or, The Artificiall Changling. 1653.

Burnet. Achilles Dissected: being a Compleat Key of the Political Characters in that New Ballad Opera, Written by the late Mr. Gay . . . . 1733.

[Coventry, Francis.] The History of Pompey the Little: or, the Life and Adventures of a Lap-Dog. 1751.

Flecknoe, Richard. Enigmaticall Characters, all taken to the Life. 1658.

Harington, Sir John. The Metamorphosis of Ajax. A Cloacinean Satire. Chiswick, 1814.

Hawksmoor, Nicholas. A Short Historical Account of London-Bridge; with a Proposition for a new Stone-Bridge at Westminster. 1736.

Howell, James. Londinopolis. 1657.

Johnson, Charles. A General History of the lives and adventures of the most famous highwaymen, murderers, street-robbers, etc.

Misson, Henri. Mémoires et Observations. 1698.

[Price, Lawrence.] Witty William of Wiltshire. 1674.

Settle, Elkanah. The Triumphs of London, performed on Saturday, Oct. 29, 1692, for the entertainment of the Rt. Hon. Sir John Fleet, Kt., Lord Mayor.

Seymour, Richard. The Compleat Gamester. 5th ed. 1734.

[Sheridan, Thomas.] The Satires of Juvenal Translated. 1739.

[Trapp, Joseph.] The Character and Principles of the Present Set of Whigs. 1711.

Ward, Edward. The London Spy, compleat in 18 parts. Ed. Ralph Straus. 1924.

A Frolick to Horn-Fair. With a Walk from Cuckold's-Point thro' Deptford and Greenwich. 1700.

DRAMA

Anonymous. The Bow-Street Opera. n. d.

[Baker, Thomas.] Tunbridge Walks: or, the Yeoman of Kent. 1703.

[Burgoyne, General John.] The Maid of the Oaks. 1774.

Breval, John Durant. The Confederates, a Farce. 1717.

Centlivre, Mrs. Susanna. Love's Contrivance. 1703.

The Basset-Table. 1706.

The Platonick Lady. 1707.

Dekker, Thomas, and Webster, John. Westward Hoe. 1607.

Etheredge, Sir George. The Man of Mode. 1676.

Fielding, Henry. Works. Ed. C. H. Maynadier. New York, 1903.

[Garrick, David.] Bon Ton. 1775.

Gay, John. Three Hours after Marriage. 1717.

Jonson, Ben. Works. Ed. Gifford and Cunningham. 9 vols. 1875.

Moore, Edward. The Gamester. 1753.

Shadwell, Charles. Works. 2 vols. Dublin, 1720.

Shadwell, Thomas. Works. Ed. G. Saintsbury. Mermaid Series, 1903.

The Virtuoso. 1704.

The Scowrers. 1691.

Steele, Richard. Plays. Ed. G. A. Aitken. 1894.

AUTHORITIES

Andrews, William. Famous Frosts and Frost Fairs in Great Britain. 1887.

Ashton, John. Social Life in the Reign of Queen Anne. 1883.

Hyde Park from Domesday-Book to Date. 1896.

Baker, David Erskine; Reed, Isaac; Jones, Stephen. Biographia Dramatica; or, A Companion to the Playhouse. 3 vols. 1812.

Beljame, Alexandre. Le Public et les Hommes de Lettres en Angleterre au XVIIIe Siècle, 1660–1744. Paris, 1881.

Beloe, Rev. William. Anecdotes of Literature and Scarce Books. 1806–12.

Boynton, Percy S. London in Literature. Chicago, 1913.

The Bystander; or, a Universal Weekly Expositor by a Literary Association . . . 1790.

Calvin, Ross Randall. The Life and Works of John Oldham. Harvard Dissertation. 1916.

[Caulfield, James.] Memoirs of the Celebrated Persons Composing the Kit-Cat Club. 1821.

Chancellor, E. Beresford. The Annals of the Strand. 1912.

The Annals of Fleet Street. 1912.

Collier, J. P. A Bibliographical and Critical Account of the Rarest Books in the English Language, etc. 2 vols. 1865.

Collins, John Churton. Jonathan Swift, a biographical and critical study. . . 1893.

The Craftsman. March 21, 1730.

Davey, Richard. The Pageant of London. 2 vols. [1906.]

Dobell, Percy J. John Dryden. Bibliographical Memoranda. 1922.

The Literature of the Restoration, etc. Bibliography. 1918.

Dobson, Austin. De Libris. 1908.

Douce, Francis. Illustrations of Shakspeare. 1839.

Elton, Oliver. The Augustan Ages. Edinburgh, 1899.

Fairholt, F. W. Costume in England. 1885.

Lord Mayors' Pageants. Percy Society, 1843.

The Female Tatler. Dec. 12, 1712.

The Flying Post. Nov. 6–8, 1712.

The Fortnightly Review. June, 1912 (article by H. M. Paull).

The Gentleman's Magazine. March, 1731, and July, 1788. (Gay letters.)

George, M. Dorothy. London Life in the 18th Century. 1925.

Halliwell, J. O. A Catalogue of an Unique Collection of Ancient English Broadside Ballads. 1856.

Hazlitt, William. Works. Ed. A. R. Waller and Arnold Glover, with an introduction by W. E. Henley. 13 vols. 1902–06.

Hazlitt, W. C. Brand's Popular Antiquities of Great Britain, Faiths and Folklore. 2 vols. 1905.
Ireland, John. Hogarth Illustrated. 2d ed. 3 vols. 1793–1804.
Johnson, Samuel. Lives of the Poets. Oxford, 1825.
Kerr, S. Parnell. George Selwyn and the Wits. 1909.
Larwood, Jacob. [Schevichaven, Herman Diederik Johan van.] The Story of the London Parks. 1872.
Mackail, J. Latin Literature. New York, 1895.
Malcolm, James Peller. Anecdotes of the Manners and Customs of London (to 1700). 1811.
Melville, Lewis [Lewis J. Benjamin.] Life and Letters of John Gay. Life of Philip, Duke of Wharton. 1913.
Mitton, Geraldine. Maps of Old London. 1908.
Montgomery, Henry R. Memoirs of the life and writings of Sir Richard Steele . . . with his correspondence and notices of his contemporaries, the wits and statesmen of Queen Anne's time. 2 vols. 1865.
Monthly Chronicle. Feb. 25, 1730 (No. 82, p. 44).
New York Nation. April 24, 1913 (article by Ernest Gay).
Nichols, John. Biographical Anecdotes of William Hogarth. 3d ed. 1785.
Literary Anecdotes of the 18th Century. 1814.
Nineteenth Century and After. Nov., 1925 (article by Major Norman G. Brett-James, on "London Traffic in the 17th Century").
Norman, Philip. London Signs and Inscriptions. 1893.
Notes and Queries. 1st Series, X, 403, and XI, 343, 496. 2d Series, VI, 532.
Orrery, Lord. Remarks on the Life and Writings of Dr. Jonathan Swift in a series of letters to his son. 1752.
Paul, H. G. John Dennis, his Life and Criticism. New York, 1911.
Pearson, Norman. Society Sketches in the Eighteenth Century. 1911.
Pendrill, Charles. London Life in the 14th Century. 1925.
Pennant, Thomas. Some Account of London. 2d ed. 1791.
The Antiquities of London. 2d ed. 1818.
Philosophical Transactions to the End of the Year 1700. Ed. John Lowthorp. 3 vols. 2d ed. 1716.
Punch. June 29, 1850.
Rowlandson, Thomas. The Microcosm of London. 1811.
Shelley, Henry C. Life and Letters of Edward Young. 1914.
Smith, J. T. The Cries of London. 1837.
The Streets of London. 1861.
Vagabondiana, or Anecdotes of mendicant wanderers through the streets of London. 1874.

Sorbière, [Samuel]. Relation d'un Voyage en Angleterre. 1667. A Voyage to England. 1709.

Spence, Joseph. Anecdotes, observations, and characters of books and men. . . . Ed. S. W. Singer. 1858.

Sprat, Thomas. Observations on Sorbière's Voyage. 1709.

Stanley, Arthur Penrhyn. Historical Memorials of Westminster Abbey. 3d ed. 1869.

Stephenson, H. T. Shakespeare's London. New York, 1905.

Stowe, John. The Survey of London. Ed. H. B. Wheatley. Dent, n. d.

Straus, Ralph. The Unspeakable Curll. 1927.

Stubbes, Phillip. Anatomy of the Abuses in England in Shakspere's Youth. 1879.

Strype. Stowe's Survey Enlarged. 1720.

Trusler, Rev. John. The Works of Wm. Hogarth in a Series of Engravings, with Descriptions and a Comment on their Moral Tendency, to which are added anecdotes of the Author and his Works [183–?]

Turberville, A. S. English Men and Manners in the XVIIIth Century. 1926.

Walpole, Horace. Letters. Ed. Mrs. Paget Toynbee. 16 vols. 1903–05.

Warton, Joseph. An Essay on the Genius and Writings of Pope. 5th ed. 2 vols. 1806.

Wheatley and Cunningham. London, Past and Present. 1891.

Wheatley, H. B. Hogarth's London, pictures of the manners of the 18th Century. 1909.

Widal, Auguste. Juvenal et ses Satires. 2d ed. 1870.

Wilkins, W. H. Caroline the Illustrious, queen-consort of George II. 1904.

Wroth, Warwick. The London Pleasure Gardens of the 18th Century. 1896.

Index

Index

A New Map of the Cityes of London, Westminster and the Burrough of Southwark